THE BUSH DYSLEXICON

THE BUSH DYSLEXICON

Observations on a National Disorder

MARK CRISPIN MILLER

W · W · NORTON & COMPANY
NEW YORK · LONDON

For information about permission to reproduce selections from this book, write to Permissions, W. W. Norton & Company, Inc., 500 Fifth Avenue, New York, NY 10110

The text of this book is composed in Bembo
with the display set in Serifa
Composition by Allentown Digital Services Division of R.R. Donnelley & Sons Company
Manufacturing by The Haddon Craftsmen, Inc.
Book design by Rubina Yeh

Library of Congress Cataloging-in-Publication Data
Miller, Mark Crispin.
The Bush dyslexicon : observations on a national disorder / by Mark Crispin Miller.
p.   cm.
Includes bibliographical references.
ISBN 0-393-04183-2
1. Bush, George W. (George Walker), 1946– Language. 2. Bush, George W. (George
Walker), 1946– Humor. 3. Presidents—United States—Language. 4. Malapropisms.
I. Title.
E903.3 .M55 2001
973.931'092—dc21   2001030726
ISBN 0-393-32296-3 pbk.

W. W. Norton & Company, Inc., 500 Fifth Avenue, New York, N.Y. 10110
www. wwnorton.com

W. W. Norton & Company Ltd., Castle House, 75/76 Wells Street, London W1T 3QT

5 6 7 8 9 0

For my parents

ACKNOWLEDGMENTS

This book was written quickly. It would have been impossible without considerable help.

I would like first of all to thank my editor, Starling Lawrence, for agreeing to this project, and Drake Bennett, his assistant. I also thank my agent, Emma Parry, for getting everything in order quickly and efficiently and always with good cheer. I was also very fortunate to be assisted by Carrie McLaren, who took time out from editing her excellent magazine, *Stayfree!*, to help me put this book together. Aside from managing a colossal research task, Carrie was an indispensable collaborator, offering many trenchant insights and editorial suggestions. Her own assistant, Ryan Creed, was kind enough to pitch in, too.

Several people read the manuscript with care and gave me counsel: Marilyn Young and Ross Posnock, close friends and colleagues here at New York University; my buddy Robert W. McChesney, who has taught me more than I can say and who added greatly to this book; my dear old friend Linda DeLibero; the wise and clever Inger Forland; independent scholar Rochelle Gurstein, a kindred spirit; and the generous Josh Ozersky. I would like especially to thank Ronald Walters of the History Department at Johns Hopkins University. Ron responded graciously—and brilliantly—to an abrupt request for guidance in the middle of what was for him a very busy time.

Many other people came through with answers to specific questions and requests: Bruce J. Miller, Angie Nosari, J. H. Hatfield, Bill Minutaglio, Garry Mauro, Sander Hicks, Katrina van den Heuvel, Richard Lingeman,

Todd Gitlin, Susan Greene, Jeff Cohen, Arvind Rajagopal, Tracy Chin, Ted Magder, Peter Beinart, Vivek Chibber, John Nichols, Eli Kintisch, Frank Bruni, Jerry Politex of Bushwatch, Jim Naureckas of Fairness and Accuracy in Reporting (FAIR), Billy Beaune and Fritz von Spüchen. I received more extensive help from Karla Hale and Andrew Elmore.

Close to home, I was extraordinarily blessed. My parents, Jordan and Anita Miller, gave me the benefit not only of their opposition research (both are hardened Democrats) but of their long experience as publishers. As Dan Quayle might say, I wouldn't be here if it weren't for them, and so I thank them from the bottom of my heart. My son, Louie Miller, was in part the inspiration for the writing of this book, which I hope heartens him, and others of his generation, to do the right thing for democracy. Louie's decency and sense of humor are a great encouragement to me in these dark times, and I would be delighted to return the favor.

Finally, I must try to find the words to thank my wife, Amy Smiley, whose rare warmth, keen intelligence, and common sense have been an inspiration to me from the day we met. She is the love of my life and my dearest friend. I hope that her sweet influence shines through in everything I do, including even this.

CONTENTS

Preface: Now More
Than Ever

Mr. Bush was at his most vivid today discussing terrorism, and the crowd was most responsive when he thanked them for aiding the war, often by sending parents or sons and daughters to Central Asia. When the subject turned to economics and jobs—the issue Mr. Bush's advisers believe the congressional elections later this year will be fought around—the attention of his audience seemed to wander.

—NEW YORK TIMES, JANUARY 15, 2002

BEFORE

The Bush Dyslexicon came out in early June 2001. It was a trying time for our new president. Suddenly, after months of adulation by the press, and only token opposition from the Democrats, the soaring Bush had been brought low by an aggrieved Republican. On May 24, Senator Jim Jeffords of Vermont announced that he would leave the party and become an "Independent," or de facto Democrat—a crossing that would shift the Senate from Republican control. The defector noted that the party had become too punitive and doctrinaire for his support on issue after issue, from education and abortion rights to "the direction of the judiciary, tax and spending decisions, missile defense, energy and the environment." However, Jeffords was offended not just by the party's far-right ideology, but also—or primarily—by his mistreatment at the hands of GOP enforcers. For balking at the size of Bush's tax cut, the senator was punished with veiled threats and petty snubs, administered, "usually anonymously, by short-sighted party operatives," as John McCain later put it, "and by some Republican members of Congress and their staff."[1] What finally tore it for the easygoing Vermonter was his noninvitation to the White House ceremony honoring Michele Forman as the nation's Teacher of the Year—education being his top concern, and she being one of his constituents.

It was small stuff, certainly, and yet that final bit of payback said a lot about the men behind the curtain. That the Bush team would allow mere vengefulness to jeopardize its own congressional agenda was, or seemed to be, a revelation. "This is a first-order disaster," said one Bush adviser. "We should have let bygones be bygones—and we certainly should have had him over for the teacher deal. The fact is, we Republicans need Jeffords a whole lot more than he needs us."[2] The story dealt a blow to Bush's much-belabored image as a sort of cracker-barrel conciliator. Beyond our borders, his antipathy to compromise had been well known since March, when foreign journalists had started to deplore his if-I-ruled-the-world approach to global matters. Here, however, he still had something of a reputation as a fella who could calm the waters—and the Jeffords episode all but destroyed it. Far from standing out as "a uniter, not a divider," Bush now appeared unable, or unwilling, to restrain the pit bulls growling in his name; and his legendary personal charm had worked no magic when the senator had come in for a final face-to-face. Those closest to him, moreover, only made things worse by aiming many nasty kicks at the departed Jeffords. While moderates rued the loss of their ex-teammate (it was a "wake-up call for our party's leaders," said Maine Senator Olympia Snowe), the Bushmen, as usual, bared their fangs. "There is only one person to blame for all this, and that's Jim Jeffords," snapped Trent Lott, who added that the turncoat "was often very liberal in his views." Andrew Card, the president's chief of staff, opined that Jeffords had been moved by "personal interest," while Karl Rove hinted that the senator was "quirky" (i.e., nuts), and that the whole mess was a piece of Democratic "hanky panky."[3]

Despite such spin—or, in part, because of it—that little crisis seemed to hit Bush hard. A CNN/*Time* poll days later held that only 45 percent deemed him "a leader you can trust," while 53 percent thought otherwise; and 50 percent said that they would not "vote for Bush if he runs for re-election," while only 43 percent said that they would. Nor did he bounce right back from that decline. Riding fairly high in April, shot down in May, he never rose again throughout that summer, but merely floated in a seeming state of grace that looked less comfortable the more one studied it. Certainly his job approval rating was not bad, especially for a president who hadn't been elected. Until the first week of September, at any rate, he racked up numbers high enough that his spinners could assert without much sweat that he was doing very well. On July 13, for example, Ari Fleischer offered this gloss on the latest Gallup poll, which showed a 57 percent approval rating: "I think this is further evidence that the President's message and his presidency has been well-received by the American people." And yet a closer reading of the polls did not support that rosy view; for the pollsters' more specific findings actually revealed a growing uneasiness about the president's abilities and widespread *dis*approval of his program.

Such disparity, in fact, had marked his term from early on. Well before the senator jumped ship, Bush's okay standing in the polls had been precarious, as clear majorities, and large pluralities, said no to him on issue after issue. "On the surface, everything is A-OK," said Marshall Wittman, of the Hudson Institute, in late April.[4] "Beneath the surface there are some disturbing trends. There is a view that he is more of a corporate conservative than a compassionate conservative, a perception that he favors big business over ordinary Americans." The media would often trumpet the good news, and play down those "disturbing trends." Around Bush/Cheney's hundredth day in office, for example, the prevailing tone was doggedly upbeat, as CNN (repeatedly), Fox (more than once), CNBC, the *Wall Street Journal, Newsweek,* AP, NPR's *Marketplace,* Scripps Howard, and, of course, the *Washington Times* ("High Poll Ratings Peeve Democrats"), as well as Rush Limbaugh and his AM/FM tribe, all hyped the president's approval ratings, while shrugging off, or leaving out, the mass awareness of his weaknesses and corporate bias. On the other hand, a CBS News poll revealed that only 43 percent of the American people thought Bush was

"really running the government" (while 52 percent thought "other people" were in charge); that only 47 percent felt sure of his "ability to deal
wisely with an international crisis" (while 47 percent did not); that 51 percent thought his economic program was "not possible" (while 38 percent
believed it was); and that only 38 percent approved of his environmental
policies, while 75 percent agreed we should "maintain our present environmental laws in order to preserve the environment for future generations." Likewise, *ABC World News* reported that, according to the polls,
most Americans perceived George W. Bush as "too close to big business,
too distant from their concerns." At that point, clearly, people could have
such specific qualms and yet still comfortably approve the president in
general. A CBS News poll of May 10–12 found that Bush enjoyed a 57
percent approval rating—although 62 percent also believed that the oil
industry exerted "too much influence" on his administration.

Until late May, the White House team appeared to have the situation
well in hand: Bush/Cheney kept on belting homers in the Capitol, and the
talking heads were very well behaved (as were the Democrats). In such a
balmy climate, few partisans were heard to fret about those chilly currents
"beneath the surface." But once Jeffords made his move, the climate
changed dramatically. Although still adequate, the president's approval ratings started fluttering downward, and the more precise statistics grew grim-
mer yet, as his performance turned off more and more of those Americans
who, after his historic nonelection, still believed in giving him a chance.
Smelling blood, the press became a bit less reverent, and the White House
edged into a new defensiveness.

While it was surely brought on by the Jeffords switch, however, Bush's
sudden slump did not result from that embarrassment alone. In fact, the
new regime was riding for a fall from the beginning of its term—or even
earlier, the sordid circumstances of the president's anointment having
deeply angered millions of Americans, who did not simply vanish once the
networks dropped the subject. With those millions disaffected, the Democrats in hiding, and "the liberal media" on bended knee, Dick Cheney
and his president launched into a reactionary drive so reckless and un-
compromising that you'd think they hadn't been defeated at the polls: nix-
ing ergonomics regulation (which would have helped cut down the

national incidence of carpal tunnel syndrome), tightening personal bankruptcy laws, imposing gag orders on women's doctors, scheming to priva-
tize Social Security, undercutting campaign finance reform, and so on.
Although such moves were often underplayed by mainstream journalists
(especially on TV), the news did get around, as different groups had mo-
bilized against them, and now spread the word. On the other hand, the
media *did* play up Bush/Cheney's worst environmental gaffes—the quick
flip-flop on capping CO_2 emissions; the infamous postponement of new
arsenic standards for the nation's drinking water; Cheney's manly sneer at
conservation as "a sign of personal virtue," nothing more. Such easy shots
enhanced the growing sense that this administration wasn't there to serve
the people (although, in fact, its policies on the environment were pretty
close to Clinton/Gore's).[5] Above all, perhaps, there was the president's
enormous tax cut, with its big favors for the very rich—a bias that many
viewers could perceive, despite the right-wing propaganda drive to obfuscate it; and when recession struck in March, the drift of the economy
began to tell against the president, as it had done against his father ten years
earlier (until a sudden war distracted everyone). And, quite apart from Jeffords, this administration was already in potential public trouble over its
connections to Big Oil. In late April, Cheney started taking heat for his refusal to identify the members of the task force he'd convened to hammer
out the nation's energy policy—a clash that was already turning into a momentous face-off. At the same time, California's energy crisis was just coming to a head; and while the polls showed little national support for that
state's government, they showed far less for Bush, whose handling of the
mess aroused or reconfirmed widespread suspicion. Such scandals would
eventually have blown wide open even if Jim Jeffords never left the fold.
(Ken Lay attended six of Cheney's task force meetings, and Enron played
a crucial role in California's meltdown.)

Even flying at its highest, then, before the Jeffords episode, the Bush
White House was accruing so much corporate baggage—as well as theocratic baggage—that eventually the weight would drag it down (unless
the people were explosively distracted). After all, those variously hurt by the
administration's policies were in the clear majority, while those who had
profited were few; and by that simple calculus Bush/Cheney's days aloft

were always numbered. But there was still another, subtler factor in the president's decline, which was a consequence not only of his flagrant plutocratic bias but of the growing obsolescence of his only selling point—that he was not Bill Clinton.

Throughout the presidential race, Bush ran hard as the un-Clinton; and while we can't say that it won him the election, it was surely key to what success he had. His base supporters were intoxicated—stupefied—by his sly daily hints that he was Clinton's total opposite. They fell completely for his ritual promise to "restore honor and dignity to the White House," notwithstanding his own highly questionable past. That Bush may, in his personal life, have had some wilder times by far than Clinton ever did, or that Bush's public ethics were immeasurably worse than Clinton's (the former having made out like a bandit as the governor of Texas, while Governor Clinton didn't make a dime beyond his salary), were thoughts that Bush's followers could not take in, so fully propagandized had they been. For it was the Manichaean view *itself* that most appealed to them—Bush/Clinton cast as total and eternal opposites, like light and dark, or life and death, the good son coming, in his father's name, to end the bad dominion of the Man from Hell. That mythic schema sowed immense political confusion, by bolstering the popular canard that Clinton—NAFTA champion, bank deregulator, tough drug-warrior, welfare terminator, friend to corporate media—was a *liberal activist,* like Franklin Roosevelt, or Eleanor. (Likewise, it reconfirmed the popular canard that Bush—crony capitalist, corporate welfare dealer, government expansionist, champion of martial law—was a *true conservative,* like Franklin's cousin Teddy.) Through that pose the governor also distorted the true history of the Clinton years, forever promising to "change the tone in Washington," as if that "tone" would now be elevated by the same Republicans who had debased it in the first place. Whatever Clinton did in private, it was not he but they who made a giant cesspool of the public sphere, by hollering ad nauseam about his genitals and that blue dress, loudly calling him a "traitor," "liar," and "scumbag," and smearing every member of his family, including Chelsea. The bland assurance that *civility* would be restored and "the finger-pointing" stopped, by such a rabble of vindictive goons, was surely Bush's most outrageous campaign promise.

And yet, despite those tacit whoppers, Bush cannot be faulted for such sly self-differentiation, which is, of course, a tactic always used by candidates who run against incumbents. Thus JFK played up his dash and vigor contra Eisenhower/Nixon, Nixon his firm hand and foreign policy credentials contra Johnson/Humphrey, Carter his modesty and frankness contra Nixon/Ford. However, those presidents did not keep battering their predecessors even after winning office; Bush stands out for the gratuitous persistence of his swipes at Clinton, which went on through the first one hundred days, and did not stop after that. He dubbed himself "the on-time president" (not like Clinton), showily declared a dress code for the White House—even for the tourists (to end the Clinton-era casualness), and kept asserting that "I don't read polls" (as Clinton did). The Bush team seemed unable to promote their own ideas without invidious reference back to You-Know-Who. Insisting, on CNN, that the Bush agenda "*is* ambitious," Karen Hughes elaborated thus: "It's the difference between school uniforms and fundamental school reform. School uniforms is a small matter that under President Bush's philosophy is best left to local districts to determine. President Bush is determined, however, to fundamentally reform America's public schools." (Clinton had called for more school uniforms.) Minutes later: "We have said, and EPA Administrator Whitman has said, that the arsenic level in water will be somewhere between 3 and 20, which is far lower than the current 50, which President Clinton allowed to stand for eight years," etc. Such comments were a little stale, since Bush had been inaugurated *three months earlier*. (Hughes also paused repeatedly to mark the altered "tone in Washington," which, under Bush, was no longer "divisive and harsh and strident" as it had been under Clinton.)

That retrospective carping may have been a ploy, used to keep us all unfocused on the Enron/Cheney team's agenda; or the belated Clinton-bashing may have been a symptom of the Bushfolks' urgent psychic *need* for such an Evil One to pit themselves against. Whatever drove it, Bush's stubborn animus, although unusual among our modern presidents, seemed completely normal at the time, because the same obsession with the Sins of Clinton also raged throughout the media. With the last election tarnished by a dark array of major scandals that had—and still have—yet to be exposed, the press was quick to change the subject to Marc Rich and his allegedly illegal pardon (and to the Clintons' mythic theft from, and trashing of, the White House). The frenzy lasted throughout Bush's honeymoon, which was exceptionally soft in part *because* of that long, loud diversion—and then, just after Jeffords's defection, the frenzy finally petered out, probably because those not-quite-scandals had begun to pull poor ratings. (Eventually, in any case, the charge of theft turned out to be unfounded, the charge of vandalism fabricated, and the Marc Rich story overblown.) Thus Bush was now obliged to face the limelight wholly unprotected by the shadow of Bill Clinton; and so began the summer of his handlers' discontent, as everything went wrong for him, now that ever more Americans could clearly see what he was all about.

In June, "enfeebled politically" (as *The Guardian* put it), he swung through Europe. While he was gently toasted by the heads of state, his rough reception in the streets, and in the media, was duly noted back at home—exposure that not only overplayed his gaffes abroad but also highlighted his eccentric stands on global warming, "missile defense," and other risky issues. On that same trip, he told us that he'd peered into the soul of President Putin, and pronounced it good—a judgment that pleased no one in this country, right or left. ("He showed a certain inexperience," said William Safire in a troubled understatement.) The trip, in short, was not a hit. Although the White House—and the Democrats—insisted that the president had had an excellent adventure overseas, the national audience didn't buy it. "Far from giving him a political lift, Mr. Bush's European tour, though it drew largely upbeat news coverage, did not appear to help him in the eyes of the public," the *New York Times* reported on June 21. "More than half of Americans say they are uneasy about Mr. Bush's ability to tackle an international crisis, and more people than not say he is not respected by other world leaders."[6]

And yet what worried people most was not such amateurishness abroad, but "Mr. Bush's inattention to matters they most care about"—and his reactionary stand "on many of those issues, including the patients' bill of rights, education, energy, the environment, raising the minimum wage, prescription drugs and judicial appointments." That clear perception of the president's elitist bias grew a little sharper through July and August, and through September 10, and so he kept on slowly falling in most polls—just as his father too had sunk when the economy was in distress before and after Desert Storm. Most importantly, it was now clear that Bush's giant tax cuts *would* mean dipping into Social Security—the very thing that he had vowed repeatedly, throughout the race, and then as president, that he would never do. ("Hear me loud and clear: A promise made will be a promise kept!") His failure to address the high cost of prescription drugs—another early promise—likewise reemphasized his long indifference to mass needs, as the nation's elder voters scorned the feeble discount plan that his administration had announced with great fanfare and little consequence. And the growing mass impression of his rich-kid's carelessness was further hardened by his unexacting work habits (he was always in the gym) and the record-breaking time he spent on holiday. It was one thing for Ronald Reagan to knock off early and take plenty of vacations—he was over seventy, and he'd been shot—but such a light load seemed improper for so young and fit a chief executive; and in any case, the restful Reagan came off like a dripping workaholic by comparison with Bush, who clocked out more than any of his predecessors.

By early August, according to the *Washington Post,* he had spent 42 per cent of his first year—ninety-six days in all—kicking back in Crawford, at Camp David, and at Walker's Point, his parents' mansion up in Maine. Although he claimed repeatedly that he was working really hard ("I'm getting a lot done"), and would often pitch his epic relaxation as a healthy rustic antidote to "Washington" (where, he liked to hint, there were no *real* Americans—the sort who live in Texas), his easy schedule didn't do him any good. According to a Gallup poll released on August 7, 55 percent of the American people thought that Bush spent too much time at play. (It hadn't helped that, in July, he had thus marveled at the time it took to run the country: "The amazing thing about this job, though, is the job seems to follow you around.") Nor was the growing national perception of his weightlessness obscured by his August 9 address on stem cell research—a moment of grand anticlimax, which his propaganda team had ballyhooed for months. As a would-be-Solomonic settlement between the claims of Faith and Reason, Bush's quick oration was a flop, disappointing the believers and bewildering the scientists. And yet, of course, its aim was not to offer a coherent argument on either side but largely to persuade the great lay public that their president could sometimes think real hard. At that propaganda purpose too, however, Bush's speech was finally unsuccessful. Although the press near-universally saluted his apparent *gravitas,* the polls continued their inexorable decline. (Most members of the audience were not distracted by TV's then-daily overemphasis on the supposed crimes of Gary Condit, the right-wing Democrat who had replaced Bill Clinton as the media's scapegoat du jour.)[7]

Now things were getting serious—literally, as the presidential spectacle no longer seemed like such a hoot. By and large, it had been a laugh a minute with George W. Bush, whose casual antics gratified his followers and also solaced many of his critics. While there were millions who, after he was chosen by the Rehnquist Five, could never even bring themselves to watch him, much less chuckle at him, there were many other Democrats et al. who liked to snicker at his gaffes because it made them feel superior. Bush's devotees, meanwhile, were simply smitten by his broader slips, unapologetic shows of ignorance, and scripted moments of self-mockery, all of which they happily mistook for evidence of populism (and, of course, as further proof that Bush was not Bill Clinton). But as the summer waned and the economy grew worse, and the White House demonstrated no awareness of the problem, the laughs died down. Now his less-committed followers were more bemused than tickled by his cluelessness. "To me, he hasn't made any real statements to the American public about how he's going to get us back on track," said an Iowan who had voted for him. "I'm not sure I have the answer, but I don't know that he does, either." Such early boosters were increasingly turned off by Bush's act. "I go around the state, and some of my Republican friends are concerned that Bush is—not that he's lackluster, but that he doesn't project confidence as much as people are expecting from a president," one Pennsylvanian noted. "He does make fun of himself sometimes, and I think that hurts him. It just reinforces an image which he needs to get rid of." And for the president's detractors, the "What, Me Worry?" caricature had finally lost its charm. On August 2, Comedy Central cancelled *That's My Bush!*—a witless sitcom that was but the latest satire to depict the president as a good-natured idiot. That termination was more meaningful than any of the show's moronic scripts, for it revealed that there was little public appetite for so benign a view of Bush, whose actions were not funny, and who was not good-natured, as more and more news items now were making clearer every day—and as this book also argues.[8]

Appearing when it did, *The Bush Dyslexicon* was both advantaged and misrepresented by the president's first slide in the opinion polls. Although it warns against the notion that George W. Bush is just a comic simpleton, it surely rode the very wave that it deplores, no doubt appealing to some shoppers as yet one more jokey item like *Bushisms* or *My First Presidentiary*. (Many bookstores put it in the humor section.) Considering how many voters felt ripped off by the Republicans, however, such inadvertent marketing was hardly necessary. The trick, rather, was to get the word out, since, by and large, "the liberal media" would not review the book, or have me on their shows to talk about it—not too surprising, since the book deals just as critically with them as with the president. (I couldn't get on NPR or CNN but did appear—twice—on Fox News Channel, where they are not afraid.) And so I traveled, and toured heavily by phone and on the Internet, doing over sixty interviews throughout the summer. Because the presidential subject was then open for discussion, I made it into venues of all kinds—Michael Medved's show as well as FAIR's and Amy Goodman's, and smaller programs right and left throughout the country. It was an exhilarating journey, although mostly sedentary; I had countless memorable exchanges (and, finally, a best-seller). And as Bush/Cheney floundered in the backwash of the ever-worsening recession, I was eventually allowed into the mainstream, to talk about the White House and its latest propaganda. On September 10, I was interviewed by Rick Sanchez on MSNBC, discussing Bush's recent celebration of America's "communities of character"—a campaign to (in Karl Rove's words) "unite Americans by focusing on children, quality of life and universally appreciated values."[9]

That drive had been unveiled a month before, but it had done the president no good. By September 10, his approval rating had slipped down to its lowest level yet—50 percent according to CBS, 51 percent according to Gallup and Zogby—and on such bread-and-butter issues as prescription drug costs, Social Security, energy policy, and the federal budget, his numbers showed minority support, which seemed to be diminishing. In short, that iffy summer was about to turn the tide. "Some House Republicans returning from recess," reported *Roll Call* on September 6, are "worried about their chances of retaining control of the chamber next year." For his part, Bush returned to Washington well rested but with unpleasant prospects. As one political observer noted: "The overall landscape is littered with potholes and land mines."[10]

AFTER

As dramatic as it was, the apotheosis of George W. Bush did not happen overnight. The process took about a week, because the president had some trouble putting on his war face. When, sitting on the dais at Emma Booker Elementary School in Sarasota, Florida, Bush learned the news from Andrew Card at 9:05 A.M., his first response was not to jump up and take charge but just to sit there in what looked like paralyzed anxiety. Facing the press at 9:30, the president compounded that impression of debility with a brief statement read out in a shell-shocked monotone, and then a jarring ad-libbed reference to the terrorists as "folks" ("those folks who committed this act"). While that performance didn't do much for the nation's confidence, it was positively bracing by comparison with what the president did next, which was to vanish for the day. Without a word to his bewildered fellow-citizens, he and his party flew a zigzag route on Air Force One, first heading east, then north, then west ("It was unclear tonight why the jet took that course," the *New York Times* reported), and then veered south to Barksdale Air Force Base in Louisiana, where Bush deplaned just long enough to tell us, from what reporters termed "an unidentified location," that "Freedom itself was attacked this morning by a faceless coward"—a feeble shot, since he did not look very brave himself just then, on the run and looking spooked. ("It was not our best moment," conceded one White House official.) He then flew northwest to Offutt Air Force Base near Omaha, where we could see the presidential entourage all being grimly hustled into a low concrete bunker, which was another image that did not do wonders for the national morale—as Bush's fellow-partisans in Washington could see. With the president AWOL and evidently incommunicado, Republicans and Democrats alike were standing right outside the Capitol and talking to the press; and Republicans deplored his flight. "This is not 1812," said William Bennett. "It cannot look as if the president has been run off, or it will look like we can't defend our most important institutions." "I am stunned that he has not come home," a Bush fund-raiser said. "It looks like he is running. This looks bad." And the next day, William Safire wrote that "Bush should have insisted on coming right back to the Washington area, broadcasting—live and calm—from a secure facility not far from the White House."[11]

To counter that perception, Karl Rove spread the story that, soon after the president flew out of Florida, someone had anonymously phoned the White House with a convincing threat: "Air Force One is next." It rattled everyone, said Rove and others (including Condi Rice and George H. W. Bush), because the caller knew the secret code for Air Force One. The tale was not believable, since no one at the Secret Service, or any other pertinent agency, remembered ever hearing such a thing; and, in any case, *why* would the terrorists phone in a prior warning? The story was so weak that, at first, some mainstream reporters openly dismissed it, which only further emphasized the same subversive question that had dogged the president since he was crowned: Was he in charge? We later read that he had wanted very badly to return but was dissuaded, or overruled, by his Secret Service detail, and by Dick Cheney back in Washington—a scene suggesting Lou Costello rather than Tom Clancy. The hint of irresponsibility related to some other questions that, although the major media would never voice them, did come up online and in the streets. Why did the president not leave the school as soon as Card informed him of the second plane? Inexplicably, he hung out on the dais for six minutes, as if waiting to be told what might come next. For that matter, why had he not just canceled the event on hearing of the *first* collision—a great disaster having struck a global landmark in the nation's largest city—and started right away to work the phones, or even make his way up north, to be nearby?*

And yet such questions were the least important of the ones that now

---

*The national scope of the atrocity was not apparent until 9:45, when the third plane hit the Pentagon.

demanded to be asked, concerning not just his behavior on that day but our whole government's ability to serve us properly. How could the CIA, the FBI, and the FAA (and, as we would soon find out, the Centers for Disease Control and Prevention) all fail us so enormously? How was it that the Air Force had allowed those planes so easily to penetrate the airspace of Manhattan—then let another smash into the Pentagon? Obvious, momentous questions—but they finally went unasked, and the questions about Bush too went unasked, as the national trauma blew the president sky-high, transforming him (once he got his act together) from a very easy punchline into something like a God.

Bush's liberation from the Jeffords Interim began at 11:00 A.M. on September 13, with his intense turn in the Oval Office, following a very public telephone exchange between himself and, seated side by side up in New York, Mayor Rudy Giuliani and Governor George Pataki. Both men had won much praise for *their* performances on 9/11—especially the mayor, whose pointed tribute to the president was therefore likely to pump up the latter's wilted reputation. With the moment carried live on all networks, the now-gigantic Giuliani spoke as follows, thereby kicking off (as he was no doubt meant to do) the great drive to recast the smarting Dubya as another Caesar:

> I can't express to you how appreciative we are of your acting so swiftly. And, also, on that terrible day when our city was being attacked, you were in immediate communication with us, Mr. President, and helped to secure the city. And the work you've done for us, we all eternally appreciate. You've been a terrific leader and we're taking direction from you, and we're following your example. You've done a terrific job, Mr. President.

After the call, Bush warmed visibly to the heroic theme of Giuliani's testament, engaging the assembled press with a surprising self-assurance. Finally, one reporter stroked him with a question that—narrowly emotional, syntactically confused—was pure TV: "Could you give us a sense as to what kind of prayers you are thinking, and where your heart is for yourself, as you—?" Bush said this:

Well, I don't think about myself right now. I think about the families, the children. I'm a loving guy, and I am also someone, however, who has got a job to do—and I intend to do it. And this is a terrible moment. But this country will not relent until we have saved ourselves and others from the terrible tragedy that came upon America.

It was a riveting performance—certainly heartfelt, as Bush is not a gifted actor. Incoherent the statement surely was (especially that final sentence), but the forcefulness of his delivery was unmistakable. "This is a terrible moment." His lips were trembling as he said it, and his hard stare glittering with sudden tears, in what appeared to be a tight outburst of genuine emotion. The man before us was, indeed, no "loving guy," and also not the genial chucklehead of *That's My Bush!* At that moment, his was the iron bearing of a holy scourge—bent on vengeance, and convinced that God Almighty had selected *him* to do the job. (That creed is evident in many of his statements after 9/11, as the Postscript demonstrates.) Whether God approved of Bush's posture is unclear, but there's no doubt that it played extremely well in these United States at that traumatic hour. Especially by contrast with his prior awkwardness, this new assurance seemed refreshing to the frightened audience, who gladly took the show of leadership that he was able to provide. While he was not built to commiserate—to "feel our pain" as Clinton would have done, or as Giuliani did, surprisingly—Bush was pretty good at promising retaliation, which was at least distracting, if not consoling. Certainly the wounded nation was suffused with rage enough to make his "war on terrorism," and his promotion of it, very popular at first. And so, from September 13, as he persisted in his new campaign to boost the national morale, his ratings kept on leaping skyward. There was, on September 14, his feisty eulogy at National Cathedral ("This nation is peaceful, but fierce when stirred to anger"), followed by his visit to Ground Zero ("The people who knocked these buildings down will hear *all* of us soon!"), and then, on September 15, his down-home promises to "to smoke 'em out and get 'em runnin'," and, on September 16, his vow to "rid the world of evildoers" in an all-American "crusade," and so on, until that postapocalyptic first week culminated in his war address to Congress, which was very winningly composed, and which he delivered with a near-aplomb that was, for him, extraordinary.

That week of oratorical bravado quite wiped out the memory of Bush's early dithering and flight into the Heartland; and it wiped out much more besides. Since 9/11, we kept hearing now, George W. Bush was *someone else*—a paragon of "leadership," a rock of "character," a fount of "splendid eloquence," etc. Countless leaders have, of course, been deified by national emergency, but few have been remade as quickly and completely as this Bush. In many cases, those who had misread him as a simple tool, braying automatically at his most trivial mistakes, now automatically revered him. Such converts suddenly agreed with those who had seen Bush's flaws as signs of latent greatness—thitherto the notion only of a large plurality, but now the common wisdom. And so, before you knew it, the seeming bozo was our nation's savior. Not only were his famous foibles magically erased, but the president's entire political prehistory also slipped right down the memory hole—the fraud and thuggery in Florida, the Supreme Court's complicity, the appointment of John Ashcroft, the budget-busting tax cuts, the moves against Social Security, the screw-you foreign policy, the slash-and-burn environmental policy, the lame prescription drug plan, the Jeffords controversy, California's power blackouts, Dick Cheney's Enron blackout and the many other signs of Big Oil's toxic spread, and on and on. Such a tacky record contradicted Bush's recent incarnation as America's Augustus, and so the record (briefly) disappeared.

Certainly the corporate media did all they could to reinforce the mass amnesia. Eager, as ever, to exploit the craze, and also to score brownie points (or still more brownie points) with our now-towering president, they glorified him with a panting desperation that recalled the wartime cult of Stalin. We had the cable operations vying to outdo each other with slick, airless "profiles" of his brilliant leadership—shows that might as well have come straight from the White House. ("And he will not waver!" Andrew Card said at the end of one on CNN.) We had the national dailies and top TV pundits, along with scores of lesser lights, promiscuously classing Bush's meager rhetoric with the most exalted works of wartime oratory. ("When he said 'Let's roll' at the end, I think there is a bit of Churchill in that, in the sense that he was saying, 'This is not the beginning of the end, it is perhaps the end of the beginning,' " Chris Matthews yelled at Larry King on November 8.) In an extraordinary act of self-abasement, *Newsweek's* Howard Fineman, in December, deemed the president "a model of unblinking, eyes-on-the-prize decisiveness," called him "eloquent," "commanding," and "astute," and treated his simplistic tag lines as articulations of a reasonable policy: "From where does George W. Bush—or Laura, for that matter—draw the strength for this grand mission, the ambitious aim of which is nothing less than to 'rid the world of evildoers'?" And, in February, there was "War and Destiny"—not a network miniseries, but a reverent spread in *Vanity Fair*, which lionized the presidential team with solemn head shots and TV wrestlers' nicknames—Cheney was "The Rock," Ashcroft was "The Heat"—while ranking Dubya with Demosthenes. ("It's been a while since presidential rhetoric could raise the hairs on your arm," wrote Christopher Buckley. "Is this really the same frat boy who choked on his tongue talking about 'subliminable' advertising? Johnny got his gravitas.")[12]

Such overt Caesarism was continually reinforced by the discreet erasure of all incongruous information. Just as the news teams prettified the "war on terrorism"—and did it gladly, as if such a whitewash were a patriotic act—so did they work to idealize the man ostensibly in charge, by tuning out or underplaying all discordant facts about him. There was, first of all, his nonelection. The media chose, in mid-October, to postpone reporting on the long-awaited recount of the votes in Florida—because, they said, we were at war, which made resources tight, and also made the whole thing "utterly irrelevant," as the *New York Times's* Richard Berke asserted. (That the war was partly in defense of "democratically elected government," as Bush himself had said to great applause, did not, apparently, strike such reporters as ironic.) Then, a month later, the media did Bush/Cheney an enormous favor, by killing the important news that *Gore* had won the vote in Florida, and so, according to the Constitution, ought to be our president. This inconvenient finding was played way, way down, as, by and large, the newsfolk either sat on it (*ABC World News, NBC Nightly News*) or brazenly distorted it, highlighting Bush's slender victory *just in those four counties* where Gore had sued for hand counts. Such disinformation came from several broadcasts, but it was the *New York Times* that started it, with a front-page obfuscation[13] that gave lots of ammo to Rush Limbaugh, Matt Drudge, and many other daily warriors against "the liberal media."

It was more as our commander in chief, however, than as the leader of a great democracy, that Bush was constantly made over by the media, whose watchdogs guarded his persona with the loyalty and zeal of presidential handlers. Thus they kept on talking up his day-to-day performance, while spiking contradictory reports. When, at the end of September, AP and CBS confirmed that Air Force One had *not* been targeted on 9/11, the other media held back, as if to certify the president's excuse for speeding out of town. Far more troubling, however, was the media's failure to report those stories that would surely complicate his posture as a pure crusader. Our press has told us very little of the links between this president and our new enemy—such links as would have had the anchors turning somersaults if it had been Bill Clinton. Concerning Bush's family, first of all, the watchdogs have been perfect lambs. Most of them spiked the news that the bin Laden family owned a small piece of the Carlyle Group, employer of the senior Bush (an awkward fact reported only by the *Wall Street Journal,* and that drove the family to sell their shares); or that Salem bin Laden, Osama's older brother, seems to have invested in Arbusto Energy, George W. Bush's fledgling oil concern, back in 1976 (a story noted in the foreign press, and, stateside, only by such plucky independents as the *On-Line Journal*). The media have also been too tactful about Carlyle's profits from the "war on terrorism," through the (aptly named) Crusader, a giant, pokey howitzer made by United Defense, a Carlyle subsidiary. Although the Pentagon itself had hoped to phase it out (in Kosovo, it proved not to be worth the cost), that $11-billion turkey was resuscitated by the terrorist attack. "On Sept. 26, the Army signed a $665-million modified contract with United Defense through April 2003 to complete the Crusader's development phase," reported the *Los Angeles Times*—and few others, including *Multinational Monitor, Red Herring,* and Paul Krugman in his *New York Times* column. (The deal was never mentioned on TV.)[14]

And while the media laid off such family ties, so did they play down, or ignore, the larger links between the evil ones and our own government. There was the poignant case of John O'Neill, the Twin Towers' security chief who died on 9/11, and prior to that one of the FBI's top counter-terrorism experts. In November, it emerged that he had finally quit the Bureau in disgust because the State Department interfered with his inves-tigation of certain of Osama's siblings, then living here in the United States. O'Neill believed that he was stopped because of oil, and our unof-ficial closeness to the Saudis. That story broke in France, in an exposé by two investigative journalists, whose findings were then carefully neglected in this country, except for one brief story deep inside the *New York Times.* (O'Neill's death inspired many patriotic eulogies, but none made mention of the reason why he changed careers.) Clearly, the U.S. media were loath to follow any leads that might somehow implicate Bush/Cheney in the great disaster.★ Such deference may explain the media's weird uninterest in the catastrophic failure of intelligence and military readiness that was so horribly revealed on 9/11. In the months after, only Seymour Hersh of *The New Yorker* looked into the CIA's malfeasance. Otherwise, the press ap-peared to share the view of President Bush, who went to Langley two weeks after the attack to *praise* the agency for its great work: "I can't thank you enough, on behalf of the American people. Keep doing it." By failing to look into it, the media have, unconsciously or not, colluded with the White House, whose big-time occupants do *not* want 9/11 publicly in-vestigated. When, in January, Congress was preparing hearings on the mat-ter, both Bush and Cheney lobbied hard to get them dropped—a move that most Republicans did not support (and that the media, by and large, did not report).[15]

While the media did take the lead in glamorizing Bush, however, they were not forcing that heroic view on everybody else but merely coming

---

★After 9/11, the U.S. media were also silent on the catastrophic failure of the Clinton State Department, in the period 1995–98, to accept assistance from Sudan, whose government tried repeatedly to give the United States ample evidence that would have helped destroy Al Qaeda. The Sudanese had also offered to extradite two suspects in the bombings of the U.S. embassies in East Africa, but that offer was turned down. "This represents the worst single in-telligence failure in this whole terrible business. It is the key to the whole thing right now. It is reasonable to say that had we had this data we may have had a better chance of preventing the attacks," a CIA official told the *Observer* (UK) on September 29 ("Resentful West Spurned Key Terror Files," *Observer,* September 30, 2001). While it was covered by the British press (MI6 had also spurned the offers from Sudan), the story was ignored by mainstream journalists in the United States.

up with the heroic view that, for the moment, many people wanted. Traumatized, the journalists and many in the audience were eager for George W. Bush to be another Roosevelt; and they were just as eager *not to know* whatever disenchanting truths an independent press would try to tell them. Thus the terrorists did land a blow on our democracy, by knocking millions, briefly, to their knees—TV journalists included. "George Bush is the president," Dan Rather said to David Letterman on September 18. "He makes the decisions—and, you know, as just one American, he wants me to line up, just tell me where. He makes the call." (Moments later, while reciting lyrics from "America the Beautiful," the anchorman broke down in tears.) That fearful, warlike mood was all-pervasive after 9/11. It was clearly visible in Bush's disparate audiences throughout that first dark week—the well-heeled congregation in the National Cathedral, belting out "The Battle Hymn of the Republic"; the weary rescue workers at Ground Zero, chanting "USA! USA!" as Bush, bullhorn in hand, vowed swift revenge; the multitude in Congress, leaping up repeatedly, ferocious in their joy at the accomplishment of Bush's war speech—Republicans and Democrats alike, the latter as if also deeply grateful that they now no longer had to deal with Bush's theft of power.

The sudden move to crown this president, in short, was not a media creation, like the never-popular campaign against the Clintons, but a widespread and spontaneous eruption of mass fear and anger. Certainly there was rare heroism, in New York and at the Pentagon, and, from the nation (and the world), a great outpouring of material assistance, and an astounding show of thoughtfulness, compassion, generosity. (Living one mile from Ground Zero, I saw such goodness every day.) But as you moved farther from the site, in both space and time, the larger animus was unmistakable—and not unprecedented in our history, despite the inescapable refrain that "everything has changed." As at those earlier moments when this country was, or felt itself to be, at risk of alien invasion or subversion, so now, again, the temper of the times became authoritarian. For criticism of the president and/or the military, journalists were fired, teachers censured, bookstores vandalized, publications threatened with attack, and certain TV programs, songs, and comic strips blacklisted; and even the most temperate public questions as to U.S. foreign policy would often get the questioner excoriated, charged with treason, communism, atheism, sodomy, or even menaced physically. Meanwhile, Bush/Cheney's apparat was quietly seconding such grassroots actions by sending agents to interrogate Americans who had been fingered for dispraising Bush and making other wrong remarks: A. J. Brown, a student in Durham, North Carolina, was questioned in her dorm for forty minutes by two Secret Service agents and a local cop for possessing "un-American materials" (on her wall, a poster critical of Bush); San Franciscan Barry Reingold, sixty, had two FBI men at his door, because someone at his gym had overheard him dissing Bush. ("He is a servant of the big oil companies, and his only interest in the Middle East is oil," Reingold had said.) Such official visits—not the only recent federal intrusion on our civil liberties—were symptoms of an antidemocratic virus that was helped along immeasurably by 9/11.* (That you may not have heard about them only makes the problem that much worse—as those cases were reported only by the *Christian Science Monitor, University Wire,* and *The Progressive,* and noted by Nat Hentoff in his column in the *Washington Times.*)[16]

In such an atmosphere, it's not surprising that people quickly scraped the bumper stickers from their cars, pulled the placards from their doors and windows, took material down off their Web sites, etc.—out of a new sense of patriotic piety, or simple fear, or both, feeling that it was now "inappropriate" to question Bush in any way. Similarly, some corporate publishers decided to drop projects of the sort that had sold handsomely when Bush was still a butt. (That books could, like TV shows, now be canceled thus, even though some people would still buy them, is one more sign of how the book business has been transformed by corporate concentration.) After 9/11, Simon & Schuster, a division of Viacom, initially axed Jacob Weisberg's *More George W. Bushisms,* which had been scheduled to come out on Christmas Day, although his *George W. Bushisms* was still going strong. (On mature reflection, the publisher decided merely to delay the book.) More controversially, just after 9/11, HarperCollins, a division of

---

*Meanwhile, the danger—of both violence and repression—was much greater for Americans and immigrants of color than for white-skinned dissidents; and for them the danger came alike from federal agents and freelancing patriots.

Rupert Murdoch's News Corporation, told Michael Moore that his book *Stupid White Men,* of which 50,000 copies had been printed, was now "too offensive" to bring out. (This from the publisher of Howard Stern.) Moore would have to rewrite certain parts of it—especially the devastating bits about the president. Bush had done a "good job" since the attack, Moore was told, and not to say so was "intellectually dishonest." If the author did not make those changes (and pay $100,000 for reprinting), HarperCollins would have no choice but to pulp the extant copies. Although reason did at last prevail (thanks mainly to some bad publicity), the episode was yet another sign of how the world had "changed completely" after 9/11.

The Bush Dyslexicon was not at such a risk—its publisher not being owned by any pusillanimous conglomerate—and yet the book's career was certainly affected by the crisis. Bookstores nationwide now canceled readings, either out of managerial concern about my personal safety or because some customers had raised a fuss. Whereas talk radio hosts of every stripe had had me on, without a qualm, to talk, or fight, about the flailing president, things got much quieter once Bush was sitting on his pedestal. Only those hosts with the most receptive following would now invite me back, and often not to talk about the book itself but to discuss the general rage. Other hosts were either too intimidated by their listeners, or too gung ho themselves, to have the sort of conversation I could offer them. And so, while the book continued selling, it did so in a strangely furtive way, as if it were illegal. Nor was I the only one to feel the heat. People who had posted positive reviews online, including their e-mail addresses, were now flamed in the vilest terms by rightist cyberwarriors. And you could ask for trouble just by carrying the book around, as I found out from someone who had had it with him on the subway, prompting another passenger to jump all over him. "How can you read that? That's disgusting! What is that?" she demanded, telling him that she had "lost people" on 9/11. The book, he told her, had been written months before the terrorist attack, and dealt with Bush's use of language during the presidential race; but she was not mollified, and went on giving him the third degree until she left the train.

Others had the same hysterical reaction, 9/11 having knocked the stuffing out of them. That gruesome shock had left them crouching low before the altar of authority, mistaking mere conformist piety for civic duty, and so detesting all irreverent works as acts of treason and dishonor to the dead:

> As I write this, the rescue workers are still removing bodies from the WTC. We have military risking their lives overseas. We are at war. The media has kept us informed concerning these events. We have a great government . . . a great country. I won't forget how the attack on September 11th brought us closer to those things we hold dear . . . family, faith, friends. We became better citizens. This book is the antithesis of these ideals.

That dramatic bit on Amazon.com, posted on January 4, was much like other such responses in its visceral intensity, blind faith in our "great government," and absolute irrelevance to anything I'd written in *The Bush Dyslexicon*. Aside from taking shots at my profession (and at Clinton), those critics would assail the book with fierce pejoratives, while saying not a word about its claims which, it was clear, they didn't know, and didn't want to know. "I haven't read this book, and I don't plan on reading it," declared one candid surfer, who found it "nauseating and unbelievable" that anyone would even think of writing such a thing. Those were expressions not of disagreement with my arguments but of a deep hostility to argument itself—an animus that also drives our president, as his hotheaded followers can see, and as this book makes clear.

NOW MORE THAN EVER

The arguments in this book are particularly relevant, now that we're "at war," and Bush has risen. Specifically, they help explain the looming mystery of his *fundamental transformation* after 9/11—a mystery that, starting in December, was only deepened by the White House.

In the beginning, there was the widespread view that Bush had *changed completely,* the crisis calling forth a strength of character that took the whole world by surprise. We didn't know he had it in him, according to this view, which has a very strong appeal, as we have seen from countless famous tales of modest fellas—Bilbo Baggins, Claudius the Emperor, Michael Corleone—rising to the grand occasion. In the eyes of those who thought he had been *fundamentally transformed* (as Haynes Johnson put it in November), Bush was one such glorious contender. "You never can tell what a terrible calamity will do to people. Some fall apart. Some dither. Some panic. Some get very focused and clear-minded, and some find out what the purpose of their life really is," wrote Margaret Wente in September. "That's George Bush. He's found his focus and his purpose, and has transformed himself into a leader." (So awesome was that seeming change that some of Bush's backers even claimed to see the Hand of God somewhere behind it. Toward Christmas Eve, Mayor Giuliani claimed, on NBC, that "there was some divine guidance in the president being elected," and Cardinal Theodore McCarrick piously concurred: "He was where he was when we needed him. And he's still there where we need him now.")*[17]

As flattering as it sounded, that view was actually insulting, since it suggested that, without the late catastrophe, the president would surely be the floundering butt we all remembered (barely) from before. To wipe away that memory, Karl Rove swung into action with a bold antirevisionary view (and one that left God out of it). "To questions about whether the attacks of Sept. 11 turned Bush into a better leader, Rove answered that Bush was a great leader all along," the *Washington Post* reported on December 12: "'I for one don't buy this theory that September 11th somehow changed George Bush,'" Rove said. "'You're just paying better attention. He is who he is.'" To get this counterview across, the White House launched a propaganda minidrive, with Rove himself remaking the point frequently, and George and Laura also chiming in. "Moments of crisis," Rove told the *New York Times,* only "bring out the best, or the worst, in people," who are *not* transformed by their ordeals. "The idea that they somehow are fundamentally changed and become smarter or more visionary, more gifted and articulate, is just wrong." "In a lot of ways he is exactly how he's always been, and I think people sort of see him now for

---

*Both men were gently disagreeing with Laura Bush, who, to her credit, had just rejected the idea that "God picks the president."

how he's always been—very steady, and very disciplined, and a lot of resolve, but also a whole lot of compassion and a way to really connect with
people," Laura told Tim Russert on December 23.[18] The whole thing
clearly nettled Bush, who, at his year-end press conference, got testy in this
brief exchange (just as he would have done *before* his total change):

REPORTER: Mr. President, some say the events of 2001 have
                     changed you, while others say that you're the same
                     person you always were.

BUSH: Yes.

REPORTER: Who's right? Or is it fair to say there's some truth in
                     both arguments?

BUSH: Talk to my wife.★

In trying to spin Bush as having *always* been "articulate" and "visionary," Rove was badly overreaching (and not for the first time, or the last).
While people en masse are indeed amnesic, they are not so forgetful, nor
was the trauma so severe, that Rove could get away with his Orwellian attempt to plant new memories in our heads: "Bush's recent performance
merely erased the 'incredibly erroneous early impressions,' Rove said. 'Oft
times we look back and with the clarity of hindsight and the passage of
time realize those judgments were erroneous,' " the *Washington Post* reported. Unsurprisingly, his grandiose attempt at mass hypnosis failed to
counter that spontaneous first view of Bush as one remade by the national
ordeal. "Has Mr. Bush changed? Of course he has, even if the line from his
White House underlings is that the public is now seeing in the man what
they always saw. Anyone who has watched Mr. Bush for the past four
months can see how confident and assured he has become in speeches and
in unscripted question-and-answer sessions with reporters," wrote Elizabeth Bumiller in the *New York Times* on January 6.[19]

It was an interesting argument—and quite beside the point, because
both views were wrong. The president's new admirers could not see, nor

---

★Bush thus ended the exchange: "I don't know. I don't spend a lot of time looking in the mir-
ror, except when I comb my hair. And—listen, I'll give you a hint: I liked coming to the ranch
before September the eleventh. I like coming to the ranch *after* September the eleventh."

would the canny Rove admit, that *they* had been the partial authors of his seeming metamorphosis, their panic driving them to see an FDR where there was only Dubya. Bush made the collective fancy that much easier, moreover, by simply doing better than expected. Compared to any skilled and charismatic orator, he did a largely mediocre job—his posture wooden, and his sentences monotonously uninflected, so that his words seemed to originate in some place other than his mind. However, it had long been his good fortune not to be compared with betters, but only to himself (see pp. 36–38)—and this traumatic time was no exception. Because he'd started out so uninspiring—looking freaked, depending on his cue cards, promising to nab the guilty "folks"—he came across like Superman just by delivering his lines without a glitch, and by seeming surer than he'd seemed before. Thus did the president, to some extent, appear to do exceptionally well by virtue of how much his terrified beholders had "misunderestimated" him.

However, his new authoritativeness was not entirely in the eyes of those beholders; for Bush, when speaking out against the terrorist attack, *did* do a better job than usual—and yet that air of confidence did *not* mean that the president had "changed" in any way. In fact, as this book demonstrates, the theme of punishment has almost always had a certain sharpening effect on Bush's manner. It's when he's had to fake ideals that he does not believe in, feign emotions that he cannot feel, that he has been most prone to gaffes. But when the blast of war blows in his ears, Bush shows the certainty of one who *likes* to go on the attack, hang tough, say "no." We saw that side of him lunge into view at certain moments during the presidential race (see pp. 50–56), and, still more often, during his unpleasant prewar summer. But once Bush found his footing after 9/11, that side of the president was *all* we saw, as he could warn and threaten almost to his heart's content, and promise global warfare without end—and do it in good conscience, and, for quite some time, to vast applause (within our borders).

His sudden rise had everything to do with television; for now that he was saying mostly what he felt, the medium was his new best friend. If the president had tried to come across through print alone, the repetitiousness and flatness of his language would have doomed him. Nor would he have excelled on radio, with his stiff-lipped delivery and tinny voice. (There Richard Nixon had him beat.) But with its tendency to foreground mere demeanor, television now did Bush the giant favor of so playing up the way he *looked* and *sounded* that—especially at that tense time—you couldn't hear what he was *saying*. Such televisual success day after day was something that the president had not enjoyed before the terrorist attack. Formerly, when he had tried to come off as experienced ("a reformer with results") and/or "compassionate," the medium would mercilessly undercut the pose, making him seem comically divided: a nasty piece of work behind the mask of kindliness, an amateur for all his pose of fitness for high office. But now that he was speaking from his wrathful heart, the medium showed us someone who appeared as thoroughly united in himself. There was, of course, some stagecraft used to help him hammer home his angry point. Day after day he advertised his *focus* and *determination* and *resolve* by telling us repeatedly about his *focus* and *determination* and *resolve*—and his appearance strongly reconfirmed that winning verbal message, his *gaze* and *stance* and *gestures* seeming just as *focused* and *determined* as he kept on telling us he was. With no laughable discrepancies between his bearing and his words, the president appeared *resolved* indeed.*

And so the president was reinvented. From the very timely spectacle of his rock-hard demeanor, many viewers—and especially the press—now extrapolated other, inner qualities, despite the lack of any evidence that he possessed them. Thus our president did not just look more "focused," but *was,* as if by magic, also eloquent, farsighted, well informed, and wise—a testament to the eternal power of wishful thinking. "These are times for serious men who bring wisdom to bear on difficult problems," wrote one critic of *The Bush Dyslexicon.* "Bush's brilliance is seen in his handling of our nation since 9/11. Evidently, he is able to get his lucid point across to

---

*And that impression was enhanced by the now-total absence of Dick Cheney, who had always been there at the president's performances, hovering in the background and looking too alert, like Britney Spears's mom. Although pitched as a security precaution, Cheney's disappearance was intended not to save him from bin Laden but to protect the president from him, the cocky veep having irked Karl Rove and Karen Hughes by talking very big on *Meet the Press* the Sunday after the attack. By bragging of his central role on 9/11, Cheney made the president look like a hapless figurehead. His punishment—internal exile—helped to make the president appear to be in charge.

those in his charge as well as the majority of Americans. Not in recent history has a president managed to impart on his branch such a comprehensive understanding and acceptance of his philosophy and vision." Nor was it only true believers who perceived the president's deliberateness as proof of surer understanding. Here again is the above quotation from Elizabeth Bumiller—but this time with its final clause included: "Anyone who has watched Mr. Bush for the past four months can see how confident and assured he has become in speeches and in unscripted question-and-answer sessions with reporters, how he has command of the issues at hand."[20]

As the Postscript to this new edition should make clear, there was, in what the president *said* after 9/11, no evidence for such conclusions, just as there was never any evidence for Karl Rove's claim that Bush had been extraordinary all along. This is not a trivial point: for the truth does finally matter, even in the culture of TV. Regardless of your views—on Bush or Clinton, Gore or Nader, Republicans or Democrats, or none of the above—some things are true and some are not, and any nation that can't tell the difference is in trouble. It is not true, for instance—although Bush repeatedly said otherwise—that American taxpayers received a "tax refund" (or "tax rebate") in the summer of 2001. What they received was an *advance,* which had to be paid back. There was a difference. Likewise, it is not true—although the president asserted it—that Iran, Iraq, and North Korea have been allies in a secret war against us. The former two have long been one another's mortal enemies, while North Korea hasn't had much truck with either one of them (although it has been armed by China, which link our president did *not* deplore). Between that actual nonalliance and the presidential fiction of an evil "axis" there's a difference. And—to move from presidential misimpressions to the president himself—it is not true that Bush was "lucid" after 9/11, or that he showed "command of the issues," or, indeed, that he was comparable *in any way* to Lincoln, either Roosevelt, or Winston Churchill—all of whom had come to power legitimately, could orate off-the-cuff (and wrote their scripts themselves), knew what was going on (and more), and acted in the interests of their people. There is, in short, a difference.

We have to tell the difference, or we're lost. If you can't distinguish "refunds" from "advances," you are likely to go broke; and if you see big bad alliances where there are none, you will end up locked in fights of your own making, and are bound to lose them. If either of those courses is disastrous, then it can't be right to hail the wisdom of a president who would urge those very courses on you—because he is unwilling, or unable, to tell truth from lie. Cut off from reality, such leadership is always headed for a fall; and when it goes, it often takes a lot of people with it. While modern history offers some spectacular examples of such hubris, we needn't wander back to Hitler's Germany to make the point. The managers at Enron also kept reality at bay by using language that befogged the minds of nearly all who worked inside the place. While ripping everybody off, those at the top obscured their thievery in part by flooding the employees' hearts and minds with lots of blather about "values"—those very "values" that the managers were just then busily violating. Working there, you could easily get yourself a coffee mug that had "integrity" imprinted on it, or a paperweight promoting "excellence." Or you could get yourself a poster that said this: "Respect: We treat others as we would like to be treated ourselves. We do not tolerate abusive or disrespectful treatment. Ruthlessness, callousness, and arrogance don't belong here." Between that gooey message and the hard reality, there was, to put it mildly, a big difference—which no one told; and when that difference did come out, it was too late.[21]

Bush's language is noteworthy, then, not merely for its formal uncorrectness, but for its substantive irrationality. Although it is embarrassing to have a president who says "not over my dead body" (January 5, 2002), or who announces that "this Thursday, ticket counters and airplanes will fly out of Ronald Reagan Airport" (October 2, 2001), such errors are only laughable because they don't pertain to anything of moment, and we do know what he meant. It is disturbing, on the other hand, to have a president who sometimes cannot tell illusion from reality—a president who isn't merely lying, but confusing spin with fact, reality with spectacle, history with TV:

I understand this is a unconventional war. It's a different kind of war. It's not the kind of war that we're used to in America.

The Greatest Generation was used to storming beachheads. Baby boomers such as myself was used to getting caught in a quagmire of Vietnam, where politics made decisions more than—more than the military sometimes. Generation X was able to watch technology right in front of their TV screens, you know, burrow into—into concrete bunkers in Iraq and blow them up.

This is a different kind of war that requires a different type of approach and a different type of mentality. (October 11, 2001)

Trying to convey a sense of poignancy that was quite foreign to him, the president here departed from the rules of English—and also from the facts of his biography, inasmuch as he was *not* "caught in a quagmire of Vietnam," but, like the hawkish Cheney, had got out of it (see pp. 100–102, 203–4). The broken grammar and the lie, however, were the least of it; for what was most remarkable about that improv was its revelation of a mind with little in it but some televisual clichés. *How* is this new war "unconventional," "different," and "not the kind of war we're used to in America"? First: "The Greatest Generation was used to storming beachheads." Such is the Brokaw/Spielberg/Ambrose view of World War II, which you might get from surfing cable—a warped view, since most of those who fought did not storm beachheads, and those who did did not get used to it. Moving on to Vietnam, the president confused some trite discourse *about* that conflict with the grunt's experience of the war itself—as if "quagmire" had referred to the actual terrain in Southeast Asia, and not merely to the war's unwinnability. Likewise, the (rightist) notion that "politics made decisions more than . . . the military" was an effort to explain why we had *lost* that war, and not a reference to the *kind* of war we fought in Vietnam. It was a protracted jungle fight against indigenous guerillas—which, in fact, may not be all that different from the "war on terrorism" that we are now fighting in the Philippines and elsewhere.

Bush then moved on to "Generation X"—as if his father's six-week Gulf War lasted long enough to have engaged a "generation." This time, Americans weren't storming any beachheads, there being few beaches in Iraq—and also, Bush suggested, no Americans, since all of them were following the action on CNN (or, as Bush put it, "right in front of their TV screens"). With everybody watching it on television, there were no U.S. soldiers fighting in the war, or any troops at all, in fact, but just "technology" attacking "concrete bunkers," every one of them precisely "taken

out" (and, of course, with no civilian casualties).* Thus did Bush nostal-
gically recelebrate the cool Atari spectacle that his dad and Dick Cheney
had concocted for the U.S. audience—a propaganda fantasy that he was
now invoking to convey the war experience of "Generation X."

And so, from those three wars—"beachheads," "quagmire," "TV
screens"—*this* war will be "different"—*completely* different. It will be "a unconventional war," "a different kind of war," it will "not [be] the kind of
war that we're used to in America," and, furthermore, it will be "a different kind of war that requires a different type of approach and a different
type of mentality." Bush having said it several times, it's only right to ask
just *how* the "war on terrorism" will be "different." Other than repeating
that it *will* be "different," the president did not come out and tell us how;
nor did his eventual military budget clear up the matter, since it apparently
included every high-tech weapon system that the Pentagon had ever
wanted—not, you'd think, the sort of thing a military would require to
fight "a different kind of war that requires a different type of approach and
a different type of mentality."[22]

By "different," what Bush obviously meant was that this war, unlike
those prior, lesser wars, *will never end.* It was a point that he kept making,
with a certain passionate insistence that seemed more and more gratuitous
as time went on. However good or bad the latest military and/or diplomatic news, and whether the prime suspects were now said to be alive
somewhere or maybe dead, the president would find a way to say—with
focus and *determination* and *resolve*—"This will go on and on and on." Such
is the terroristic subtext of the call-to-arms so frequently reiterated by the
president and his lieutenants. Scripted, Bush would make it sound as if this
struggle will *not* last forever.

> To all the men and women in our military, every sailor, every soldier, every air-
> man, every Coast Guardsman, every Marine, I say this: Your mission is defined.
> Your objectives are clear. Your goal is just. (October 7, 2001)

---

*In fact, the "bunkers" bombed by the United States, at Al Amerriyah, were full of women
and children.

Extemporizing, on the other hand, he and his fellow-warriors were not that clear—or rather, their intention was *quite* clear, although their language was obscure. Consider this reply by Donald Rumsfeld, who shortly after 9/11 was asked how we might know when we have won the "war on terrorism":

> Now, what is victory? I say that victory is persuading the American people and the rest of the world that this is not a quick matter that's going to be over in a month or a year or even five years. It is something that we need to do so that we can continue to live in a world with powerful weapons and with people who are willing to use those powerful weapons.
> And we can do that as a country.
> And that would be a victory, in my view. (September 12, 2001)

He said it with his usual craggy fervor and ostensible lucidity, as if he knew what he saying; and there was no follow-up, which bolstered the impression that it might have been a reasonable answer. And yet what Rumsfeld said was this: that "victory" in this war will mean convincing everybody in the world that we may have to fight forever, so that we can keep living in a world where we might have to fight forever. We will have won when we have made the people, here and elsewhere, understand that we can never win. Thus victory will be ours not when we have won some territory, or destroyed some army, or negotiated peace, but only when we have converted all the world to an apocalyptic faith—an aim that sounds uncannily familiar.

What we have learned from 9/11, then, is that it *can* happen here. Even here, where we have ads and anchorwomen, Wal-Marts and televangelists, full-frontal nudity and endless racks of DVDs, unreason can pervade the atmosphere just as it has done in more monotonous places. For it ultimately makes no difference whether the predominating media are mosques and audiocassettes or cable TV and the Internet—or even if the media are not owned by a few huge corporations (although such ownership does make things worse). What makes the difference, finally—and what makes everything the same—is the imperative of war, here in this peace-loving nation no less than in Baghdad, Pyongyang, or George Orwell's Oceania. The candidate who used to stammer so amusingly about "compassion" has now found his voice at last, because we have a war that's made him popular, that's made it dangerous to disagree with him, and that, as far as he's concerned, has placed God on his side. And as the war has sharpened up his act, so has it been a killer story all throughout the media, and made a lot of good Americans feel proud again. But none of that is any reason for the rest of us to go along with it.

—Mark Crispin Miller
New York City
February 2002

The firmness with which the people have withstood the late abuses of the press, the discernment they have manifested between truth and falsehood, show that they may safely be trusted to hear everything true and false, and to form a correct judgement between them. As little is it necessary to impose on their senses, or dazzle their minds by pomp, splendor, or forms. Instead of this artificial, how much surer is that real respect, which results from the use of their reason, and the habit of bringing everything to the test of common sense.

—THOMAS JEFFERSON TO JUDGE JAMES TYLER,
JUNE 28, 1804

See, I believe in the power of the people. I truly do. I do.
—GEORGE W. BUSH, MARCH 6, 2001

LOOK WHO'S TALKING

On picking up *The Bush Dyslexicon,* you may think you've seen this sort of thing a hundred times before—and not only in bookstores but on TV.*
This book, you figure, must be just another snickering ad hominem attack on yet another U.S. president—a blast of easy satire, meanly motivated. On the one hand, it might be a piece of laughing propaganda by, or for, the party out of power, in this case the Democrats now doing to George W. Bush what, say, the Republicans, and/or the Christian Coalition, did to Bill Clinton or what the Democrats had done to Richard Nixon or what the right had done to FDR: putting out a mocking version of "the record," full of campaign lies and comic gaffes and damning statements taken out of context. Or this book might be a mere commercial venture, with no partisan affiliation—a lite anthology of famous bloopers, offering a bound equivalent of an evening's worth of campaign-season stand-up, TV's sharpest wiseguys taking on the latest round of flubs and pratfalls. Thus this *Dyslexicon* would fall into the rich—and often lucrative—tradition of David Frye (doing Nixon), Chevy Chase (doing Gerald Ford), countless mimics doing Jimmy Carter, and so on, right up through the last campaign, when everyone was doing the "robotic" Gore and Bush the Bumbler. And so whether you regard it as a partisan assault or an attempt at cashing in, this book may strike you as either a cheap shot or a guilty pleasure, de-

---

*By and large, I use "television" to denote the medium per se, and "TV" to indicate the medium as we know it: owned by multinational corporations, dominated by commercial advertisers.

pending on which man you voted for—assuming you could vote, or even wanted to.

First impressions often tell the truth, as I will argue here. Your first impression of this book may be off the mark, however. For one thing, the *Dyslexicon* is not a piece of party propaganda. Its aim is not to move the masses to take some simple action, nor is it part of any broader effort by the Democrats. (As a New Yorker, I could vote safely for Ralph Nader, and I did so with a certain wary pride.) Nor does this book play any propaganda tricks. It includes no items altered or abbreviated, nor is it cunningly selective, but rather reprints passages at length and places entries in their proper context—at times even debunking certain unfair raps against this Bush or his father. Most important, this book does not promote the dangerous simplicity that marks *all* propaganda, good or bad, backward or enlightened. ("All propaganda is a lie, even when it is telling the truth," as George Orwell put it.) While it is clearly "anti-Bush," in other words, it is not a tacit advertisement for some simple other way. (Indeed, its tacit purpose is to warn *against* the sort of warlike either/or that is destroying our democracy, through both the GOP and major media.) On the contrary, this book admits complexity, honoring paradox and ambiguity—a flexible approach that doesn't make for propaganda, which tightly answers every question so as to leave you grinning in assent.

While it promotes no party line, neither is this book a mere anthology of funny bits. Amusing as it often is, *The Bush Dyslexicon* has not been crafted just for laughs, although that would have been an easy job. For one thing, such manipulation would have been dishonest—and irrelevant, because the situation that we're in today is really not so funny. Even if our president were the cheery cretin that such satire makes him out to be, it wouldn't make our plight a comic one, for he has a highly seasoned, wholly ruthless, and, for that matter, deeply humorless cabal of rightist pols and operatives around him—and that's no joke. In any case, our president is not an imbecile but an operator just as canny as he is hard-hearted—which is to say that he's extraordinarily shrewd. To smirk at his alleged stupidity is, therefore, not just to miss the point, but to do this unelected president a giant favor since, as Shakespeare's Prince Hal reminds us—and as Bush himself has often said—it suits a politician to have everybody thinking he's a dunce, especially if he wants to do things his way. The satire that sells him short, therefore, can only work to his advantage, by blinding us to his team's big-time plans and causing us to overlook his own prodigious skill at propaganda.

Far from merely goofing on this president, then, this book is meant to shed some light on propaganda in our time. The *Dyslexicon* attempts to give the lie to that enormous wave of propaganda—a joint production of the GOP and major media—whereby George W. Bush was forced on us as president, and then, after his inauguration, hailed almost universally for his amazing charm, his democratic ease, his rare ability to be all things to all Americans, and so on. Our experience of this transparent coup has been disorienting from the start. On the one hand, TV has clearly shown the truth about him—with his own inadvertent help, since Bush is strangely frank about himself. His body language bellows his uninterest, his distraction, his uneasiness, his callousness; and he tends to blurt out all or part of what he's really thinking, even as he's trying to lie about it (a linguistic struggle that intensifies his incoherence). Meanwhile, his handlers and the mainstream media all keep on trying to play the revelations down, forever countering the obvious with lots of upbeat spin and tactful silence. Thus TV keeps on sending us an eerie double message, by showing us one thing and telling us another. Those who want to buy the pitch prefer the latter, naturally, while those who just can't buy it feel as if they must be going crazy, what with all those smooth authoritative voices claiming that this man *should* be our president—when we can see, and have seen all along, that that is simply not the case.

Thus we are the victims of a strange new national disorder. It is as if the U.S. body politic were itself afflicted with a corporate version of dyslexia. The individual dyslexic cannot learn to read because he is unable, for whatever reasons, to translate letters into sounds. Because he can't decode those printed symbols for their phonic content, the writing on the page can make no sense to him. Today our body politic is comparably disabled, although it isn't written language that's the problem. The head that drives that body forward is, of course, the media machine—the busy neural network of producers, editors, anchors, journalists, and pundits, all subtly guided by the propagandists of the right. While it has no trouble scanning press releases or providing copy for the TelePrompTers, that swift, collective mind is fatally dyslexic when it comes to doping out the very spectacle that it presents to us. Unable to perceive the glaring daily evidence of absolute hypocrisy and cynical manipulation, it cannot read the writing on the wall—which, meanwhile, is crystal clear to many of the rest of us. The dyslexics at the top may be extremely savvy, yet they lack (to quote Orwell again) that all-important knowledge "in the bones" whereby we try, down here, to make our way. Seeing that it's all gone wrong yet always hearing, from on high, that everything is perfectly all right, we each feel—whether we can read or not—as helpless and perplexed as any undiagnosed dyslexic faced with street signs, menus, newspapers, and exams.

Against all that, *The Bush Dyslexicon* is meant to set the record straight: to remind us of the truth that TV shows us, even as it keeps on lying about it—much like the president himself, who, unless he knows his script by heart, often tells the truth despite himself, and does it most transparently when he is lying. (In this he is much like his dad, as we shall see.) By thus corroborating what TV so viscerally conveys, the book may also help dispel the great myth of "the liberal media"—a preposterous notion (or Big Lie) that Rush Limbaugh and his screaming brethren have long since sold to millions of Americans. And, more subtly, by pointing out the truths that television has revealed to us, this book may also shed some light on the bizarre postmodern form that propaganda often takes today, here in the culture of TV—wherein the falseness of the spectacle before us is a sort of open secret, obvious to any viewer who wants to see it and, strangely, all the more deceptive for that fact.

FIRST IN HIS CLASS

Of all his flaws, the president's illiteracy is—or was—the one most noted by the media. Governor Bush's way with words (and logic, and books) got prominently covered in the months before Election Day, although journalists eased off as time went on. His bite-sized gaffes were perfect for TV, which duly replayed some of them, while Frank Bruni of the *New York Times* tracked the candidate's most flagrant boners. (Meanwhile, long lists of Bushisms—carefully compiled for *Slate* by Jacob Weisberg—criss-crossed the country via e-mail so that the Democratic precincts of all cyberspace were finally saturated by November 7.) More influentially, the televisual concentration on Son of Bushspeak—George H. W. Bush having had a similar problem—extended quickly to the realm of late-night comedy, which is the surest way to the nation's consciousness. (Of course, the shtick on Bush was more gleeful, and far more insulting, than the tittering journalistic bits.) Such reportage-cum-stand-up did the trick, to some extent. Soon everybody knew that Bush could not pronounce "subliminal," while few had heard—or ever would hear—of his neglected military service, his many shady business dealings, or his close ties to the likes of Representative Tom DeLay, to name a few of his more substantive and complicated failings.

The governor was not the first American presidential candidate to stand accused of gross illiteracy. In the fierce campaign of 1828, the genteel supporters of incumbent John Quincy Adams—that dour, standoffish veteran of the Harvard faculty—tried to beat back the advance of Andrew Jackson, the much-loved hero of the War of 1812, by casting him as far too rough-edged and unthinking to "discharge the complicated and arduous duties of President," as one Whig politician put it. To make their case that Jackson was a man "who cannot spell *more than about one word in four*," to quote one piece of Adams propaganda, the Whigs circulated letters that included stark examples of Old Hickory's faulty English—proof that he was too coarse, too "savage," to be entrusted with the nation's leadership. The general was "a barbarian who could not write a sentence of grammar," Adams later hotly reminisced, "and hardly could spell his own name."[23]

There are, however, some big differences between the anti-Jackson campaign and the recent coverage of the governor's defective English. First of all, the Whigs themselves invented those "examples" of the general's illiteracy—as they were forced to do, since Jackson was in fact an eloquent haranguer, whether at the podium or at his desk, even if his syntax wasn't always perfect. The governor's linguistic record, on the other hand, is all preserved on video and/or audio. It is therefore as authentic as the secret tapes of Richard Nixon or as any flub or pratfall broadcast on *America's Funniest Home Videos*.

As the *Dyslexicon* makes clear, this president would seem to be the most illiterate in U.S. history. His is not the merely technical illiteracy of most Americans, who, irrespective of their class or education, routinely make grammatical mistakes so slight that only pedants mind them: George W. Bush is so illiterate as to turn completely incoherent when he speaks without a script or unless he thinks his every statement through so carefully beforehand that the effort empties out his face. His eyes go blank as he consults the TelePrompTer in his head, and he chews uneasily at the corner of his mouth, as if to keep his lips in motion for the coming job, much as a batter swings before the pitch. Thus prepared, he then meticulously sounds out *every . . . single . . . word,* as if asking for assistance in a foreign language. Without such hasty mental planning, Bush is liable to make statements that either don't mean anything ("I will have a foreign-handed foreign policy") or require unscrambling ("Families is where our nation finds hope, where wings take dream") or say the opposite of what he means ("Well, I think if you say you're going to do something and don't do it, that's trustworthiness") or are just dead wrong ("The legislature's job is to write law. It's the executive branch's job to interpret law").

Indeed, our president's illiteracy is something of a miracle, as rich in its own way as the expository genius of the Founding Fathers. His incapacity does not reflect one problem in particular but several kinds of verbal defect. As Gail Sheehy has argued, the president may actually suffer from dyslexia. (For Governor Bush's response to that diagnosis, see p. 102.) Surely that condition may explain his tendency to transpose words and to blurt out the opposite of what he means. It may also explain his frequent malapropisms ("hostile" for "hostage," "arbitrary" for "arbitration," "preserve" for "persevere," "cufflink" for "handcuff," etc.). However, dyslexia would not account for his incessant violation of the fundamental rules of grammar ("The question is, how many hands have I shaked?"), his syntactic accidents ("It's not the way America is all about"), or his utter prepositional confusion. Nor—far more important—would dyslexia explain the president's thorough unacquaintance with the system that he now purports to lead or his unawareness of the world beyond our borders (except for northern Mexico). To believe that Social Security is somehow not a federal program, that the word "insurance" is mere Washington bureaucratese, to think that Kosovars are "Kosovarians" (and the Greeks "Grecians," and the East Timorese "East Timorians"), and to confuse Slovenia with Slovakia—and the judicial branch of our own government with the executive—is to suffer from no disability but ignorance.*

Clearly, we have come a long way from the discursive model of the Founders, those broadly educated and "profoundly reasonable people" whose language was exemplary for its "everyday businesslike sanity," as Bernard Bailyn has observed. Of course, it is unfair to measure Bush against the likes of Madison, Monroe, and Jefferson since, as expositors, they surely have *no* peer among the modern tenants of the White House. Perhaps, then, we should compare Bush not with the very greatest of his literate predecessors but with those who tend to place *last* in historians' rankings of American presidents. Yet even in comparison with most of them as users of the language, this Bush does not compete. The one likely peer who comes to mind is Zachary Taylor, an arrogant patrician dunce renowned for his contempt of learning. Otherwise, even the least of our premodern presidents are daunting in their eloquence and erudition, since all of them were well instructed in the art of rhetoric (which back then denoted far more than "baloney"—the colloquial meaning of the word today). The well-read James Buchanan could make thorny legalisms understandable to common folk; Franklin Pierce—a distant forebear of our president on Mother's side—was fluent in Greek and Latin, like so many of his peers, and an adept of Locke's philosophy; John Tyler was also a cultivated lawyer; and the autodidact Millard Fillmore was assiduous in compensating for the rudimentary education of his early years. (Throughout his unimpressive stint as president, Fillmore was never "heard [to] utter a foolish or unmeaning word," claimed his attorney general.) The disastrous Andrew Johnson was a first-rate speaker, while his bibulous successor, Ulysses Grant, could boast some literary genius, as readers of his *Memoirs* know. In the last century, the dim and genial Warren Harding—although a stunning wind-

---

*Here it should be noted that dyslexia bears no relation to acuteness, eloquence, or the capacity for knowledge. The dyslexic population has included brilliant figures boasting high intelligence of every kind—Albert Einstein, George S. Patton, Winston Churchill, and Thomas Edison among them.

bag—at least had what it took to edit several newspapers, and the hapless Herbert Hoover was a copious and able author.[24]

For all their faults as chief executives, none of those men could ever have said anything like "A leadership is someone who brings people together" or the celebrated "Is our children learning?" Yet here again it may be unreasonable to hold Bush—a child of television and a product of modern education—to the vanished standards of nineteenth-century schooling. Against them, such precise and ready talkers as Bill Clinton also fail, and so do nearly all the rest of us. ("If we wish to become great and useful in the world, we must improve our time in school," wrote Grover Cleveland, age nine, in 1846.) Perhaps, then, we should measure Bush against those postwar presidents who in their time also took flak for verbal failure. Eisenhower was often ridiculed for the syntactic murk of his ad-libbed remarks—but such obfuscatory rambling was deliberate, a canny way to dodge the question without seeming to. Despite his folksy aspect, Eisenhower was a subtle and exacting rhetorician, as Emmet John Hughes, his top political adviser, points out in *The Ordeal of Power,* and at his best a vivid writer, as *Crusade in Europe* demonstrates. Obsessively prolific, the mad Nixon was throughout his public life often faulted—rightly—for the deep dishonesty and egocentric bias of his output, both written and spoken; yet even his most violent memos were drafted in sound English, and in his lucid intervals he could indeed be "perfectly clear," as we can see from his debates with Kennedy. And even Ronald Reagan, although much mocked for his simplicity, was in fact an avid reader—albeit one with a hearty appetite for anti-Soviet propaganda—and (when he knew his lines) an excellent speaker—a talent that depended on the vast archive of quips and anecdotes stored in his head. "His mental cassettes," Lou Cannon writes, "were crammed with odd scraps of information and obscure insights that he had acquired from his reading [and, of course, his viewing] and committed to memory." Thus Reagan did have an absorptive and inquiring mind of sorts—even if he did think that the singular of "indices" was "indice".[25]

And yet without a script, of course, the Great Communicator tended either to fall mute or make no sense at all, nor was he capable of writing books or full-length speeches by himself. However, Ronald Reagan was another Winston Churchill by comparison with George W. Bush—whose only competition for the anticrown of presidential barbarism would appear to be the gentleman who sired him. In his day, the frenetic and uneasy George I was just as tongue-tied as the laid-back W. Throughout the 1988 campaign, in fact, his penchant for "Bushspeak" was a subject of much tittering coverage, which pushed the contrast between his awkwardness and Reagan's way with (scripted) words. Just like his son, the elder Bush was ridiculed for meaningless assertions worthy of Sam Goldwyn ("It's no exaggeration to say the undecideds could go one way or another"), for mangled syntax (he claimed to oversee the writing of his speeches, "inarticulate as though I may be"), for using the wrong word (the Democrats had "cramped down on any discussion of individual initiatives"), and for non sequiturs, mixed metaphors, and wild allusions ("You cannot be president of the United States if you don't have faith. Remember Lincoln, going to his knees in times of trial and the Civil War and all that stuff. You can't be. And we are blessed. So don't feel sorry for—don't cry for me, Argentina"). He was also given to bizarre remarks whose psychic roots are best left unexplored: "We have made mistakes, we have had sex," he once claimed in a public testimonial to Ronald Reagan. (For his part, the son once told a crowd of Iowans, "The most important job is not to be governor, or first lady in my case.")[26]

Despite their similarity, however, Bush *père et fils* are not coequals at the mangling of the mother tongue. If Bush the Elder spoke "like a sixteen-year-old from Andover," as one political consultant sneered in 1988, the son often sounds like an even younger child—and one who hasn't been to any school at all, so much more basic are his errors. ("Will the highways on the Internet become more few?") In the annals of executive unlearnedness, in fact, the only figure near identical to Bush the Younger is, of course, his dad's unfortunate vice president (whose choicest flubs are frequently confused with W's). Like past bloviators beyond number, his running mate included, Quayle excelled at grave assertions of the wholly obvious. "This election is about who's going to be the next president of the United States!" he once exulted on the stump. ("More and more of our imports come from overseas," the governor of Texas once observed.) Quayle was also an impressive malapropist—noting, for example, that "We [Republicans] understand the importance of having the bondage between the parent and the child." ("We cannot let terrorists or rogue nations hold this nation hostile or hold our allies hostile," warned the governor.) And yet Quayle's English was, like W's, a brew so rich and strange that no specific types of defect can explain its dizzying effect. As every gaffe collector knows, Quayle's richest bits are idiotic gems, each one as exquisitely perplexing as a Zen koan or line of Hegel. "Bobby Knight told me this: 'There is nothing that a good defense cannot beat a better offense.' In other words, a good offense wins." ("This is a world that is much more uncertain than the past. In the past we were certain, we were certain it was us versus the Russians in the past. We were certain, and therefore we had huge nuclear arsenals aimed at each other to keep the peace. . . . You see, even though it's an uncertain world, we're certain of some things," explained the governor of Texas.)[27]

Even in this contest our president stands out, however. He has outdone his dad's clueless second-in-command in part because his goofs are so much more abundant than the much-derided Quayle's, and also because his bloopers often are so much more grammatically primitive than those of Quayle—who, even if he couldn't spell "potato," never seems to have said anything quite like this: "Laura and I really don't realize how bright our children is until we get an objective analysis."

And yet the true distinction of our president lies not in his illiteracy per se but in the fact that he could not care less about it. He shows a perfect grinning unconcern that is unprecedented in the history of American leadership. There was no such princely callowness about Bush/Quayle, those other rich kids at the top. After his terrific hazing at the outset of the '88 campaign, the Indianan knuckled down and made a manful effort to improve his mind—or at least his standing—by plowing through a lot of heavyweight biographies and publicly regretting having goofed off at De-Pauw: "Looking back, I should have pursued philosophy and history and economics and things of that sort in college more, but I didn't." Marilyn Quayle had also tried to help, by telling journalists out on the stump that Dan "really is the studious sort," a guy who "tries to read Plato's Republic every year." ("He isn't an egghead intellectual, which I find very refreshing," she added hastily.) Although George Bush also was a lightweight, he came across like Lincoln next to his frenetic little running mate, and so there was no need for him to play the scholar once elected.[28]

Yet even he took pains to seem as if he cared about the precincts of the mind. He claimed to want to be "the education president," and Barbara Bush pitched in by making "literacy" her major issue as first lady. In a pinch, Bush could even shoot the breeze about his reading, which included Tom Clancy (a Reagan favorite), nonfiction about flyers in World War II (Bush having been one), business sagas like *Barbarians at the Gate* and *Liar's Poker,* prophetic works like *Megatrends 2000,* the fishing magazine *Bassmaster,* and, for laughs, Dave Barry. Bush was frankly put off by anything too challenging (*War and Peace,* an Andover assignment, had flummoxed him, but then so did the movie *Field of Dreams*) or just "too fat." Although his reading wasn't highbrow, it was a miracle that he could read at all, considering his wild hyperactivity and minuscule attention span. "He jogged and drove his boat *Fidelity* and played tennis and pitched horseshoes with the restlessness of a teenager," writes Dan Quayle, capturing a speedy adolescent spirit that just wasn't made for reading books— or any text much longer than a thank-you note. Bush was even tired out by his own speeches if they weren't bite-sized. "He usually got bored in the middle, even if it was only two pages long," writes John Podhoretz.* And yet the father still was far more literarily inclined than his impatient eldest son. Our president stands out not merely for his lifelong inability to sit and read (a feature of dyslexia, after all), but for his proud uninterest in the pleasures and rewards of reading.[29]

Such deep indifference was apparent in Bush the Younger's own half-hearted efforts to persuade the audience that it was otherwise. On the one hand, he, or Karen Hughes, his communications capo, was always ready to assert his Barbara Bush-like dedication to the world of letters: "Our capacity for discovery is never lost as long as we continue to read," he (or someone) told the *American Spectator.* He would also rattle on about his

---

*"Clark Judge, who had written for him when he was vice-president, would deliver a speech to Bush and the first thing he would do was weigh it in his hands; if it was more than a five-minute peroration, he would say, 'I don't know, this looks pretty heavy to me.' " John Podhoretz, *Hell of a Ride: Backstage at the White House Follies, 1989–1993* (New York: Simon & Schuster, 1993), p. 82.

"love" of "history" (as he did on C-SPAN), and insist that he did "read books all the time," and yet was seldom able to come up with any titles. Repeatedly that unconvincing pose of his would break apart when someone asked him—sometimes meanly, sometimes innocently—for details. In December 1999 Bush took up a disarming prop: a nice new copy of James Chace's *Acheson,* which he schlepped everywhere he went and which he cited ostentatiously at the Republican debate in Manchester, New Hampshire. Asked just what the book had taught him, he came up with a windy C+ answer (and then John McCain upstaged him with a pointed reference to an anecdote in Chace's book: see pp. 127ff.). As a constant reader, Bush fared no better in the world of children. "I can't remember any specific books," he 'fessed up in South Carolina to a schoolchild who asked him what he'd liked to read when he was small. (In fact when he was small, the only thing he read was baseball cards.)★[30]

Bush was not only unembarrassed by such revelations, but was clearly miffed that anyone would even care, since he was "a guy who's been an accomplished governor of the second-biggest state in the union," as he put it to the *Washington Post.*[31] Furthermore—although he didn't say it outright—he was, after all, George Bush. (On Bush's reading, see "Curious George," pp. 123ff.) Such brazenness reflected badly not just on the candidate per se. That Bush could be so cavalier about his ignorance, whereas the brainless Quayle had felt obliged to mime profundity, suggests a certain decadence within the culture of TV—a serious decline in "standards," as Bush himself would say.

★That gaffe only worsened Bush's credibility problem over children's lit. A few weeks earlier, responding to a Pizza Hut survey of the nation's governors, the candidate claimed that his very favorite children's book had been Eric Carle's *The Very Hungry Caterpillar*—which came out in 1969, when Bush was almost twenty-three years old. And of the seven titles Bush (or someone) had sent in to Pizza Hut, another three—*James and the Giant Peach* (1961), *Tuck Everlasting* (1975), and *Sarah's Flag for Texas* (1993)—were all published some years after Bush left grade school. That snafu clearly was not Bush's fault. The titles on his list were books that had been read to his own daughters. Several other governors (that is, their staffs) had made the same mistake, which suggests an ambiguity in the questionnaire from Pizza Hut. Nevertheless, what counted was the mass perception of the error—a mass perception that, as in Bush Sr.'s case, was basically correct, since Governor Bush, as it turned out, could not remember any books from his own childhood. Nor, off the cuff, could he recall his daughters' favorite childhood books, since Laura clearly was the one who had always read the girls to sleep.

THE PLOWMAN

Such frank boobery would seem to represent a culmination of the long, strange history of anti-intellectualism in America. Certainly George W. Bush has always postured as a good ole boy, who don't go in fer usin' them five-dollar words like "snippy" and "insurance." That pose recalls, again, the case of Andrew Jackson, whose campaign was the first one to deploy the Jeffersonian distinction between "the plowman and the professor," casting Adams as a European sort of fancy-pants, book-smart and effete, while praising General Jackson as a man of mighty deeds and lightning intuitions. "Behold, then, the unlettered man of the West, the nursling of the wilds, the farmer of the Hermitage, little versed in books, unconnected by science with the tradition of the past, raised by the will of the people to the highest pinnacle of honor, to the central post in the civilization of republican freedom," gushed one Jackson propagandist. "What wisdom will he bring with him from the forest?" Although such ripe encomia were based less on the candidate's biography than on the writings of Rousseau, they did the trick; and they helped set up a hardy paradigm that's still persuasive after all these years, at least in certain circles. Because of it, the shiftless W could seem, to some, a viable alternative to the far more seasoned and intelligent Al Gore—whose very strengths could be perceived, or spun, as weaknesses by contrast with the Texan's "naturalness" and "likeability" (as TV's punditocracy kept on asserting).[32]

However, the comparison with Andrew Jackson is, to put it mildly, problematic. That military hero was, of course, a fiery democrat, whose unaffected style bespoke an ardent dedication to the common people over all.* He thought it was his aim to serve them, and he said as much and said it clearly. (Indeed, such "calculated bluntness" was quite typical of nineteenth-century democratic oratory, as Kenneth Cmiel observes.) When "the laws" are used "to make the rich richer and the potent more powerful," Jackson wrote in 1832, "the humble members of society—the farmers, mechanics, and laborers—who have neither the time nor the

---

*Naturally, that group did not include the slaves—or the Indians, whom Jackson slaughtered with a gusto quite extraordinary even by contemporary standards.

means of securing like favors to themselves, have a right to complain of the injustice of their Government." Our president, on the other hand, is at the service only of the haves—as any cursory study of his record will make clear, and as even he himself acknowledged often, inadvertently, out on the stump. "I'm trying to protect my invest—my contributors from unscrupulous practices," he said in one interesting slip of the tongue. And as he famously put it up in New Hampshire: "I know how hard it is for you to put food on your family"—which, if what he'd meant to say were true, he probably would not have said. "This campaign," he said in Iowa, "not only hears the voices of the entrepreneurs and the farmers and the entrepreneurs, we hear the voices of those struggling to get ahead." That "the farmers," in his view, belong among "the entrepreneurs"—a subgroup so important to him that he named them twice—tells us where this "unlettered man of the West" is really coming from, despite the twang and cowboy boots. (For more on his oblique class consciousness, see "It's the Economy, Your Excellency," pp. 212ff.)[33]

Although the GOP machine has spun his elementary goofs as signs of kinship with the Common Man, they are in fact an insult to the people. Every bit of broken English, every flash of comfy ignorance, reminds us of a privilege blithely squandered: Bush attended Phillips Andover Academy, then Yale—olympian institutions that would never have admitted him if he were not a Bush (both schools are heavily shadowed by the family), and surely rigorous enough to have taught him English and a little history, if he had been receptive to the benefits of such a gift. However, he was both too limited and too secure to take full advantage of an opportunity that countless brighter, poorer folks have worked for, prayed for, and then been denied. Bush did the minimum at Yale, mainly partying and making good connections.* (Bush himself has chucklingly conceded that he was "never a great intellectual" at Yale.) Thus, in the matter of his education, this president, despite his folksy pretense, is something of an anti-Lincoln—one who, instead of learning eagerly in humble circumstances, learned almost nothing at the finest institutions in the land. When he comments on how

---

*Whereas Bush's Yale transcript was published in *The New Yorker,* his grades at Andover are in protective custody, kept in a safe in the registrar's office.

many hands he's "shaked," or frets that quotas "vulcanize" society, or claims that he has been "miscalculated," he is, of course, flaunting not his costly education but his disdain for it—much as some feckless prince, with a crowd of beggars watching from the street, might take a few bites from the feast laid out before him, then let the servants throw the rest away.

The insult is compounded by the myriad successes that Bush met with after graduation, following a stint at Harvard Business School. Having been admitted first to Andover, then to Yale, then to Harvard, all despite a mediocre record, he now succeeded brilliantly despite a mediocre record at those schools, performing just as if he'd studied like a monk and graduated with full honors. Like his dad before him, Bush did very well because the Family always went to bat for him, pulled strings for him, shelled out for him, and let him freely trade on his relations: getting him that plum assignment to the Texas Air National Guard so that he wouldn't have to go to Vietnam; pumping capital into his failing company Arbusto Energy, which never made a dime—although it did enable giant write-offs; letting him exploit the family name to merge his way to wealth despite a downturn in the oil business, helping him to exit that same business at a hefty profit, even though his corporation was about to tank; letting him exploit the family name to set up the consortium that bought the Texas Rangers and to rebuild the stadium at Arlington, which feat of networking enabled his political career; helping him to get elected, and then re-elected, chief executive of Texas, in part by working their connections to provide him with the largest gubernatorial war chests in American history; and so on. Indeed, it was such lofty patronage that would soon convey the lucky W into the White House, the election having been decided for him by those jurists whom his dad and Ronald Reagan had conveniently appointed to the Supreme Court. Again the case of Andrew Jackson comes to mind, for its absolute *dis*similarity to what we have today. "Little versed in books," this president of ours was *not* "raised by the will of the people to the highest pinnacle of honor" but ended up there thanks to an enormous effort (managed by his brother the governor of Florida, his brother's comrade Katharine Harris, and by his dad's old friends Jim Baker and Dick Cheney) to *suppress*—through bureaucratic trickery, selective force, and unrelenting propaganda—the people's will; for although that race was close (too close), a bare majority of voters still could see that this man is not one of them, and hasn't got the wherewithal to serve them as their chief executive (or "chief executive officer," as he has put it tellingly). Many of them could perceive, in other words, that his sloppy speech was not a way of saying, "I am one of you," but rather of asserting, "The rules just don't apply to me."

Indeed, the candidate's transparency was sometimes overwhelming, so unapologetically did he present himself; and President Bush has been extraordinarily self-revealing, his natural indolence and unabashable complacency up front for all to see. ("I'll answer some questions, and I'm going to head home and take a nap," he told a group of Democrats soon after his inauguration.)[34] Although this president's transparency is often wonderful, it is not unprecedented. Certain prior chief executives have also stood before us naked on TV, while others have been magically ennobled by the medium. The history of this postwar phenomenon is worth recounting for the light it sheds on television's sometime veracity. That history may also help illuminate the true ancestry of our see-through leader—who is, as we shall see, the child not only of George Herbert Walker Bush but also of Richard Nixon.

FIRST IMPRESSIONS

They say the camera doesn't lie. Of course, that axiom requires elaboration in the culture of TV, wherein "the camera," while it may not "lie" outright, does routinely stretch the truth. This is not just a matter of transforming physical traits, as television, like all photography, tends to do, making people appear heavier/taller/older/younger than they do when you run into them. More pervasively, the medium is an acute and unrelenting caricaturist, the Mother of all late-night stand-up. Whomever it presents to us, it instantaneously magnifies some tic or feature that we might not even notice in that person face-to-face—but which is *all* we'll see in the persona jabbering and blinking on the screen, especially once we've seen that tic or feature worked into the repertoire of TV's wiseguys. Often the outstanding trait—like Katharine Harris's face-lift, Al Gore's lisp, Ted Koppel's hair, the wizened elfishness (i.e., big ears) of Ross Perot—is a material particularity (authentic or cosmetic) that marks the person whether he or she is televised or not, even if it's not so ostentatious off the air. Such televisual tags are not in themselves necessarily revealing. When parties are at war, however, such accidental details take on an acute significance for the livid fighters on the other side, who see that superficial oddity as a profound reflection not just of the person through and through but of an evil ideology that threatens all the world. Thus did Mme. Harris's thick rouge and rigid smile (and flirty eagerness to do the boss's dirty work) appear to half of us symbolic of a Southern-style coquettishness that might set feminism back to the days of the Missouri Compromise, while Parson Gore's censorious lisp and schoolmasterish affect seemed to the other half expressive of a haughty top-down liberalism that would tax every breath you take and padlock all the righteous churches. That such ostensible dead giveaways might be mere televisual accidents, quite without significance— and, indeed, irrelevant—is a possibility that cannot come to many minds in time of war. In any case, there is no doubt that television urges us to overestimate the fine points of appearance—a bias that now rules out a career in national politics for anyone who doesn't look like he or she could be an anchor on CNBC. What with those eyebrows and the funky clothes, Honest Abe would never be allowed into Dick Cheney's GOP—and not just because its honor roll includes Trent Lott, Bob Barr, and other white supremacists.

While the candid camera does exaggerate, it also makes some big mistakes, for there are gifted actors who can fool it just as easily as certain hardened types can fool the lie detector. There are among us (and above us) charismatics who are able to project a high or deep or comfortable "humanity" that's sheer illusion—a sort of magic trick played by nice looks and subtle acting on an audience eager to be scammed. (The trickster might be perfectly, or partially, sincere.) Such magnetic personalities have been with us forever—Socrates and Jesus each discuss the type—but they have come to thrive especially through the electronic media, radio and television each having radically empowered them, keeping them as inaccessible as gods while vastly spreading, and unaccountably enhancing, their seductive influence. Conversely, such ingratiating players have exactly what it takes to break through in the culture of TV, their narcissistic drive and inexhaustible appeal enabling them to make it to the top—and usually to stay there.

Our most successful postwar presidents have been such ultrasmooth performers—as Machiavelli would agree.* In each of them the camera could discover nothing of the inner man (if any), except for glimpses now and then in times of crisis. Eisenhower was just such a marvel, with his unassuming ways and plainsman's grin. Those telegenic properties helped the Man from Abilene to wrest his party's nomination from the large and frosty Robert Taft, who looked like some heartless banker in an old Frank Capra movie, while Ike—although not really warm at all—came off like everybody's Grandpa. His air of folksy affability allowed the GOP to wear a human face throughout the years of Joe McCarthy, the House Un-American Activities Committee (HUAC), nuclear proliferation, and the rise of Allen Dulles's CIA. The global threat of John Foster Dulles's "brinksmanship," in other words, was softened somewhat by the president's "aw-shucksmanship." ("He was a far more complex and devious man than most people realized," Nixon later wrote, with the usual hint of rancor.) As an impregnable persona, Ike was followed, and surpassed, by John F. Kennedy—the smoothest of them all. With his wry wit and kingly gaze, that young bronzed god (the golden glow a sign of Addison's Disease) offered not a hint of his distracting appetite, nor could any viewer of his urbane performances on television have divined how risk-averse he really was (as on race relations) or how vengeful (as toward Cuba). Cut down prematurely—and with his luster posthumously burnished to a blinding sheen by the authors of the Camelot mythology—JFK went out with his mystique intact, and all those tawdry revelations have not quite dispelled it yet. The next chief executive to put on the impenetrable mantle was Ronald Reagan, our Teflon President, who never once appeared to peek out from behind his happy mask. The camera failed to glorify him only at those

---

*Such players are ubiquitous not only in politics, however, but also in the movies, TV, advertising, the music business, on Wall Street, and in the nation's jails.

moments when it mercilessly showed that there was *no one there* (because
of Alzheimer's, perhaps), his ruddy and anachronistic visage standing empty,
like an old brick high school soon to be converted into loft apartments.
(This happened at his first debate with Walter Mondale—"I'm all confused
now"—and once again when, having been asked out at his ranch what was
being done to free the hostages in Lebanon, he just stood there, beaming
vacantly, with Nancy tensed up next to him. "We're doing everything we
can," she muttered at the ground through gritted teeth, and he, uncom-
prehendingly, repeated it, still smiling.) And recently there was Bill Clinton,
whose epic durability owed so much to his iron self-possession on TV. (He
was also greatly aided by the toxic hatefulness of his attackers.) Whether
belting out a State of the Union speech, riffing on some policy detail, or
working a crowd Oprah-style, the Comeback Kid always maintained his air
of genial equanimity, never showing so much as a flash of weakness and
very little of his famous temper. The camera hurt him only by recording
Clinton's trivial yet epoch-making lie about "that woman, Miss Lewinsky"—a flagrant whopper that would haunt him, and the rest of us, for years
to come. Tellingly, it was only after he was safely out of sight that his enemies could finally dim his glow by harping on the ill-considered pardon of
Marc Rich, and charging that he "stole" gifts from the White House.

  Those winning presidents each had something of the regal mien of
FDR, whom all four honored, despite their differences (and although two
of them did plenty to dismantle Roosevelt's achievement). Of course,
FDR's heroic air of dauntless optimism was, to some extent, a product of
reportorial discretion, the members of the press back then remaining silent
on such proofs of frailty as the president's paralysis and his relationship with
Lucy Page Mercer. A like tactfulness marked JFK's press coverage, despite
his thin achievement, serious illnesses, and raging satyriasis. And the Gipper, although completely out of it, was also treated reverently by a press
corps that let Michael Deaver and his propaganda elves run rings around
them. Yet such forebearance by the press does not itself explain those
politicians' rare ability to stand tall in the camera's eye; Clinton, after all, received no such indulgence. The fact is that the television cameras loved
him, much as they had loved Eisenhower, Kennedy, and Reagan, and as the

newsreel cameras (and radio transmitters) had loved FDR for years. And love, as we all know, is blind.*

Most politicians aren't so blessed. Lacking the invisible armor that protects the special few from televisual embarrassment, those mortals run the risk—if they appear more often than the average pol—of being *seen*. It is, in short, about such lesser players that the camera never lies. Whereas each gifted heir of FDR was clearly "comfortable in his own skin," as the cliché has it, the common strugglers often suffer deep and fatal insecurities that somehow come across on television, just as a hidden tumor shows up on the X ray.

Such flaws have shone most glaringly in those post-Camelot pretenders who have strained to mimic JFK. The harder Lyndon Johnson worked at aping Kennedy, the less like Kennedy he seemed—and the more apelike, the earthy Texan only looking clownish and constrained in so Hyannisport a guise, like an orangutan in a tuxedo. For all his genius as a politician—and his great accomplishments on the domestic front—LBJ just couldn't hack it with the national audience, through *any* medium.† But it was Kennedy's main forum that obsessed him: "TV is still to him a sort of bête noire," Lady Bird noted in her diary in early 1964; and after the election it was downhill all the way. He tried to wow the journalists as JFK had

---

*Of course, not everyone succumbs to such televisual charm, whose sway requires a mass predisposition that is merely general, not universal. Only those already inclined to adore that face and voice will do so, while those who, for whatever reason, just can't see it never will. Here it is pertinent to note Oliver Sacks's memorable account of how an audience of aphasic mental patients reacted to a speech of Ronald Reagan's: "There he was, the old Charmer, the Actor, with his practiced rhetoric, his histrionisms, his emotional appeal—and all the patients were convulsed with laughter." Deaf to his words, but acutely sensitive to all his "extraverbal cues," those viewers saw him only as a comic charlatan.

"Here then was the paradox of the President's speech. We normals—aided, doubtless, by our wish to be fooled, were indeed well and truly fooled. . . . And so cunningly was deceptive word-use combined with deceptive tone, that only the brain-damaged remained intact, undeceived." *The Man Who Mistook His Wife for a Hat* (New York: Simon & Schuster, 1985), pp. 80–84.

†As the war blitzed his ratings, LBJ took to posing wildly out of character for magazines like GQ and *Life*—lounging on his front porch in a nicely tailored suit (like Jack), frisking heavily "among the young people" (one aide having urged him thus to replicate "the Kennedy image"), and even going boating in a bathing suit (like Jack and Bobby). "Reviews were poor," notes Jeff Shesol. See his *Mutual Contempt: Lyndon Johnson, Robert Kennedy, and the Feud That Defined a Decade* (New York: W. W. Norton, 1997), pp. 310–13.

done at *his* press conferences—which LBJ referred to, with envious contempt, as "vaudeville"—and postured as a modern Medici, à la Jack and Jackie, by throwing fêtes for intellectuals and artists, but such efforts never worked.[35] (In the elite consensus there was, of course, an element of Northern snobbery, which was encouraged among the pundits by the Kennedy machine.) And Johnson also had another, larger television problem: the "credibility gap," which grew still wider as he kept on sending more and more Americans to Vietnam—and as ever more of them came home in body bags, while LBJ gabbed on about how bright the outlook was. Surely no one could talk away that national agony, but Johnson was especially bad at trying. His backroom style of politics was literally hands-on, a domineering one-on-one approach that television obviated, although the urge to twist your arm was visible. Moreover, as we now know, his attempts to sell the war were strained by his own secret qualms about it—an ambivalence that television also showed the viewers, more and more of whom could see that he was lying. In short, as he sat facing us, bespectacled and huge, and drawling out his pious homilies, you sensed the same dishonest bully who on the one hand was grimly raping Vietnam★ and on the other hand so deftly forced the Congress into realizing all of those heroic domestic feats that Kennedy had only talked about. Like the body count inexorably mounting on the nightly news, Johnson's evident bad faith was a major televisual strike against him.

And yet compared to *his* successor, LBJ was as inscrutable as the Mona Lisa, for we have had no president as naked to the camera's X-ray eye as Richard Nixon. "I'm not a bit thin-skinned," he once privately asserted, and although the claim was ludicrous, it told an accidental truth, since Nixon really had no skin at all.[36] Thus television was finally one of his great enemies—along with the Eastern WASP elite, the Kennedys, the Democrats, "the Jews," "the intellectuals," the "bastards" in the press, "the bums on the campuses," and the "vipers" in the federal bureaucracy. On televi-

---

★"During a private conversation with some reporters who pressed him to explain why we were in Vietnam, Johnson lost his patience. According to Arthur Goldberg, 'LBJ unzipped his fly, drew out his substantial organ, and declared, 'This is why!' " Robert Dallek, *Flawed Giant: Lyndon Johnson and His Times, 1961–1973* (New York: Oxford University Press, 1998), p. 491.

sion the man of cover-ups was so transparent that the nation could see everything that he kept laboring to conceal: his bone-deep awkwardness, his festering resentment, and the hot joy he took in sticking it to "them."

Until 1960 Nixon had no television problem. As Eisenhower's top agitator, he managed to defame the "pinks" and flay the nonexistent Reds with a certain tidy zeal that played well with many viewers (unlike the jeering, slovenly McCarthy, whose gross judicial manners finally did him in, once people got a look at them). In full control of his resentments back then, Nixon could perform them brilliantly—as in the "Checkers speech," that little masterpiece of petit-bourgeois grievance (and Nixon's *only* televisual triumph).* But things changed, changed utterly, when Kennedy went national, with his amazing looks and money and that ineluctable aplomb. Thus equipped, the Kennedy machine turned televisual politics into a whole new game, one that the man from Whittier could never play. This was apparent at their first debate, where CBS's cameras did a job on Nixon that in fact destroyed him. As most viewers know by now, that night "the fighting anti-Communist"—although he sounded fine on radio—looked like a neglected mental patient next to Kennedy, who seemed as hale and masterful as his opponent looked awestruck and underfed.

Several factors had contributed to that effect, as Nixon later wrote. He wore no makeup, pulled his punches, had lost weight and had banged his knee, while Jack was tanned and fit and fought unfairly. Moreover, he did better in the second two debates. And yet that glaring contrast was not just a televisual construction. The spectral bumpkin glimpsed on CBS that night *was* Richard Nixon at his most abject—the shabby, furtive Nixon facing his worst nightmare in the form of the resplendent Kennedy, who now towered over him, a glowing incarnation of the caste that Nixon had always hated more than anything. (That Jack had for years been his friend and comrade only made his plight more galling.) The exclusive network

---

*His famous television speech of November 3, 1969, to "the great Silent Majority of my fellow Americans," received tens of thousands of supportive calls and letters—most of them secretly arranged for by the White House. "Nixon Team Contrived Response to Speech," AP, January 23, 1999.

of great Yankee dynasties—Lodges, Mellons, Rockefellers, Roosevelts, et al.—had always been the sharpest thorn in Nixon's mind. "I don't think you can possibly overestimate the importance of all that," Robert Odle Jr. has observed. "It's at the core of understanding Nixon."[37] The Kennedys, of course, had also long resented those imperious WASPs. Nevertheless, that family—and Jack especially—now became the focus of Nixon's grand resentment, which thenceforth grew beyond his power to control it, or conceal it.

Traumatized by Jack's hypnotic savoir-faire, the haunted president kept on trying, impossibly, to be as smooth a player as his departed nemesis.* Deeply humorless, he labored to be effortlessly funny, just like Jack—a mission he could carry out, he thought, with just a few good hires. "One weakness in our research shop is on the humor side," he wrote H. R. Haldeman, urging that they siphon some new blood into the operation. Until then, it would help "if I could get a few suggestions from time to time for either humor or just warm color which might trigger an extemporaneous comment or two."[38] Yet not even Mark Twain could have helped the uptight Nixon with his humor problem, which was apparent every time he lobbed a jest, deadpanning broadly in a stiff impersonation of Bob Hope. He was inadvertently quite funny, on the other hand, when he tried to be majestic, like Jack. For example, there was a picture of him standing pensively at the seashore, the image strongly reminiscent of those famous shots of JFK relaxing at Hyannisport—except that Jack was dressed for a vacation in the sun, while Nixon wore a suit and tie and dress shoes as he stood there grimly eyeing the horizon. Thus he looked not like a lonely visionary dreaming of a better world but a federal agent out to bust a boatload of illegal immigrants. The clueless president was again attempting glamour when he had the White House police dressed up in double-breasted tunics with gold braid and buttons, and topped with high-crowned military caps festooned with plumes. Nixon thought it was the

---

*Nixon's emulation was, however, tellingly selective. His mimicry of JFK included none of the familial touches: at play with Caroline, John-John under Daddy's desk. Nixon wanted to project not warmth but an imperial augustness and therefore kept the wife and girls off camera.

sort of thing that Kennedy would do, but those costumes smacked less of Camelot than of *The Merry Widow.* (They were used just once, then retired to gales of laughter.)

And yet such propaganda slipups weren't just funny. They were the chronic errors of a mind inflexible and grandiose, and fatally inclined to *force* the issue. Although he deemed himself a whiz at "public relations," he was built only for attack.* He had a peerless instinct for the jugular, rare stamina, and a fanatic's single-mindedness—the very gifts that he admired in other "sons-of-bitches," American and Soviet alike. And yet he lacked those subtler qualities that propaganda warriors require as well. He had no detachment. He could shrug off nothing as "just politics," or let bygones be bygones, or agree to disagree, but instead took every counterthrust as a vicious swipe at *him,* and so bore countless grudges through the years. He was also militantly unadaptable, a lifelong total square whose unsophistication was a sign not, as he thought, of innocence but of a sharp provincial bent that made him always the divider, never a uniter—despite his early vow to "bring us together." And, finally, Nixon was a man without ideals, although he did some twilight maundering about "a higher purpose." His only program was the imposition of his will—a goal that he pursued on every front with equal brutal clumsiness. Thus was his flatfooted drive to shine like JFK continuous with his attempts to flatten Southeast Asia, strangle Chile, wipe out all dissent at home, and sweep himself to re-election by whatever means.

We could see all those defects; the nastiness, the morbid sensitivity, the deep unhappiness, and the will to win at any cost would now and then all flash forth on television, his cute slogans notwithstanding. It was therefore not all that surprising when his dark TV persona was eventually authenti-

---

*His approach was poundingly aggressive, whether the campaign was positive or negative. Sherman Adams describes a telling moment during the Eisenhower cabinet's "post-mortem discussion" of the 1954 midterm elections. "He pulled out of his pocket a toy figure of a drummer, released its mechanism and placed it on the Cabinet table. While the President and the Secretaries stared at it in surprise and amusement, the toy drummer marched briskly across the table, banging on its drum. 'We've got to keep beating the drum about our achievements,' Nixon said." It was, Adams writes, "a scene unique in the annals of the Eisenhower cabinet." *Firsthand Report: The Story of the Eisenhower Administration* (New York: Harper, 1961), p. 168.

cated by the documentary outpouring after Watergate, the secret tapes, internal memos, frank memoirs, and diaries all starkly certifying that what we saw was what we got. The man behind that gloomy scowl, it now turned out, was just as furious *in camera* as he often looked on camera, the rancor flowing out of him in a fetid torrent of hateful epithets, sadistic threats, and scatological eruptions. Likewise, the obviously tricky Dick turned out to be a propaganda micromanager psychotically intent on absolute dictation of his image, the president devoting nearly all his time—before *and* after Watergate—to crafting cover stories, rehearsing spin, conceiving and stage managing "big plays," and otherwise conniving at his exaltation in the viewers' eyes and in the eyes of "history."* What *was* a bit surprising was the fact that Nixon was already livid, and already scheming, long before the big leaks and the Plumbers. As early as July 1969 the president—fired up by NASA's landing on the moon—launched into a proleptic three-hour monologue on what his men now had to do to make him awesome. "Need now to establish the mystique of the presidency," scribbled Haldeman as Nixon ranted that "we haven't used the power of the White House to reward and punish," that U.S. authority "must be used more effectively, at home and abroad or we go down the drain as a great power," and that the time had come for systematic " 'dirty tricks.' "[39]

And the revelations keep on coming, each new batch reconfirming that the cameras never lied about him, and so refuting, again, the stubborn efforts of his epigones to prettify the picture. It is his tragicomic fate that all such posthumous PR is swiftly wrecked by further nauseous evidence of his true nature. In 1998, for example, Monica Crowley published *Nixon in Winter,* the second of two glowing memoirs of the four years that she spent ingenuously taking down his spin. The best part of that vicarious self-advertisement is its long account of Nixon's putative adventures in political philosophy. "When I walked into his study, he had Aristotle's *Politics* marked and open in his hands," writes Crowley, an acolyte as credulous as

---

*No detail was too trivial for his concern: "the George Washington painting over the fireplace" ("It should either be moved up or the clock should be moved out"), "the horrible modern art in some of our embassies" (should be "cleaned out" ASAP), "the portions of meat" served at official dinners ("too large"), and so on. See Bruce Oudes, ed., *From the President: Richard Nixon's Secret Files* (New York: Harper & Row, 1989), pp. 32, 86, 156 *et passim.*

the ex-president was calculating. He had his views on all the greats from Machiavelli ("Boy, there's the truth!") to Hegel ("It's so complex, so German!"), but it was "the ancient Greeks" whom he most revered: "No wonder the Greeks are timeless! They were asking the timeless questions!" Such theatrics would be slightly more convincing if we didn't know what Nixon really thought about the Greeks, and how he'd talked about them back when Monica was not around. In 1999 the National Archives released 445 hours of White House tapes, including one in which the president, having vented on the subject of "these little Negro bastards on the welfare rolls," turns to the subject of *All in the Family,* which he complains is "glorifying homosexuality"—a giant leap toward national decline and fall. "You know what happened to the Greeks!" he yells at Haldeman and John Ehrlichman. "Homosexuality destroyed them. Sure, Aristotle was a homo. We all know that. So was Socrates." And, he goes on, "the Catholic Church" was also "homosexual, and it had to be cleaned out," and so's "the upper class in San Francisco" ("I can't shake hands with anybody from San Francisco"), and so are all the "decorators" and "the goddamned designers," who "hate women" (which is why they keep designing all those "sexy things"). The release of that moronic tirade, coming, as it did, soon after Crowley's whitewash, confirms the truth of JFK's own terse appraisal of his ever-flailing adversary—a judgment just as apt since Nixon's death as it had been in 1962: "He went out like he came in. No class."[40]

Although LBJ and Nixon were both daunted by the Kennedys' big money, the sort of presidential "class" that plays well on television is not an economic but a temperamental factor. This is clear not only from the televisual successes of Ike Eisenhower, Dutch Reagan, and Bill Clinton, all men of humble origin, but also from the televisual disasters of George Herbert Walker Bush, a scion just as privileged as Jack Kennedy yet nowhere near as smooth. Indeed, Bush's posh class background *was* his major TV problem, the cameras mercilessly outing the big pantywaist within. Thus that stilted princeling also suffered by comparison with Kennedy, who had the common touch—a contrast that has galled the noble House of Bush almost as much as it enraged the shabby Nixon.

This is not to say that Bush was too "aristocratic" for the medium and/or for postmodern times—a frequent claim by journalists, who make (too) much of the famous reticence that Dorothy Walker Bush drummed into her patrician son. In fact, the Bush clan, although fabulously wealthy, is not aristocratic *enough* to do well on TV, if by that modifer we mean elegant and polished. First of all, the Bushes often have let fly in the most boorish way—as when Barbara Bush hinted coyly that Geraldine Ferraro was a "bitch," or when the president, losing it completely in the late campaign of 1992, called Clinton/Gore "two bozos" and dubbed Gore "Ozone Man" (or when the younger Bush addressed obstructive staff and uncooperative journalists as "assholes," which he did routinely when co-managing his dad's campaign in 1988).* Such crudity is obviously not aristocratic (even if aristocrats are often crude)—nor, more importantly, is it aristocratic to make everyone around you conscious of your plummy background: on the contrary. As one who could not help but wear his class advantage like a letter sweater, the elder Bush was no aristocrat. Such was the fatal flaw that television kept exposing—with his help—although it was a problem that predated his encounters with the medium. There was an exemplary moment back in 1950, when young "Poppy" Bush, who had lately moved to Midland, Texas, where he sold oil drilling rigs, stepped out one day to run an errand, then ran back in and quickly changed his clothes. "He had on Bermuda shorts, and the truck drivers were whistling at him," writes Barbara. "I don't believe he wore shorts ever again, except to play tennis."[41]

And yet those shorts were almost always in your face, whatever he might do to cover them. Throughout the 1988 campaign, his top imagineers—Roger Ailes and Lee Atwater, the latter heatedly abetted by George W.—worked manfully to keep him, as it were, dressed up in overalls and cowboy boots, but on TV those prissy knee-length jobs kept glowing through the denim. The ambivalent Nixon (Bush had been his protégé) said as much to Monica Crowley: "It's not that he doesn't like people; it's just that he's not very comfortable out there on the stump trying to connect with them. He tries too hard to be one of them, eating pork rinds and the rest, but he is not one of them, and it comes across. He's better off just

---

*The elder Bush also betrayed a certain impropriety when, as vice president, he boasted, after his debate with Representative Ferraro, "We kicked a little ass tonight."

being himself." That advice would not have helped, since Bush's true self only raised guffaws whenever it skipped into view. When asked if, as U.S. envoy to China, he had gotten close to any of the natives, he replied: "Oh, yes. They gave us a boy to play tennis with." He had made that lordly statement in a private conversation in the 1970s, but he also sounded that way on the stump a decade later. His hoity-toity slips were justly famous—as when he asked for "just a splash" of coffee at Cuzzin' Ritchie's Truck Stop in New Hampshire, or thus explained why he had lost the straw poll in Ames, Iowa: "A lot of people who support me were at an air show, they were off at their daughter's coming-out party, they were teeing up at the golf course," he speculated philosophically, apparently mistaking Iowa for Greenwich.[42]

By Election Day of 1988, Bush and his propaganda team had finally managed to democratize his image just enough to get him into office. (He feigned a hearty appetite for pork rinds and country music, while his flacks played up the chilly, technocratic vibe of Governor Michael Dukakis). His shorts were also hidden well in times of war, which he therefore brought about as often as he could. In general, however, the cameras tended to expose his inner twit, even when they misconstrued him. This had been true all along—as, for example, when Vice President Bush threw out the first pitch at the Houston Astrodome to open the National League Championship Series in 1986 and did a really half-assed job (a bit caught brilliantly by Richard Ben Cramer in *What It Takes*). Watching that slow, spastic dance on ABC, you had no way of knowing that Bush had been a champion baseball player at Yale or that he was still quite an athlete. That early flub was just embarrassing, however. At the end, his major gaffes helped do him in—although, strictly speaking, they were not his fault. At a convention of the National Grocers Association in Orlando, Bush took a tour of the exhibits, then paused to marvel courteously at a state-of-the-art supermarket scanner: "This is for checking out?" It was that gizmo's new ability to read torn labels, and not the thing itself, that Bush was lauding; but the *New York Times* front-paged him as "amazed" by the very notion of a scanner, as if he'd never been inside a supermarket, and the videotape appeared to bear that out. The White House protested, but the damage had been done, because, let's face it, George Herbert Walker Bush was not a supermarket kind of guy.★ Similarly, the president lost points when, in his second debate with Clinton and Perot, he made a big deal out of looking at his watch—an impatient gesture to suggest that Clinton had run on too long: "Times's up," Bush meant to say, but it looked like he was saying, "I have better things to do," and that apparent display of haughty boredom turned off many viewers. And yet while they were wrong, those viewers were also right; for Bush *did* think himself above such lowly rituals—especially after having worn the laurels of Desert Storm.[43]

As with Nixon, so with Bush, the quirks accentuated by the medium were not just funny. That sense of high entitlement was dangerously aggravated by a need to show the world—to show his sons—that he was not a softy but a guy as hard as Dorothy and Prescott Bush had raised their kids to be. Such upper-class machismo was, of course, a common feature of the monied East; it had marked the Kennedys and all those buccaneering Ivy Leaguers who had made the CIA (which Bush ran under Gerald Ford, and whose headquarters is now named after him). And yet Bush seems to have felt especially bedeviled by his insecurity. It drove him, strangely, into Nixon's arms, as if he craved the fatherly approval of that bitter, low-born character. Bush was a Nixon man by 1968, sharing Nixon's hard-line anticommunism and taking his political advice. (Both players used the same ad man to help them win elections in the 1960s.)[†] After losing his first senatorial bid in Texas—a bad idea proposed by Nixon—Bush went on to front wholeheartedly for the beleaguered president throughout Watergate, that crafty operator having asked him to direct the Republican National Committee, so that Bush's pedigree and moderate ties might help defuse the crisis. Bush put his straight persona wholly at the service of the

---

★Shortly after moving back to Houston after Clinton's swearing-in, George and Barbara "made an amazing discovery: You can call out for pizza!" Barbara Bush, *Barbara Bush: A Memoir* (New York: Scribner's, 1994), p. 517.

†This was Harry Treleaven, who had handled the accounts of Ford, Singer, and PanAm for J. Walter Thompson. He approached the tasks of selling Bush (as a Congressman in 1966) and Nixon (as presidential timber two years later) with the same expert disregard for anything of "substance." For Treleaven's views on pitching Nixon, see his memos in Joe McGinniss, *The Selling of the President, 1968* (New York: Trident Press 1969), esp. pp. 171–80 et seq. Elizabeth Mitchell quotes Treleaven's plan for pitching Bush in *W: Revenge of the Bush Dynasty* (New York: Hyperion, 2000), pp. 90–92.

crooked White House ("He takes our line beautifully," Charles Colson noted) and otherwise sought Nixon's manly reassurance that he was no Yalie faggot but a serviceable thug. "I am convinced that deep in his heart he feels I'm soft, not tough enough, not willing to do the 'gut job' that his political instincts have taught him must be done," Bush wrote ruefully to his boys.

The charge that he was sissified—a creature of "privilege and softness in a tea-sipping, martini-drinking, tennis-playing sense"—was one that he could not shrug off, whether he inferred it from the guarded Nixon or, years later, read it in *Newsweek*'s cover story on "the wimp factor"—a piece that drove him (and his eldest) permanently up the wall. Indeed, his presidency was distinguished *only* by his violent serial efforts to disprove the charge, from his Nixonian run against Dukakis ("card-carrying member of the ACLU") to his unnecessary, ruinous invasion of Panama ("a political jackpot," Lee Atwater called it) to the overhyped, atrocious, and half-finished war against Iraq ("Saddam is going to get his ass kicked") to the propaganda drive to smear Anita Hill and salvage Clarence Thomas ("the best man for the job"). And yet not even all those victories could ease his sense of impotence. Even after Desert Storm, which had boosted his approval ratings to a stratospheric 89 percent, the president was still grousing about *Newsweek*'s cover story. Nor did those wins exalt him in the camera's eye. After all the countless handsome photo ops, the television image that defined Bush in the end came from that unlucky moment when he tossed his cookies on Japan's prime minister, and then collapsed.[44]

A VERY GENEROUS ALLOWANCE

As a TV performer, President George W. Bush is in the same camp with his father and his father's mentor—and yet without their superficial flaws. While both Bushes do speak much the same amusing lingo, this president is, of course, infinitely better at the grip-and-grin of retail politics, having been reared not back East but in West Texas. (He is also made of sterner stuff, his character reflecting less of the compliant George I than of Queen Barbara, a blunt, ferocious partisan despite the pearls and silver crown.)* Whereas his father, like Nixon, just could not get down, this George doesn't have to fake the sort of pseudopopulist roughhousing that it takes to charm a lot of voters in the Sun Belt, the farm states, the Rocky Mountain states and other strongholds of far-right Republican emotion. A jolly veteran of the DKE frat house and the Austin statehouse, and a seasoned traveler of the dusty roads between them, Bush the Younger has no trouble givin' strangers jokey nicknames or grabbin' fellas by the neck or squeezin' folks in big bear hugs or—more important—talkin' the draconian talk of hard-right ideology, which always sounded just a little funny on his father's famous lips.

Thus Bush can easily play the game that stumped his dad. What places him among the televisual losers is the obvious fact that that's his *only* talent—and it's one that doesn't count for much, unless he finds the time, these next four years, to go out and fondle every voter in the United States. Beyond the campaign trail (or certain sections of it), Bush's chummy manner cannot hide the fact that he's an amateur in way over his head, as the political cartoonists and late-night comics have all merrily observed. TV is their authority, with this president's unfitness coming through as clearly as the logo in a thirty-second spot, whenever he attempts to handle an unforeseen question or free-associates a bit too long. Of course, his flacks and partisans and most members of the mainstream press say otherwise, attempting endlessly to hitch his little wagon to the presidential stars of yesteryear. "He connects with people like a Jack Kennedy," said one Bush propagandist early on, and we also heard repeatedly that this Bush represents the Second Coming of the Gipper, who was also written off as inexperienced and slow, a cipher, "just an actor."[45] And yet it is precisely Reagan's histrionic talent that this president lacks.† He is unable to feign

---

*Bush did inherit one political talent from his father: a prodigious knack for remembering people's names. Once when he and other pledges at Yale's DKE house were ordered to recite as many names as possible of that year's fifty new initiates, "George got up and named all fifty," recalls a classmate. "He just has such an interest in people that he remembers their names, which is his medium, like writing numbers are [*sic*] for somebody else." George Sr. has throughout his life displayed the same ability.

†While it exaggerates our president's charisma, that comparison also belittles Reagan's prepresidential record. By 1980, Reagan was, as a leader, far more experienced than Bush was by 2000, having served two full terms as governor of California, where that post is constitu-

"presidentiality" or put on gravitas or even to project much confidence —
despite his famous smirk (which only reconfirms the sense that this is all a
terrible mistake). In short, such incapacity is the defining feature of W's TV
persona. As LBJ was *insincere,* as Richard Nixon was *vindictive,* and as
George Bush was *effete,* this president is *undeserving.*

Of course, that impression was forever burned into the record by the
sedentary putschists of the Supreme Court on that Day of Infamy, December 12, 2000. And yet the governor seemed undeserving long before
he got the ultimate in undeserved rewards. From the outset of the presidential race in 1998, if not before, TV ruthlessly played up the candidate's
peculiar air of groundless egotism. His propagandists therefore had their
work cut out for them, because Americans—however they may vote—
don't like rich slackers or anybody else who gets by without paying for it.
And so, under the command of Karl Rove (who started out doing dirty
tricks for Nixon), the governor's spinmeisters got to work denying the obvious—trying to talk away his bratty aura with loud paeans to his "likeability," and carefully suppressing, or dismissing, all the evidence of the
numerous special favors that had finally put him where he was.

The latter task was easy, since throughout the race "the liberal media"
laid off the lucky candidate.[46] While there was much solid work done by
print journalists, it never took—i.e., it wasn't picked up by the networks.
Those giant players politely walked around the gaping potholes in the governor's record, a marked departure from the telejournalistic MO of the
not-so-distant past. On Bush's easy entry into the Texas Air National Guard,
and then his lax observance of that outfit's rules, reporters were discreet (as
they had not been with Dan Quayle or with Bill Clinton vis-à-vis *their* draft-
dodging). And unless you searched, you might know nothing about Bush's
shady self-enrichment down in Texas, both in business and in politics—a
fortune based entirely on his link to Dad. (The contrast with Whitewater,
that epoch-making nonstory, is instructive.) The only news that threatened
to confirm the obvious about the overprivileged sprout came from an in-

---

tionally stronger than in Texas; and he oversaw a number of reforms—both liberal and conservative—much more impressive than the legislative feats of Governor Bush, whose six
years in office paid off largely for his friends.

dependent author—and W's men fixed him but good. The darkest aspect of the governor's career was its Texas-sized hypocrisy, the rich kid keenly punishing the poor for crimes that he himself had once (or twice) committed with impunity. That sin stands out in J. H. Hatfield's *Fortunate Son,* a sound biography whose afterword alleges—via three unnamed sources—that the twenty-six-year-old was busted down in Texas for cocaine possession in 1972 and that his father had the crime expunged by an obliging judge. The boom dropped fast and hard. Just before the book was to be published by St. Martin's Press, the Bush team hit the mattresses, hollering indignantly ("mindless garbage," Dad exploded) and leaking word that Hatfield had done time for attempted murder. Although that item was, albeit true, beside the point, its propagation—and whatever other pressures *la famiglia* brought to bear—induced St. Martin's not just to withdraw the book but to promise publicly to *burn* it.* Thus the campaign ruined Hatfield so as to kill that inconvenient story—which, despite the uproar, may not go away.

There was usually no need for such rough stuff, however, since Bush was good at shrugging off his priors—brawling, drunk driving, and whatever else—as mere youthful friskiness, which seemed to satisfy the press—although it did clash somewhat with his motto of "accountability," and also failed to square with his big crackdown on juvenile crime in Texas. That what-the-hell-now-let's-move-on approach to his own checkered past also helped to enhance the governor's "likeability"—the campaign's main objective, since it was necessary to promote the fiction that this lazy child of wealth was really "just like you and me," Odessa-style. This was, of course, the same stylistic strategy that had elected George H. W. Bush in 1988; and, like Dad back then, this George was also blessed with an opponent tight-assed and mechanical (and also linked with Harvard)—traits that, by contrast, enhanced the grand illusion that George Walker Bush is just a good ole boy. Formerly, both Bushes got their candy-asses whupped when they made runs at Texans who were more convincing than themselves: Senator

---

*Despite that archaic pledge—which roused little protest from the punditocracy—St. Martin's actually did not turn the unsold copies into "furnace fodder." They sold them off so that the remaindered copies ended up competing with the new edition, published by the independent Soft Skull Press.

Ralph Yarborough in the elder Bush's case, Representative Kent Hance in W's. Skilled at populist derision, and gifted with the drawls and faces for it, such men played the Bushes' Yalie heritage for laughs—whereas the Massachusetts bureaucrat Dukakis, and the overeager Beltway Bandit Al Gore, made it all too easy for the Bush machine to play it low and rural, notwithstanding the estates in Greenwich, Kennebunkport, and on Jupiter Island, an exclusive Florida enclave near Hobe Sound. George Bush took special pleasure in out-shufflin' the fastidious Gore, and was surely better at that posture than his father; but his success at it owed less to his own acting talent than to *Gore's* exposure by the camera. An oversharp perfectionist who could not play it cool to save his life (or the Republic), the inner man as televised was far too glaringly intent on making just the right impression on the audience—a major propaganda no-no, since we must never be reminded that the actor has designs on us. Gore's deportmental zigzag was too obvious, the air of strain sometimes embarrassing.* By contrast, the addled one-note Bush appeared—that is, could be depicted—as a reg'lar sorta guy, never mind that his family fortune puts Gore's in the shade.

In its effort to conceal the governor's gilt-edged bonds, the Bush campaign went well beyond playing up his affability. In order to affirm the boy's egalitarian credentials—thereby turning his celebrated weaknesses into a strength—the Bush/Cheney operation supervised a grand revival of the anti-intellectual diatribe that flourished in the heyday of McCarthy/Nixon, then reblossomed with the national careers of Spiro Agnew and George Wallace. (The diatribe recurred a bit when Bush's dad—despite his Yale degree—joined Danny Quayle in taking childish shots at "Harvard Yard.") The Bush/Cheney drive was easily the biggest and the slickest in our history, however, since it used such smart technologies to spread the word, and had the help of *all* the propaganda armies of the right—"free market" and neocon as well as Christian fundamentalist. Guided by the campaign's daily talking points, all those loud Judaeo-Christian soldiers were unanimous in

---

*This ceased to be the case after Election Day. Although he made some major tactical mistakes, Gore weathered the five-week postelection crisis with extraordinary dignity, behaving just as graciously and tactfully as the stalwarts of the GOP were bellicose, intransigent, and snide. Perhaps it will be said one day of Gore that nothing so became his public life like the leaving of it.

arguing that George Bush was a second Andrew Jackson, braving the elitist smarty pants "Prince Albert." They cast the governor's thick tongue as a sign of unpretentiousness, his ignorance as strength—as if he'd come to talk that way from working long hours on the docks and in the fields, not from drinking heavily—at least—and blowing off his studies, the sky-high tuition notwithstanding.

In its divisiveness, the tactic was pure Nixon. Cunningly, and quite absurdly, it identified the much-mocked W with those midwestern elders who had also been derided by the snooty Pharisees of Washington, New York, and Hollywood—the infernal "they" so damningly invoked by countless all-American rabble-rousers and certain demogogues elsewhere.*
"I remember what *they* did to Ronald Reagan. *They* belittled him, and *they* said, 'Oh, he can't possibly be smart enough to be president of the United States,' " the governor told Larry King (emphasis added). Predictably, the propaganda also placed this Bush alongside Eisenhower—whom *they* had likewise taken for a "dumbie" [*sic*] but who "twice mopped the floor with . . . Adlai Stevenson, the darling of the smart-set [*sic*]," wrote Dennis Byrne in the *Chicago Sun-Times*. "The intelligentsia said the bovine electorate had been beguiled by Eisenhower's smile," wrote George Will, without naming names. The Nixonian subtext of such seething discourse was that "they" are fewer by far than "we" and therefore lord it over "us" not democratically but through Satanic guile. Intelligence itself, in this equation, is a sign of wickedness, as in the Great Awakening some years before our Revolution. Thus Bush's plain unbookishness was taken to evince his godliness, while Gore was just too goddamn smart for our own good—his complex clauses a temptation and a snare, like the devil

---

*Dan Quayle depended heavily on the same quasi-Nixonian tactic in his last quest for the Republican nomination—as he had in 1988 and 1992. ("I wear their scorn as a badge of honor!" he had railed against "them" during the *Murphy Brown* affair.) As the *Wall Street Journal* reported in May 1999, time had not dimmed the mass perception of Quayle's thickness, which was still getting easy laughs on TV and elsewhere: "But fresh derision serves the Quayle strategy perfectly. 'When the establishment laughs at Dan Quayle,' says spokesman Jonathan Baron, 'they're laughing at people who are prolife, who go to church, who believe in core conservative values.' The campaign's strategic challenge, says campaign manager Kyle McSlarrow, is 'to channel what's happened to Quayle into an emotional response' among GOP voters." Since Quayle had no appeal beyond the rightist "core," that masochistic "strategy" could not succeed.

Clinton's.★ "The country can afford a forty-watt president. It cannot allow the Clinton-Gores, corroded to the core, to further define corrosion down," warned Michael Kelly tartly (and unclearly). For George Will, the governor's "modesty" was preferable by far to all those "clever people" in the Democratic Party—which has *no* popular support, unlike the GOP, a party deeply rooted in our richest soil. "A Gore administration would have the mentality of Washington's Northwest quadrant; a Bush administration would have a West Texas attitude," wrote the boyish, bow-tied buckaroo, whose burst of prairie populism ought to give us pause.[47]

For there was a vast self-contradiction in the rightist snow job on behalf of the unlettered governor—a contradiction that explodes the right's conservative pretensions. All at once those nativists and highbrows—Rush Limbaugh, William Bennett, Robert Bork, et al.—who had long bemoaned the colored masses' inability to speak "grammatical English" (to quote Limbaugh) were now saying nothing—publicly—about the governor's West Texas version of Ebonics ("Is our children learning?") or about his weird vocabulary or syntactic haplessness.[48] Likewise, the governor's supporters adamantly looked away from his bald ignorance of U.S. and world history, U.S. government, world geography, and literature in general as well as his peculiar way with "fuzzy math." Such forebearance is surprising, given the reactionary zest with which those partisans—Lynne Cheney, for example—have long deplored the ignorance of our young about the glories of our history in particular, and Western culture generally. Toward the privileged governor, in short, the tribunes of the right have happily extended just the sort of condescending tolerance that they attack in anyone who would make the same allowances for poor black children. Thus Bush himself is a big-time beneficiary of what he likes to call "the bigotry of soft expectations"—an indulgence that his champions never grant to any politician who would speak up for the underprivileged.

★That quaint formulation was by no means new. The conception of intelligence itself as somehow un-American—an ancient notion in our history—found especially loud expression in the presidential race of 1952, in which, for example, Senator Richard Nixon charged that Adlai Stevenson "got his Ph.D. from Dean Acheson's College of Cowardly Communist Containment." On the anti-intellectual subtext of that campaign, see Richard Hofstadter, *Anti-Intellectualism in American Life* (New York: Knopf, 1963), pp. 3–51.

George Will, for example, was among the staunchest of the governor's postdebate defenders. Although the Bush performance was, by any reasonable gauge, not good (see below), the rootin'-tootin' Will adeptly skirted the reality by making up quaint allegories based on his fanatic's view of how the candidates appeared: "Bush's ambling on the stage and his low-voltage delivery exhibited a kind of behavioral modesty, analogous to and expressive of conservatism's modest expectations for the uses of government," while Gore "strode and gesticulated and generally overflowed with the sort of confidence with which liberalism would wield government for grant purposes," etc.[49] Even before he made that sort of case in many columns and TV appearances, however, Will had already been quite generous with the befuddled candidate. On a broadcast of ABC's *This Week* in January 2000, Bush told Will that he was "not sure" whether Congress should naturalize Elian Gonzalez: "I really haven't thought through the, a— a—a law that would make him a citizen." Then, moments later, Bush told Cokie Roberts that he would advise the senators to pass the law. "So you've n—so you now think citizenship is a good—?" Roberts wondered, and the governor said this:

> Well, I think—I—It—listen, I don't understand the full ramifications of what they're going to do. But I—I—I think it'd be a—a—a wonderful gesture. I guess the man c—the boy could still go back to Cuba as a citizen of the United States. I'm concerned about, you kn—you know, family relations, and I think the dad ought to come here. And I think the dad ought to be given time to understand the greatness of America. I don't think—I—I would suspect he's not—he's not able to make a rational decision in Cuba. I'm sure the pressure's enormous on this man, an—t—t—t—to toe the Castro line. But I— as I said to George, I hadn't really thought about the citizenship issue. It's an interesting idea, but if I were in the Senate, I'd vote aye.

Although both illogical and ill-considered (if Elian were made "a citizen of the United States," his Miami relatives could then *prevent* his going "back to Cuba"), that dim reply earned no rebuke from his bespectacled inquisitor—who had taken an entirely different tack with Jesse Jackson. On ABC's *This Week* in 1988, during the contest for the presidential nominations, George Will did everything but try to rope and brand that uppity contender, hitting him with questions of a sort that would have knocked the governor unconscious. "As president, would you support measures such as the G-7 measures in the Louvre accords?" he asked sharply, then looked well pleased that Jackson didn't understand the question (which referred to the ongoing GATT negotiations). Will also homed in on some of Jackson's leftist economic claims with a pedantic ruthlessness entirely absent from his later puff pieces on Bush—although the latter could not even clarify the fuzzy math in his own plans. (Jackson's economic answers made some sense, despite the interviewer's jeering.) The set-to caused a stir, with Jackson charging racism, whereupon Will wrote a column boasting of how gutsy he had been to blow the whistle on that candidate—which Jackson's fellow Democrats, he claimed, were all afraid to do: "Because he is black, his white rivals sit silently beside him, leaving his foolishness unremarked."[50] Faced with a peerless "foolishness" some twelve years later, the smitten pundit did not just leave it "unremarked" but praised it as the highest wisdom. Thus George Will showed himself to be a stalwart double-standard-bearer for the GOP—one of many who were willing to say anything to represent the rich kid as a populist, the novice as experienced, the ignoramus as a proper heir to Thomas Jefferson.

NIXON'S REVENGE

The anti-intellectual appeal goes way back in American history and is still a potent one; and the Bush team made it with enormous skill, alleging W's rusticity and hyping Gore's aggressive braininess with all due unanimity and vehemence. It is therefore remarkable, and cause for optimism, that that drive ultimately failed, although it surely did a lot to redden all those middling states where Bush's act played well. Despite Gore's inability to warm the cockles of the national heart—and, more importantly, despite the media's gigantic bias against him—the majority of voters did *not* find W so "likeable" or, if they did, were not convinced that he was any deeper or more able than he seemed. Television's daily revelation of his absolute unfitness was, or should have been, a killer. Just as Nixon's men could never make him seem like fun, Bush's propagandists couldn't make that party animal seem capable of running the United States; and so it finally took five members of the nation's highest court, and the journalists' blind eye to what went down in Florida, to place him in the nation's highest office.

And yet TV's exposure of the governor's unfitness was itself misleading; for it allowed the quick construction of a caricature that has served to *idealize* the candidate, however cruelly it's been rendered. The dim bulb played by Will Ferrell on *Saturday Night Live,* and roasted nightly by Jay Leno, David Letterman, Conan O'Brien and the rest, and satirized by countless political cartoonists, is, on the one hand, an appalling figure—the sort of idiot prince who might slouch in the throne of some exhausted monarchy, perhaps, but who should never sit in charge of our democracy. While shockingly out of his depth, however, that plain half-wit is himself benign—a danger only insofar as evil others might manipulate him (as in *SNL's* mock soap *Palm Beach*). For all his faults, that butt *is* kind of "likeable," a simpleton as genial, blithe, and innocent as Alfred E. Neuman (to whom our president has often been compared). In short, that cheerful moron is a figure not much different from the smirking anti-Gore extolled by the Republicans throughout the recent contest. ("You don't have to be smart to be president!" yelled Representative J. C. Watts in introducing W at a rally in South Carolina.)[51] He may be dumb, in other words, but he's not ambitious, and he's a real nice fella, wouldn't hurt a fly.

The overall good-naturedness of that cartoonish image has been subtly amplified by Bush's own public response to such derision. Like all postmodern politicians from Ronald Reagan on, this Bush has understood that, in the culture of television, there is no balm like "self-effacing humor." However much the satire galls him—and it's obvious that it does—he has managed somewhat, and so far, to rise above it—and ensure its harmlessness—by seeming to take part in it himself. Thus he started early on to use that weary little joke about his tendency to "stress the wrong syl-LAB-ble," and told Letterman that he "would make sure the White House library has lots of books with big print and big pictures." Likewise, just before Election Day, he and Al Gore co-starred in the opening bit on *Saturday Night Live*—he riffing broadly on his own dyslexia (he said he was "ambilavent" about appearing on the show, which he at times had found "offensible"), while Gore sat stiffly sighing. That defensive comic pas de deux brought down the house—which made it clear, if further proof were needed, that such self-parody has no subversive edge at all. Indeed, such frank cooperation often works to power's advantage, since it appears to demonstrate a kingly magnanimity by showing the world that such burlesque is really licensed by the sovereign. Thus Ronald Reagan had Rich Little doing Ronald Reagan at his big inaugural bash in 1984, the Gipper richly laughing through it all; and the elder Bush was just delighted to have Dana Carvey come and do him at the White House, no hard feelings—and not very funny, either. Real satire always draws a little blood or else it's just court entertainment: Harry Shearer would never have been asked to play the Reagan White House, nor would Governor Bush have visited *The Daily Show;* and the Clintons got a bit more than they bargained for—as did all the other attendees that night—from Don Imus when he gave his raucous keynote at the annual dinner of the Radio/TV Correspondents Association in 1996. The comedy that's politician-friendly, on the other hand, is always trivial (even if it's sort of funny)—as are the politician's self-inflicted jabs. Far from being self-critical, in fact, the politician who cracks wise about himself—it seems to be a male thing, by and large*— is actually thereby betraying a certain shamelessness, both in himself and in the culture that sits laughing with him. (For examples, see "The Wit and Humor of George W. Bush," pp. 120ff.)

And so to snicker at this president for his stupidity is not productive, for his unfitness isn't really funny—and in any case he isn't stupid. True, he is the most ignorant president in U.S. history, probably the most illiterate, and easily among the least concerned about the contents of his mind. Moreover, his off-the-cuff remarks betray what is apparently an inability to reason—an intellectual handicap much worse than, say, a lack of interest in the sort of wonkish fare that he himself has always gleefully dismissed.

---

*Of course, there are exceptions. Concerning Katherine Harris's "mischievous sense of humor," Katherine G. Seelye tells this story: "In a recent television interview with Diane Sawyer, Ms. Harris told a story about Christmas shopping at Target one night when she could not sleep. 'The woman looked at my credit card and looked at me and she goes, 'Katherine Harris.' And like, she didn't, she said, 'Are you Katherine Harris?' And I said, 'Yeah. I only have on one layer of makeup. I'm incognito.' " "Katherine Harris Redux: No Longer Larger Than Life," *New York Times,* February 5, 2001.

("Sitting down and reading a five-hundred-page book on public policy or philosophy or something" is just not his thing, he told Tucker Carlson.) At issue here is not the president's distaste for slogging through tough prose but the incessant hints of a profound confusion that ought not to cloud the mind of anyone who has his finger on the trigger: a penchant for non sequiturs, a hard time making elementary distinctions, a tendency to merge cause and effect. Tautologies abound in Bush's speech: "In terms of being a president that says there is no place in [i.e., for] racism, it starts with saying there's no place for racism in America." "If you don't stand for anything, you don't stand for anything." And when asked about the prospect of there not being sufficient unity at his Republican convention, he replied: "I am confident there will be. I'm confident people are coming together. And the reason I believe this is because our party is united." (For more on Bush's illogic, see "Let Me Make One Thing Perfectly Clear," below.)

We can cite such examples till the cows come home, but it won't change the fact that George W. Bush *is* our president, despite his obvious lack of interest in, or preparation for, the job (and despite the fact that the American people didn't vote him into office)—a momentous sign that he is by no means the cheery imbecile that many people would prefer to think he is. That he performs as front man for Dick Cheney's shadow government does not mean that he's a figurehead, like Henry Pu Yi or Paul von Hindenburg. Although he is as overwhelmed as he appears, this president is neither as dim-witted nor as easygoing as TV makes him out to be. That first impression now requires a clear corrective because—as he might say— we misunderstimate him at our peril. For just beneath that "What, Me Worry?" grin there burns the adamant, ill-shaven glare of Richard Nixon. Uncannily, the vengeful spirit of that most *un*likeable of presidents is back upon us once again—reincarnate in our hyperchummy chief executive, who, television keeps telling us, is *marvelously* "likeable."

By his own description "a political animal"—or, in Mary Matalin's admiring phrase, a "political campaign terrorist"*—Bush, like Nixon, has

---

*"He is not as ham-handed as the typical terrorist," Matalin told Bill Minutaglio. "He's much more of a stiletto as opposed to an ax murderer. He comes into a room, you know he's there." *First Son: George W. Bush and the Bush Family Dynasty* (New York: Times Books, 1999), p. 260.

exactly what it takes to win elections at their dirtiest: a taste for blood and a sharp sense of how to agitate his base, the right. He is also driven by ferocious tribal loyalty—a trait entirely missing from the loner Nixon, who had "the soul of an alley cat," as William Rusher put it once. The feudal urge to glorify his clan, exalt his vassals, and reward his friends has taken Bush a long, long way. Moreover, although bored stiff by governance, he is capable of SWAT-like focus in the war room. As J. H. Hatfield—alone among biographers—has pointed out, the first son exerted a great influence on the Bush/Quayle campaign in 1988, giving it his terroristic all. He joined the team to keep an eye on Lee Atwater, whose lowbrow antics—he appeared on the cover of *Esquire* with his pants down—had offended Mother Bush. Soon, however, young George was working closely with the dirty trickster, working hard to give offense on a far grander scale. The two of them devised the tactics, then George would urge the necessary measures on his then-reluctant dad. "He'll do positive things, but that's all," Nixon noted of the loyal George H. W. fifteen years before. The first son helped the candidate get past such inhibitions. It was he who got the elder Bush to go ballistic on Dan Rather in a live exchange on CBS so as to stifle any further talk of Iran-Contra, and to show off the candidate's king-sized *cojones* for the media-hating right (a gambit that restored the campaign's faltering momentum). Thus W aggressively exploited the old anti-telejournalistic animus that Nixon was the first to take advantage of, through the medium of Spiro Agnew. (See p. 75.) It was also W who persuaded Dad to go along with the strategic smear of Jimmy Swaggart just two weeks before the South Carolina primary, where Swaggart's man Pat Robertson was threatening Bush's chances; and so Bush/Atwater leaked word of Swaggart's motel assignations to the local press—a covert op that saved the state for Bush Sr. And, crucially, it was W who ensured that the notorious—and effective—Willie Horton ads could be blamed plausibly on mavericks unaffiliated with the Bush campaign. The first son raised the money for those ads and devised the cover operation that could then be said to have produced them on its own (a ruse that—to paraphrase our president—allowed Bush/Quayle to claim the high horse while taking the low road).[52]

While he has the sort of smarts required for work of that clandestine sort, our president has also long been sharp enough to keep his disparate warriors inside the GOP's big tent. This, too, is a Nixonian ability—although our president is actually much better at it, since the necessary schmoozing comes much easier to him than to his dad's uneasy mentor. It was the younger Bush who in the 1980s made the peace between the Christian far right and his Episcopalian father—no mean feat since, as far as those believers were concerned, George Bush, with his membership in Skull and Bones and the Trilateral Commission, was about as worthy a Republican as Che Guevara.★ As the man responsible for outreach to the Pentecostalists and Southern Baptists and their brethren, W forged many bonds secure enough to see him through the last election, his victory throughout the red states owing everything to that connection; and yet even as he always talked the talk of Christian rectitude, Bush has also walked the walk of Wall Street—and in him the twain do meet. Thus he has shown the sort of coalition-building savvy that defined his idol, Ronald Reagan. As long as all the players are on the right, W can talk to 'em—as in Texas, where Governor Bush *did* work with some Democrats, but where he did *not* work with any Democrats who weren't essentially Republicans. (There are quite a few such players in Texas politics.) Whoever can pull off such diplomatic coups cannot be half retarded, however comical his grammar.

Bush's link to Nixon is not merely temperamental, for his team has long included operatives who made their bones in Nixon's service. Lee Atwater was a Nixon acolyte—and devotee of both the Gipper and Strom Thurmond—who transferred to the Bush machine in 1988, after having used Jew-baiting tactics to get Carroll Campbell into Congress. Likewise, there was Roger Ailes, who got his start in 1968 producing *Ask Richard Nixon!*—a series of canned television forums that placed the candidate "in the arena" with a hand-picked audience of grinning milquetoasts—and ended up coordinating Bush/Quayle's media drive while coaching Bush on how to come off manly at the podium. (Ailes now runs Rupert Murdoch's Fox TV.) For his part, W was mentored by Atwater, whose early cohort, Karl Rove, has been with Bush the Younger from the start. Known

---

★That W was able to stay tight with the Christian Coalition even after having worked to sink Pat Robertson (by smearing Jimmy Swaggart) is an indication of his rare adroitness.

to the inner circle as "Turd Blossom" (the nickname came from Bush), the war-addicted Rove is just the sort of "mean, tough son-of-a-bitch" whose dedication Nixon always craved: "If you're not with Karl one-hundred percent, you're an enemy," as Texas GOP chair Tom Pauken has marveled. From his early days as a dirty trickster for the College Republican National Committee in 1973—stealing stationery, forging invitations to fictitious parties, sifting garbage for discarded memos, etc.—Rove went on to do his number for the Texas right (while also handling other clients, including Phillip Morris), working his black magic as required. Just hours before the one gubernatorial debate in 1986, with the campaign of his boss, Republican Bill Clements in trouble, Rove charged dramatically—and with no evidence—that he had found a hidden microphone in his office, and accused the incumbent, Democratic governor Mark White, of having had it put there. Four years later Rove made news again when it emerged that he'd been meeting privately with ultraright FBI agent Greg Rampton, who had been supplying him with secret information on Agriculture commissioner Jim Hightower. (Rove was working then for state representative Rick Perry, who wanted Hightower's job.) Such Watergate-style operations have recurred since Rove began to work full time for W. The crude attempt to tar the Gore campaign before the first debate (by anonymously mailing them a training video that supposedly only Bush was meant to see) appeared to be pure Rove—and certainly was vintage Nixon.[53]

So much for our president's Nixonian abilities and personnel. But *what* makes W run that way? It seems anomalous indeed that Richard Nixon— who "went up the walls of life with his claws," as Bryce Harlow once remarked—should have exerted such an influence on this or that George Bush, who, to quote Ann Richards, "was born on third base and thought he hit a triple." The simple answer to this mystery is quite important, since it will help us understand exactly what we're living with today. Surprisingly, the large and very wealthy House of Bush, with its sterling fourteenth-century pedigree (the Queen of England is a cousin) and its decades of high influence on Wall Street, is driven by much the same resentment that compelled—and in the end destroyed—the threadbare Californian, son of Hannah and the loser Frank. That shared hositility explains the otherwise bizarre entanglement between the golden Poppy and the brazen Nixon, who evidently saw Bush as the son he'd never had: "A total Nixon man—first," he enthused at the outset of his second term. "Doubt if you can do better than Bush." And yet the heart of Nixon beats more strongly in the breast of our new president, who lacks those dated scruples that he once had to talk his father out of honoring.[54]

The Bushes' resentment is more complicated than the plain class grudge that drove the underprivileged Nixon. Like him, they were angrily fixated on the Kennedys—not out of thwarted aspiration, certainly, but from dynastic envy, George the Elder having longed for years to transform Prescott, retroactively, into an American patriarch like Joe Kennedy: "Just wait till I turn these Bush boys out," he promised proudly back when Jack was president. Over the years after Camelot, the cult of JFK became more galling than inspiring, as it appeared to leave the Bush ménage forever in the shade, and grumbling tightly on the patio of their own mammoth seaside compound. Seeking to define themselves as somehow better than the competition, they took—preposterously—to trumpeting the family's modest origins, their frontier diligence and pluck—just like Nixon. "While Kennedy was running for the Senate in 1952 with a healthy inheritance to back him," wrote Bush friend Fitzhugh Green, in an early presidential hagiography, "Bush was struggling to build his own bankroll"—a "struggle" that in fact entailed much generous investment by the folks back home (primarily Bush's dad and Uncle Herbie). Such invidious mythology loomed large in Poppy's presidential spectacle, what with the pork rinds and the cowboy boots and the canny exploitation of his clumsy way with words ("I may not be eloquent," etc.). And yet, while disavowing the Camelot mystique, Bush Sr.—like Nixon—also tried at times to reproduce it, strongly echoing JFK in his own inaugural address (penned by Peggy Noonan, who as a girl had been "in love with the Kennedys") and even picking Dan Quayle as his running mate in part because he thought the Indianan's youthfulness would call Jack Kennedy to mind. (He was wrong.)*[55]

---

*In *Man of Integrity* (1988), a family-sponsored propaganda volume meant to sell the Christian right on Bush's presidential bid, there is this revealing passage, at the start of Chapter 7, "Family Comes First":

It is impossible to understand the Vice President outside the context of his own family. There is an electricity, a special magic, when Barbara and the children are nearby.

Worked up by their lesser status as a rival house, the Bushes, once they'd settled down in dusty Midland, also found themselves offended by the high disdain that many Eastern liberals felt toward Texas. Unlike Nixon, who never longed to go back where he came from, the transplanted Bushes loved their neighborhood as they loved themselves, and that allegiance sharpened their Nixonian hostility toward sophisticated coastal types. Barbara writes of one telling face-off at a Georgetown dinner party in early 1968, when she and George had just moved to Washington for his first stint in Congress. Sitting next to her was some nostalgic Camelot survivor who kept taking shots at LBJ, then said, "I hate all Texans." When Barbara told him she was one, he said that she was obviously different, having grown up in the East. "I said that he was right, but that he was talking about my children, who were lucky enough to be born Texans. I turned my back and never spoke to that whining, pompous man again." With that, "George and I crossed 'inside Washington' dinners off our list."[56]

Fed by his clan's imperial ambitions, and shaped by his experience as a very wealthy kid in segregated Texas, the eldest son could only come to hate the East—or any other precinct outside Nixon country. This had to do primarily with the 1960s. Bush's time away from home—at Andover, then Yale—was tolerable only insofar as he could replicate the sort of nonstop fun-time and homogeneous companionship that he knew while growing up in Midland. As head cheerleader at Andover, then as president of Delta Kappa Epsilon—Yale's drunkest frat house—and as a loyal Bonesman (like his dad), Bush had a ball. The currents of the time, however, were all against such puerile institutions—and eventually against his father, and against the president whom his father was serving with that anomalous steadfastness. The elder Bush became a Nixon surrogate as soon as he joined Congress in 1968—the year of the Tet Offensive, the Chicago Seven, *Soul on Ice,* and the *White Album,* to name just a few manifestations

---

When all four boys recently appeared with their father on a morning television talk-show, the telephone lines lit up for hours. Some said that they were reminded of the Kennedys, that they had never seen so many young men in the same family so bright and handsome and personable.
—George Bush with Doug Wead, *Man of Integrity*
(Eugene, Ore.: Harvest House, 1988), p. 111

of the global trends that seemed to spell the end of everything that Nixon *and* the younger Bush had both believed in.

And yet there is, of course, a difference between Bush's anti-'60s beef and Nixon's. For the thirty-seventh president, as for millions of other Americans, the schisms and innovations of that decade were apocalyptic, threatening everything with mere destruction, and so requiring a defensive movement *back* toward that exclusive tidy Eden that "we" enjoyed before the rise of Lyndon Johnson, Martin Luther King, the Beatles. "The country—we turned away from the Great Society," Nixon raved to Alexander Haig in May 1973. "It turns away from an obsession about the blacks. And it's starting to turn away from the crime and drug syndrome, the dirty movies, etc. It turned away from, you know, the whole [unintelligible] peace thing. I mean, it turned a little character."[57] The villains of the piece were not "the blacks" per se, not even the Communists, but all those affluent liberals who had made things go so wrong—the permissive parents and their snotty college kids, the pompous bleeding hearts who let the Reds and negroes get away with murder, the pseudointellectuals with their big words and "dirty movies." Nixon's rage at that elite expressed, among other things, a class-based sense of grievance, piqued to fury by the spectacle, or thought, of privileged types who, even though they had it all, were blithely dumping on the values that had made this country great and that he'd worked his whole life long to honor—or so he liked to think.

For George W. Bush, on the other hand, the 1960s represented not a vast barbarian invasion but a pretty big impertinence. The turmoil was annoying to him largely for its threat of interference with his faux-aristocratic life of buddy rituals and heavy drinking; but he was most irked by the general disrespect for George Bush Sr., a famed alumnus whose support for Nixon and the war in Vietnam were naturally well-known at Yale. Of course, it was also a matter of taste for young Bush, who didn't groove to *Sgt. Pepper* any more than Nixon did. ("The Beatles went through that kind of a weird, psychedelic period, which I particularly didn't care for," confessed the governor, who went on to have Wayne Newton help inaugurate him.) But it was all the somber questioning that most aggrieved him—the sudden vocal skepticism toward the wisdom of the Fathers, for their errors, or crimes, in Vietnam and on the ground at home. The younger Bush could not abide such antipaternal sentiment, much less share it, since his own dad was—and still is—his guide in everything. "There is an arrogance about some Ivy League connections that is bad," the father wrote the son in 1974, referring to the student enemies of Richard Nixon. "I saw an intellectual arrogance that I hope I never have," said W in 1992, describing Yale precisely as his dad (and Nixon) did.[58]

That there was some "arrogance" among the campus left is surely true—although far less than in the White House at the time. However, to thus write off that whole explosion of dissent itself betrays a certain smugness, especially considering Bush's own frank lack of any intellectual *or* moral engagement in those painful years: "I don't remember any kind of heaviness ruining my time at Yale." To be that cavalier about the war, the global influence of U.S. corporate power, the plight of blacks, and the demands of "women's liberation" was to be absurdly out of step—a careless Bourbon among Jacobins, Girondists, fretful moderates, and active royalists. His own beloved dad was more affected by the issues of the day: Representative Bush voted, bravely, for the Civil Rights Act of 1968, with its "open housing" provision—a stand that won him lots of hate mail from his native Houston—and although a dedicated hawk, he took the protestors seriously, meeting with them often in D.C. and even standing up for them before Republicans at home, pointing out the moral basis of the demonstrations and reminding his constituents that "we in Texas certainly can't stand to be without the right to dissent." (That respectful view was very different from the absolute contempt that would pervade the Nixon White House.)* For his part, the son, through all his years in Jim Crow Texas, was never moved to take a stand on civil rights—unlike Joe Lieberman, Pat

---

*Roger Morris recalls the Nixon team's dismissiveness: " 'Look,' [they might have said], 'these people in the streets are thoughtful, they may have *a point* about the war, it may behoove us to rethink some of our assumptions.' They never did that. They thought [the demonstrators] were insubstantial and capricious, they thought it was basically a draft protest, they thought they were cowardly, they thought they were there for frivolous reasons. . . . They just never took the protest seriously in an intellectual sense. . . . And their disdain and their contempt for the anti-war movement was part of the defense mechanism for keeping them out. . . . If you could dismiss them as a bunch of flukes and phonies and kids, you didn't really have to think seriously about what they were saying.' " Quoted in Tom Wells, *The War Within: America's Battle over Vietnam* (Berkeley: University of California Press, 1994), p. 307.

Schroeder, Edward Garvey, Barney Frank, Clinton, Gore and many other white members of the generation that our president has often deprecated for its selfishness. Nor did the younger Bush say anything, pro or con, about the war back then. His silence on the subject struck his brothers in the DKE house as remarkable, since he was not the silent type, and they were talking endlessly about it. He refused to sign an antiwar petition, but otherwise did nothing about Vietnam, except keep from going there by taking full advantage of that plum assignment to the Texas Air National Guard.[59]

Thus was all the era's idealism quite lost on our president, who staggered through that fiery epoch partying and making good connections. (When they first saw *Animal House,* some of Bush's college pals were struck by his strong undergraduate resemblance to the woozy, boozy "Bluto," played by John Belushi.) The chaos and the disrespectfulness he noticed, and deplored, while simply tuning out the grand utopian impulse that was throbbing everywhere. Indeed, his only impulse vis-à-vis "the [unintelligible] peace movement" was—just like Nixon—to *attack* it. For its "arrogance" in challenging his own complacent views and in dissing his beloved father, Bush became a surly and half-conscious sort of counterrevolutionary, who would ultimately work that grudge into his platform. This explains the basis of his own relationships with other bitter sons (and daughters) of the lower middle class—Nixon's spiritual children, whose hard alliance with the wealthy W is but the next step down from George the Elder's more ambivalent—and less destructive—partnership with Tricky Dick himself. Our president's most devoted operatives are those ex-kids who saw their parents' values spit on by the haute-bourgeois protesters of the 1960s, and who are still seething after all these years: the toxic Rove, mad Mary Matalin, and other livid shadowboxers. Moreover, Rove long ago provided Bush with some simple broadsides that enable the illusion of an intellectual basis for the anti-'60s fervor that impels the whole cabal: Myron Magnet's *The Dream and the Nightmare* and David Horowitz's *Destructive Generation.* Such screeds offer a veneer of sober doctrine (a very thin veneer in Horowitz's case) for what is nothing more than a belated, and gratuitous, assault against the vanished counterculture—that is to say, an endless venting of self-righteous wrath *for its own sake.*

BULLY PULPIT

Such, after all, is Nixon's spiritual legacy: "Study of revenge, immortal hate, / And courage never to submit or yield," as Milton's Satan puts it. Our president's continuation of that legacy is manifest not only in his firm reliance on such implacable destroyers as Rove, Matalin and Horowitz, but— as this *Dyslexicon* makes clear—in his own language. Both in his gaffes and in his lucid statements Bush consistently betrays the raging animus that also drove our thirty-seventh president, and that Nixon also tried, and failed, to keep concealed from public view.

While Nixon's rage is famous, Bush's boiling anger is—as of this writing—still known only to insiders and to the readers of his best biographies. That anger was, in fact, his salient feature back when he was working in his dad's campaigns. As George Bush's self-styled "loyalty enforcer," W took on the job of blowing up at those reporters who may have been, or seemed to be, "unfair" in their coverage. He evidently did that job with zest, if not much lucidity: "You no good fucking son of a bitch, I will never fucking forget what you wrote!" he ranted at Al Hunt of the *Wall Street Journal,* who was sitting down to dinner in a Dallas restaurant with his wife, Judy Woodruff, and their four-year-old son. (See pp. 107–8.) Such pique is not unusual, of course; Bobby Kennedy was also known to lose it— often—in defense of Jack. Bush's tantrum was unusual, however, for its complete irrationality. Hunt recalls that Bush was "quite clearly lubricated," but this was in itself not so remarkable—although it was a year since Bush's famous pledge to give up drinking. More striking was the fact that Hunt had written nothing to offend George Bush. It was April 1987, and in the most recent issue of the *Washingtonian,* Hunt was one of many journalists offering a forecast of the next year's presidential line-up: "Kemp and Indiana Senator Richard Lugar against Hart and Robb," was all he wrote— an item whose exclusion of George Bush could seem offensive only to a mind unhinged by filial devotion.* (The vice president had not declared his candidacy yet.) "This," Hunt thought, "is a guy who's got problems."

---

*Years later, Bush betrayed a similarly groundless animus against another journalist. Onstage with Dick Cheney for a Labor Day campaign event in Naperville, Illinois, the governor

Bush thus allowed his wrath to carry him away throughout his father's presidential quests. ("I'm a warrior. I'm not very objective," he confessed to Larry King in 1992.) By the time he ran against Ann Richards for the Texas governorship, however, Bush had learned to bite his tongue and smile—a deliberate feat of self-restraint that he terms "feisting out."* Considering how hot he burned within, it was an astonishing achievement—especially since the caustic Governor Richards went all out to try to piss him off. (So amazed was Bush's cousin Elsie Walker at the sight of the contender calmly taking all those blows that she cabled her Aunt Barbara: 'WHAT HAS   WHAT DID HE DO?') Such self-discipline has so far served him well. Although he did at times get snappish during the campaign—especially at those moments when Al Gore ripped into him—he never blew up on camera, as Nixon did. Taken all in all, however, his language gives the game away, almost as clearly as those tapes incriminated Nixon.[60]

For Bush, despite his many howlers, is *not* always inarticulate. There are in fact two kinds of speech at which he does quite well. First, he can be good at talking policy, albeit not at length. When he is entirely confident about his subject and wholly comfortable with those around him, he can be just as clear and well-informed as any other politician. He seemed to know what he was saying, for example, at his gubernatorial debate with Garry Mauro in 1998—although he also came across as slightly nuts, jabbering as if on speed and violently listing to the side, eyes rolling skyward—and he did well at the little "education forum" that he chaired on C-SPAN during the transition. That round table was clearly modeled on the "economic forum" that Clinton held in 1992, and Bush did suffer by comparison. He could not talk for very long, and often got so fidgety when others

---

made this comment to his running-mate: "There's Adam Clymer, major-league asshole from the *New York Times.*" ("He is, big-time," agreed Cheney.) The exchange took place in front of a live microphone. The ensuing flap concerned the candidate's imprudence—and not the strangeness of his grudge, the wholly inoffensive Clymer having written nothing that could possibly explain the wrath of Bush (and Cheney). See the coverage of the episode, posted at www.adamclymerfanclub.org.

"It was, some people in Texas later said, an odd way of putting it—'feisting out'*—something you might hear in the South when someone was talking about feisting curs, small mongrel dogs that could corner wild boars or snarl for hours at a squirrel they had sent up a tree." Minutaglio, *First Son*, p. 229.

spoke that they got nervous. Still, the sight of him so ably nattering was rather a surprise, considering how incoherent and ill at ease he often is in other circumstances.

Secondly—and more commonly—Bush is almost always clear when he's speaking cruelly. For example, when his subject is the punitive infliction of great pain, there is no problem with his syntax, grammar, or vocabulary, even if he happens to be lying. There was the sudden clarity of his aside, at the Winston-Salem face-off with Al Gore, on the fate of James Byrd's murderers in Texas—which the governor brought up by way of a response to Gore's remarks about the need for hate crimes legislation. "You have a different view of that," Jim Lehrer prompted him.

BUSH:	No, I don't, really.
LEHRER:	On hate crimes laws?
BUSH:	No. We've got one in Texas—and guess what: The three men who murdered James Byrd—guess what's going to happen to them? They're going to be put to death. A jury found them guilty and—it's going to be hard to punish them any worse after they get put to death. And it's the right cause, so it's the right decision.

The speech stood out for its rare pithiness—and for the joyous leer with which the governor made that statement, which was disingenuous as well as scary, since he had in fact opposed the hate crimes law that James Byrd's family had wanted him to pass.* His bald pleasure at the prospect of those executions—a gleefulness so flagrant that he was asked about it at the next debate—had everything to do with the unwonted clarity of those re-

---

*The governor displayed the same stone-heartedness in turning that petition down. Renee Mullins, James Byrd's daughter, traveled from Hawaii to Austin to ask Bush to approve the law. She was escorted by Diane Hardy-Garcia, Texas lobbyist for the Lesbian & Gay Political Caucus. According to Hardy-Garcia, who accompanied Mullins to the meeting, the governor seemed very uncomfortable. Mullins asked Bush why he opposed the bill, and he told her he hadn't read it. "She gave him a copy and he threw it on his desk," Hardy-Garcia said. Then she asked, "Will you help us?" He said, "No."

" 'She was crying, and he didn't try to console her or even offer her a Kleenex,' Hardy-Garcia said. 'He was cold, icy, to her.' " Molly Ivins and Lou Dubose, *Shrub: The Short But Happy Political Life of George W. Bush* (New York: Vintage, 2000), p. 100.

marks. Like all the rest of us, however well or badly educated, Bush can talk quite clearly on the subjects that most interest him: baseball, football, campaign tactics, putting men to death.

On the other hand, our president is extraordinarily tongue-tied when he's trying, off the cuff, to sound a note of idealism, magnanimity or—especially—compassion. For all the maudlin yammering about his "heart" and his success at vending that Orwellian oxymoron "compassionate conservatism," the higher sentiments—Judaeo-Christian or chivalric—are so completely foreign to his nature that he can't even express them in plain English, much less make them sound convincing. For example, minutes after his plain-spoken promise to despatch James Byrd's murderers, the governor, in yet another move to play down gun control, said this about the need to get ourselves a kinder, gentler culture:

> Columbine spoke to a larger issue, and it's really a matter of culture. It's a culture that somewhere along the line we've begun to disrespect life. Where, for a child can walk in and have their heart turn dark as a result of being on the Internet [sic], and walk in and decide to take somebody else's life. And so gun laws are important, no question about it. But so is loving children and character-education classes and faith-based programs being a part of after-school programs. Somebody, some desperate child that needs to have somebody put their arm around him and say we love you and so there's a—this is a society of ours that's got to do a better job of teaching children right from wrong. And we can enforce law, but there seems to be a lot of preoccupation on, not necessarily in this debate, but just in general in law, but there's a larger law [sic]: Love your neighbor like you'd like to be loved yourself. And that's where our society must head if we're going to be a peaceful and prosperous society.

While he speaks pure gibberish when he tries to *care,* Bush is clear not only when he's frankly brutal but also in his jokes—which aren't exactly kind. The president does boast a certain ready wit but has a hard time flexing it onstage unless he trusts the audience. At his ease—or in his cups— the guy can be a riot. For example, there's a Web site (thesmokinggun.com) that features sixty seconds of a 1992 wedding video that shows Bush, "quite clearly lubricated," ad-libbing a deadpan mock testimonial to the happy couple as the interviewer, another wedding guest, cracks up at the insulting spiel. What's most interesting about the tape is not his drinking—although it had been six years since his pledge to give that up—but his off-beat and sardonic putdown humor. You can see from that surprising bit (which as of this writing no one from the mainstream press has ever mentioned) why Bush was always such a hit at frat parties and finally made it as a politician.

His humor has an edge to it, and always has, reportedly. Bush was a relentless kidder as a child, then went on to other funny places. At Andover—where he was nicknamed "Lip"—the drollery of choice was sarcasm, which the future chief executive wielded with unusual frankness. "He would call people names, derogatory nicknames," one classmate recalls. "Other people would use them behind people's backs, but he was more open about it."[61] During the campaign, Rove and Company spun that habit as another sign of Bush's natural ease with all folks great and small; but in fact that teasing edge connects with something truly nasty in the president's sense of humor. There is, of course, his snickering mockery of Karla Fay Tucker's final plea for life—the sort of joke that she herself would probably have liked, back when she was killing folks with pickaxes. (See p. 121.) Although his other public jests have not been quite as shocking as that one, his humor often tends toward the sadistic, seeking chuckles in the most unlikely situations: David Letterman's heart surgery, the slaughter of animals, the Russians massacring Chechnyan women and children, the perdition of the Jews, etc. (See "The Wit and Humor of George W. Bush," pp. 120ff.) The candidate claimed that his taste for laughs reflects his interest in "the lighter side of life," but that *Reader's Digest* way of putting it does not do justice to the man's peculiar wit, which smacks of very different magazines.

Bush has often protested that we cannot see or judge what's in his "heart," and he gets testy when observers try. Like his father—and, indeed, like Nixon—he abhors psychologizing, often using "psychobabble" as a term of grim opprobrium. (He abhors such treatment of himself but not of others: John Rocker's mandatory "counseling" didn't bother him a bit. See "Freedom of Expression," pp. 155ff.) However, it takes no Freudian speculation to perceive that there's a bit of darkness in that famous heart of his, as we can tell not only from his language but from the nastier bits of his biography. As president of DKE, for instance, he went public in defense of the fraternity's sadomasochistic hazing rituals, which included branding each initiate just above and in between the buttocks with the red-hot tip of a wire coathanger. The on-campus stir over such practices inspired some coverage in the *New York Times,* which quoted the young Bush as pointing out dismissively that "the resulting wound is 'only a cigarette burn.' "[62]

Such biographical details confirm the rather kinky picture that we also get from Bush's language, his fuzzy discourse snapping into focus at the gratifying thought of someone else's punishment. ("We added beds. We're tough! We believe in tough love!" he crowed poetically in Winston-Salem, referring to the expansion of Texas's prisons.) The point here is not to hint at as-yet-undiscovered sins. Someday there may be tawdry news about this president's private life, or, of course, there may be none. Such revelation is forever likely in the culture of TV. For our purposes, what matters is the evidence, in Bush's language and life story, of a rage that *will* keep coming out, no matter how ingeniously he tries to mask it, either with religious turns of phrase or with pacific promises of "unity" or "healing." That inner wrath is what we'll see and what we'll hear, despite its endless efforts to conceal itself. Thus the Bush team's showy gestures of conciliation always ended up exploded utterly—and pretty quickly: "I'm a uniter, not a divider," a reassurance not convincing to begin with, turned into an easy punchline from the morning of November 8, as all Bush/Cheney's mighty propaganda forces started working overtime to demonize Al Gore, all of his fellow Democrats, and everyone who voted for him (or who tried to vote for him). Likewise, on December 13 Bush grandly vowed a spirit of "reconciliation and unity," promising to be the president of *all* the people, when he made his first acceptance speech—a pledge he quickly followed up by nominating the fanatic John Ashcroft to be attorney general, and James Watt's protégée Gale Norton to be secretary of interior. Throughout the transition, meanwhile, Bush continued taking shots at the departing team as if the race had not been settled in his favor. But when he took the national spotlight yet again on January 20, 2001, yet again he hailed "our unity, our union," giving his "solemn pledge" to "work to build a single nation of justice and opportunity," etc. (That day Karl Rove grinningly announced "the return of civility and respect.") And then, as if he'd never made that pitch for "unity," Bush's team continued hunkering down, working just as hard as ever for an ultrarightist victory, smearing every effort to find out the truth in Florida and otherwise pursuing the *attack*—which, finally, is the only thing they really want to do. And that, of course, was also Nixon's way. On the night he won in 1968, he, too, postured as an altruistic mediator—pledging solemnly to "bring us together"—while longing to take care of "them" once and for all.

ON MESSAGE

However, there is one crucial difference between Bush's show and Richard Nixon's. Back then, the president's hypocrisy, while dimly apprehensible to the untrusting audience, did not become explicit until Watergate, which finally made his falseness unmistakable to all—even his most fervent champions. (Trent Lott was an exception.) By contrast, this president's hypocrisy is so apparent that when he says things like "unity," "bipartisan," and "reconciliation," he might as well have on a sandwich board that says, "I'M TALKING BULLSHIT." The same was true of the whole rightist propaganda mill that ran the country ragged following Election Day. Its bad faith was so blatant, and the propaganda so pervasive, that you couldn't *not* notice the hypocrisy—unless you were a part of it, in which case you believed that the hypocrisy was wholly on the other side. Thus it is, of course, with all hermetic propaganda systems, be they democratic or authoritarian. Indeed, that big, loud network of Republicans—shifting ground from one hour to the next, bitterly attacking principles that they had just now bitterly defended, and screaming at the Democrats for doing things that they themselves had done or were about to do—behaved exactly like their erstwhile enemies in Moscow (and New York), executing endless swift voltefaces to toe the party line.

Thus we had the GOP—the long-time bastion of states' rights—now demanding, then defending, the use of Federal power to overturn a ruling by the high court of the state of Florida. The party that had long decried—

and was *even now* decrying—"judicial activism" was also gratefully applauding the Supreme Court's highly activist decision to itself elect the nation's president. The party that was *even now* decrying judicial interference with the legislative branch was also now applauding the Supreme Court for having halted a state recount on the grounds that there was "no clear standard" for the process—when the standard had been written by the Florida legislature. The party that was vehemently arguing that hand recounts are wholly unreliable and absolutely not to be allowed was *at the same time* calling for hand recounts in New Mexico, and was supporting, as its leader, the very man who had approved the passage of a Texas law permitting hand recounts in close elections. The party that had just pulled off a massive keep-out-the-vote campaign in Florida's most heavily Democratic precincts, disenfranchising tens of thousands of black, poor white, and Hispanic voters, now hailed the Supreme Court's decision to abort the recount under the equal protection clause in the Constitution. And even as they frantically demanded, then defended, all those shifts and gimmicks, the Republicans assailed Al Gore as one "who would do anything to get elected" and the Democrats as fiendishly intent on making some historic "mischief."

Such flagrancy was quite a shock—a show of overt, unapologetic propaganda that was certainly unprecedented in our history. And yet the weird transparency of that manipulative drive was not entirely new, for the candidate, in his own laid-back way, had always been transparent in *his* daily propaganda effort; and when he talks to us as president, he is transparent still. In short, his public speech has always blandly advertised the fact that it *is* propaganda, this insincere and incoherent politician selling us by telling us how hard he works at selling us—as if he merits our support exclusively because of what a first-rate job he's done at acting as if he merits our support. Thus he spoke at the beginning of the race. "So it should be grueling?" Larry King asked him. "Yes, it should be grueling," he replied:

> I'm not so sure length necessarily equates to grueling, but it should be a tough process. You need to be scrutinized and questioned. There needs to be debates, like we're going through. There needs to be town-hall meetings. There needs to be travel. This is a huge country.

And a candidate's got to be able to travel the country with a consistent message that rallies people for a better tomorrow.

As a statement of political intention, that bit was, typically, as empty as it was illiterate. On the other hand, as a simple overview of the most effective propaganda practice, it made some sense, since it is sadly true that, to get elected in the culture of TV, "a candidate's got to be able to travel the country with a consistent message that rallies people for a better tomorrow," and that's about it. That thin truism won't take us very far. What *else* should a candidate "be able" to do, aside from fly from state to state and say the same thing every day? Can a "message" that "consistent" really tell us anything? And how can our "tomorrow" be any "better" than today if we're all out there getting "rallied"—hypnotized by buzzwords and catch-phrases?

Bush never ceased to push his message or to keep us posted on how it was going. After the controversy over his appearance at Bob Jones University, he thought about the implications of his having worked that hateful room and realized the error of his ways—he hadn't sent the proper message. "I readily concede I missed an opportunity at Bob Jones; I [could] have been a hero," he said in March. "If I had gone down there and said, 'We're all God's children; we can receive redemption in all different kinds of ways; the Catholic religion is a great religion, Judaism is a great religion.' It's all I would have needed to have said. One sentence." Things eased up by the summer, when he looked forward to the big event in Philadelphia and to the upbeat message that the show would send the audience if all went well: "The convention is important because it gives a sense of who I am, and I think if we do our job right, to lead our party and lead the country, I think what you are going to find is that this is going to be a convention that spells out what we're for," he told Fox-TV's Carl Cameron, who seemed to understand that statement. At the debates, Bush did a fairly good job staying on message, even though that pushy know-it-all Al Gore did kind of rattle him. From time to time he managed to highlight a "theme." Explaining at the third debate why he is "absolutely opposed to a national health care plan," he told us this: "I trust people. I don't trust the federal government. It's going to be one of the themes you hear tonight. I don't want the federal government making decisions on behalf of everybody."

That last one was a pip, considering the "trust" that Bush's operation ultimately showed in "people" over "government." In retrospect, it's all too obvious that that "consistent message" was completely false—a pseudo-PC circus meant to mask the true intentions of a deeply antidemocratic movement. He has "opposed . . . a national health care plan" not out of a populist concern for individual freedom but because he's resting comfortably inside the pocket of insurance. The "message" of the GOP convention was no less deceptive: a prime-time picture of "inclusiveness," with many folks of color at the podium—albeit very few out on the floor—and lots of eager music black and brown, making for an antiseptic miniseries that could have been entitled, *It Takes a Potemkin Village*. This from the party of Strom Thurmond, Jesse Helms, and Bob Barr, a party managed by Trent Lott and Tom DeLay, and dedicated to the proposition that all men of color were created for the slammer. If Bush was ever troubled by the gap between his democratic "message" and the hard elitist interests backing him, it was because his "message" hadn't been delusory *enough*. He'd "have been a hero" after speaking at Bob Jones if only he had had the foresight to have Rove or Karen Hughes cook up "one sentence" for the cameras—just a quick I'd-like-to-give-the-world-a-Coke-type sentiment, and he would have been a visionary. Of course, the school itself would still have been the place it was: a fortress of medieval bigotry and—worse—a crucible of just the sort of theocratic ideology that drove the forces of Team Bush, however bright and tolerant his "message." (For more on Bush's "message," see "Message: I'm Real," pp. 246ff.)

And yet it almost seems a waste of time to set the record straight like this, because the candidate was always so disarmingly upfront about the crafting of his misimpressions.* He tended not so much to say that he *believed* in this or that, as to make clear to us that this or that would be, or

---

*For a vivid evocation of Bush's frank theatricality, see Nicholas Lemann's brilliant profile: "The Redemption," *The New Yorker,* January 31, 2000, pp. 48–63.

was, his "theme" or "message." The actual point of all such propaganda—
the matter that we now call "substance"—comes up only as an after-
thought if it comes up at all.

> Well, there'll be a health-care debate, and there'll be a health-care issue that I'm
> going to—I mean, a health-care speech and policy that I lay out. I talk about
> health care all the time at these one-on-ones when asked. It's on people's
> minds.

WHAT YOU SEE IS WHAT YOU GET

If Bush had won legitimately, we could say that we'd gotten the president
that we deserve. His "message" having played well on TV, and the audience
having picked him by a clear majority (both electoral *and* popular), he
would be the people's choice, and there would be no ambiguity about it.
But the situation now is highly complicated—and not just because of the
shenanigans in Florida and on the Supreme Court. For Bush owes his unlikely victory not only to those party flacks and goons who forced the
issue, nor only to the Rehnquist Five, but also to TV. Although he never
played well on the medium per se, TV was very, very good to him, because
the network that controls the medium—from above, and from the anchor
desks and pundit chairs—embraced him, and implicitly endorsed him, for
several reasons.

First of all, there is the great extrinsic factor of the media's corporate
ownership, the top managers and major shareholders preferring the aggressively big-merger-friendly GOP to the less-aggressively big-merger-
friendly Democrats. Al Gore had many champions in Hollywood, of
course, including all the top pro-Clinton heavyweights from Michael Eis-
ner on down. A tough New Democrat somewhat to Clinton's right,
Gore was never threatening to the interests of the corporate media, for
all his pulpit thumping with Joe Lieberman. (Indeed, even Rupert Murdoch was a quiet Gore supporter, the Democrats having used the Staples
Center—40 percent owned by News Corporation—as a gift for their

convention.)*[63] Nevertheless, the media's parent companies will do much better, and clean up much faster, now that they have Bush to play with, since he's for corporate concentration above all (literally), nor will his FCC—now chaired by Colin Powell's son, Michael, an adamant free-marketeer—discuss even the feeblest sort of regulation, whereas Powell's predecessor, Bill Kennard, did try now and then. (Under Bush, we will soon see the final merger of newspaper chains with media corporations—a move that Gore would not have made without a lot of prior shilly-shallying.) The media–corporate bias toward the governor was evident, for example, in MSNBC's decision to show repeatedly, throughout the five-week civil war in Florida, its dubious hail-Caesar documentary on Desert Storm—an obvious stroke of pro-Bush programming, certainly approved, if not dictated, by the network's corporate Dad and Mom: General Electric (a huge defense contractor, likely to do well from NMD) and Microsoft (whose antitrust woes Governor Bush did not approve of and will surely end).

Certainly such bias at the top does not translate directly into bias on camera. The influence is for the most part atmospheric rather than direct, the smartest, most ambitious employees inferring how the wind blows from on high and suiting up accordingly. This is true of all large corporations (including universities), but such impact is especially momentous in the culture industries, from which we tend to garner all we know about the world. In TV's case, the problem is compounded by the rightist conquest of the news divisions—a sweep that Nixon long ago envisioned and took some steps to realize, bullying the networks into mere cheerleading. ("ABC and CBS have improved considerably over the past couple of months since my visit with them," Chuck Colson reported to Bob Halde-

---

*After the election, Gore taught a course at the Columbia School of Journalism. For the class on February 28, 2001, which he devoted to the ills of media concentration, Gore recruited Murdoch as guest lecturer. The blunt Australian—who had prepped himself, in part, by reading some of my own writings on the subject—assured the students that the current corporate domination of the media is not a problem. With something like sincerity, he also boasted of the "objectivity" of the baldly pro-Bush Fox News—an odd assertion, what with Al Gore sitting there beside him.

men in late 1970.)[64] The system once assailed by Spiro Agnew (his tirades penned by William Safire and Pat Buchanan) as pro-Red is now solidly right wing, its frequent talking heads including Ollie North, Bob Novak, Peggy Noonan, William Bennett, George Will, Tucker Carlson of the *Weekly Standard,* Rich Lowry of the *National Review,* Alan Simpson, William Kristol, John Sununu, Paul Gigot, Ed Rollins, David Frum, David Brooks, Linda Chavez, Andrew Sullivan, John McLaughlin, Tony Blankley, Armstrong Williams, John Reilly and the whole prime-time ménage at Fox, John Fund of the *Wall Street Journal, Time's* paranoid Hugh Sidey, and Reagan Democrat Chris Matthews. (Mary Matalin has gone back to work directly for the Bush machine.) Opposing that dark legion are a few wan pseudoliberals, like Bob Beckel and Bill Press, some genuine articles like Eleanor Clift, Mark Shields, Joe Conason, and Robert Reich, and here and there some true—and very lonely—people of the left, such as Katrina van den Heuvel of the *Nation,* the provocative Christopher Hitchens, Jim Hightower, and (on weekends) Jeff Cohen. Otherwise, TV's punditocracy (like radio's and like the brain trust in the think tanks) is firmly on the right—i.e., not conservative but *radical* in its support for private privilege and, to some extent, a theocratic state.

Always well armed with Bush/Cheney's talking points, that chorus worked efficiently to change the subject when the governor's incapacities came up—which was not often. And their canned views were generally seconded by those nervous nellies who worked with them—the anchors and reporters who, although not necessarily on the right themselves, could not afford to seem unsympathetic. Certainly the national press corps in D.C. is, on economic matters, largely to the right of the American majority—a fact documented by Fairness and Accuracy in Reporting—because those members of the Fourth Estate are in some pretty high tax brackets and would therefore benefit from a return to Reaganomics.[65] And yet even the moderates and liberals of the press deferred to the pro-Bush consensus, for their careers depend on such compliance. What mainly drives them is a general fear of seeming "liberal"—as countless rightists (many of them *in* the media) have long been charging, notwithstanding the abundant counterevidence, from TV's long love affair with Ronald Reagan to the coverage of the 1988 campaign to the news divisions' loud huzzahs for

Operation Desert Storm to the journalistic drives to make "Whitewater," "Filegate," "Travelgate," and "Chinagate" look like worthwhile stories and not propaganda fabrications. The media's refusal during the recent coup to call a spade a spade reflected the anxiety of those professionals, who all keep bending over backward not to be accused of "liberal bias."* Such a tag would be a killer in the corporate news biz, since it would mean that you'd have no more *access* to those inside players who tell you what the news should be.

And yet there is another, deeper reason for TV's support of Governor Bush. On the one hand, as we have noted here, he is not telegenic unless his turns are very tightly choreographed, when he sticks closely to his script and shows no tension or bewilderment. It is worth noting here that Bush's incapacity is so apparent that it was gently conceded by his own supporters, once he had the job sewed up. "He has made sure that he has a high-powered team around him to make up for any deficiencies, though I'm not saying he has big deficiencies," said the GOP's Robert Michel vis-à-vis the president-select's impending cabinet. And William Safire, in a piece on the relationship between Don Rumsfeld at the Department of Defense and Colin Powell at the Department of State, offered this not-comforting conclusion: "What happens in those crises when State and Defense disagree? Bush can consult Dick Cheney or get George Shultz on the phone or, in due course, trust his own judgment."[66]

And yet while Bush per se plays badly on the medium, the TV system as we know it is his natural ally—because both it and he are all about mere "message." Both of them, in other words, are all *about* TV and nothing else. This is nothing new for him, a calculating sort from way, way back, but on TV it was not ever thus. For many years—indeed, from McLuhan's day—both observers and practitioners of campaign propaganda entertained the

---

*The media's marked deference to the Bush team following Election Day was also an expression of mere arrogance. In many instances, the power exerted by the telestars has gone straight to their heads—a self-regard that has, of course, been heightened by their whopping salaries. Such conceit may help explain the quickness of Tim Russert and Chris Matthews, among others, to instruct Al Gore to pack it in, even though the ballots were still being counted. In an editorial, the *New York Times* gave Gore the same premature advice, for whatever reasons.

question of exactly where to find the proper balance between word and image, argument and spectacle, issue and impression. The comfortable assumption was that those two categories were entirely separate, fixed, both resilient and both perfectly amenable to expert handling by the news professionals who, if they were sober, civic-minded and meticulous enough, could strike the crucial balance, at once instructing and entertaining their audience.

But now there is very little place for "substance"—indeed, for any rational discourse—on TV (or throughout the other large commercial media), for formal, political, and economic reasons. As the networks have developed it, the medium is far too speedy, loud, disjunctive, and sensational to permit even the resonance, much less the discussion, of a complex sentence (never mind an idea). Furthermore, the heavy pressure of the advertisers forbids the airing of whatever issues might be either too depressing or too complicated, or too threatening, for the venue's crucial atmosphere of light festivity—a nonstop pseudocarnival that never can slow down, or someone might lose money. Into this tightly regulated riot of commercial propaganda every politician has to fit his/her own propaganda "message"—and, if s/he's lucky, also has to fit him- or her*self*, looking "nice" enough (with just the right amount of self-effacing humor) and sounding "clear" enough (without alarming anyone) to keep from coming off as "stiff," "robotic," "wooden," or in any other way ridiculous. All "political" success has everything to do with such smooth integration— which by and large leaves out telling truth or making sense.

Thus Bush belongs here in the culture of TV. He fits in, not despite his open calculation and the utter superficiality of his (overt) concerns, but because of them. Such defects don't disturb the pundits of today, most of whom—whatever medium they work in—cannot even see what's wrong with Bush, so steeped are they themselves in TV's trivial world-view. Our president's most calculating predecessors weren't so lucky, their overconcentration on mere spin arousing strong objections back in those less TV-saturated days.

For example, Emmet John Hughes, one of Eisenhower's top assistants, was blown away by Nixon's straining effort to project a natural identity. Hughes quotes from Nixon's account, in *Six Crises*, of his resolution following his first debate with JFK: "I went into the second debate *determined* to do my best to *convey . . . sincerity. . . .* If I succeeded in this, I felt my 'image' would take care of itself." Hughes—who added those italics—found the contradiction there amazing and yet typical: "Only the most shallow exercise in self-scrutiny could conclude with such a resolve to appear 'sincere.' Yet it was characteristic of the candidate, the politician, and the man." Like his mentor, George H. W. Bush conceived "sincerity" as a performance. "I can't be as good as Ronald Reagan on conviction," he confessed during the 1988 campaign. "There's nobody like him at conveying what it is like to strongly feel patriotism and love of country." Just as it marks his son's, such ingenuous theatricality marked much of that failed president's public speech—a self-reflexiveness that many journalists noted at the time. "Bush is always telling you how to look at what he is doing, or what the impression is that he is trying to create," Meg Greenfield wrote in *Newsweek* back when George I was king. That tendency got lots of laughs when Bush, in the middle of a campaign speech in New Hampshire, accidentally read one of his stage directions: "Message: I care." And yet he did that all the time, and quite deliberately: "We have—I have—want to be positioned in that I could not possibly support David Duke because of the racism and because of the bigotry and all of this." Such dim transparency amounted almost to a kind of honesty, as Michael Kinsley wrote in 1992: "What these tics share is a clear view of the mind at work. Bush's mental processes lie close to the surface."[67]

Our new President Bush is also endlessly explaining what the "theme" or "message" is—but in the new millennium our journalists don't seem to notice it. While Bush's comic flubs did get some press, his constant commentary on his own self-presentation raised no qualms or questions. "I think probably the best thing I've done is interface with the press," he told *Brill's Content* in September 2000. "They get to see the human—that I'm a human person, that I've got feelings, I care, I've got priorities. It gives them a better sense of who I am as a person. . . . I think the more somebody gets to know a person, the more likely it is they'll be able to write an objective story." The entire interview went like that, the candidate discoursing at great length on what a dandy job he had been doing keeping the whole press corps off the subjects of his record, his sponsors, his affiliations, and his ultimate intentions—and the *Brill's* reporter, Seth Mnookin, played right along, asking Bush no question that might spoil the mood of chummy candor. As any journalist should know, "the more somebody gets to know a person" the *less* likely it is that he or she will write objectively about him. If Mnookin had been listening to the candidate instead of watching him, he might have asked Bush to explain the meaning of "objectively" or, for that matter, what his "feelings" really had to do with anything, or what he meant by that all-too-familiar "message," "I care."

By now, the mainstream press has quite forgotten the important differences between what's on TV and (what we might call) reality. Instead of trying to interrogate the photo op, asking what it *isn't* saying or how it's fiddling with the truth, journalists—or those who have been granted the appropriate credentials—often actively *collaborate* with those who set up the picture so as to help the audience discern the proper "theme." When Bush presented certain choices for his cabinet, he was asked helpfully if his "diverse" selection might not indicate "a message that you're sending to America." "You bet," replied the president-select without missing a beat: "That people who work hard and make the right decisions in life can achieve anything they want in America."

At another such unveiling two weeks later, Bush was once again assisted big-time by the press: "You've now named a cabinet that is very diverse in terms of gender and ethnicity and experience in the private sector and the federal government. What does your cabinet say, do you think, about your management style, about how you intend to make decisions as president?" "It says I'm not afraid to surround myself with strong and competent people," Bush shot back, and then expanded on that "theme" by adding that he knows "how to recruit people and how to delegate, how to align authority and responsibility, how to hold people accountable for results and how to build a team of people." It was a memorable lesson, which Bush concluded with a stirring pledge: "And that's exactly what we're going to do."

The journalists' collusion has extended well beyond such servile prompting. On TV itself, the eternal "expert" nattering on "politics" deals mainly—and often exclusively—with what some still call "image" but what is really just TV. The networks' journalistic stars go on and on and on about the politicians' failure or success at pleasing—or at not displeasing—

viewers. Reflexive and impressionistic, such interminable yakking tells us nothing, dwelling on details of bearing, posture, voice, and makeup, instead of dealing with what anybody did, said, or failed to say. And yet such discourse is not merely empty. By reducing all discussion to the level of the taste test, wherein "likeability" is all that counts, it tacitly discredits all intelligent discussion, while favoring those figures who can rile us without challenging or, as it were, taxing us. In other words, it is not just TV itself that works against the rational position but those never-ending propagandists *on* TV who *tell* us who is likeable and who is not. That influence will work on those inclined already to agree with it, especially when it manages to get in the last word.

Thus TV functioned after each of the debates. On CNN, for example, after the third encounter on October 17, Bob Novak got the ball rolling by suggesting that "there might have been a defeat for Gore on the likeability factor. I haven't seen all the numbers, but I understand he didn't do well on credibility or likeability." Of course, the wish was father to that thought, as Novak is among the steeliest of commandos, saying nothing that will not advance the Cause: cutting taxes. From there Jeff Greenfield took the ball and ran a long way with it, wondering whether "Gore's clear decision to be aggressive, to try to define very sharp differences," might make him seem "assertive and tough minded" or "rude and smug"—although "we're going to have to wait forty-eight hours or so to find out." He then moved on to Bush, who "clearly was trying to stage a conversation with both the people here and to [*sic*] the country, and, in effect, to say: Look, I'm a regular, soft-spoken guy. And Al Gore just wants this too much." *Time*'s Tamala Edwards then weighed in: Gore had learned the "lesson" that he can't "out-soften George Bush on compassion and talking about his heart" and therefore worked this time to "strike a contrast." She seemed, however, to differ with Bob Novak: "In this forum, where he was answering questions and being that aggressive, it will be interesting to see whether or not it plays as [if] he was a little terrier running out and trying to answer this person's question versus standing back and saying: You know, let me talk down to you [*sic*]." Bill Schneider then talked for what seemed like a week about a snap poll CNN had done just then. Novak summed up: "I don't think it's a win for Al Gore." And as for Bush: "I don't think that Governor Bush is very good in this kind of a format. . . . But I don't think he hurt himself."

That Novak would admit that much about the governor's inane performance confirms how bad it really was. Bush was vague on the details of his own voucher plan, his own position on the Patient's Bill of Rights, and on affirmative action, among other issues, while Gore was certain— and relentless. It was at that third debate that Bush's various evasive tactics were most blatant—crying out that he was being attacked, using ancient lines that didn't answer ("Well, you know, it's hard to make people love one another; I wish I knew the law because I'd darn sure sign it," he said regarding the accountability of schools), and at one point even needing Jim Lehrer to rescue him from Gore's persistent inquisition. Nevertheless, the "analysts" at CNN said not one word about the *substance* of the candidates' exchange but just kept harping on the general "statements" that the candidates were putatively "trying" to make about themselves, through their tone and body language.

Although a waste of time, that postdebate bull session was at least not strongly biased, nor was its anti-intellectualism too pronounced. On ABC there was a far more noxious session on the subject of the third debate. We will do well to reproduce that episode in its entirety because it captures perfectly the barbarous synergy between the right and TV news, each feigning populism for its own elitist purposes. It took place two weeks before Election Day 2000, on the October 22 broadcast of *This Week* with Sam Donaldson and Cokie Roberts, joined by George Will and George Stephanopoulos. The topic was the Dingell Norwood bill, which would provide a patient's bill of rights, including the right to sue your HMO. In the debate, Bush had claimed to be in favor of a patient's bill of rights, and Gore then challenged him to say if he would back that piece of legislation.

DONALDSON: Well, talk about the message. I mean, remember during the last debate, Gore kept talking about "the Dingell-Norwood bill, the Dingell-Norwood bill." And we thought, as a public service, we'd just show you who Dingell and Norwood are. Let us tell you about them. Representatives Dingell and Norwood introduced the

Patient's Bill of Rights favored by Gore and the House of Representatives. John Dingell, from Michigan, is the longest-serving Democrat in the House. His father, who was a House member before him, was a sponsor of Social Security in the 1930s and pioneered the idea of national health insurance back in 1943. Charlie Norwood, from Georgia, a Republican, is a dentist. He served in Vietnam and was first elected to the House in 1994 as part of the Republican revolution.

So that's who Dingell and Norwood are. Now I'll tell you—

STEPHANOPOULOS: But the important—

ROBERTS: Yeah, but—

DONALDSON: But there's a guy named Greg Ganske who's also on the bill. It's actually the Dingell-Norwood-*Ganske* bill!

STEPHANOPOULOS: But the import—the *important* point—

DONALDSON: But I don't have time to start telling you about him!

ROBERTS: He's from Iowa!

STEPHANOPOULOS: The important point there is that George Bush didn't answer the question about the Dingell-Norwood bill, which is a patient's bill of rights that allows people to— the right to sue.

ROBERTS: Actually, I don't think that *is* the important point there.

STEPHANOPOULOS: Why not?

ROBERTS: Because that's not what comes across when you're watching the debate. What comes across when you're watching the debate is this guy from *Washington* doing *Washington-speak.*

STEPHANOPOULOS: But it's—

ROBERTS: And you know, it's having an effect not just at the presidential level but at the congressional level, as well. Because the Republicans did a very smart thing, which is that they voted for *their* version of a Patient's Bill of Rights, and they voted for *their* version of prescription drug coverage. So they get to go out and tout all these issues, and then the Democrats are left saying, "But you didn't do *Dingell* and *Norwood!*"

STEPHANOPOULOS: Well, then they—but what gets lost there—wait a second, what gets *lost* there is that George Bush *did* oppose a patient's bill of rights in the state of Texas. And he did—and he's *not* for the Dingell-Norwood bill.

ROBERTS: It was lost because Al Gore didn't *say* it.

STEPHANOPOULOS: Yeah, well, he did say it, actually, in the course of the debate.

DONALDSON: This is very cerebral. George Will, you are, but it doesn't be—helping Gore [*sic*].

WILL: It's not helping Gore in part because people find him overbearing and off-putting and all the rest. But also the fact—I think the issues are beginning to break, finally, for George W. Bush. The reports in the papers are that—that Gore is going to stress Social Security from now on. I think he's going to find that when p—I'm surprised that Bush hasn't been stressing his plan to allow people to invest a portion of their Social Security taxes in the stock market. Since 1992, Sam, the number of Americans with—owning stocks, largely through mutual funds, has doubled. Two-point-two million more Americans joined the stock-holding ranks last year alone. And I think you're going to find, and he's going to find, that it helps.

THE POWER OF FORGETTING

Amid all that sparkling repartee, Stephanopoulos's earnest efforts to *recall* and *explain* could not go anywhere—and neither could the issue of the Patient's Bill of Rights, a total bore as far as Sam and Cokie were concerned (and, in George Will's eyes, a portent of Communism). Stephanopoulos's colleagues couldn't possibly relate to Dingell-Norwood since they're far too wealthy to concern themselves with HMOs and therefore wouldn't ever need to sue one. However, Stephanopoulos's problem wasn't just the privileged superciliousness of his particular co-workers but the heavy anti-democratic bias of the entertainment system that employs them all. The partnership of Donaldson and Will reflects the perfect union of two complementary probusiness forces. On the one hand, there is the incessant upscale emphasis of ABC News, which, like every other TV news division (and newsmagazine and national newspaper), is an advertising medium pitched at shoppers and investors and therefore devoid of labor coverage—unless a strike should inconvenience the commuters—and serious consumer news. (Case in point: The born-again anticonsumerist John Stossel does his let's-be-fair-to-agribusiness "exposés" on ABC.) On the other hand, we have, in Will, the outright plutocratic presence of the GOP, which doesn't want too many of the natives getting restless—or voting. Although Dingell-Norwood is not even slightly leftist (Charlie Norwood [R.-Ga.] was a Gingrich ally), the issue of the Patient's Bill of Rights, with its allowance for litigation by the masses, was just a bit too Bolshevik for the gang on ABC. And so the effervescent Sam and Cokie laughed it off, and the grave Will deftly changed the subject—to the stock market and all those glad Americans who own a piece of it, which upbeat subject Sam and Cokie and both Georges all discussed until the next commercial.

Thus that broadcast, in its light-hearted way, attempted to preserve the status quo by getting everybody to *forget* a democratic possibility and just go back to sleep. Whether they work brutally or entertainingly—or both— *all* antidemocratic forces see the people as extremely thick and basically oblivious—and work on them accordingly. "The receptivity of the great masses is very limited, their intelligence is small, but their power of forgetting is enormous," Hitler wrote.[68] As that example will remind us, the effort to exploit the masses' feeble memory can be violently crude, with just one party taking over all the nation's media, its hooligans attacking dissidents, and all contrary books turned into "furnace fodder." Here in the United States, the mass forgetfulness is by and large more peaceably exploited, as those in power—economic or political—don't just overwhelm the audience with their own propaganda or send thugs to trash books and beat up writers. Rather, those powers rely on the media to carry out such labors for them—and to do it with finesse, hyping the authorities and killing off the opposition without violence (and without having to be told). This is a distinction that our president understands. Asked by Mnookin if there "should be some kind of redress in the courts" when writers such as Hatfield publish "rumors and gossip," Bush first answered that there should ("Yeah, I would hope so at some point"), then came up with a subtler, smarter answer:

> Well, I don't know that, I don't know that question [*sic*]. . . . I think there ought to be some—I think the press corps ought to self-police, and I think there ought to be—in order to enhance the integrity of the press corps, it seems like to me [*sic*] that when they catch, when they catch these fraudulent acts, these scurrilous attacks, they ought to rise up in indignation, and I don't know if that—you know, I think that maybe might have occurred when they started condemning this guy for writing the story.
>
> There's a little—you know there's kind of a deep—in the consciousness of the press corps there's still this gotcha element. It seems like it's improving.

It did improve, as we have seen, with the mainstream press consistently forgetting all the governor's weaknesses and thereby urging us to do the same. And yet the telejournalists' oblivious work on his behalf throughout the race was nothing by comparison with what they managed after his inauguration. Once installed, and having made the proper "unifying" gestures at his swearing-in, Bush was born-again again, as all of his past history went straight down the memory hole. Not only was his record utterly forgotten—and with it all his ultrarightist ties—but so was the chicanery in Florida, and so was all the party's brazen postelection propaganda, and so was the Supreme Court's arbitrary and unprecedented move to choose the nation's president. Once Bush had been enthroned, it was as if all that had never happened, so ravishing were his new clothes. On CNBC's *Hardball* just a week into the Bush regime, Chris Matthews gave historian Robert Dallek and *USA Today* reporter Doris Page his view on why the Democrats had "lost": Gore did not blast Clinton for his Oval Office dalliance back in '96 (Matthews meant '98), and Gore/Lieberman's campaign was too left-wing. Page tried politely to remind her bumptious host that Gore had actually not lost the national vote, and there even was some question as to whether he had lost in Florida; but Matthews was unfazed by those reminders—or, rather, couldn't hear them, but kept explaining why the

Democrats had "lost" while Page and Dallek sat there, their perplexity apparent through their smiles.*

Such forgetfulness, it seems, should not be quite so easy in the culture of TV. After all, there's so much stuff on tape, and so much of that is all so readily available—at least to those of us who can afford to be on-line—that journalists have no excuse for blanking out on what occurred, say, twenty years ago or even just last week (as long as what occurred was televised). Equipped with such an archive, journalists could do a lot to fight the institutional tendency to prettify our past. Indeed, unless they do such crucial work, that tendency will soon take over absolutely, hiding our whole history in a fog of fragrant myth. Certainly the videos can shed no light on matters too complex to have been televised (e.g., the savings and loan scandals of the 1980s) or that were largely hidden from the public (e.g., Iran-Contra) or that took place long, long ago, before the dawn of television. A grasp of history requires, of course, a knack for understanding things that were complex *and* secretive *and* happened long ago (e.g., Prescott Bush's business dealings with the Nazis).[69] And yet there's still a great deal that the videos can teach us if we bother to look closely at them. They tell us much that books cannot—about the character of certain men and certain times.

There are, for instance, many telling moments of the Nixon era that you can't appreciate by reading, in part because they go unmentioned in most books and in part because the cold print doesn't do them justice. There was, for example, the Senate floor fight over Nixon's nomination of G. Harrold Carswell, a judge from Georgia, to the Supreme Court in early 1970. Rankling over the Democrats' rejection of Clement Haynsworth (who had opposed desegregation efforts in Virginia and shown an antilabor bias), Nixon sought to "shaft" the liberals by picking Carswell, an unrepentant white supremacist and patent mediocrity. The national outcry was immense, and yet what finally finished Carswell was the statement made

---

*The telejournalists were not the only ones afflicted with amnesia. "I think one of the key reasons he won is because people could relate to his style a lot better than they were able to relate to Al Gore, and I think that's continuing in the presidency," said Leon Panetta, formerly Bill Clinton's Chief of Staff, three weeks after the inauguration. "Presidency Takes Shape With No Fuss, No Sweat," *New York Times,* February 10, 2001.

in his defense by Senator Roman Hruska of Nebraska, the Republican floor manager. "Even if he is mediocre," grumbled Hruska on April 8, 1970, "there are a lot of mediocre judges, and people, and lawyers. They are entitled to a little representation, aren't they? And a little chance? We can't have *all* Brandeises, Cardozos, and Frankfurters, and—stuff like that there."

That truculent assessment (which showed up on the network newscasts) proved a fatal blow to Carswell's chances. Its defiant lowbrowism, its weird assertion that the Supreme Court ought to include a special seat to represent the stupid, and its not-so-tacit thrust against the Jews ("stuff like that there") were too much even for the White House, and Carswell went down to defeat. Although the system certainly survived the episode (the next man chosen by the president was Harry Blackmun), Nixon's scorched-earth move to nominate so base a candidate, and Hruska's shocking testimonial, were just a few examples of the vengeful spirit of the White House in those years—a spirit that *did* do harm to the republic. Like the image of the president accepting, with a smile, an honorary hard hat from a delegation of construction workers visiting the Oval Office (shortly after many of their buddies had punched out a lot of demonstrators in the streets of New York City), the sight of Senator Hruska praising Carswell for his lack of any pertinent experience or intellectual distinction said all too much about the temper of those times.

And as TV has lately shown us, the simian spirit of those times is with us still—and even more predominant, for now the defects that disqualified a Carswell really aren't that big a deal, as long as the defective one can help the haves to get still more. Thus it was with Bush the Elder's nomination, and Congress's confirmation, of the undistinguished Clarence Thomas, whose prior judicial record was far skimpier than Carswell's; and thus it was, again, when Thomas helped appoint the younger Bush our president, and most Republicans approved the putsch.★ Such widespread tolerance of clear unfitness represents a great leap *backward* from the mainstream principles of 1968, when even Roman Hruska's fellow party

---

★There were some honorable exceptions, including John DeIulio of Princeton and Justice John Paul Stevens.

members knew that they should give it up. And yet the difference between then and now is still more striking. For it is not the GOP alone that drives the anti-intellectual reaction but also, and ironically, the mainstream media—Nixon's biggest and most powerful enemy (or so he thought) and now a helpful and forgiving friend to President Bush. As his coverage has made clear, the media no longer minds the sort of mediocrity and inexperience that ruled out Harrold Carswell, nor do the telejournalists much disapprove the racist ideology that also told against that nominee. Far from looking down upon the ignorant masses, as Spiro Agnew charged unforgettably and wrongly, today the media itself applauds such ignorance and does as much as possible to strengthen it—by gleefully indulging in the same snide pseudopopulism that the Nixon White House used to tar its public enemies, the media included. As Agnew (using Pat Buchanan's words) assailed the TV newsmen as an out-of-touch "elite" whose views "do *not* represent the views of America," etc., so did Sam and Cokie loudly jeer Al Gore for even knowing what "Dingell-Norwood" was and for his tiresome "Washington-speak"—which, Sam and Cokie seemed quite sure, just doesn't interest average folks. And just as Agnew (and Buchanan) lashed out at the "intellectuals" as "an effete corps of impudent snobs," so Sam dimissed Gore's point, and Stephanopoulos's attempt to clarify it, as "cerebral."

Thus TV's news stars, and the many pundits to their right, kept urging us, and urge us now, to lighten up and join the party—or at least let the winners party on. In other words, they want us to forget what TV has itself made clear to us, thereby moving the majority to vote *against* that party.* TV revealed the candidate's unsuitability (although he claimed to be "more suited") and revealed his constant calculation (which he kept imputing to his adversary). TV showed us how thin-skinned he really is—despite the endless hype about his "likeability"—and even that sadistic streak, which stood out most when he was trying to show his "lighter side." Moreover, TV had already shown us what the movement backing him is really all about—the crazy hatred and fanatical resolve on full display

---

*The combined totals of the Democratic and Green votes put the anti-Bush vote at close to 52 percent of the electorate.

throughout the great mock epic of the failed impeachment (which Governor Bush was always very careful never to bring up).* That same crusading madness was apparent on TV throughout the postelection crisis—a spectacle not easy to forget, whatever TV's newsmen say, and however charming this new president can be behind closed doors.

Given all that TV had to show us, it seems a little strange that, in the culture of TV, it takes a book to emphasize the obvious. And yet this book is only doing what TV did all along, despite the efforts of its managers: urging you, through all of Bush's "themes" and "messages," his half-truths and his slick, distracting lines, his endless shots at "them" for being "calculating," devious, and "irresponsible," to look who's talking.

---

*Nor did any of the liberal media ever ask him to explain his own position on the Republicans' long anti-Clinton drive, in light of Bush's many promises to end "the bickering and rancor," "the finger-pointing," the "partisan" hostilities in Washington, which had cast the United States into "a season of cynicism." "I know millions of Americans are sick of the politics of personal destruction, when people are able to float rumors in the political process with one thing in mind, and that is to destroy somebody," he said on *Meet the Press* in November 1999—referring to the pesky story of his own past use of drugs.

THE MADNESS
OF KING GEORGE

In the New World, the Bush heritage represented the mergers of well-established families. George's maternal ancestors, the Walkers, who were early arrivals in America, settled on the coast of Maine in the seventeenth century before moving on to Maryland and St. Louis, which became central to their Midwestern dry goods business. Devout Catholics, they named the man who became George Bush's maternal grandfather after a seventeenth-century poet and Anglican priest, George Herbert.

—HERBERT S. PARMET,
GEORGE BUSH: THE LIFE OF A LONE STAR YANKEE

It is oddly fitting that the father of our president should bear the name of England's great religious poet; for the elder Bush is certainly the most poetic of this era's leading malapropists. Although they've been no less prolific, neither George W. Bush nor Dan Quayle—the one a natural, the other an adoptive son—has shown the older man's unique stylistic flare. While W has often had Quayle's flubs ascribed to him, and vice versa, no one could mistake the voice of Poppy Bush, who has always had a wacky lyricism all his own.

That style owed much to Bush's temperament—the unself-conscious gabbiness bespeaking, literally, his all-around hyperactivity. He talked the way he golfed and ran and fished, played tennis and tossed horseshoes. (As Michael Kinsley has ob-

served, Bush is by no means "a quiet man," which—thanks to Peggy Noonan—
was what he called himself in his acceptance speech at the 1988 Republican convention.) His talk betrayed not just his natural speediness, however, but also the
central fact of his biography—his hothouse adolescence in the wealthiest enclaves of
the East. When Bush ad-libbed, those shorts of his would start to glow right through
his suit, his monied past atwinkle in the schoolboy references to "deep doo-doo," the
playful abbreviations ("the Big Mo"), and all the other blueblood mannerisms. His
generational affiliation had an influence, as well. A very highly privileged man of
yesteryear, Bush would make no bones about how hip he wasn't, but would often
flaunt it with a certain proud abandon. Those factors—and, no less, his politician's
sense of what he should or shouldn't say—all helped produce his weird patois: the
pidgin English of an old preppy on acid.

And yet as with the son, so with the father, it is unwise to notice only what
might make us laugh. As funny as his gaffes have often been, there is a dark side
to his clubby babble. The same stiff patrician who ingenuously burbled on about
"deep doo-doo" and "the vision thing" was also capable, it seems, of doing anything
to guard the privilege of his caste. His deeply antidemocratic instincts are quite obvious throughout his verbal record as they are in all his main achievements, from his
dirty run in 1988 through his postpresidential efforts at a Restoration, by whatever
means necessary, twelve years later. To apprehend his oligarchic impulse, we must look
beyond his lightest verse and take note also of his darker works.

First, however, we should pause for an appreciation of those celebrated gaffes,
wherein, despite himself, he showed the world his shorts.*

THE B'S KNEES

This Bush's gaffes were often striking for their sheer inanity, their metaphorical
confusion, and/or their trivializing stream of consciousness.

---

*The best of George H. W. Bush's comic lines are all collected, and wittily presented, in
Bushisms: President George Herbert Walker Bush, In His Own Words (New York: Workman, 1992),
compiled by the editors of The New Republic.

"It's no exaggeration to say the undecideds could go one way or another."   —AT A CAMPAIGN RALLY IN TROY, NEW YORK,
OCTOBER 21, 1988

"I don't want to get, you know, here we are close to the election—sounding a knell of overconfidence that I don't feel."
—ON TELEVISION WITH DAVID FROST, ELECTION DAY,
NOVEMBER 6, 1988

"All I was doing was appealing for an endorsement, not suggesting you endorse it."   —MEETING OF THE NATIONAL GOVERNORS
ASSOCIATION, FEBRUARY 3, 1992

Bush made this remark to Colorado's Governor Roy Romer, who had criticized the economic plan that the president had just pitched to the group.

"Please just don't look at part of the glass, the part that is only less than half full."   —ON THE OUTCOME OF THE GUBERNATORIAL
ELECTIONS THE DAY BEFORE, NOVEMBER 6, 1991

"I don't really think—I think I respected certain components of one's presidency—Lincoln for his fairness, his determination, I'm going to preserve the Union. Then his equity that came with the freeing of the slaves. That's so big and so strong that obviously it had to be inspiring. Teddy Roosevelt's commitment to the great outdoors, and his, you know, kind of zest for life. His kids were around this very lawn out here. We have ours out there now. I mean, there's some examples of that kind. In fact, I'm not going to be driven off the golf course. Didn't affect Ike, and it isn't going to affect me, either. I can do two things at once: mind the country's business and then every once in a while play golf. So I—I think there's a lot of examples in previous presidencies, pros and cons.

—ON HOW HE HAD BEEN INFLUENCED BY OTHER U.S.
PRESIDENTS, C-SPAN INTERVIEW, DECEMBER 22, 1991

Bush's ramblings were especially embarrassing when he would try to project sympathy for working people—an effort that would often end up demonstrating just how out of touch he really was.

"And the other thing, and I guess—is that I expect it's difficult for somebody working in a plant here in New Hampshire to wonder, to know if the president really cares about what's happening in the economy. And I think I know this state. I went to school a thousand years ago across the border and—would go up every summer of my life, except 1944, to Maine, spending a fair amount of time. Almost—you could see it, practically, coming in on the plane. So when you get clobbered on the seacoast by a storm, I get clobbered by a seacoast on the storm. It goes further than that. When you get hurting because you worry whether you're going to have a job or you get thrown out, I do care about it, and I just wanted to say that."

—AT A DAVIDSON TEXTRON PLANT IN DOVER,
NEW HAMPSHIRE, JANUARY 15, 1992

In his patent inability to empathize with those beneath him, the father was forerunner to the son, who also has a hard time showing that he "cares." (See pp. 213ff.)

Often Bush's utterances turned comic at the end, as he would topple from the sentimental heights into an anticlimax that revealed the calculation underneath it all. Speaking in Ohio, Bush reminisced about his close call as the navy's youngest flyer in World War II:

"I was shot down, and I was floating around in a little yellow raft, setting a record for paddling. I thought of my family, my mom and dad, and the strength I got from them. I thought of my faith, the separation of church and state."   —DECEMBER 5, 1987

Not yet taught to feign the sort of piety that would attract the Christian right, Bush was evidently worried that his reference to "my faith" might sound unconstitutional, so he tossed in that last item.

The wackiness of Bush's monologues would often help to mask their propaganda purpose, which was usually not funny. Although it isn't likely that he meant to do it, his zanier improvisations sounded kind of cute—suggesting an ingenuousness that could disarm his inattentive listeners, while his critics sometimes concentrated less on what it was he was proposing than on how foolishly he put it.

"If you're worried about caribou, take a look at the arguments that were used about the [Alaskan oil] pipeline. They'd say the caribou would be extinct. You've got to shake them away with a stick. They're all making love lying up against the pipeline, and you got thousands of caribou up there."

—BUSH/QUAYLE FUND-RAISER, HOUSTON, OCTOBER 31, 1991

Here Bush was trying to justify his plan to let the oil companies start drilling in the Alaskan National Wildlife Reserve—a controversial plan that Bush the Younger is now set to realize, with the help of his secretary of interior, radical antienvironmentalist Gale Norton.

THE DARK SIDE

"I will never apologize for the United States of America—I don't care what the facts are."

—AT A PRESS CONFERENCE INTRODUCING THE COALITION OF
AMERICAN NATIONALITIES, AUGUST 2, 1988

The Coalition of American Nationalities was not the most felicitous of venues for a promise never to apologize for any national misdeeds. An "outreach" group established by the GOP to help get out the Bush/Quayle vote in certain ethnic neighborhoods, the coalition was dominated by pro-Nazi émigrés, as the Washington Jewish Week *reported on September 8. The newspaper named several European fascist activists among the coalition's advisers to Bush/Quayle, including Nazi collaborator Laszlo Pasztor, who had served as junior envoy in Berlin for the Arrow Cross regime in his native Hungary; Florian Goldau, who had been a recruiter for the Romanian Iron Guard; Bohdan Fedorak, who had headed a Ukrainian pro-Nazi group involved in wartime pogroms; and Croatian-born agitator Jerome Brentar, a fixture on the Holocaust-denial circuit.*

The bad press forced the resignation of seven Bush advisers (although some of them—including Fred Malek, who had compiled the infamous "Jews list" for Richard Nixon—were soon back on the job). Weeks later, just before Election Day, yet another fascist had to quit the coalition: Aleksis Mangulis, identified by the Philadelphia Inquirer *as a veteran of the Latvian Legion, an affiliate of the Nazi SS.*

"Boy, they were big on crematoriums, weren't they?"★
—AFTER TOURING THE AUSCHWITZ DEATH CAMP,
CHICAGO SUN-TIMES, JANUARY 29, 1992

Although shocking, the relationship between Bush/Quayle and European fascism should come as no surprise, since it evidenced two subterranean traditions in postwar U.S. history. Since the 1950s, on the one hand, the GOP had quietly culti-

---

★The superciliousness of that remark would seem to have betrayed a lifelong inability to grasp the immorality of fascism. His biographer recounts the following anecdote about Bush's years at Andover:

"One Latin teacher remembered by [Bush friend] George Warren was 'quite a horror' and 'rather a fascist.' . . . He had his class depart from Latin one day of each month and spent the time instead on current events and politics. 'He was a Nazi. He'd talk glowingly of Hitler. This was in 1939, 1940, the Battle of Britain had been fought and we were going into that period of the Phoney War.' All this was no problem for Poppy, who 'seemed to have enjoyed the teachers and accommodated himself rather easily to even the most authoritarian. Bush would never defy.' " Herbert S. Parmet, *George Bush: The Life of a Lone Star Yankee* (New York: Scribner, 1997), p. 39.

vated the most sympathetic elements in U.S. émigré communities as a way to win large blocs of urban votes and so offset the Democrats' advantage among blacks and Jews. That partisan effort, moreover, grew out of an older venture by the CIA, which from the end of World War II deliberately absorbed large numbers of Nazi and pro-Nazi fugitives to help out in the anti-Soviet crusade. (The Soviets, too, relied on fascist brains and brawn.)[70]

As both a ranking party member and long-time confederate of the CIA (which he ran briefly, and most sympathetically, for President Ford), George Bush was in an excellent position to recruit the sort of talent that it takes to pull off antidemocratic coups of various kinds. With such a background, Bush was well suited for his deep involvement in Iran-Contra—the most serious of all the postwar presidential scandals, because its perpetrators had turned U.S. foreign policy into a massive private covert operation.

Questions about Bush's role in that affair continued to annoy him up until January 26, 1988, when Dan Rather tried to interview him on the subject in a live exchange on the CBS Evening News. The candidate responded with a furious exhibition of indignant stonewalling, even going after Rather in a bold—albeit irrelevant—ad hominem attack.

BUSH:	Now, Dan, let's be careful here, because you're trying—
DAN RATHER:	Yes, I want you to be careful, Mr. Vice President, because the problem here—
BUSH:	I *am* being careful!
RATHER:	The problem here is, you repeatedly sat in the meetings. You sat in the meeting in which Secretary Shultz in the most forceful way raised his objections—and then you said you never heard anybody register objections.
BUSH:	I wasn't there for a most forceful way. If it was a most forceful way, I've heard George Shultz be very, very forceful and if I were there and he was very, very forceful at that meeting, I would have remembered that and I don't remember that and [unintelligible]—

RATHER: Then how do you explain you can't remember what other people at the meeting say [unintelligible]—?

BUSH: Because I wasn't there at that point!

RATHER: You weren't in the meeting?

BUSH: I'm not suggesting. I'm just saying I don't remember.

RATHER: I don't want to be argumentative, Mr. Vice President—

BUSH: You do, Dan. This is not a great night because I want to talk about why I want to be president. Why those 41 percent of the people are supporting me.

RATHER: Mr. Vice President—

BUSH: And I don't think it's fair to judge a whole career, it's not fair to judge my whole career by a rehash on Iran. How would *you* like it if I judged *your* career by those seven minutes when you walked off the set in New York? Would you like that? I have respect for you, but I don't have respect for what you're doing here tonight.

RATHER: Mr. Vice President, I think you'll agree that your qualifications for president, and what kind of leadership you'd bring the country, what kind of government you'd have, what kind of people you'd have around you, is much more important than what you've just referred to. I'd be happy—

BUSH: I just want to be judged on the whole record, and you're not giving me an opportunity.

RATHER: I'm trying to set the record straight.

BUSH: You invited me to come here to talk about, I thought, the whole record.

RATHER: I want you to talk about the record. You sat in a meeting with Secretary George Shultz. He got apoplectic when he found out that you and the president were being party to some of these missions to the Ayatollah Khomeini, the Ayatollah of Iran. Can you explain how you were supposed to be—you are the antiterrorist expert. Iran was officially a terrorist state, and you went around telling [unintelligible]—in the—

BUSH: I've explained that. I wanted [CIA agent William] Buckley out of there before he was killed.

RATHER: Mr. Vice President, the question is you've made us hypocrites in the face of the world. How could you sign on to such a policy? How could you [unintelligible]—?

BUSH: I'll tell you how I could. The same reason the president signed on to it. When a CIA agent is being tortured to death, maybe you err a bit on the side of human life. But everybody's admitted mistakes. I've admitted mistakes. And you want to dwell on them. And I want to talk about the values we believe in, and the experience and the integrity that goes with all of this. And what I'm going to do about education. There's nothing new here. I thought this was a news program!

RATHER: Well, I had hoped, Mr. Vice President, that you would tell us to whom you expressed your reservations—

BUSH: Yes, I did—

RATHER: —when you expressed them, and what the reservations were.

BUSH: [unintelligible]—under oath!

RATHER: What were your reservations?

BUSH: Reservations about getting the control of an operation in the hands of a foreign power. Don Regan stated the other day—and I never heard a word of it on CBS—that the vice president, in the presence of the president, spoke up about his concern about the whole cover of an operation being

blown, and secrets and people which you're dealing with and putting their lives in jeopardy [unin-
telligible] every covert action—

RATHER: And you weren't concerned about selling missiles
to the Ayatollah Khomeini?

BUSH: The president has explained that. The committee
looked at that, and so there is nothing new on this.

RATHER: Mr. Vice President, I appreciate you joining us
tonight. And I appreciate the straightforward way
in which you engaged in this exchange. There are
clearly some unanswered questions remaining. Are
you willing to go to a news conference before the
Iowa caucuses, answer questions from all comers?

BUSH: I've been to eighty-six news conferences since
March—

RATHER: I gather that the answer is no. Thank you very
much for being with us, Mr. Vice President. We'll
be back with more news in a moment.

—*CBS EVENING NEWS,* JANUARY 26, 1988

"When Dan Rather had tried to pin Bush down on Iran–Contra,
the candidate had blustered, said that it was old stuff, and accused
Rather of unfairness. Bush's campaign telephone banks had then
stimulated calls to CBS affiliated stations complaining about Rather.
As [Anthony] Lewis noted, 'It was a carefully prepared gambit and it
worked. Through the rest of the 1988 campaign, reporters hardly
raised the Iran question. It is still working. President Bush brushes off
questions on the subject as dated, unfair, silly. He makes the press feel
uncomfortable for asking. . . . But this was the worst government
scandal in years, a true violation of the Constitution that damaged
the national interest. It matters whether Mr. Bush is telling the truth
about his part in it.' "

—LAWRENCE WALSH, *FIREWALL: THE IRAN-CONTRA
CONSPIRACY AND COVER-UP,* P. 456

That "gambit" was, as we have seen (see p. 42), urged on the president by his canny eldest son, who saw the opportunity to boost his father's sagging effort for the nomination.* (Going mano a mano with Dan Rather helped Bush win the Iowa caucuses soon afterward.) In any case, the cover-up itself was finally covered up for good when Bush extended presidential pardons to Caspar Weinberger and several other major players in the scandal.

Here it's worth recalling that the elder Bush enjoys a well-earned reputation for politeness and considerateness. He has sent out gracious notes and letters by the tens of thousands, and in dealing with his peers has always taken pains to do the decent thing. (He skipped Nixon's first inauguration, for example, to go and see off LBJ, who would otherwise have left D.C. with no farewells.)

Such thoughtfulness seems disconcertingly at odds with the insensitivity that has marked many of George Bush's public statements. Like his eldest son (see pp. 120ff. and 213ff.), Bush would frequently betray a disconcerting callousness when speaking from the "heart."

"Obviously, when you see somebody go berserk and get a weapon and go in and murder people, of course, it troubles me."

—OCTOBER 17, 1991

A gunman had massacred twenty-three people in a cafeteria in Killeen, Texas. The president was explaining why the shootings would not alter his position against gun control.

On the other hand, Bush could always muster towering and infectious outrage, when it was necessary to help sell the public on a war.

"Look, if an American Marine is killed—if they kill an American Marine, that's real bad. And if they threaten and brutalize the wife of an American citizen, sexually threatening the lieutenant's wife while kicking him in the groin over and over again, then, Mr. Gorbachev, please understand, this president is going to do something about it."

—WHITE HOUSE PRESS CONFERENCE, DECEMBER 21, 1989

---

*When faced with a persistent questioner about his knowledge of world leaders, the governor tried to use the most disorienting of his father's tactics: shifting the inquisitorial spotlight to the questioner. In that later case, the gambit didn't work. (See pp. 196–97.)

Thus Bush obliged a reporter who had asked him how he planned to tell the So-
viet leader why he had invaded Panama. The president was always able to rouse
vigilantist sentiment in favor of a righteous cause. Such rabble-rousing is no less
effective for its illogic, incoherence, or falseness: on the contrary. For getting audi-
ences hot and bothered, there's nothing like the image of some colored brute abus-
ing a white woman—a charge so potent that it tends to obviate the need for any
evidence.

Bush first deployed his talent for such Jim Crow demagoguery in the summer
of 1988, when he introduced the tale of Willie Horton into the campaign against
Governor Michael Dukakis.

"What did the Democratic governor of Massachusetts think he was
doing when he let convicted first-degree murderers out on weekend
passes, even after one of them criminally, brutally raped a woman
and stabbed her fiancé?"

—ILLINOIS REPUBLICAN STATE CONVENTION;
NATIONAL JOURNAL, JUNE 18, 1988

"Horton applied for a furlough. He was given a furlough. He was
released. And he fled—only to terrorize a family and repeatedly rape
a woman."   —NATIONAL SHERIFFS ASSOCIATION CONVENTION,
LOUISVILLE; *WASHINGTON POST,* JUNE 22, 1988

Such accusations were just true enough to serve their purpose: Horton, serving a life
sentence in a Massachusetts prison, had been convicted of first-degree murder, did flee
while on furlough and did commit those crimes against a couple down in Maryland.
Otherwise, the story was a classic of disinformation, based on the sloppy coverage
of the case by the Lawrence Eagle-Tribune. *Contrary to the Bush/Quayle prop-*
aganda, the infamous furlough program had not been started by "the Democratic gov-
ernor of Massachusetts" but by Governor Francis Sargent, a Republican, in 1972.
Nor was it Dukakis who "let convicted first-degree murderers out on weekend

passes" but the Massachusetts Supreme Court, which had ruled in 1973 that such prisoners must be included in the furlough program.

Moreover—and more important—prison furloughs had dramatically reduced recidivism. Such effectiveness explains why thirty-five states were using similar programs (i.e., extending furloughs to first-degree murderers) by the time the Bush/Quayle team had started to attack Dukakis/Horton. The furlough system also helped reduce escape attempts. When Horton fled to Maryland (which occurred on his tenth furlough), the escape rate for lifers who had committed murder was .0008 percent—a rate considerably lower than it was before the program started.[71]

Bush used the same old racist plot, and with the same regard for truth, in trying to mobilize the audience against Saddam Hussein:

"And that's what we're dealing with. We're dealing with Hitler revisited, a totalitarianism and brutality that is naked and unprecedented in modern times. And that must not stand. We cannot talk about compromise when you have that kind of behavior going on this very minute. Embassies being starved, people being shot, women being raped—it is brutal. And I will continue to remind the rest of the world that this must not stand."

—GOP CAMPAIGN RALLY, MANCHESTER,
NEW HAMPSHIRE, OCTOBER 23, 1990

"Will we insist that Saddam Hussein get out of Kuwait, that the government of Kuwait be restored, that the rape and the pillage and the plunder of Kuwait stop, and that aggression not be rewarded? It isn't oil, it is aggression—naked, brutal aggression."

—GOP CAMPAIGN RALLY, LOS ANGELES, OCTOBER 26, 1990

"They literally—literally, not figuratively—literally raped, pillaged, and plundered this once-peaceful land, this nation that is a member of the Arab League and a member of the United Nations. . . .

"They've tried to silence Kuwaiti dissent and courage with firing squads, much as Hitler did when he invaded Poland. They have committed outrageous acts of barbarism. In one hospital, they pulled twenty-two premature babies from their incubators, sent the machines back to Baghdad, and all those little ones died."

—GOP CAMPAIGN RALLY, MASHPEE, MASSACHUSETTS,

NOVEMBER 1, 1990

"We are talking about brutal, naked aggression. We are talking about brutal, naked aggression."

—GOP RECEPTION, CINCINNATI, NOVEMBER 2, 1990

At this point it may seem a pedantic exercise to note that Saddam Hussein had lately been a big-time client of the Reagan/Bush administrations, which had generously answered the petitions of the U.S.–Iraq Business Forum, a large consortium of major U.S. corporations, by showering Iraq with covert aid—although back then our friend Saddam Hussein had been no nicer than he was once he had invaded Kuwait City. (Moreover, that invasion had been preapproved by Secretary of State James Baker.)

It may also seem irrelevant to observe that, although the forces of Iraq's dictator did indeed commit some heinous crimes against Kuwaitis, they actually committed none of the offenses that the U.S. and Kuwaiti propaganda charged them with. No pregnant women were impaled on bayonets, no crowds of innocents were crushed by tanks, no firing squads killed groups of "dissidents." (The Iraqis worked with more efficiency—leaving a mangled body in a street where everyone would recognize it, for example.) Nor was there any widespread vandalism or dismantlement of Kuwait City—until after the Iraqis started to retreat. That tale of the twenty-two discarded babies soon turned out to be a bald canard. The story had them shocked and ranting in the halls of Congress, after it was told—with much pathetic weeping—by the daughter of Kuwait's ambassador to the United States (the girl posing as your average patriotic teen from Kuwait City).[72]

But there's no need to quibble: Operation Desert Storm was an extraordinary victory. Not since World War I had the American people been so expertly bamboo-

zled. (Militarily, the war was by no means as clean a sweep as advertised—and po-
litically the job was botched.) The campaign gave a huge boost to morale through-
out the weapons industries and therefore inside the Pentagon, and it also gave our
national spirits—and the president's approval ratings—a major lift that lasted
through the summer of 1991.

"By God, we've licked the Vietnam Syndrome!"

—*LOS ANGELES TIMES,* APRIL 19, 1991

And yet, for all that vast applause throughout the nation and the military (and the
media), and despite his now-imperial standing—a rise in popularity so daunting
that all hands predicted easy re-election in 1992—the president was still burned up
about what "they" had said about him four years earlier.

"You're talking to the wimp. You're talking to the guy that had a
cover of a national magazine, that I'll never forgive, put that label on
me."   —*NEW YORK TIMES,* JUNE 27, 1991

Bush followed his achievement in Iraq with a far more lasting contribution to the
American judicial system.

"I am very pleased to announce that I will nominate Judge Clarence
Thomas to serve as associate justice of the United States Supreme
Court. Clarence Thomas was my first appointee to the U.S. Court of
Appeals for the District of Columbia, where he served for over a year.
       "And I believe he'll be a great justice. He is the best man for this
position."   —PRESIDENT'S NEWS CONFERENCE,
                                  KENNEBUNKPORT, JULY 1, 1991

Reporters could not help but notice that the nominee, a black Republican, had been
a judge for all of fifteen months.

REPORTER: Mr. President, last year you vetoed the civil rights
              bill, saying it could lead to quotas. Today you've
              made a nomination that could easily be seen as
              quota-based. How do you explain this apparent
              inconsistency?

BUSH: I don't even see an appearance of inconsistency
              because what I did is look for the best man. And
              Clarence Thomas's name was high on the list
              when the previous nominee went forth—Judge
              Souter, Mr. Justice Souter now.
                   And so, I don't accept that at all. The fact that
              he is black and a minority has nothing to do with
              this in the sense that he is the best qualified at this
              time. And we had a very thorough screening
              process then; we had one now that we put into
              forward gear very fast, but we didn't have to start
              from square one.
                   So, Clarence Thomas, seasoned now by more
              experience on the bench, fits my description of
              the best man at the right time—or the best person
              at the right time because women were considered,
              as well.

REPORTER: But do you see how it could be perceived so?

BUSH: No, I can't see it.

REPORTER: Was race a factor whatsoever?

BUSH: I don't see it at all.

—IBID.

In his 1992 campaign against Bill Clinton, Bush replayed the Nixon card by hinting broadly that the governor of Arkansas had been a youthful creature of the
KGB. (That smear had entailed the Bush/Quayle team's illegal use of Clinton's
state department passport file.) While hammering away at his opponent's draft
record, Bush also deplored the fact that Clinton had participated in an antiwar protest
while studying at Oxford. The president did not say why it was especially repre-

hensible to stage a protest "in a foreign land," but, then, the charge was meant merely to sound damning, not to make a lot of sense.

Although that effort to tar Clinton was a failure in the short term, it helped kick off the long Republican jihad that eventually dragged the nation through the near-impeachment farce and, two years later, helped defeat Al Gore.

On Larry King's show—which had a live audience that evening—Bush responded to a caller's question about Iran-Contra.

KING:	Iran-Contra—fair issue?
BUSH:	Fair enough. I've answered every question. If Bill Clinton would do on the draft what I've done on Iran-Contra, we'd have the facts out there.

> [*Applause*]
>
> That Iran-Contra has been looked at to the tune of $40 million of investigation. I've testified to the commissions and everybody else, and *leveled* with the American people. Now, I see a lot of distorted campaign rhetoric, like this [caller's question], and I'm sorry, I don't—If this guy had a specific question instead of a speech—

KING:	Yes, his question is trust.
BUSH:	Well, trust. That's what this election is going to be about: Who do you trust to lead this country? I served this country, and I served it in uniform, and I believe I've earned the trust in that capacity from the American people.

> I have made tough decisions. I have not waffled, been on one side or the other—on the war or on right-to-work laws or spotted owls or NAFTA agreements. Every position these guys take, they're on one side—"Oh, by the way, I see the point over here." You can't do that when you're president. So I think I have earned the trust of the American—
>
> *This* guy, I mean, you know, he's part of the

campaign apparatus or something like that. [laughs]

KING: What do you make of the Clinton Moscow trip thing? Do you think that's a—

BUSH: Moscow?

KING: He says it was just a student trip.

BUSH: Larry, I don't want to tell you what I really think because I don't have the facts. I don't have the facts. But to go to Moscow one year after Russia crushed Czechoslovakia, not remember who you saw, I think—I really think the answer is, *Level* with the American people.

I've made a mistake. I've said, "I made mistakes." But don't try to—You can remember who you saw in the airport in Oslo, but you can't remember who you saw in Moscow—

KING: So, in other words, you're saying—

BUSH: I'm just saying, *Level* with the American people—

KING: —Say you're sorry you went?

BUSH: —on the draft, on whether he went to Moscow, how many demonstrations he led against his own country from a foreign soil [*sic*]. *Level,* tell us the truth, and let the voters then decide who to trust or not.

[Applause]

KING: How about the missing pages in the state department records? He implied the other night that that may have been Republican hanky-panky. He didn't even know there *were* state department papers.

BUSH: Well, I'm sure there are passport files. But why in the world would anybody want to tamper with his files, you know, to support the man? I mean, I don't understand that. What would exonerate him—put it that way—in the files?

KING: Do you really have deep-down suspicions about
             the Moscow thing? I mean, just gut suspicion?

BUSH: I'm just concerned about it. No, I don't have it as
             a federal case. I'm just concerned about it because
             it's a pattern here.

KING: Judgmentwise?

BUSH: Yes. I'll tell you what concerns me, and I really
             feel viscerally about this: demonstrating against
             your own country in a foreign land. I have
             demonstrators in front of the White House every
             single day. If you go up there right now, there are
             probably some sitting out here.

KING: And that's fine.

BUSH: In the war, when I was trying to mobilize world
             opinion and United States opinion, we had a lot
             of people marching and demonstrating in front of
             the White House—ministers and guys that op-
             posed the war. And I understand that. But I cannot
             for the life of me understand mobilizing demon-
             strations and demonstrating against your own
             country, no matter how strongly you feel, when
             you're in a foreign land. I just don't believe it. I
             don't think you should do that.

                    [*Applause*]

             That's what gets me. Moscow—I don't know
             what he did in Moscow.

KING: Well, what you're saying is: "Do it at home, OK.
             Over there, no"?

BUSH: Sure. I mean, but I just—Maybe I'm old-
             fashioned, Larry. But to go to a foreign country
             and demonstrate against your own country when
             your sons and daughters are dying halfway around
             the world? I'm sorry, I—I just don't like it. I think
             it is wrong. I think it is wrong to do that.

             —*LARRY KING LIVE,* CNN, OCTOBER 7, 1992

On January 15, 1993, the White House belatedly released a copy of Bush's diary, which the independent counsel, Lawrence Walsh, had been struggling to obtain for many months.

"The White House yesterday released excerpts of a long-secret diary President Bush started the day after covert arms sales to Iran were first disclosed in November 1986 and in which he said, 'I'm one of the few people that know fully the details.' That private statement of Bush's knowledge while vice president was made on November 5, 1986, months before a newspaper interview in which Bush said he had been 'out of the loop' on the covert dealings with Tehran to gain the release of American hostages then being held in Lebanon by pro-Iranian terrorists.

"The excerpts show Bush professing less and less knowledge as the furor over the Iran–contra affair intensified."

—*WASHINGTON POST,* JANUARY 16, 1993

Later on the sixteenth, Bush held his last press conference, where he appeared with his old friend Brian Mulroney, prime minister of Canada. UPI reporter Helen Thomas asked the president about that coda to the Iran-Contra tragicomedy.

THOMAS: Mr. President, on your diary, do you think you got
             a fair shake?

BUSH: I don't like any stuff about that.

MULRONEY: Helen, what we want to do is read *your* diaries.
             That's what *I'm* waiting for!
                  [*Laughter*]

THE YOUNG PRETENDER

Dan Bartlett, deputy counselor to the president, said Mr. Bush believed he owed his victory, "despite the narrowness of the election, to the power of his ideas."   —*NEW YORK TIMES*, FEBRUARY 7, 2001

"I Am Who I Am":
Bush on Bush

CHRIS
MATTHEWS: When you hear Al Gore say, "reckless, irresponsible," what do you hear from him, really? What's
the real words, the real message there?

BUSH: I hear a guy who's not confident in his own vision, and, therefore, wants to take time tearing me
down.

Actually, I—I—this may sound a little West
Texan to you, but I like it when I'm talking about
what I'm—what I—

MATTHEWS: Right.

BUSH: —when I'm talking about myself, and when he's
talking about myself, all of us are talking about
me.

MATTHEWS: Right.   —HARDBALL, MSNBC, MAY 31, 2000

*In the culture of TV, it is impossible to do the sort of absolute and lasting propa-
ganda job that, say, Parson Weems did for George Washington (with a lot of help
from the general's friends). The printed fiction of the lad who could not tell a lie
would never have withstood TV's nonstop up-close-and-personal, with its childish
preference for good looks and winning body language. If Sam and Cokie had gone
back in time to cover Washington the man, they would have killed him for his frosty
manner and big, ugly dentures. (On the other hand, they would have overlooked his*

business deals and military record and any other complicated "issue.") As many students of the media have noted, TV's easy and habitual intrusiveness and great deglamourizing tendency do not permit the sort of mountainous charisma that were once possible through print, then through radio and cinema—and through television itself, pre-1964. Thus the sort of monumental grandeur that we still associate with FDR and Winston Churchill—and, in certain circles, Hitler—and that Nixon always craved is now passé.

Video's demythifying effect annoys the right, because it ravages their dearest myths. It's hard to feel that war is swell, for instance, when you can see the corpses smoking; and so the Pentagon has long forbidden all press coverage of the battlefield (a policy enforced with special vigor by Defense Secretary Cheney throughout Operation Desert Storm), while Rush Limbaugh, Ollie North, et al. routinely charge the telejournalists with treasonous intent, so that any unexpected gruesome sight will come across as enemy propaganda. Notwithstanding Adam-12 *and* ChiPS *and* Cops, *TV has also dimmed the sheen of law and order by airing the explosive video of Rodney King's near-fatal beating by the LAPD—images assailed by Rush (and others), who predictably charged that they were "taken out of context." Likewise, any televisual revelation of high corporate crime—not that we see much on TV these days—is automatically dismissed by probusiness flacks as "gotcha journalism," the all-important images impugned as "staged." Thus TV gets battered by the right whenever it appears to balk the powers that be. (When TV's antiglamour aids their cause, meanwhile, the right takes full advantage: Bush "won" Florida in part because TV was there to make the recount look suspicious, what with all those shots of people lofting ballots and laboriously peering at them—an innocent display that Bush's propagandists loaded with malign significance.)*

While disapproving of such inconvenient revelation, the right also dislikes television's anti-imperial effect on the facade of leadership. Like certain of their forebears (like John Adams), they prefer a high monarchic finish to theatrics lower-key, and therefore put down Jimmy Carter's modest style, as well as Clinton's, much preferring the retro silk-top-hat-and-mink-coat grandiosity that made a big comeback with Reagan/Bush, and—with the addition of a lot of cowboy hats—Bush II, whose inaugural weekend was as ostentatious as it was unmerited.

The taste for kingly presidential style accompanies a preference for a wholesome and uplifting presidential story. Thus Bill Clinton was despised for the vulgar strain in his biography: the hard times, the alcoholic stepfather, the mother punched around, the ne'er-do-well half-brother in and out of clinics—and all in Arkansas! Such a background, for which Clinton tended to be unapologetic, would not be likely to appeal to moralists in search of pretty stories to beguile the nation's subjects. By stark contrast with the Clinton narrative, the Bush biography, as it has thus far been purveyed, is all pretty sunny, despite an early cloud or two. There was the devastation of his baby sister's death ("a sharp pain in the midst of an otherwise happy blur") and then, in his twenties, a vague period of personal "drift" that entailed a bit of boozing, a drunken drive over a neighbor's garbage can (followed by a tough-guy face-off between him and Dad, all soon forgotten), and now and then a reefer—maybe. But then the young man clambered out of that distressing puddle, with the help of wife Laura ("a rock") and Jesus Christ. He went straight, put his best face forward, got rich, then got elected governor. And the rest is history.

The story is a little thin and—given Bush's temperament and lifelong license— too good to be true. (Our first lady's bio is even emptier.) Given what hints have survived the propaganda blackout on this politician's past, it's possible that his biography would make Bill Clinton's seem like good clean fun from start to finish. Bush's whole life story may eventually come out—or it may not, since there are no Republicans to peddle it, and the watchdogs of the media have, oddly, lost the urge to sniff out scandal. Such silence—call it Teflon—helps protect the president from television's X-ray eye, which cannot do him harm as long as everyone refuses to discuss what it reveals.

Even if the lid stays clamped on tight, however, the official version of the Bush biography is at some risk as long as Bush himself talks off the cuff. His statements variously contradict the slight and tidy narrative that the journalists have largely bought so far. Such statements start to limn the outline of the actual person there behind that Norman Rockwell/Billy Graham façade—a man who never tried, and doesn't care.

"HELL, NO, I DON'T KNOW."

The other reality in spring of 1968 was Vietnam. The war became increasingly personal as friends who had graduated the year before went into the military. The war was no longer something that was happening to other people in a distant land; it came home to us.

—GEORGE W. BUSH, *A CHARGE TO KEEP,* P. 50

"I don't remember debates [about the war]. I don't think we spent a lot of time debating it. Maybe we did, but I don't remember."
—*WASHINGTON POST,* JULY 27, 1999

"I just don't remember much protest. The only protest I remember that had a big impact on the East Coast was the Columbia protest. That was in 1968. But maybe I just missed it. I wasn't looking for it. I wasn't much of a protester. I'll be frank with you, I don't remember any of my friends protesting."
—IBID.

"Of some dozen Bush associates from that time, none recalls a conversation with Bush about his views of the war."
—*CHICAGO TRIBUNE,* JANUARY 18, 2000

"Among the questions Bush had to answer on his application forms was whether he wanted to go overseas. Bush checked the box that said: DO NOT VOLUNTEER.
    "Bush said in an interview that he did not recall checking the box. Two weeks later, his office provided a statement from a former, state-level Air Guard personnel officer, asserting that since Bush 'was applying for a specific position with the 147th Fighter Group, it would have been inappropriate for him to have volunteered for an overseas assignment and he probably was so advised by the military personnel clerk assisting him in completing the form.'
    "During a second interview, Bush himself raised the issue.
    " 'Had my unit been called up, I'd have gone . . . to Vietnam,' Bush said. 'I was prepared to go.' "★
—*WASHINGTON POST,* JULY 28, 1999

★The article continues: "But there was no chance Bush's unit would be ordered overseas. Bush says that toward the end of his training in 1970, he tried to volunteer for overseas duty, asking a commander to put his name on the list for a 'Palace Alert' program, which dispatched qualified F-102 pilots in the Guard to the Europe and the Far East, occasionally to Vietnam, on three- to six-month assignments.
    "He was turned down on the spot. 'I did [ask]—and I was told, "You're not going," ' Bush said."

"I was prepared to do it . . . but no—if I'd wanted to, I guess I would have. It was in my control."

—*LOS ANGELES TIMES,* JULY 30, 2000

A HANDICAP

"That woman who knew I had dyslexia—I never interviewed her."

—*NEW YORK TIMES,* SEPTEMBER 16, 2000

Bush was referring to Gail Sheehy, whose piece in Vanity Fair *proposed the diagnosis of dyslexia. This gaffe was celebrated for its inadvertent wittiness: a dyslexic denial of dyslexia. ("He did not appear to be making what would have been an incredibly clever joke," wrote Frank Bruni of the* New York Times.*) Overlooked in all the merriment was the statement's inadvertent confirmation of the Sheehy thesis: "That woman who knew I had dyslexia" makes clear that the reporter got it right—otherwise, Bush would have used "said" or "claimed." Moreover, the candidate's inverse assertion that she had never interviewed him was not true, since the profile begins with an exchange between them and includes other quotations of his answers to her questions.*

(For more on the Bush/Sheehy relationship, see "Freedom of Expression," pp. 156–57.)

LARRY KING:	The dyslexia thing, did that bother you?
BUSH:	Oh, that was just fiction.
KING:	But did it bother you? Because, first of all, millions of Americans have it.
BUSH:	Of course they are. My little brother, Neil, is dyslexic.
KING:	Successful people have it.
BUSH:	Very much so. Winston Churchill, one of my—
KING:	So how did you react when a thing like that made—
BUSH:	I just smiled. I just thought it was silly, you know.

We've got a writer who just made something up.
And, you know, I'm—even if I were, I would
be a good president. But I'm not.

—*LARRY KING LIVE,* CNN, SEPTEMBER 29, 2000

SAVE THE CHILDREN

Throughout the presidential contest, Bush was dogged by rumors of his past drug use—rumors that were only strengthened by his adamant refusal to discuss them. Rather than just bite the bullet and confirm them (with a televangelistic anti-'60s mea culpa), or deny them hotly à la Nixon ("I am not a crook") or Clinton ("I did not have sex with that woman"), Bush refused even to talk about them on the grounds that doing so would do major moral damage to the nation's children.

It was an unsuccessful gambit since it only dragged the whole thing out, the governor having to address repeatedly—and, worse still, defensively—*the very subject he was trying to avoid. At those moments, his was an image not too likely to impress the young, who were surely smart enough to see that he was hiding something.*

Although it was a PR dud, that move exemplified a kind of fakery that pervaded Bush's propaganda overall—a tendency to ideologize his self-protective tactics. Rather than just dodge the question, he tends to cast his flight as a reaffirmation of some principle that few could argue with, although he probably does not believe in it (see "Bring Us Together," pp. 143ff.). In this case, Bush was cleverly, if ineffectively, appropriating Myron Magnet's argument in The Dream and the Nightmare *that the poor were catastrophically corrupted by the hedonistic "message" of the bourgeois counterculture. (E.g., " 'Turn on, tune in, drop out' was the slogan of the 1960s counterculture, and the underclass duly turned on.")[73] Thus Bush argued that he had a certain generational* responsibility *to lie about his past.*

STEVE COOPER: What about alcohol?

BUSH: Probably no more so than others that you know.
But I quit drinking. I quit drinking for a couple of
reasons. One, I was drinking too much at times.
But remember, during this period of life I was a

Sunday-school teacher. I was a Little League coach. I was a husband. I was a dad. But alcohol began to compete with my energies.

COOPER: Have you ever used drugs? Marijuana, cocaine?

BUSH: I'm not going talk about what I did as a child [*sic*]. What I'm going to talk about, and I'm going to say this consistently: It is irrelevant what I did twenty to thirty years ago. What's relevant is that I have learned from any mistakes that I made. I do not want to send signals to anybody that what Governor Bush did thirty years ago is cool to try.

—CNN, FEBRUARY 2, 1999

TIM RUSSERT: Senator Bill Bradley was asked: "Does it matter if a presidential candidate has used cocaine, an illegal drug?" Bradley: "I do think that if someone violated the law, they should state whether they did or not."

BUSH: Yeah.

RUSSERT: Do you agree with Senator Bradley?

BUSH: I've said all I'm going to say about what I may or may not have done. Here's the important thing that I think baby-boomer generations ought to be saying: If we've made mistakes, we've learned from our mistakes; if we made mistakes when we were young, that we've learned and we're responsible citizens. And we're willing to say to children, who are listening to words that people like me utter, "Don't use drugs." I don't want to provide any excuse, Tim, for your fourteen-year-old child to say, "Hey, maybe if old Governor Bush did something, I think I'm going to try it, Dad." That is irresponsible behavior. Those of us who have got positions of leadership must have a loud, unified voice, saying, "Drugs will destroy you." Secondly, "Abusing alcohol will ruin your chances."

—*MEET THE PRESS,* NBC, NOVEMBER 21, 1999

BARBARA WALTERS:	I know you're going to hate this discussion, but I've got to do it anyway. The whole issue of whether or not you took drugs may not be as important as your refusal to discuss it. I mean, Al Gore has admitted he smoked pot. Bill Bradley admitted he smoked pot. Why are you afraid to discuss it? I mean, what's the difference between discussing drinking and discussing drugs—pot, for example?
BUSH:	I made up my mind before I got into this race that I wasn't going to try to disprove negatives because I know how the system works. People—
WALTERS:	But you talk about alcohol.
BUSH:	—people will float a rumor. People have made me talk. And I've decided I'm not going to talk about it. And you know what? I'm not going to talk about it.
WALTERS:	Even though—you know it's sort of the mystery became more important than whether you did it or not. You don't think so?
BUSH:	No, I think it's time for people to hear this voice out of me. Drugs will destroy you. It's time to have somebody stand up to say to baby-boomer parents, "Join me in saying to our children, drugs will ruin your life." But I'm not going to talk about the gossip and rumors about my own— what may have happened years ago.

—*20/20,* ABC, MAY 5, 2000

Shortly before Election Day, it came out—the story broken by a Fox-TV affiliate in Maine—that Bush had once been arrested for drunk driving. Again, the candidate explained his years of silence on the subject by invoking his parental obligations. Note also how deftly Bush changed the subject of the question—"Why wait till now?"—from himself to the perfidious "they."

UNIDENTIFIED REPORTER:	Governor, why wait till now? Why wait till now?
BUSH:	Well, it came out now because a news TV station in Maine broke the story. But I made the decision that, as a dad, I—I didn't want my girls doing the kinds of things I did, and I told them not to drink and drive. It was a decision I made. I've been very up front with the people of the state of Texas that I, you know, that I had been drinking in the past, that I had made mistakes. And the story broke. I think—I think that's an interesting question: Why now? Four days before an election. . . .
UNIDENTIFIED REPORTER #2:	Governor, did the girls know about this?
BUSH:	No, the girls did not know until tonight. . . . I've talked to them. I'm a dad. I'm trying to—trying to teach my children right from wrong. I chose the course that—that to my daughters I was going to tell them [*sic*] they shouldn't drive and drink and that's the course of action I took.

—PRESS CONFERENCE; CNN, NOVEMBER 2, 2000

A MESSAGE OF
"DISCIPLINE" AND "FOCUS"

"On a summer night in 1986, spent with his wife and friends at the Broadmoor resort in Colorado Springs in celebration of his and some friends' fortieth birthdays that year, Bush partied heartily. He woke up with a raging hangover. To his stunned friends, he simply began announcing that he had made a decision never to drink again. "It was a spontaneous pledge but one he has kept, says Bush. As he put it to me a few years ago when I was preparing a story about the contrasting ways in which he and [Ann] Richards viewed addiction-treatment programs in the state prison system (in sum, he has much more faith in the cold-turkey approach): 'I quit for the rest of my life and if you catch me drinking, it's not going to be a good sign for your old buddy George.' "

—SAM HOWE VERHOVEK, "IS THERE ROOM ON THE
REPUBLICAN TICKET FOR ANOTHER GEORGE BUSH?"
NEW YORK TIMES MAGAZINE, SEPTEMBER 13, 1998

BARBARA WALTERS: Do you ever take, like, a glass of wine at a wedding or something?

BUSH: No, I've had no alcohol since I decided to quit.

WALTERS: Are you afraid you're an alcoholic?

BUSH: No.

WALTERS: Then why wouldn't—couldn't you take, you know, I don't know, a "Happy New Year, here's a sip of champagne"?

BUSH: Because I just decided to quit.

WALTERS: Period.

BUSH: When I said I was quitting, I was quitting. And I think that speaks to my discipline and my focus.

—*20/20,* ABC, MAY 5, 2000

"One afternoon [in 1987] at a Mexican restaurant in Dallas, [Bush] spied Al Hunt, the *Wall Street Journal*'s Washington bureau chief. Hunt and his family, including his four-year-old son, had just settled into their seats.

"Now Hunt spotted the thirty-nine-year-old Bush [*sic*] winding over to his table.

" 'You no good fucking sonofabitch, I will never fucking forget what you wrote!' he heard the vice president's son sputtering as he stepped up to Hunt and his family.

"Hunt stared at him, nonplussed. He didn't know Bush very well, had hardly seen him around the campaigns or at the White House. Lingering for thirty seconds by Hunt's table, Bush mentioned the *Washingtonian*. Hunt was confused. He hadn't thrown any darts, let alone any hatchets, at Bush's father. He also assumed that Bush was drinking heavily, that 'he was quite clearly lubricated.' "

—BILL MINUTAGLIO, *FIRST SON*, PP. 208–9

(As this episode took place the spring of 1987, "the vice president's son" was not thirty-nine, as Minutaglio painstakingly asserts: Bush's fortieth birthday, with its famous vow of abstinence, had been on July 6, 1986.)

ON J. H. HATFIELD'S
FORTUNATE SON

In October 1999, Bush's propaganda team swung into action to suppress an ugly story: In 1972 he had been busted for cocaine possession down in Houston, and his dad then managed, with the help of a compliant local judge, to have the crime expunged from the record, on the condition that the twenty-six-year-old perform a few months of community service at Project P.U.L.L., a nonprofit that helps troubled youths in inner-city Houston. (See p. 33.)

Thereafter Bush would often rail against the author J. H. Hatfield, whose For-tunate Son had made the charge. In this passage from an interview with Seth Mnookin of Brill's Content, the candidate addressed the case again, and in the process made a few intriguing slips.

MNOOKIN: Now, speaking of rumors and gossip, the St. Mar-
            tin's Press, the book they put out, should there be
            a legal—should there be some kind of redress,
            when publishers print that stuff, either in . . .
            should there be responsibility in the courts?

BUSH: Well, I don't know that, I don't know that ques-
            tion. You know, I would hope there would—*to*

save, to protect the innocent. But the problem is I'm a public figure, and the question is, where do you draw the line?

I think there ought to be some . . . I think the press corps ought to self-police, and I think there ought to be . . . in order to enhance the integrity of the press corps, it seems like to me that when they catch, when they catch *these fraudulent acts, these scurrilous attacks,* they ought to rise up in indignation, and I don't know if that—you know, I think that maybe might have occurred when they started condemning this guy for *writing the story.*

—*BRILL'S CONTENT,* SEPTEMBER 2000

(EMPHASIS ADDED)

Nowhere in his statement—nor in any other statement—did Bush claim that Hatfield's story was untrue. In fact, he inadvertently all but confirmed it. The press condemned Hatfield, Bush said, "for writing the story"—not for inventing it but just for daring to report it. Moreover, the governor began his answer with a typically revealing slip of the lip: "You know, I would hope there would [be some legal means] to save—to protect the innocent." "To save" implies not protection of the innocent but mere damage control, as in "save my campaign"—or "my ass."

"Scurrilous" does not mean "untrue," furthermore, but "vulgar," "low," "indecent," "mean." Tellingly, the only word that Bush did use to denote untruth was "fraudulent"—but it refers to "acts" rather than writings; and the only "acts" at issue were, of course, Bush's own.

Although Hatfield's standing has been hurt beyond repair (even champions of free speech joined in the media's assault on him), his story merits close attention. First of all, Bush's altruistic stint at Project P.U.L.L. is wildly out of character—a charitable sojourn unlike anything he'd ever done before or has done since. (Sometimes, the story is that Poppy made him to do it, as a lesson in noblesse oblige. But that soft father never made his eldest son do anything, except drop certain girlfriends who failed to make the grade; and such cold orders came from Mom and Dad together.)

What Bush doesn't say, moreover, is as telling as the things he says—and so it's rather striking that he has so rarely mentioned, publicly, his time at Project P.U.L.L. For all his efforts to "reach out" to African-Americans, and his heavy volunteerist pitch, as a candidate for governor, then president, Bush seldom talked about his noble months of service to the poor—an odd silence for a savvy politician, who one might think would mine that bit of his biography for every ounce of credit.

JESUS LOVES ME

Bush was, by his own account, transformed completely by his partnership with Jesus, who, through the sturdy medium of Billy Graham, entered Bush's famous heart sometime in 1985. It was a timely conversion. Vice President Bush was gearing up for his presidential run in 1988 and had a mammoth image problem with the Christian right, who had never thought him to be one of them; and it was the unofficial duty of the first son—Poppy's "loyalty enforcer"—to rectify the situation. As the family's chief liaison to the Christian Coalition, Bush would clearly do way better as a born-again than as a wimpy mainline Protestant. Considering his own apt self-description as "a political animal," it is hard to believe that his decision to get "right with God" bore no relation whatsoever to his all-consuming drive to put his father in the White House.*

To point out the political convenience of his spiritual move is not to hint that Bush was insincere in his profession of renewed belief. He is no doubt a deeply pious man, boasting long and close relationships with many other deeply pious men. Indeed, his political and spiritual commitments do not contradict but rather reinforce each other: "I've heard the call. I believe God wants me to run for president," he told James Robison, the right-wing Fort Worth televangelist, in 1998. Bush feels "a sense of destiny," observes Ed Young, Bush's Houston pastor. "It's mystical. He will look right at you and say, 'I'm going to be the president of the United States.' And there's no ego in it. He is just reporting facts." Bush identified especially closely with Jesus'

---

*Similarly, George's brother Jeb, a Catholic convert, had fallen from the faith—but then came straight home to the Church right after losing his first bid to be the governor of Florida: "Starting in November 1994, two weeks after his bitter defeat, he attended classes under the Roman Catholic Church's Rite of Christian Initiation of Adults. He went once a week for five months to [wife] Columba's church, the Epiphany Catholic Church in Miami, and was received into the faith at Easter 1995." *Time,* June 8, 1998.

*most devout apostle, and Christianity's greatest propagandist. "We talked a lot
about Paul," Don Evans has recalled.*[74]

*Thus the authenticity of Bush's faith is not in doubt. Indeed, it would be bet-
ter for us all if he were faking it, this being a constitutional democracy (whose greatest presidents have not been deeply pious men). While Bush's zeal is certainly for
real, there's still good reason to approach his spiritual engagement with the utmost
skepticism. Specifically, the deep convergence of his turn-the-other-cheek philosophy
and kick-ass politics (and, of course, peculiar zest for executions) raises questions as
to how he understands the Savior's "message."*

*This section pertains to Bush's own religiosity. For more on his views of Chris-
tianity—and other creeds—see "That Old-Time Religion," pp. 147ff.*

*The governor boldly introduced his faith into the national campaign at the
Iowa Republican debate on December 13, 1999. The contenders there were each
asked by NBC's John Bachman to name "the political philosopher or thinker . . .
you most identify with and why."*

BUSH:	Christ, because he changed my heart.
BACHMAN:	I think the viewer would like to know more on how he's changed your heart.
BUSH:	Well, if they don't know, it's going to be hard to explain. When you turn your heart and your life over to Christ, when you accept Christ as the Savior, it changes your heart. It changes your life. And that's what happened to me.

[Applause]

*No thoughtful Christian could be happy with that answer, since Jesus was defini-
tively not a "political philosopher or thinker"—as the Pharisees and Romans also
failed to understand.★ As a piece of worldly cunning, on the other hand, it was brilliant, since it turned the governor's ignorance to his advantage, even making it appear to be a sign of grace that he could not "explain" his transformation. Given the
applause, his answer surely helped him with the Christian right throughout the nation—and especially there in Iowa, where Bush won big soon after the debate.*

★"God, of course, is the greatest philosopher of all"—Richard Nixon, quoted in Monica
Crowley, *Nixon in Winter* (New York: Random House, 1998), p. 341.

Of course, such secular advancement is not what Jesus ever had in mind—as we might recall from a pertinent passage in the Gospel of St. Luke. Fearing that his words were threatening them with worldly, not eternal, punishment, the Pharisees despatched agents provocateurs *to try to get the Savior to endorse a sweeping tax-cut plan—a verbal crime that would permit them to "deliver him unto the power and authority of the governor."*

> *And they asked him, saying, "Master, we know that thou sayest and teachest rightly, neither acceptest thou the person of any, but teachest the way of God truly:*
> *"Is it lawful for us to give tribute unto Caesar, or no?"*
> *But he perceived their craftiness, and said unto them, "Why tempt ye me?*
> *"Show me a penny. Whose image and superscription hath it?" They answered and said, "Caesar's."*
> *And he said unto them, "Render therefore unto Caesar the things which be Caesar's, and unto God the things which be God's."*
> *And they could not take hold of his words before the people: and they marveled at his answer, and held the peace.*
>
> —LUKE 20:21–26

Three weeks later in New Hampshire, Bush was given an opportunity to reconfirm his piety when Tim Russert, in a multicultural spirit—and somewhat dyslexically—asked about the millions of believers in the nation's other faiths.

RUSSERT: Governor Bush, in the last debate, when you talked about Jesus being the most philosopher thinker that you respected [*sic*], many people applauded you. Others said, "What role would religion have in the Oval Office with George W. Bush?" Fifteen million atheists in this country, five million Jews, five million Muslims, millions more Buddhists and Hindus—should they feel excluded from George W. Bush because of his allegiance to Jesus?

BUSH: No. I was asked what influenced my life, and I

gave the answer the way—an honest, unvarnished answer. It doesn't make me better than you or better than anybody else, but it's a foundation for how I live my life.

Some may accept the answer, and some may not. But, Tim, I really don't care. It's me. It's what I'm all about. It's how I live my life. It's just a part of me.

—GOP DEBATE, DURHAM, NEW HAMPSHIRE,
JANUARY 6, 2000

Here again, "they marvelled at his answer, and held the peace"—despite the fact that Bush had gone on record with his personal belief that non-Christians will not make it into heaven. (See pp. 147–49.)

Bush's fervent claim to have been made anew by Christ—"It's what I'm all about"—does not quite square with the abundant evidence of a bitterly un-Christian temperament.

"Several months after his father lost the 1964 Texas Senate campaign to Ralph Yarborough, the incumbent Democratic populist, Bush said he met Yale's prominent campus chaplain.

" 'I ran into William Sloane Coffin, who was the preacher at Yale, supposedly the guy that was there to comfort students,' said the governor. 'I introduced myself and he said, "Yeah, I know your father, and your father lost to a better man." '

"Even today, 33 years later, Bush is clearly offended by the statement, and it is one of the many reasons, he says, that he couldn't wait to get back to Texas, after his graduation in 1968: 'Texas people are more polite. I don't think a Texan would do that to a son.' "

—SAM HOWE VERHOVEK, *NEW YORK TIMES MAGAZINE,*
SEPTEMBER 13, 1998

Coffin's offhand comment to the boy, if he did make it, was indefensible. Nevertheless, the lingering ferocity of that grievance does raise questions as to just how thor-

oughly Jesus Christ had purified Bush's heart twelve years before. Indeed, the record indicates that Bush's whole career in politics was motivated by a thirst for payback that belies the candidate's assertion that Christianity is "how I live my life."

"When Bush first announced his plan to run for governor, Randy Galloway, sportswriter for the *Fort Worth Star-Telegram,* asked him why. Ann Richards was 'too popular,' said Galloway. 'You can't beat her.'

" 'Randy, I'm not runnin' against her,' Bush said. 'I'm runnin' against the guy in the White House.'

"The venom in his voice conveyed a very personal motive: Bush had to avenge his father's humiliation in losing to Bill Clinton. Galloway remembers, 'The way he said it was like a blood oath.'

". . . Lacey Neuhaus, a Houston friend, agrees with this analysis. 'His dad had just lost. It ate him up. He was driven to go after the people who had trashed his dad. Ann Richards was tied to Clinton—or a surrogate for him—and therefore a perfect target. . . . Running gave George a way to vent.' "

—GAIL SHEEHY, "THE ACCIDENTAL CANDIDATE,"
VANITY FAIR, OCTOBER 2000

The chasm between Bush's Christian scruples and Nixonian vindictiveness does not suggest plain old hypocrisy but a profound blindness to the meaning of the Sermon on the Mount.

" 'There are some great admonitions in the Bible, talking about, you know, don't try to take the speck out of your neighbor's eye when you've got a log in your own. I'm mindful of that.' "

—SAM HOWE VERHOVEK, *NEW YORK TIMES MAGAZINE,*
SEPTEMBER 13, 1998

Judge not, lest ye be judged.

For with what judgement ye judge, ye shall be judged: and with what measure ye mete, it shall be measured to you again.

And why beholdest thou the mote that is in thy brother's eye, but considerest not the beam that is in thy own eye?

Or how wilt thou say to thy brother, Let me pull the mote out of thine eye; and, behold, a beam is in thine own eye?

Thou hypocrite, first cast out the beam out of thine own eye; and then shalt thou see clearly to cast out the mote out of thy brother's eye.

—MATTHEW, 7:1–5

That verse bears directly on the great self-contradiction at the heart of Bush's whole political career—i.e., his lifelong immunity to punishment for crimes that, as the governor of Texas, he enthusiastically nailed others for committing. The busts for brawling (as an undergraduate) and drunk driving (in his twenties), and his postgraduate drug use (a practice that he claimed he had not indulged past 1974) might well have meant the end of him, if he had been a poor young fella living under Bush's rule, not the child of privilege that he was.

Whatever the true history of Bush's crimes (and punishments), he could not discuss the contradiction even hypothetically when Larry King attempted to engage him on the subject. Rather than approach the issue of hypocrisy abstractly, and acknowledge, in a Christian spirit, the inequity that King was trying to address, Bush could only treat the questions tactically—that is, as attempts to worm something out of him.

The tension between King's emotional inquiry and the governor's impatient wariness spoke volumes about Bush's "heart." (It also suggests that, as Bush reads it, Matthew 7:1–5 pertains not to himself and his rash judgements but to anyone who would judge him.) Faced with a question that pertained directly to the Christian "admonition" that he mentioned to the New York Times, *Bush could only keep on parroting his Christian message.*

KING: You took a hit on the drug issue.

BUSH: Yes.

KING: And one of the things that was raised was that, I
           guess, the hypocrisy question. If you did—and it's
           none of our business if you did or didn't—if you
           did, is it fair to have anyone in prison who did [get
           arrested on a drug charge] in Texas?

BUSH: I—you see—

KING: Now, that's a fair hypothetical.

BUSH: No, but I think—look—no—what you're trying
               to do is to get me to talk about my past, and I re-
               spect your attempt to do so. I'm not willing to
               do so.

KING: [unintelligible]

BUSH: Here's what's important in life. Here's what's im-
               portant in life for a parent or a leader is that you
               learn from your mistakes.

KING: Correct.

BUSH: That's important, and that's the most important
               thing for leadership.

KING: So if I were, let's say—I don't want to make it per-
               sonal—if I'm governor, and I did something ille-
               gal, whatever it was, and anyone in my state is in
               jail for doing the same thing, and I didn't get
               caught and they did, I'd go nuts.

               That would bother me—it was hypocrisy. That
               guy sitting behind the bar[s] who did the same
               thing I did and I—he got caught and I didn't, and
               I'm the governor. It would drive me nuts.

BUSH: Yes, well—

KING: If that's true, seriously.

BUSH: Well, I appreciate your attempt to get me to talk
               about my past and—

KING: But that wouldn't bother you?

BUSH: Here's what people need to know about me: that
               I'm going to bring honor and dignity, that I've
               learned from mistakes made, that I am prepared to
               send a message of personal responsibility, and that's
               what I'm going to do.

               —*LARRY KING LIVE,* CNN, DECEMBER 16, 1999

BUSH FAMILY VALUES

Like his Christianity, Bush's fierce devotion to his big, happy family is as political as it is personal. This is in part a propaganda matter. Bush uses his big, happy family to send the "message" that he comes from a big, happy family—the same big, happy message that Bush Sr. sent the voters back in 1992, when, at the climax of the Republican convention, he (or someone) had the whole toothsome clan troop out onto the stage and affluently beam upon the hall of roaring delegates. It was a not-too-subtle dig at Clinton, whose wee ménage and fractious marriage seemed to mark him as unfit by contrast with the happy Papa Bush and all those happy sprouts.

Like that propaganda spectacle, our president's loud devotion to his family—and, specifically, his dad—is not just a cheery ad for "family values" (or "togetherness," the coolly sentimental concept that Barbara's father, Marvin Pierce, who ran McCall's, promoted through the magazine back in the 1950s). Bush's grand fixation on his father speaks profoundly to the right, whose longing for a more paternal kind of chief executive has much to do with their weird loathing of the boomer Clinton and of the kids-are-all-right '60s. Thus our president's obsessive emulation of George Sr.—servicing Big Oil, employing Baker/Cheney/Powell, having Laura stump for reading (just like Barbara), choosing "education" as a way to soften the agenda, and so on—expresses more than his ambivalent desire to shore up Poppy's masculinity. This Bush's desperate father-worship speaks to all of those uncomfortable souls who wish that Dad—whether he might look like Ronald Reagan or someone else—would come back home to lead them, and the rest of us, in straight paths for his name's sake.

Of course, such motives are unconscious. Bush's service to and for the Family is, first of all, dynastic. As J. H. Hatfield meticulously demonstrates—which may have been another of his sins—our president's selection was the upshot of a long-term plan that used the family's full financial and political resources to attain the Oval Office. That plan entailed (1) Bush's landslide re-election as governor in 1998, with (2) a major push to win a strong majority of the Hispanic vote (so as to sell the "message" that the Bush GOP is "inclusive"), and (3) a drive to get Rick Perry, a Republican, elected as lieutenant governor to make sure the GOP retained control of Texas's government if and when Bush moved up into the Oval Office. The plan's final step was the election of Jeb Bush as governor of Florida, so as to lock up those twenty-five electoral votes. To ensure Jeb's victory, the Big Oil machine *in Texas, at W's urging, gave the Florida campaign over $1 million (that we know of)—a move that many Democrats, and environmentalists, deplored. "Why would anyone in Texas want to give money to Florida?" asked Florida's Democratic Party chairman. "Obviously, it's his brother. They're playing politics with Florida's future." The first son responded to such carping with a message of fraternal loyalty. "If the Democrats in Florida don't understand brotherly love, then they better reassess their emotions. I help my brother because he is my brother. If he asked for help, I'm more than willing to help him."[75]*

With Florida-and-Texas always on his mind, the latter's governor was prone to certain gaffes.

BUSH:	I talked to my little brother, Jeb—I haven't told this to many people. But he's the governor of—I shouldn't call him my little brother—my brother, Jeb, the great governor of Texas.
JIM LEHRER:	Florida.
BUSH:	Florida. The state of the Florida.

—NEWSHOUR WITH JIM LEHRER, PBS,
APRIL 27, 2000

Bush has always been as eager to deny his clan's ambition as he has been to grat-ify it.

" 'Dynasty' is the wrong word. There's a history, but dynasty has got this sense of royalty." *—USA TODAY,* JULY 28, 2000

By "the wrong word," Bush meant "the wrong message" since "dynasty" reminded viewers of everything about this Bush that he was trying to get them to forget: the deep pockets, the fancy schools, the lifelong easy ride. Above all, "dynasty" would have implied that the Bush family wanted him to be our president—assuming that post to be theirs, as a sort of birthright. Typically, George H. W. Bush betrayed that feeling by denying it: "I'm not like Joe Kennedy sitting there: 'Here's a couple of hundred thousand—go out and win the West Virginia primary,' " he told CBS in

1996, about his son the governor's presidential chances. "I—you know, it's not a
scheme. It's not a dynasty. It's not a legacy."

Karl Rove, on the other hand, had been less coy about the family's dynastic long-
ings. "On this day, George W. Bush clearly comes into his own, and no one can dis-
pute that," Turd Blossom told the Dallas Morning News *the day of Bush's*
swearing-in as governor of Texas. "We really do have a generational passage here.
Sort of like Joe Kennedy handing off to young John." (The Bushes' keen aware-
ness of Joe Kennedy's influence in West Virginia raises further questions vis-à-vis
their influence in Florida.) (Minutaglio, First Son, *pp. 300, 304.)*

A FOLLOW-UP QUESTION, PLEASE?

" 'You mean to tell me, Mr. Vice President, you're retracting your
concession?' Mr. Bush asked, his tone incredulous, one aide said. The
Texas governor had already begun preparing his victory remarks.

" 'You don't have to be snippy about it,' Mr. Gore responded,
according to several of those who heard Mr. Gore's side of the conversation.

"Mr. Bush told Mr. Gore that his brother Jeb, the governor of
Florida, had just assured him that Florida was his, Gore aides said.

" 'Let me explain something,' Mr. Gore said. 'Your younger
brother is not the ultimate authority on this.' "

—*NEW YORK TIMES,* NOVEMBER 9, 2000

Here Bush's tendency to blurt things out might well have gotten him in trouble, if
any members of the press had bothered paying attention. The vote was still in
doubt, with many tens of thousands of Florida ballots still uncounted, and the exit
polls all pointing to a victory for Gore. How, therefore, did Florida's governor know
that Bush had won?

The Wit and Humor of
George W. Bush

One of the things in the public arena, a lot of people take themselves so seriously.

And they've got the sullenness.

And everything is so heavy.

And humor, I think, is such a key ingredient to life.

—GEORGE W. BUSH, JANUARY 2000

Q: When you're not talking politics, what do you and
            [your father] talk about?

BUSH: Pussy.

            —TO DAVID FINK OF THE *HARTFORD COURANT*
            AT THE 1988 REPUBLICAN CONVENTION
            (*SALON*, APRIL 9, 2000)

"Desert Storm. We sold a lot of tickets."

            —JOKING ABOUT THE COMMERCIAL ADVANTAGES
            OF BEING GEORGE BUSH'S SON *AND* PART-OWNER OF
            A BASEBALL TEAM AND STADIUM
            (*LARRY KING LIVE*, CNN, AUGUST 16, 1992)

"[You're all] going to hell."

—JOKING ABOUT WHAT HE WOULD SAY TO ISRAELI JEWS
UPON ARRIVING IN THE MIDDLE EAST IN 1993
(*AUSTIN-AMERICAN STATESMAN,* DECEMBER 1, 1998)

"Republican gubernatorial candidate George W. Bush admitted
Thursday he was guilty of a fly-by shooting when he mistakenly
killed a bird that is on the protected-species list. Bush received a
$130 misdemeanor fine in The Case of the Badly Bagged Bird.

" 'I killed a killdee,' confessed Bush, who was hunting with a
borrowed 20-gauge shotgun on the opening day of dove season. 'I
thought it was a dove.'

"What Bush actually killed was a killdeer, known colloquially as
a killdee because that is the cry the tiny plover makes. Asked the difference between a killdee and a killdeer, Bush said, 'One's dead and
one's alive.' "   —*HOUSTON CHRONICLE,* SEPTEMBER 2, 1994

"In the end it did not hurt, and it may have helped. I think it
showed a side of me that voters had not seen. I was able to laugh at
myself, to make a mistake, admit it, and poke fun at it. People watch
the way you handle things; they get a feeling they like and trust you,
or they don't. The killdee incident helped fill in blanks the voters
may have had about what type of person I was. Plus it gave me great
joke material."   —GEORGE W. BUSH, *A CHARGE TO KEEP*
(NEW YORK: HARPERCOLLINS, 1999), PP. 37–38

"I'm glad it wasn't deer season, I might have killed a cow."

—AP, OCTOBER 17, 1994

"Please . . . don't kill me!"

—MOCKING WHAT KARLA FAYE TUCKER SAID
WHEN ASKED, JUST BEFORE HER EXECUTION, "WHAT WOULD
YOU SAY TO GOVERNOR BUSH?" (*TALK,* SEPTEMBER 1999)

" 'If the Russian government attacks innocent women and children in Chechnya,' Bush told an AP reporter, 'it cannot expect international aid.' The reporter asked the Governor if such attacks were taking place. Phone in hand, Bush turned to foreign policy advisor Condoleezza Rice: 'They *are* attacking women and children, aren't they?' Rice nodded yes.

"When Rice appeared on ABC's 'This Week' the following Sunday, she said that Bush's question was a 'little joke.' 'One thing that I've learned about the Governor,' she said, 'is that he has quite a sense of humor. So you have to be ready for that.' "

—AP, NOVEMBER 17, 1999; *THIS WEEK,* NOVEMBER 28, 1999

(BUSHWATCH.COM)

DAVID LETTERMAN: Let me remind you of one thing, Governor: the road to Washington runs through me.

BUSH: It's about time you had the *heart* to invite me.

—*LATE NIGHT WITH DAVID LETTERMAN,*
MARCH 1, 2000; TAPED SHORTLY AFTER
LETTERMAN'S OPEN-HEART SURGERY

"I'm a uniter, not a divider. That means when it comes time to sew up your chest cavity, we use stitches as opposed to opening it up."

—IBID. (THIS JOKE—WHICH MAKES NO SENSE—
WAS BOOED BY THE STUDIO AUDIENCE.)

"If this were a dictatorship, it'd be a heck of a lot easier, just so long as I'm the dictator."   —CNN, DECEMBER 18, 2000

Bush had also used that gag in 1996, in a speech before a business group in Texas: "It would be a heck of a lot easier to work in a dictatorship than a democracy" (Hatfield, p. 173).

"Who's that goosing me with that stick?"

—GEORGE H. W. BUSH, WHEN HIS ELDEST POKED HIM
IN THE REAR END WITH A FISHING ROD; *WASHINGTON POST,*
DECEMBER 28, 2000

Curious George:
Bush on Books

DOUG WEAD: Your Mom Loves books, and the Vice President does too. I've had conversations with them about their favorites. Did she get the boys reading or did that happen on their own?

BUSH: I think it kind of happened on our own. I was never a great intellectual. I like books and pick them up and read them for the fun of it. I think all of us are basically in the same vein. We're not real serious, studious readers. We are readers for fun.

—GEORGE BUSH WITH DOUG WEAD, *GEORGE BUSH: MAN OF INTEGRITY* (EUGENE, OREGON, 1988), P. 132. (WEAD, THE INTERVIEWER, WAS A CHRISTIAN POLITICAL OPERATIVE WORKING FOR THE BUSH FAMILY.)

"I love history. I just finished reading *The Sword of San Jacinto,* about Sam Houston. I like occasional social commentary. I say occasional; I occasionally read social commentary. But I love history. I was a history major in college, and I spent a lot of time on history. I'm trying to wrack my brain now that you asked me to think of all the great history books. Well, I mean, *The River Also Rises,* the book about the

Mississippi River that flooded; the '27 flood, I believe it was, of the Mississippi. It's a great book. . . . It's amazing to be interested in history and living—making history. It's an interesting coincidence."

—C-SPAN INTERVIEW, QUOTED IN *JEWISH WORLD REVIEW,* FEBRUARY 5, 1999

"When I was growing up, I preferred reading biographies about historical figures and baseball players. I still enjoy books about history, especially Texas history: *The Raven: A Biography of Sam Houston,* by Marquis James, is one of my favorites.

"I also like studying forces that helped shape today's economy and social structure. *The Good Life and Its Discontents: The American Dream in the Age of Entitlement, 1945–1995,* by Robert J. Samuelson, and *The Dream and the Nightmare: The Sixties' Legacy to the Underclass,* by Myron Magnet, each provide food for thought and discussion.

"Laura and I often read to our daughters when they were young. One of their top requests was *The Very Hungry Caterpillar,* by Eric Carle. A few more of my favorite books for children are: *Sarah's Flag for Texas,* by Jane Alexander Knapik; *James and the Giant Peach,* by Roald Dahl; *My Side of the Mountain,* by Jean Craighead George; *Tuck Everlasting,* by Natalie Babbitt; *The Wind in the Willows,* by Kenneth Grahame; *Just So Stories,* by Rudyard Kipling.

"Our capacity for discovery is never lost as long as we continue to read."   —*AMERICAN SPECTATOR,* DECEMBER 1998

"He reads at night, another habit (current bedside books, according to former librarian Laura: *The Color of Night,* the latest thriller by David L. Lindsey; *Hadrian's Walls,* a novel by Robert Draper; and John C. Waugh's *Reelecting Lincoln*)."

—*TEXAS MONTHLY,* JUNE 1999

"I can't remember any specific books."   —AP, AUGUST 26, 1999

Thus Bush replied, when asked, by a schoolchild in South Carolina, to name the book he liked the most when he was small.

"The Bible has influenced me a lot. I read it every day. I've sought redemption and believe I've found it. I get great strength from the Bible. There's a book called *Modern Times* by Paul Johnson, which had an effect on my thinking. It's just one of those books that catches your attention, and you go, Whoa—this thing is powerful."
—*NATIONAL REVIEW,* DECEMBER 31, 1999

"He reads the Bible every morning. 'I've got what's called the *One-Year Bible,* and I read it every other year all the way through. In the off years I'll pick and choose different parts of the Bible.' "
—AARON LATHAM, "HOW GEORGE W. FOUND GOD,"
GEORGE, SEPTEMBER 2000

Despite the high importance of religion in his political agenda, Bush's daily reading of the Scriptures seems rarely to have been reflected in his speeches. In this he is remarkably unlike other Fundamentalist politicians, who routinely quote the Good Book in their homilies, both written and extemporaneous.

BRIT HUME: Governor, there are a great many people who have said that they couldn't have done any better on that pop quiz on world leaders than you did. [See pp. 196–97.] But it does seem, fairly or not, to have raised the issue of your knowledgeability of the world and your interest in that. Could you tell us, sir, what do you read every day for information?

BUSH: What do I read?

HUME: What do you read for information?

BUSH: Well, I read the newspaper.

HUME: Which?

BUSH: I read the *Dallas Morning News,* I read the *New York Times,* I read the *Wall Street Journal,* and I read the *Austin American-Statesman*. I'm not so sure I get a lot of knowledge out of there, but I read them every day.

HUME: And what else?

BUSH: Well, I read books all the time. I'm reading a book on Dean Acheson right now. I like to read mysteries, I like to read novels.

But look, here's the test of a leader. A test of a leader is, When given responsibility, can you perform? And I've got a record of leading. It's the second biggest state in the Union. If it were a nation, it would be the eleventh largest economy in the world. And I've had confirmation about my leadership style. The people of Texas overwhelmingly voted for me for the first time—for a person to be elected for the first time to back-to-back four-year terms. I've been able to reach across racial lines in my state. I got nearly 50 percent of the Hispanic vote. I got a significant part of the African-American vote. People appreciate the fact I know how to lead.

—NEW HAMPSHIRE GOP DEBATE, DECEMBER 2, 1999

Bush had said the same thing earlier in the same debate, in answering a question on his lack of foreign policy experience. (See pp. 197–98.)

"I ask this national candidate what he reads in the morning. '*New York Times.* For news. Good foreign coverage. I don't read stories about myself, which *sometimes* have news.' He smirks. '*Chronicle,* of course'—he nods to the *Houston Chronicle* reporter. 'Sometimes read clips from the *Wall Street Journal.* Course we get the wire service.'"

—GAIL SHEEHY, "THE ACCIDENTAL CANDIDATE," *VANITY FAIR,*
OCTOBER 2000

"Sitting down and reading a 500-page book on public policy or philosophy or something."   —*TALK* MAGAZINE, SEPTEMBER 1999

*Bush thus replied, without a pause, when Tucker Carlson asked him to name some-
thing he isn't good at.*

**JUDY
WOODRUFF:**   Governor Bush, while we are considering America's place in the world. You volunteered at last
week's debate that you were now reading the biography of Dean Acheson. And my question is: What
lessons do you take from the successes and the failures of Acheson and George Marshall during that
critical period in U.S. history? And how would you
apply that to a Bush international policy?

BUSH: The lessons learned are that the United States
must not retreat within our borders—that we must
promote the peace. In order to promote the peace,
we've got to have strong alliances: alliances in Europe, alliances in the Far East. In order to promote
the peace, I believe we ought to be a free-trading
nation in a free-trading world because free trade
brings markets, and markets bring hope and pros-
perity.

And in order to keep the peace, the United
States must be strong militarily. In a speech I gave
at the Citadel in South Carolina, I talked about
the need to not only make sure that the morale in
today's military is high but also to make sure that
we reconfigure our military. You see, if we get to
redefine how war is fought, we get to redefine
how peace is kept.

The lessons of Acheson and Marshall are—is
that our nation's greatest export to the world has

been, is, and always will be the incredible freedoms
we understand in the great land called America.
[*Applause*]

*CNN's Candy Crowley asked Sen. Orrin Hatch about the World Trade Organi-
zation, and then:*

JOHN KING: Senator McCain, tonight there is an emotional
              kind of diplomatic drama playing out about a five-
              year-old boy from Cuba, who lost his mother as
              they tried to enter the United States by water. The
              boy's father back in Cuba says he wants his son
              back. If you were president of the United States,
              what would you do?

McCAIN: I'd say to Mr. Castro, let his father come to the
              United States and enjoy peace and freedom and be
              reunited with his son. We don't want his son to
              grow up under communist tyranny.
                  Let me talk about Dean Acheson a second.
              When Dean Acheson walked into Harry Truman's
              office in June of 1950 and said, "North Korea's at-
              tacked South Korea," Harry Truman didn't take a
              poll: Harry Truman knew what we had to do. If
              he'd a taken a poll, maybe Americans wouldn't
              have let us go.
                  This administration is poll-driven and not
              principle-driven. We didn't have to get into
              Kosovo. Once we stumbled into it, we had to win
              it. And the fact is that this administration has con-
              ducted a feckless photo-op foreign policy for
              which we will pay a very heavy price in American
              blood and treasure.
                  You have to have a concept of what you want
              the world to look like, where our interests and our

values lie and how we are going to bring this
world into the next century and call it, again, the
American century.

WOODRUFF: Thank you, Senator McCain.

—GOP DEBATE, PHOENIX, DECEMBER 6, 1999

*The senator's point was not exactly clear. (Invading Cuba wouldn't be too popular,
but we should do it anyway?)* And yet the true purpose of his Great Leap Backward from Havana to Pyongyang was not to ace the question about Elian but to em-
barrass the front-runner by coming up with a* specific *from the book—James
Chace's* Acheson—*that the governor had so vaguely paraphrased.*

*McCain got high marks for that shot at Bush, who later bristled at the specu-
lation that he hadn't read the book at all. "I mean, what kind of world is this?" he
lamented to the* Washington Post. *"I guess people are so used to being lied to in
Washington that they think I'd get up on national TV and make up some book.
Where have we gotten to?" The governor then took a tardy countershot at Senator
McCain's performance: "Maybe I should have picked out one little bitty detail of
the book. I don't think so. I thought my answer was the right answer, otherwise I
wouldn't have given it. I don't get it. I don't understand this cynicism."*[76]

*That defensive self-appraisal says it all, capturing what's wrong not just with
Bush's way of reading but also with his education plans and with his sort of governance. There could be no one "right answer" to the open-ended question Woodruff
asked. There's much to say about "the successes and the failures" of the Truman team
throughout "that critical period in U.S. history." Her further question—on how the
"lessons" of Dean Acheson's Cold War accomplishments pertain to U.S. foreign policy today—was also quite a good one, meaning that it offered Governor Bush the
opportunity to think aloud on a rich and timely subject (and one that he himself
had raised). But all that Bush could do was quickly rummage through his little bag
of "themes" for "the right answer"—coming up with a pastiche of lines he'd used
a hundred times, loosely fitted to the circumstances.† Whereas he should have en-*

---

*This would have been in keeping with the foreign policy agenda that he pushed through-
out the contest for his party's nomination: "rogue state rollback."

†Moreover, that bit about "exporting freedom" ran directly counter to what Dr. Rice, his
tutor and prospective National Security Advisor, was saying at the same time.

tertained *the question, he only tried to* nail *it—Bush told the* Post *that he had "absolutely hammered" it, as if he were a sophomore who'd been memorizing answers all the night before. Thus, if he* had read *Chace's book, he read it just as he has always read (or had his staffers read) the memos and reports that cross his desk: in search of simple, handy bits for later use. That is not the way to lead or read— or to teach children how to read. And yet the president sees "education" mainly as intensive training for an annual test—a vision just as narrowly utilitarian as his approach to Chace's Acheson.*

Bush blew it. His take on Acheson *was obviously not germane, however clear his point was to himself. And yet his answer was no worse than Senator McCain's. The governor's assessment was right on the money: McCain did just "pick out one little bitty detail from the book" and run with it—all the way from Cuba to Korea, to Kosovo and home again, then stood there panting praise for Henry Luce. The illogic of his riff begged many questions (e.g., didn't the Korean War exact "a very heavy price in American blood and treasure"?), but the press asked none of them, so wowed they were by Senator McCain's apparent mastery of the text.*

But no reporter, then or later, thought to question James Chace's Acheson. *Because it was* a book, *one written by* a known historian *and on the subject of* a great American, *all hands assumed it to be* serious stuff. *And yet the book itself—much like the answers of McCain and Bush—is weak throughout, a hagiography based heavily on secondary sources. Unlike other recent studies of the early Cold War,* Acheson *provides a highly partial view of its intriguing subject, and of "that critical period in U.S. history." And here it was the very ground of a debate between two would-be presidents, on U.S. foreign policy today.*[77]

Thus that moment could not possibly shed light on anything. Far from demonstrating only Bush's difficulties with the world of books, it was a propaganda triple whammy, stupefying at every level.

"Reading is the basics for all learning."

—*ALL THINGS CONSIDERED,* NPR, MARCH 28, 2000

The governor made this statement in announcing his "Reading First" initiative in Reston, Virginia.

"This is Preservation Month. I appreciate preservation. It's what you do when you run for president. You gotta preserve."
—*LOS ANGELES TIMES,* JANUARY 28, 2000

Thus spake Bush in honoring "Perseverance Month" at Fairgrounds Elementary School in Nashua, New Hampshire.

But in the end, the candidate's illiteracy just didn't matter much, this being the culture of television. Bush did some stand up on the subject at the Al Smith Memorial Dinner on October 19, 2000.

"And I see Bill Buckley is here tonight, fellow Yale man.
[*Applause*]
"We go way back, and we have a lot in common. Bill wrote a book at Yale—I read one."
[*Laughter*]

Let Me Make One Thing
Perfectly Clear

Intelligence is can you think logically.

Intelligence is do you have a basis from which to make decisions.

Intelligence in politics is do you have good instincts.

—GEORGE W. BUSH, *WASHINGTON POST,*
JANUARY 19, 2000

As a creature of TV, Bush is prone to flashes of illogic of a kind not based in any neurological disorder. He is especially given to tautologies—"A is A because A is A." While this tendency may well bespeak an inability to reason, it's just as likely to reflect on Bush's understanding of the fact that reason isn't needed on TV. "Talk on television isn't meant to be listened to," writes Peter Conrad. "The words merely gain for us the time to look at the talker." [78] *Any able propagandist knows this instinctively. He therefore orates not to make an argument but just to be there talking firmly on the screen—showing us that he is talking, and, ideally, emphasizing just those words that—focus groups have shown—make just the right impression.*

Tautology is the inevitable product of such spectacle.

BRIT HUME: What if there isn't any unity at the Republican convention?

BUSH: I am confident there will be. I'm confident people

132

are coming together. And the reason I believe this
is because our party is united.

—*FOX SPECIAL REPORT WITH BRIT HUME,*
FOX TV, JULY 19, 2000

"A reformer with results is a conservative who has had compassionate results in the state of Texas."

—*NEW YORK TIMES,* FEBRUARY 10, 2000

"There is a lot of speculation and I guess there is going to continue
to be a lot of speculation until the speculation ends."

—ON WHETHER HE'LL RUN FOR PRESIDENT,
AUSTIN AMERICAN-STATESMAN, OCTOBER 18, 1998

LARRY KING:	Only 1 percent of Americans are even affected by [the death tax], right?
BUSH:	Well, if that's the case, let's do it.
KING:	Yes, but when 1 percent convinces 99 percent that it's in their best interest to lower their—
BUSH:	Well, maybe we ought—maybe we ought—I don't know the figure of 1 percent or 99 percent, but if that—if it's good public policy, it's good public policy. —*LARRY KING LIVE,* CNN, JULY 20, 2000

"If you don't stand for anything, you don't stand for anything. If you
don't stand for something, you don't stand for anything."
—*AUSTIN AMERICAN-STATESMAN,* NOVEMBER 2, 2000 (SEE P. 178.)

"Dick Cheney and I do not want this nation to be in a recession. We
want anybody who can find work to be able to find work."

—*60 MINUTES II,* CBS, DECEMBER 5, 2000

"One of the common denominators I have found is that expectations rise above that which is expected."

> —*LOS ANGELES TIMES*, SEPTEMBER 27, 2000 (SEE ALSO P. 139.)

Some tautologies are very subtle, embedded in a single word:

"It is clear our nation is reliant upon big foreign oil. More and more
of our imports come from overseas."

> —BEAVERTON, OREGON, SEPTEMBER 25, 2000; *SLATE*

"Now, by the way, surplus means a little money left over, otherwise
it wouldn't be called a surplus."

> —KALAMAZOO, MICHIGAN, OCTOBER 27, 2000;
> FCDH TRANSCRIPTS

Bush also tends to surprise the audience with a bald self-contradiction. For this ten-
dency there may be some physiological explanation; or it may express the muffled
protests of a very deeply buried conscience.

"I don't care what the polls say. I don't. I'm doing what I think
what's wrong."   —*NEW YORK TIMES*, MARCH 15, 2000

Bush was referring here to his economic policies.

"Well, I think if you say you're going to do something and don't do
it, that's trustworthiness."   —CNN ONLINE CHAT, AUGUST 30, 2000

"If you're sick and tired of the politics of cynicism and polls and
principles, come and join this campaign."

> —HILTON HEAD, SOUTH CAROLINA, FEBRUARY 16, 2000; *SLATE*

"I'm a strong candidate because I come from the baby-boomer generation recognizing that we've got to usher in an era of responsible
behavior."   —*NEWSHOUR WITH JIM LEHRER,* PBS, APRIL 27, 2000

*That inversion of the Myron Magnet thesis was the opposite of what Bush had
meant to say—and what he did say all the time. For example:*

"The culture of my generation, our generation, has clearly said, 'If it
feels good, do it, and be sure to blame somebody else if you have a
problem.' "   —*VANITY FAIR,* OCTOBER 2000

The Education President: The Sequel

Each student should leave twelfth grade reading English at a twelfth-grade level or better. He should have read great English writers such as Shakespeare, Dickens, the Brontës, and, in translation, great Russian writers such as Tolstoy, Spanish writers such as Cervantes, Latin American writers such as Borges. Black students should know something about Hobbes, Locke, and Rousseau, and white students should know about Ghandi and Martin Luther King, Jr. In short, every student should know a little bit about everything, so he can make an intelligent decision about what he wants to study in greater depth in college.

— RICHARD NIXON, *IN THE ARENA: A MEMOIR OF VICTORY, DEFEAT AND RENEWAL* (1990), PP. 99–100

I had to read *War and Peace* when I was like 16 or 17. Don't give me a quiz on the thousands of characters in it, but I guess it had an influence because it was a discipline. It was more that than remembering anything in it. And of course, we had to read Shakespeare in school. It was required.

— GEORGE H. W. BUSH, *NEW YORK TIMES*, OCTOBER 27, 1988

Higher education is not my priority.
—GEORGE W. BUSH, *SAN ANTONIO EXPRESS-NEWS*, MARCH 22, 1998

*As noted above, Bush's view of education is overfocused on "results"—a clear re-
flection of his fierce probusiness fundamentalism. Students must be educated for the
work force, and that's it. They must have the basic skills and solid "character" to be
reliable employees and, therefore, energetic shoppers. Any higher instruction and they
might turn "arrogant"—or "uppity," as some folks used to put it.*

*Throughout the campaign, Bush took lots of credit for the great improvements
in Texas's once-abysmal school system. As Molly Ivins, Paul Begala, and others have
demonstrated, those great improvements all predated Bush's term in Austin. The best
that can be said for him is that he didn't interfere with them, although he did place
an inordinate new emphasis on standardized tests, an innovation that leaves some
kids behind since not all children test as well as others, regardless of their gifts.*

*As to education, the biggest questions are these: Can an ill-read and semiliter-
ate president really grasp the meaning, or importance, of true education? And is it
possible for one so tightly bound to corporate interests to promote education at its best?
(As chief of Houston's independent schools, Rod Paige, Bush's secretary of education, was quick to give the corporate marketers, like Channel One, full access to the
classrooms.)*

"Illiteracy is a problem that needs to be dealt with, and all of us need
to pitch in and help. It's something that can be cured. As a nation, we
need to bind together and unify to help our brothers and sisters
learn to read."
—G.W.B., *GEORGE BUSH: MAN OF INTEGRITY,* P. 133

"Laura and I really don't realize how bright our children is sometimes until we get an objective analysis."
—*MEET THE PRESS,* NBC, APRIL 15, 2000

"My education message will resignate amongst all parents."
—*NEW YORK POST,* JANUARY 19, 2000

"Governor Bush will not stand for the subsidation of failure." —IBID.

"How do you know if you don't measure if you have a system that simply suckles kids through?"

—BEAUFORT, SOUTH CAROLINA, FEBRUARY 16, 2000; *SLATE*

"We want our teachers to be trained so they can meet the obligations, their obligations as teachers. We want them to know how to teach the science of reading. In order to make sure there's not this kind of federal—federal cufflink."

—MILWAUKEE, MARCH 30, 2000; *SLATE*

"What's not fine is, rarely is the question asked, are, is our children learning?"

—*LOS ANGELES TIMES,* JANUARY 14, 2000

LARRY KING: One of the things [Gore] said is you're the forty-fifth—thirty-seventh in per capita spending on education in America. That's pretty low for a state that big.

BUSH: You know, he's critical of everything. I mean, this is a campaign really where he'll tear down every single aspect of what is a very positive record. And you know, he may want to look at it—I mean, listen, you can talk about numbers all the time, but what matters are results. And we lead the nation when it comes to improvement. Say, for example, amongst minority students, Texas and North Carolina are ranked the two best states when it comes to improving in test scores for Hispanic youngsters or African-American youngsters. We've got a great record here.

—*LARRY KING LIVE,* CNN, JULY 20, 2000

"As governor of Texas, I have set high standards for our public schools, and I have met those standards."

—CNN ONLINE CHAT, AUGUST 30, 2000

"One of the reasons I came to this school was because I love to highlight beacons of hope, centers of excellence that challenge the odds. One of the common denominators I have found is that expectations rise above that which is expected."

—LOS ANGELES, SEPTEMBER 27, 2000;

FCDH POLITICAL TRANSCRIPTS

"The federal government ought to have maximum flexibility."

—*WASHINGTON POST,* OCTOBER 1, 2000

Bush was referring to education funds. By "federal government," he meant "the states."

CREATIONISM

Evolution is as well documented as any phenomenon in science, as strongly as the earth's revolution around the sun rather than vice versa. In this sense, we can call evolution a "fact." (Science does not deal in certainty, so "fact" can only mean a proposition affirmed to such a high degree that it would be perverse to withhold one's provisional assent.)

—STEPHEN JAY GOULD, *TIME,* AUGUST 23, 1999.

In August 1999 the Kansas Board of Education voted to remove the subject of evolution from the state's science curriculum—a stroke of faith-based censorship much more effective than an outright ban, which would have been unconstitutional. The six-to-four decision was the upshot of a propaganda drive spearheaded by Celtie

140 Mark Crispin Miller

Johnson, a Christian Fundamentalist completely innocent of scientific training. "To Johnson, evolution simply makes no sense," the Kansas City Star reported. "She rejects the evidence most scientists say supports the theory that all living things share common ancestors."

As "young Earth creationists," Johnson and her co-religionists on the state's board of education believe that our multibillion-year-old planet was created about seven thousand years ago and, of course, in just six days. They seek to spread this superstition not by means of rational discourse but through intimidation and a pounding sophistry. Aside from their insistence on the literal truth of Scripture, they offer nothing but inflammatory rhetoric ("Do you want to believe your ancestors were monkeys?") and a heady potpourri of partial truths. For example: It takes up to one thousand years to form an inch of topsoil. The average worldwide depth of Earth's topsoil is seven to eight inches. Ergo, the Earth has been around for just a few millennia. As evolutionists point out, that tidy proof ignores the crucial factor of erosion.

Such outright propaganda tactics have no place in any proper classroom—a fact apparent to most Kansans, who were and are embarrassed by the move. (The state's Republican governor also deplored it.) And yet because of its effect on textbook publishers, the local victory of those creationists is likely to hurt public education far beyond the state of Kansas. "Developing any book is an expensive undertaking and publishers cannot afford to print separate texts to meet each curriculum," noted the distinguished naturalist Gerry Rising. "For that reason most cover only the non-controversial concepts included in all curricula. So religious fundamentalists have won an important skirmish in their national battle with scientists.[79]

Bush responded to the zealots' coup as if he had been part of it. By implying that the vote had had widespread popular support, and that its aim had been to broaden the curriculum, he merely made more propaganda for their cause—an odd move for a self-styled champion of education.

"It's a state issue. The people of Texas can resolve that issue as can the people of Kansas. . . . Should the people choose in my state [to adopt a similar rule], I have no problem."

—*KANSAS CITY STAR*, SEPTEMBER 9, 1999

"I think it's an interesting part of knowledge [to have] a theory of evolution and a theory of creationism. People should be exposed to different points of view." —IBID.

"I believe children ought to be exposed to different theories about how the world started." —*TIMES UNION,* AUGUST 30, 1999

"I have absolutely no problem with children learning different forms of how the world was formed."
—*NEW YORK POST,* NOVEMBER 5, 1999

"I personally believe God created the earth."
—*KANSAS CITY STAR,* SEPTEMBER 9, 1999

"After all, religion has been around a lot longer than Darwinism."
—*GEORGE,* SEPTEMBER 2000

AT THE HELM

"You teach a child to read, and he or her will be able to pass a literacy test."
—TOWNSEND, TENNESSEE, FEBRUARY 21, 2001;
THE NEW REPUBLIC, MARCH 5, 2001

"*Washington, D.C.*—The Committee for Education Funding (CEF), a nonpartisan coalition of 100 education organizations, is concerned that President Bush's proposed 5.9% increase in the Education Budget FY 2002 falls short of growing needs and expectations. . . .

"CEF is responding to 'A Blueprint for New Beginnings,' President Bush's budget plan released on Wednesday. According to the blueprint, when advance funding for FY 2001 is counted, the total increase for the Department of Education is not $4.5 billion or 11.5%, as widely reported, but $2.5 billion or 5.9%. This increase would represent the smallest percentage increase for the Department of Education in five years if enacted."

—PRESS RELEASE, COMMITTEE FOR EDUCATION FUNDING,
FEBRUARY 28, 2001

"Bring Us Together"

There is a problem with heart in America. One of the great frustrations of being a governor is I wish I knew the law to make people love one another, because I would sign it.

—GEORGE W. BUSH, DES MOINES, IOWA, DECEMBER 13, 1999

Although the last two sections seem to reconfirm the general impression that Bush is just a dope, a careful study of his speech reveals a certain genius at equivocation.

Of course, all politicians must master that evasive art. Often Bush stands out, however, for the peculiar cynicism of his answers. In particular, when asked about one of his more divisive policies, he doesn't always merely tell a lie or change the subject. At his best, he takes the question of his party's homophobia or racism, or of his own hard line on gun control, and ends up answering by affirming his own tolerance and love of children. Although he does it with his usual West Texas quasi-mellowness, the move is reminiscent of the sort of propaganda that the Inner Party makes in 1984. (For examples of a similar trick, see "Save the Children," pp. 103ff.)

DIANE SAWYER:	Mrs. Clinton has said it's time for the American-people to write their senators and congressmen and say, "Buck the gun lobby." Do you want Americans to write their senators and say that?
BUSH:	I don't know what that means. I do know that mothers and dads have got to say and understand

the most important job they will ever have, they
will ever have, is to love their children.

—*GOOD MORNING AMERICA,* ABC, MAY 10, 1999

*In just saying no to some progressive cause, Bush would often cast his answer as a
heartfelt pitch for universal brotherhood. He made this move a few times in dealing
with the tricky issue of the Log Cabin Republicans, an affluent gay lobbying group.*

TIM RUSSERT: Would you meet with them?

BUSH: Oh, probably not.

RUSSERT: Why not?

BUSH: Well, because it creates a huge political scene, I
mean, that this is all—I am someone who is a
uniter, not a divider. I don't believe in group
thought, pitting one group of people against another. And all that does is create kind of a huge
political, you know, nightmare for people. I mean,
it's as if an individual doesn't count, but the group
that the individual belongs in is more important.

—*MEET THE PRESS,* NBC, NOVEMBER 21, 1999

*While he professed to be indifferent to "the group" that any "individual belongs in,"
Bush was always quick to welcome that group into his big tent—as long as he did
not have to shake hands with any of them.*

LARRY KING: You didn't speak to the Log Cabin Republicans,
the gay group. Was that—should you have?

BUSH: Well, they asked me of whether or not [*sic*] I'd
meet with them, I said, probably not, because I
didn't want to create a ruckus. I believe someone's
sexual orientation is their personal business.

KING: But they're Republicans. They want to vote for
you.

BUSH: Sure. Of course, and I've got a lot of members of the Log Cabin Republican club that support me. I welcome gay support.

—*LARRY KING LIVE,* CNN, DECEMBER 16, 1999

We can best appreciate Bush's special knack for making "Get away from me" sound warm and friendly by comparing his act with the zombielike performance of his spokesman Scott McClellan, who was interviewed by The Advocate *on the subject of gay rights.*

THE ADVOCATE: How does Governor Bush's slogan "compassionate conservatism" apply to the gay and lesbian community?

MCCLELLAN: Governor Bush is outlining an agenda that will help improve the lives of all Americans. It focuses on improving public schools so every child can learn, strengthening Social Security, increasing access to medical care for working families; and ushering in an era of personal responsibility.

THE ADVOCATE: Can you be more specific? Gay and lesbian students, for example, often report facing a hostile environment in school.

MCCLELLAN: Governor Bush believes in treating all individuals with dignity and respect. He does not tolerate discrimination in any form or fashion.

THE ADVOCATE: What's the best way to fight sexual orientation discrimination in the workplace?

MCCLELLAN: Everyone should be treated with dignity and respect.

THE ADVOCATE: What's the place of gays and lesbians in American society?

MCCLELLAN: Governor Bush is a uniter. The governor believes in focusing on our common objectives. He welcomes the support of all individuals who support a compassionate conservative agenda. At the recent meeting in Austin, he felt he was a better man for meeting with them [gay Republicans]. There are areas where he disagrees, such as gay marriage, but there are a number of areas of agreement, such as improving schools and access to health care.

THE ADVOCATE: How did the governor react to the religious conservative critics of the meeting?

MCCLELLAN: I addressed some of those [criticisms]. Governor Bush has always been clear and consistent in views and philosophy. He makes his decisions based on what he believes is right for America. He does not believe in pitting one group of people against another. He has said he believes in strong families and the importance of the sanctity of marriage. He believes marriage is between a man and a woman.

THE ADVOCATE: Don't gay people have their own strong families?

MCCLELLAN: Every individual should be treated with dignity and respect.   —*THE ADVOCATE,* JULY 4, 2000

Bush was always quick to sound the theme of racial harmony, albeit as a way to keep from doing, or endorsing, anything specific. (See also "The Color Line," pp. 226ff.)

LARRY KING: Can a president do something about [racial profiling]? There was a movement that Bill Clinton can sign an executive order dealing with it. To your knowledge, can you?

BUSH: I don't know about that, but yes, I think the president can call upon racial reconciliation in America.
—*LARRY KING LIVE,* CNN, SEPTEMBER 26, 2000

That Old-Time Religion

I know thy works, that thou art neither cold nor hot: I would thou wert cold or hot.

So then because thou art lukewarm, and neither cold nor hot, I will spew thee out of my mouth.

—REVELATION 3:14–15

Bush's true divisiveness is most apparent in his faith—despite the crowds of nuns and imams at his photo ops. His blithe assertion that non-Christians cannot make it into heaven—a tenet of his creed that he has never disavowed—bespeaks a cold and absolute self-righteousness that has always posed a danger to democracy, whatever ideology may cloak or drive it. The militant Christian is as bad a democrat as any other true believer; Marvin Olasky, Bush's chief Fundamentalist guru and the coiner of the phrase "compassionate conservatism," was once a hard-line Marxist-Leninist—and no doubt just as flexible and open-minded then as he is now.

The risk posed by the president's religiosity is not an abstract matter of the necessary separation of church and state—although Bush is unmistakably intent on breaking down the wall between them, as when he made "Jesus Day" an official holiday in Texas. Nor is the danger merely one of possible intolerance toward this or that minority—although the Jew-free zone that is his cabinet does not betoken an enlightened spirit. The real threat, rather, is that bone-deep conviction of almighty rectitude—the dead certainty that God Is On Our Side. Such martial piety divides the world in two, in the good old Manichaean tradition. "When you have no king but Caesar, you release Barabbas—criminality, destruction, thievery, the low-

est and the least. . . . When you have no king but Jesus, you release the eternal, you release the highest and best, you release virtue, you release potential," John Ashcroft told them at Bob Jones (adding, "I thank God for this institution.") "If America is to be great in the future, it will be if we understand that our source is not civic and temporal, but our source is godly and eternal."

Against the "bad," all means are justified, since it is God's will that we do away with "them." Unless it is constrained by democratic ways and common sense, that world-view always leads to war, both beyond our borders and among ourselves. The same crusading spirit that impelled the drive to nail the Antichrist, Bill Clinton, also motivated W to seek the presidential chalice for the GOP. "It's Redemption Time!" he cried when he decided to reclaim the White House for his father.[80] Such piety spells trouble for the Constitution—just as it did when Bush's dad was in the White House. "Sometimes you just have to obey a higher law," as Fawn Hall put it in her blunt defense of the illegalities of Iran-Contra.

   " 'Mother and I were arguing—not arguing, having a discussion— and discussing who goes to Heaven,' recalls the Governor, who at the time had religion very much on his mind. Having dealt with a gathering drinking problem by abruptly swearing off alcohol, he had vowed a renewed commitment to his family and his faith. Bush pointed to the Bible: only Christians had a place in Heaven. "I said, Mom, look, all I can tell you is what the New Testament says. And she said, well, surely, God will accept others. And I said, Mom, here's what the New Testament says. And she said, O.K., and she picks up the phone and calls Billy Graham. She says to the White House operator, Get me Billy Graham.'

   " 'I said, Mother, what are you doing?' " Bush continues, chuckling at the memory. "Seriously. And about two minutes later, the phone rings, and it's Billy Graham, and Mother and I are on the phone with Billy. And Mother explains the circumstances, and Billy says, 'From a personal perspective, I agree with what George is saying, the New Testament has been my guide. But I want to caution you both. Don't play God. Who are you two to be God?' "

           —SAM HOWE VERHOVEK, *NEW YORK TIMES MAGAZINE,*
                                 SEPTEMBER 13, 1998

Bush had also told a version of this story to a Houston Post reporter back in 1994.

TIM RUSSERT: In 1993 [*sic*], you suggested that unless you accept Jesus Christ as your Lord and Savior you couldn't go to heaven.

BUSH: No, no. What I said was, my *religion* teaches—my religion says that you accept Christ and you go to heaven. That was a statement that some interpreted that said *I* get to decide who goes to heaven. Governors don't decide who gets to go to heaven. No, sir. God decides who goes to heaven, Mr. Russert.

RUSSERT: Even non-Christians?

BUSH: God decides. And far be it from the politician who tries to play God.

—GOP DEBATE, DURHAM, NORTH CAROLINA,
JANUARY 6, 2000

"I mean, that's the Southern Baptists. But I don't think that this is a government function."

—*SLATE,* DECEMBER 6, 1999

Bush was referring to efforts of the Southern Baptists to convert Jews. He evidently meant that the government ought not to do it—or at least he didn't think so.

"That school was based upon the Bible."

—*PALM BEACH POST,* FEBRUARY 4, 2000

"That school" was Bob Jones University, whose ban on interracial dating, strident anti-Catholic teachings and candid anti-Semitism all were justified by Holy Writ, according to the governor.

The most glaring contradiction in Bush's personal/political religious program was, and is, his wholehearted embrace of the death penalty.

DENNIS
RYERSON: Here's the question: How do you post the Ten
              Commandments in schools without telling chil-
              dren who are not in the Judeo-Christian heritage
              that their form of religious expression is invalid?

BUSH: Well, it seems like to me "Thou shalt not kill" is
              pretty universal. I think districts ought to be al-
              lowed to post the Ten Commandments, no matter
              what a person's religion is. There's some inherent
              values in those great commandments that would
              make our society a better place for everybody.
                        —GOP DEBATE, JOHNSTON, IOWA,
                                        JANUARY 15, 2000

*Here Bush was lauding that commandment not as a "universal" moral principle—
which would require him to have followed it—but as a universal sort of "message"
to be tacked up in the nation's classrooms, along with the other nine. Aside from violating the Constitution's antitheocratic spirit, Bush's answer also evidenced his
usual obtuseness on the subject of capital punishment.*

Fox-TV's Bill O'Reilly urged the governor to meditate upon that subject.

O'REILLY: OK. Now in—so far in this campaign, the thing
              that sticks in my mind with you is the Jesus Christ
              political philosopher remark. Everybody remem-
              bers that. It's been played many, many times. When
              I heard you say that, I—I had no problem with it.
              I said, you know, that's a legitimate answer. Cer-
              tainly, Jesus Christ was a[ll?] that. But somebody
              might say, "Gee," you know, "if Governor Bush
              has been so influenced by Jesus Christ, how can he
              support the death penalty—"

BUSH: Sure.

O'REILLY: "—for example, so *hard?*" Because Jesus Christ
              would not have. How do you answer?

BUSH: Well, first, let me say the question was really, you know, who influenced me the most, and I didn't—this was not a calculated answer. It's one of those moments of time where somebody—"Who influenced you most?" And—

O'REILLY: Off the top of your head.

BUSH: —"Christ" came out of my mouth because Christ has influenced me, thanks to Billy Graham. It planted a seed in my heart, and it changed my life. It really did. I'm   I'm   I take great solace—I recognize I'm a humble—I'm a lowly sinner who sought redemption.

O'REILLY: But what about the death penalty?

BUSH: Let me—

O'REILLY: Texas leads the—

BUSH: Yeah, we can have a lot of issues that relate to Christianity. I—you know, I don't want to put words in Jesus Christ's mouth. I believe that the death penalty when administered surely, swiftly, and chilling signal [*sic*] that if you kill somebody in my state in the commission of another crime, there's going to be a consequence, and you're not going to like it.

O'REILLY: So you might disagree with Jesus on this one if he said—

BUSH: Well—

O'REILLY: —"I don't believe in that."

BUSH: Well, I—yeah, and I'm not so sure he addressed the death penalty itself in the New Testament. Maybe he did.

O'REILLY: No, he didn't, but I don't believe he would be for it if he were here today. But I could be wrong. I mean, I could be wrong. But he was one of those—

BUSH: This—this—we both can agree on this. Far be it
                 from me and you to put our—put words into the
                 Savior.
                           —*THE O'REILLY FACTOR,* FOX, MARCH 6, 2000

TONY SNOW: Is the Nation of Islam a faith-based organization?
BUSH: I think it is. I think it's based upon some universal
                 principles. It's certainly not the religion I accepted.
                 But I believe that the folks—the Muslims who ac-
                 cept, you know, love your neighbor like you'd like
                 to be loved yourself—
SNOW: So you wouldn't mind having taxpayer money go
                 to the Nation of Islam for—
BUSH: Well, let's make sure you understand something. I
                 don't like taxpayer money to support any religion.
                 What I like is taxpayers' money to support people
                 who are seeking some kind of help, people that
                 are trying to find some kind of better answer to
                 their lives. I don't believe government ought to
                 fund religion. I believe government can and
                 should fund people who are trying to help and
                 programs that help change people's lives.
                           —*FOX NEWS SUNDAY,* JANUARY 30, 2000

A few weeks later, just before the New York primary, the Governor's spokesman, Ari Fleischer, sought to make clear what Bush would have said if someone had prepped him properly.

"He answered about the religion of Islam. He has said previously he does not believe Louis Farrakhan preaches peace. He interpreted the question to be about Islam, not Farrakhan, not the Nation of Islam. The governor doesn't think anybody who preaches hate would qual-ify for the program's funding. And Farrakhan preaches hate."
                           —*NEW YORK TIMES,* FEBRUARY 24, 2000

"I'm going to lead the country to understanding the value of life—
the preciousness of life. Life for the living and life for the unborn."
—*THIS WEEK,* ABC, JANUARY 23, 2000

"Throughout the world, people of all religions recognize Jesus
Christ as an example of love, compassion, sacrifice, and service.
Reaching out to the poor, the suffering and the marginalized, he
provided moral leadership that continues to inspire countless men,
women, and children today.

"To honor his life and teachings, Christians of all races and de-
nominations have joined together to designate June 10 as Jesus Day.
. . . Jesus Day challenges people to follow Christ's example by per-
forming good works in their communities and neighborhoods."
—FROM GOV. BUSH'S PROCLAMATION OF "JESUS DAY"
AS A TEXAS STATE HOLIDAY, JUNE 10, 2000

AT THE HELM

*At his joint press conference with Tony Blair, Bush was asked by UPI's Helen
Thomas about the appropriateness of his "faith-based initiative" to give federal
funds to social programs run by religious groups.*

THOMAS: Mr. President, why do you refuse to respect the
wall between the church and state? And you know
that the mixing of religion and government, for
centuries, has led to slaughter. The very fact that
our country has stood in good stead by having this
separation—why do you break it down?

BUSH: I strongly respect the separation of church and
state.

THOMAS: Well, you wouldn't have a religious office in the
White House if you did.

BUSH: I didn't get to finish my answer, in all due respect.

I believe that so long as there's a secular alternative
available, we ought to allow individuals who we're
helping to be able to choose a program that may
be run by a faith-based program or can—will be
run by a faith-based program. I understand full
well that some of the most compassionate missions
of help and aid come out of faith-based programs.
And I strongly support the faith-based initiative
that we're proposing because I don't believe it vio-
lates the line between the separation of church
and state. And I believe it's going to make America
a better place.

Thomas tried again, but Bush curtly interrupted her, and moved on to another questioner.

THOMAS:	Well, you are a secular official—
BUSH:	I agree. I am a secular official.
THOMAS:	—and not a missionary.
REPORTER:	Sir, on the air strikes in Iraq, the Pentagon is now saying that most of the bombs used in those strikes missed their targets. . . .

—*NEW YORK TIMES; WASHINGTON POST;
LOS ANGELES TIMES,* FEBRUARY 23, 2001

Freedom of Expression

It concerns me. As much as I'd like to stifle it occasionally.
—BUSH ON "STIFLING THE PRESS," *NEW YORK TIMES,*
JANUARY 14, 2001

Bush's position on free speech is flexible. On the one hand, he supports free speech for media corporations and well-fixed political campaigns (i.e., his own). He is therefore opposed to campaign finance reform (see pp. 161ff.). Likewise—despite his sermonettes against the "dark" stuff on the Internet and peddled by "big Hollywood"—Bush is utterly opposed to any regulation of the media for public-interest purposes. This puts him squarely in the laissez-faire tradition of Ronald Reagan, whose FCC chairman, Mark Fowler, once notoriously claimed that television is just an appliance, "a toaster with pictures." On such issues Bush is also not that far from Clinton/Gore, whose record is an awful lot like that of Reagan/Bush. (See p. 358, n. 63.) Colin Powell's son, Michael, Bush's choice to chair the FCC, is an unabashed free-marketeer convinced that Clinton/Gore's procorporate policies on media were somehow bad for business.

While adamant in his support of "free speech" for himself and friends, Bush has no qualms about silencing the opposition—or anyone who might mess with his "message." Like Nixon, he is quick to deny access to any publication that might dare to scrutinize his record or his policies. One reporter, who had tried to cover Bush in depth, told me that the campaign's iron curtain was unprecedented in his own professional experience: "I can honestly say that I never encountered so much resistance in so many arenas in my twenty-three years of being a working journalist."

As the Hatfield episode demonstrates, moreover, Bush will use whatever spooky strategems it takes to "neutralize" an inconvenient voice. In general Bush favors the prerogative of management over the free speech rights of individuals who work for them, as his take on the John Rocker episode made clear (see pp. 159ff.).

"When it comes to the overall story, the long-term view of the campaign, it's so important for the campaign to set the long-term view."
—*BRILL'S CONTENT ONLINE,* SEPTEMBER 2000

"Obviously, the less publicity I'm able to achieve in California . . . the more I'm able to continue to send the message that my head and heart's right here in Texas." —CNN, MAY 12, 1998

This was Bush's explanation of his decision to bar coverage of a recent speech of his in Hollywood.

In the course of researching her Vanity Fair *profile of Governor Bush, Gail Sheehy found herself abruptly frozen out by his campaign—and long before she "knew" he had dyslexia. Her crime was to have discovered the horrific consequences of the governor's polluter-friendly rule. In Odessa, she saw the residents of that blue-collar city suffering the tortures of the damned—darkness at noon, soaring rates of respiratory illness, windows taped shut in the thick of summer—because of copious omissions by the Huntsman plastics factory right in the heart of town. "The Huntsman operation in Odessa is not the worst case of alleged environmental recklessness in Texas, but it is a classic example of how the interests of the oil and power and petrochemical industries are protected by the Bush administration, while the population is virtually helpless against the dangerously mounting pollution levels." As the conclusion of her article reports, her effort to get some germane response from Bush led to her immediate alienation from his presence.*

"I hoped to have an opportunity to ask Governor Bush about his learning difficulties, his religious awakening, and his environmental policies. Coming out of the celebratory Republican convention, I joined Bush's whistle-stop train tour through the Midwest, expecting a real grassroots trip. Instead, it was a long string of privately owned railroad cars. The campaign had hired a top Philadelphia caterer, who was told to 'take care of the press, first class,' which meant laying on heavy hors d'oeuvres—smoked-salmon napoleons and caviar on crème fraîche—while the train purred through traditionally Democratic states. Crowds were huge and highly charged, but the faces were almost exclusively white.

"Running down the roadbed at one stop, I collared Don Evans. I asked him how Bush, as president, would balance his loyalty to the oil, gas, and petrochemical industries with the nation's growing concerns about environmental policy. The pause was long. 'We'll have a policy position on the environment and energy—it's being worked on.' Evans emphasized that the governor has taken 'enormous constructive steps to reduce pollution.'

"The next morning I was told by Karen Hughes, 'The governor will not be able to participate in your profile.' "
—GAIL SHEEHY, "THE ACCIDENTAL CANDIDATE,"
VANITY FAIR, OCTOBER 2000

As he explained throughout the GOP debates, Bush has no qualms about trade with China, whose repression of free speech (and other) rights doesn't seem to faze him.

"Imagine if the Internet took hold in China. Imagine how freedom would spread. I told—in my earlier answer I said our greatest export to the world has been, is, and always will be the incredible freedom we understand in America"
—GOP DEBATE, PHOENIX, DECEMBER 6, 1999

Such tolerance of the Chinese way is not surprising, since Bush himself is no more tolerant of heresy than are the rulers in Beijing.

"There ought to be limits to freedom. We're aware of this [Web] site, and this guy is just a garbage man, that's all he is."
—AP, MAY 21, 1999

Thus the governor explained his complaint filed with the Federal Election Commission, to shut down a parody site, gwbush.com.

Perfectly at ease with media concentration, and therefore quite untroubled by the prospect of a few huge corporations ruling all the culture industries, online and off-, Bush was typically unable to use simple English in attempting to feign deep concern at such a threat to free expression:

> "Will the highways on the Internet become more few?"
> —CONCORD, NEW HAMPSHIRE, JANUARY 29, 2000; *SLATE*

Bush often would lament the gross and exploitative product of the media, especially when it was aimed at children:

> "It's important for us to explain to our nation that life is important. It's not only life of babies, but it's life of children living in, you know, the dark dungeons of the Internet."
> —ARLINGTON HEIGHTS, ILLINOIS, OCTOBER 24, 2000; *SLATE*

However, such product doesn't bother him enough to take the side of parents who like to see some programming not dictated purely by commercial logic:

> "Put the 'off' button on."   —AP, FEBRUARY 14, 2000

Such was the governor's advice to parents troubled by the graphic fare on television.

I MAY AGREE WITH WHAT YOU SAY, BUT I APPLAUD THE RIGHT OF MANAGEMENT TO TEACH YOU NOT TO SAY IT

In October 1999, John Rocker, a gifted pitcher for the Atlanta Braves, created a considerable ruckus when he gave Sports Illustrated *a rich sample of the contents of his mind. He was especially vivid on the subject of New York, "the most hectic, nerve-racking city," where he had found the Mets fans especially unlikeable—although the catcalls in Shea Stadium were not the only local color that offended him. "Imagine having to take the [Number] 7 train to the ballpark, looking like you're [riding through] Beirut next to some kid with purple hair next to some queer with AIDS right next to some dude who just got out of jail for the fourth time right next to some 20-year-old mom with four kids. It's depressing." The ebullient Georgian also noted, "The biggest thing I don't like about New York are the foreigners. I'm not a very big fan of foreigners." Although universally condemned for such remarks, Rocker later heatedly denied any kinship with the controversial Knicks guard Latrell Sprewell, who had taken similar heat for choking P. J. Carlesimo, his coach, two years before, when he was playing with the Golden State Warriors. "That guy should've been arrested, and instead he's playing basketball," exploded Rocker. "Why do you think that is? Do you think if he was Keith Van Horn—if he was white—they'd let him back? No way." It was not just New Yorkers who got Rocker's goat, however. He casually referred to one black teammate as "a fat monkey."*

Rocker's free-associations prompted many calls that he be sensitized ASAP. "Something should be done about this, so that Mr. Rocker is held accountable for his vicious and bigoted remarks," said Mayor Rudy Giuliani, whose delicate regard for others' feelings is well-known. The mayor advised "some kind of training, where he becomes more educated." Such calls had their effect. Soon the management of the Atlanta Braves decided to have Rocker "counseled," so that he might go and sin no more.

At the GOP debate in Michigan, journalist Suzanne Geha asked Governor Bush for his opinion on the Braves's decision. His approval of the company's position was remarkable. First of all, it indicated a departure from the libertarian ideals of most American conservatives, who generally deplore the tendency to treat hate speech as a crime or illness. Bush's take on the outspoken Georgian was a little disingenuous, moreover, inasmuch as Rocker's diatribe was not the sort of thing that a Republican would mind. (See "The Color Line," pp. 226ff.)

SUZANNE GEHA: As a former owner of a baseball team, the Texas Rangers, and as a candidate for president, would you defend Rocker's right to say whatever he wanted short of making a threat, or would you support and require him to undergo psychologi-

	cal testing? Would you call for his firing or demotion?
BUSH:	Listen, I think it's a free—this is a case of a player needs help [*sic*]. And I appreciate the fact that the Atlanta Braves are getting him counseling. But this is a world of—in athletics, this is a world of some young men who make a lot of money who don't—who aren't responsible for their behavior.

What I'd like to do, as the president of the United States, is usher in the responsibility era so that each American, whether you be a baseball player or a—anything, wear the uniform of the United States, are responsible for the actions you take in life; that each of us must understand with certainty that we are responsible for the decisions we make.

And it starts, by the way, with having a president who behaves responsibly in the Oval Office.

[Applause]

GEHA:	Governor Bush?
BUSH:	Yes.
GEHA:	Do you think that it is fair to order someone to undergo psychological testing if that individual says something that is so offensive?
BUSH:	I think in this case it made sense to do so, and I appreciate what the Atlanta Braves have decided to do. I appreciate that.

Geha asked the governor if Rocker might have been immune to such forced "testing" if he played for a publicly supported institution rather than a private corporation.

BUSH:	Look, I think—I think that—I don't know the particulars about this particular person. I think the Braves made the right decision, though. I mean,

they know the man better than you and I do. The fellow said some incredibly offensive things. He is a public person. And I appreciate them trying to get the man help.

I understand in America we can say what we want to say, but that doesn't mean that if the man needs help, he shouldn't get it. And I appreciate their efforts to provide psychological counseling for him.

—GOP DEBATE, GRAND RAPIDS, MICHIGAN,
JANUARY 10, 2000

CAMPAIGN FINANCE REFORM

"I'm trying to protect my invest—my contributors from unscrupulous practices."   —*HOUSTON CHRONICLE*, JULY 18, 1998

The governor was explaining why he had resisted having the names of his campaign donors posted on-line.

Although he'd vigorously resisted publicizing his donors' names, the governor was all for public information of some kind—the vaguer and more limited, the better. Indeed, such unenlightening revelation was the one "reform" that Bush would ever recommend.

"I think a good reform would be for any group that decides to put money up on TV, they need to let us know something about their group and who their treasurer is, for example."

—*THIS WEEK*, ABC, MARCH 5, 2000

"On the one hand he preaches campaign finance reform. On the other hand he passes the plate."

—*NEW YORK TIMES*, FEBRUARY 8, 2000

Bush was here referring to Senator John McCain—who had received "more money than anybody" from D.C. lobbyists, the governor charged. In fact, the governor, in working lobbyists and their immediate families, had raised almost five times as much as Senator McCain in the first three quarters of 1999, according to the Center for Responsive Politics.

When Al Gore endorsed McCain's crusade, the governor again responded with ad hominem derision—and an outright lie about his own unprecedented campaign war chest.

GORE: This current campaign financing system has not reflected credit on anybody in either party. And that's one of the reasons I've said before, and I'll pledge here tonight, if I'm president, the very first bill that Joe Lieberman and I will send to the United States Congress is the McCain-Feingold campaign finance reform bill. And the reason it's that important is that all of the other issues— whether prescription drugs for all seniors that are opposed by the drug companies, or the Patients Bill of Rights to take the decisions away from the HMOs and give them to the doctors and nurses, opposed by the HMOs and insurance companies—all of these other proposals are going to be a lot easier to get passed for the American people if we limit the influence of special interest money, and give democracy back to the American people. And I wish Governor Bush would join me this evening in—in endorsing the McCain-Feingold campaign finance reform bill.

JIM LEHRER: Governor Bush.

BUSH: You know, this man has no credibility on the issue. As a matter of fact, I read in the *New York Times* where he said he cosponsored the McCain-Feingold campaign fund-raising bill. But he wasn't in the Senate with Senator Feingold.

And so I—Look, I'm going to—What you
need to know about me is, I'm going to uphold
the law. I'm going to have an Attorney General
that enforces the law, that if the time for—the
time for campaign funding reform is after the
election.

This man has outspent me. The special interests are outspending me. And I am not going to
lay down my arms in the middle of the campaign
for somebody who has got no credibility on the
issue.

—PRESIDENTIAL DEBATE, OCTOBER 3, 2000

*Although beside the point—and false to boot—the crack about Gore's claim to have
cosponsored the McCain-Feingold bill functioned to distract us from the issue, by invoking the effective propaganda legend of Al Gore as a "serial exaggerator." Having thus used up his only ammunition on the campaign-finance front, Bush flailed
around, resolving vaguely "to uphold the law" and urging the postponement of the
whole discussion until "after the election." The governor then made a desperate lunge
for the high ground with his preposterous claim that his opponent, and "the special
interests," had "outspent" him. In fact, Bush raised and spent more money than any
presidential candidate in U.S. history—just as he had done both times he ran for
governor of Texas. In the last election season, Bush/Cheney raised $193,088,650
and spent a total of $132,900,252. For their part, Gore/Lieberman had raised
$185,860,812 and spent $120,369,160. Although the governor's almighty fund-
raising apparatus was well-known to the telejournalists, his claim to have been
"outspent" by Gore inspired no snide remarks from them about his tendency to gild
the truth.*[81]

"Bush partisans would have you believe that his $63 million (as of
December 20 [1999]) represents nothing so much as a vast outpouring of public support. 'The media's monomania about Bush's
fund-raising,' wrote George Will in a recent column, 'reflects an ob-
durate refusal to recognize that Bush has lots of money because he

has lots of supporters, not vice versa.' Will, whose penchant for Republican front-runners is legendary, may want to fire his research assistant: According to the latest Federal Election Commission filings, Bush has managed to raise more than twice as much as Al Gore with about 20,000 fewer donors. And it's no surprise that of Bush's top-10 fundraising zip codes, one is in Greenwich (his père's home turf), one is on New York's Upper East Side, one is in Saint Louis, and seven are in Texas. Like any mainstream Republican, Bush gets most of his money from the usual collection of establishment and business types, with added boosts from Texas oil and gas interests and from his father's old fund-raising network."

—*THE AMERICAN PROSPECT*, JANUARY 31, 2000

The exchange on campaign finance at the first debate continued, with Al Gore suddenly reverting to a notion of reform far more effective than the weak provisions of McCain-Feingold—which actually would raise the limits on individual donations. The governor's hysterical response to his opponent's sally is worth noting.

JIM LEHRER: Senator McCain said in August that it didn't matter which one of you is president of the United States in January. There's going to be blood on the floor of the United States Senate, and he's going to tie up the United States Senate until campaign finance reform is passed that includes a ban on soft money. First of all, would you support that effort by him, or would you sign a bill that is finally passed that included soft—

BUSH: Well, I would support an effort to ban corporate soft money and labor union soft money, so long as there was dues checkoff. I've campaigned on this ever since the primaries. I believe there needs to be instant disclosure on the Internet as to who's giving to whom. I think we need to fully enforce the law. I mean, I think we need to have an attor-

	ney general that says if laws are broken we'll enforce the law, be strict about—be firm about it.
GORE:	Look, Governor Bush, you have attacked my character and credibility. And I am not going to respond in kind. I think we ought to focus on the problems, and not attack each other.
	And one of the serious problems—hear me well—is that our system of government is being undermined by too much influence coming from special interest money. We have to get a handle on it. And, like John McCain, I have learned from experience. And it's not a new position for me. Twenty-four years ago I supported full public financing of all federal elections. And anybody who thinks I'm just *saying* it'll be the first bill I send to the Congress, I want you to know—
BUSH:	All right, let me just say one thing—!
GORE:	—I care passionately about this, and I will fight until it becomes law.
BUSH:	I want people to hear what he just said! He is for *full public financing* of Congressional elections! I'm absolutely, adamantly opposed to that! I don't want the government financing Congressional elections!

—PRESIDENTIAL DEBATE, OCTOBER 3, 2000

The governor's outrage was understandable, since full public financing of federal elections would eliminate the vast electoral advantage of the rich and finally cleanse our airways of the heavy fog of propaganda that benights our politics throughout every campaign season. (Such radical reform would irk the broadcasters no less than it would hobble certain politicians, because it's the media machine itself that takes in all that money—a payoff that explains why the National Association of Broadcasters is the top lobbyist against campaign finance reform.)

Faced with that surprising challenge by Al Gore, Bush resorted to a bit of tacit red-baiting, by equating actual reform with Big Brother-type control of general elec-

tions. (Of course, as things turned out, our electoral system was subverted by the governor's own campaign.)

"Show me the money!"   —*TEXAS MONTHLY,* JUNE 1999

The governor shouted out that cinematic jest on seeing two lobbyists on the steps of the Capitol in Austin, Texas.

MOVING RIGHT ALONG . . .

"This is an impressive crowd, the haves, and the have-mores. Some people call you the elite. I call you my base."
        [*Laughter*]
            —AL SMITH MEMORIAL DINNER IN NEW YORK,
                                OCTOBER 19, 2000

God's Green Earth

Mammon led them on,
Mammon, the least erected Spirit that fell
From heav'n, for ev'n in heav'n his looks and thoughts
Were always downward bent, admiring more
The riches of heavn's pavement, trodden gold,
Than aught divine or holy else enjoyed
In vision beatific. By him first
Men also, and by his suggestion taught,
Ransacked the center, and with impious hands
Rifled the bowels of their mother earth
For treasures better hid.

—*PARADISE LOST*, BOOK I, 678–88

Of all the blots on Bush's record (his "victory" excepted), none is quite as large, or evil-smelling, as his six years of environmental work in Texas. A man of oil and gas, the governor was—as it were by nature—always sympathetic to the planet's dirtiest polluters: the big oil, petrochemical and automobile industries. His innate sympathy was much intensified by the gigantic campaign contributions that those and other toxic interests dumped into his coffers when he ran against Ann Richards in 1994 and against Garry Mauro four years later. His favor thus secured, Bush did all he could to gut the state's regulatory apparatus in order to enrich the likes of Exxon, BP Amoco, Phillips, Texaco and Mobil, Dow and DuPont, Lockheed and

Apache—*and, among the dirtiest, Alcoa (whose CEO, Paul O'Neill, Bush made his secretary of treasury). Such collaboration paid off handsomely for his investors, which meant the vast contamination of the air and water throughout Texas—or rather, all throughout its major cities and its poorest pockets, where the toxins leave no healthy child behind.*

*Under Bush, Texas had the nation's highest volume of air pollution, with the highest ozone levels of any state—while ranking forty-sixth in spending on environmental problems. Moreover, after 1994 Texas was the nation's leading source of greenhouse gases, accounting for 14 percent of the annual U.S. total while boasting only 7 percent of the U.S. population. Under Bush, Texas's oil refineries became the nation's dirtiest, with the highest level of pollution per barrel of oil processed. And because all such industrial effluvia are concentrated in or near the state's poorest neighborhoods, Bush's Texas also led the nation in the number of Title VI civil rights complaints against a state environmental agency—in this case, the Texas National Resource Conservation Commission (TNRCC), which Governor Bush staffed brazenly with staunch anti-environmentalists like Ralph Marquez, a veteran of Monsanto Chemical, and Barry McBee, of the pro-business law firm Thompson & Knight.***

However shocking, such statistics cannot quite convey the ugliness of Bush's legacy as steward of the environment in Texas—a story not just of poor numbers but of townships darkened by thick toxic fogs, of schools shut down because of airborne poisons, of children suffering from damaged lungs as if they were heavy smokers. Gail Sheehy, for example, offered up a vivid picture of Odessa as a city ravaged by the governor's extreme indulgence of such outfits as Alcoa, Dow, and Exxon—a crime for which she was forbidden access to the candidate (see pp. 156–57).

While Bush's grim environmental record is his worst offense, it is also one that could have hurt him badly as a national candidate if it had ever been reported with due clarity. Most Americans are flaming liberals on environmental issues—as Bush himself was well aware, having helped to mount Bush/Quayle's strong assault on Governor Dukakis for the latter's putative neglect of the disgusting Boston Harbor.[82]

---

*For a detailed overview of Bush's true environmental record, see Rick Abraham, *The Dirty Truth: The Oil & Chemical Dependency of George W. Bush* (Houston: Mainstream Publishers, 2000).

If the viewers had known more about the Texas governor's hard-nosed let-them-eat-smog approach to the environment (and his aggressive efforts to impose a radioactive waste dump on the unwilling citizens of Sierra Blanca way out West), his canned assurances about the perfect sweetness of his "heart" would not have helped him much.

In Bush's playbook, then, the less said about his views on the environment, the better. That policy explains why he said very little on the subject throughout his two years as a presidential candidate. Whenever he was forced to talk about it, his actual views were all too clear.

Campaigning in Saginaw, Michigan, the governor tried softening his usual pro-business spiel with what he evidently thought to be a green improvisation.

"Texas Gov. George W. Bush has been using a TelePrompTer recently to help him sharpen his speech delivery. But why stick to a script all the time?

"In a speech, Bush said he would not tear down energy-producing dams merely to protect fish.

" 'I made it clear to the citizens of the Pacific Northwest that I oppose breaching those dams,' the governor said. And then he ad-libbed: 'I know the human being and fish can coexist peacefully.' "

—AP, SEPTEMBER 29, 2000

That gaffe has been much ridiculed—and its true import therefore overlooked. The remark is striking not because it's silly but because it casts a threatened creature as a national enemy. A relic of the Cold War, the phrase "peaceful coexistence" was a predétente Soviet coinage, meant to pitch conciliation between the world's two rival superpowers; Bush would have heard the phrase a million times in Midland and at Andover. Thus its application to "the human being and fish" is, although bizarre, not terribly amusing. The candidate's preposterous call to "coexist peacefully" with the fish suggests that he now sees "us" as being somehow at war with them. Here we could psychologize, but it is more germane to observe that such a warlike view of nature has for centuries defined the white man's progress through the world. Of course, that view has largely fallen into disrepute, its catastrophic consequences—for "the human being and fish," God's other creatures, and the planet overall—having now become so clear. Only within Bush's moral universe is that view still re-

spectable—among the zealots of the Christian right and throughout the automo-
tive and extractive industries, whose luminaries see the fish (and every other living
creature that moveth) as nothing more than obstacles to further profit.

On those few occasions when the governor was forced to speak at length on the
environment, his epic incoherence was, in its own way, as telling as his brief ad-lib
in Saginaw.

DENNIS RYERSON:	We have time for one more question, but we'll just have to have quick answers of thirty seconds each. This is from Burt Miller of Mount Pleasant [Iowa], and he asks, "Do you think tougher laws are needed to protect our environment?"
BUSH:	I think we ought to have high—high standards and set by—by agencies that rely upon science, not by what may feel good or what sound good [*sic*]. And I think it's important to give people time to say we're going to conform to standards, and if they don't, I think we ought to fine them. I mean, I think we ought to be tough when it comes to our environmental laws. But I don't—I don't believe that this administration has got it right when it comes to the environment. They try to sue our way to clean air and clean water or regulate our air—way to clean air and clean water [*sic*]. I think we need to lead our way by bringing stakeholders to the table and rely upon the new technologies that are coming—
RYERSON:	Thank you, Governor.
BUSH:	—so that we can have clean air and clean water.

—GOP DEBATE, IOWA, JANUARY 15, 2000

Once in office, President Bush remained incapable of sounding like he could ap-
preciate the natural world as anything but an exploitable resource. A few weeks after

his inauguration, Bush thus began a White House briefing to allege the fragile state of the economy:

> It's good to see so many friends here in the Rose Garden. This is our first event in this beautiful spot, and it's appropriate we talk about policy that will affect people's lives in a positive way in such a beautiful, beautiful part of our national—our national—really, our national park system, I guess, is you'd want to call it [*sic*].
>
> —WHITE HOUSE BRIEFING, FEBRUARY 8, 2001★

On the environment as on so many other subjects, Bush spoke relatively clearly only when reciting certain lines.

> Gas is a clean fuel that we can burn to—we need to make sure that if we decontrol our plants, that there's mandatory—that the plants are—must conform to clean air standards. The grandfather plants, that's what we did in Texas, no excuses; I mean, you must conform. In other words, there are practical things we can do. But it starts with working in collaborative effort with states and local folks. You know, if you own the land, every day is Earth Day. And people care a lot about their land and care about their environment. Not all wisdom is in Washington, D.C. on this issue.
>
> —PRESIDENTIAL DEBATE, OCTOBER 11, 2000

★That stammering salute betrayed the president's low esteem for "our national park system." Bush's Texas ranked forty-eighth in the nation for spending on state parks, and his proposed federal budget of 2001 was no more generous. Most of the $4.9 billion allocated for the national parks was dedicated to road repair and other non-natural improvements—a big blow to conservationists:

"Since the presidential campaign, the National Parks Conservation Association has been lobbying the Bush team about a new vision for funding the parks that focuses on protecting and managing the wilderness and wildlife.

"The new administration gave the group hope that it would be the one big environmental winner in the Bush presidency. Instead, Ron Tipton, the conservation association's vice president, said: 'This is sure the wrong direction to go. The plan spends 98% on roads and buildings and only 2% on birds and bunnies.' " ("The Federal Budget; Bush's Parks Plan Worries Watchdog Group," *Los Angeles Times,* March 1, 2001.)

The first, most incoherent part of that statement culminates in an outrageous lie about what Bush called "the grandfather plants" in Texas.

"The failure of George W. Bush's 'voluntary' approach to environmental protection is . . . illustrated in Texas where it was tried with old, outdated industrial facilities for almost 30 years. When the Texas Clean Air Act was passed in 1971, existing power plants, refineries and chemical plants were 'grandfathered' and exempted from the law. Facilities built later were covered by the law and required to have better pollution controls. In 1971 these 'grandfathered' polluters said that over time, they would voluntarily comply with the law, to the same standards imposed on newer facilities. Instead, most continued business as usual. By 1998 these industrial facilities, some of the oldest, biggest and dirtiest in Texas, were responsible for 36% of the state's industrial air pollution, or over 900,000 tons. They emit as much ozone pollution-causing chemicals as 18 million automobiles."

—RICK ABRAHAM, *THE DIRTY TRUTH*, P. 36

Only when he found himself docked back in the safe harbor of his campaign bromides ("If you own the land, every day is Earth Day") could Bush speak anything like lucid English on the subject of the suffering Earth.

GLOBAL WARMING

While deaf to all that science has to say on the Creation (see pp. 139ff.), Bush purports to be enormously concerned that something he calls "science" should very strictly guide our national policies on other issues. "The science is still out on issues like global warming," he said in March 2000. Although he did claim to "believe there is global warming," as he said a few months later, he also noted that a "number of conservative people . . . disagree about its cause and impact."[83]

Such excessive cautiousness should come as no surprise, given Bush's long devotion to the very system—fossil fuels and automobiles—that has lately warmed our planet to the point of crisis. Although he made a few progressive noises as a candi-

date—and even, for a day or two, after his inauguration—it soon became quite clear that as long as he and Cheney are in charge, the giant oil and coal and petrochemical concerns will always win out over every other interest—civic, scientific, economic. On this issue, our president will no more heed the warnings of the health care and insurance industries than he will listen to the great majority of scientists—or the public.

It is not merely Bush himself that is the problem here, however, but the larger TV culture that in part produced him. In his second debate with Al Gore, when the discussion turned to global warming, Bush's personal obtuseness on the subject meshed quite nicely with the stupefying triviality of the entire production. What with Gore's agonized attempts at self-effacement after his flamboyant sighing in the first debate, and Jim Lehrer's niggling overemphasis on the ground rules of that particular nonconfrontation, the spectacle itself distracted everybody from the clear and present danger that is global warming.

LEHRER: What about global warming?

BUSH: I think it's an issue that we need to take very seriously. But I don't think we know the solution to global warming yet, and I don't think we've got all the facts before we make decisions [sic]. I'll tell you one thing I'm not going to do is I'm not going to let the United States carry the burden for cleaning up the world's air, like the Kyoto treaty would have done. China and India were exempted from that treaty. I think we need to be more even-handed as, evidently, ninety-nine senators—I think it was ninety-nine senators—supported that position.

LEHRER: Global warming, global warming. The Senate did turn it down.

BUSH: Ninety-nine to nothing.

GORE: I think that—well, that vote wasn't exactly—a lot of supporters of the Kyoto treaty actually ended up voting for that because of the way it was worded, but there's no doubt there's a lot of opposition to it in the Senate.

. . . But I disagree that we don't know the cause of global warming. I think that we do. It's pollution, carbon dioxide and other chemicals that are even more potent but in smaller quantities that cause this.

Look, the world's temperature's going up, weather patterns are changing, storms are getting more violent and unpredictable. And what are we going to tell our children? And I'm a grandfather now. I want to be able to tell my grandson when I'm in my later years that I didn't turn away from the evidence that showed that we were doing some serious harm. In my faith tradition, it's written in the Book of Matthew: "Where your heart is, there is your treasure also." And I believe that we ought to recognize the value to our children and grandchildren of taking steps that preserve the environment in a way that's good for them.

BUSH: Yeah, I agree. I just, I think there's been some, some of the scientists, I believe, Mr. Vice President, haven't they been changing their opinion a little bit on global warming? A profound scientist recently made a different—

LEHRER: Both of you now

BUSH: But the point is—

LEHRER: Excuse me. Both of you have now violated your own rules. Hold that thought.

GORE: I've been trying so hard not to [violate the rules].
       [*Laughter*]

LEHRER: I know, I know, but about—under y'all's rules, you are not allowed to ask each other a question. I let you do it a moment ago—

BUSH: Twice.
       [*Laughter*]

LEHRER: Twice, sorry. OK.

GORE: That's an interruption, by the way.

             [*Laughter*]

LEHRER: That's an interruption. OK. But, anyhow, you just
             did it, so now we're—

BUSH: I'm sorry.

LEHRER: That's all right. It's OK.

BUSH: I apologize, Mr. Vice President.

             [*Laughter*]

LEHRER: No, you're not allowed to do that either, you see.
             No, no. I'm sorry, go ahead. Finish your thought.
             People care about these things, I've found out.

BUSH: Course they care about—Oh, you mean the *rules*.

Bush thought that Lehrer had meant global warming.

LEHRER: Right, exactly right. Go ahead, sir.

BUSH: What the heck. I—of course there's a lot of—I
             mean, look, global warming needs to be taken
             very seriously, and I take it seriously. But science—
             there's a lot of—there's differing opinions, and be-
             fore we react, I think it's best to have the full
             accounting, full understanding of what's taking
             place. . . .

LEHRER: New question.

BUSH: Yes.

LEHRER: Last question for you, Governor—and this flows
             somewhat out of the Boston debate. You, your
             running mate, your campaign officials have
             charged that Vice President Gore exaggerates, em-
             bellishes, and stretches the facts, etc.

                  Are you—do you believe these are serious is-
             sues, this is a serious issue that the voters should
             use in deciding which one of you two men to
             vote for on November 7?

BUSH: Well, we all make mistakes. I've been known to
                 mangle a syl-*lab*-ble or two myself, you know.
                 [*Laughter*]
                 But you know what I mean. I think credibility is
                 important.
                 —PRESIDENTIAL DEBATE, OCTOBER 12, 2000

"Impacts of climate change will be far worse than previously
thought and beyond the capacity of mankind to adapt unless greenhouse gas emissions are cut substantially, 700 scientists say in a report
published yesterday.

"Loss of food crops, disappearance of fisheries, melting of gla-
ciers which provide millions of people with summer water supply,
and a rise in sea levels will cause massive economic disruption and
migration, it says.

"The Arctic, which is already known to be suffering ice loss,
could be completely ice-free in summer and the melting giant ice-
cap on Greenland may cause faster sea level rise than previously
thought. . . .

"The Intergovernmental Panel on Climate Change report is intended to guide politicians on problems they face as temperatures
rise. Yesterday's assessments mean the world is heading for disasters
on an unprecedented scale.

" 'Climate change, amongst other issues, threatens basic human
needs of food, clean water and a healthy environment,' said Robert
Watson, co-author of the report."
                 —*THE GUARDIAN* (UK), FEBRUARY 20, 2001

AT THE HELM

"The Bush administration, some influential Republicans in Congress, and several big owners of coal-burning power plants have
joined in advocating something long sought by environmental

groups and Democrats: cuts in the plants' emissions of carbon dioxide, a heat-trapping greenhouse gas widely thought to contribute to
a global warming trend."   —*NEW YORK TIMES,* MARCH 10, 2001

"Under strong pressure from conservative Republicans and industry
groups, President Bush reversed a campaign pledge today and said his
administration would not seek to regulate power plants' emissions of
carbon dioxide, a gas that is widely considered to be a key contributor to global warming."   —*NEW YORK TIMES,* MARCH 14, 2001

White House spokesman Scott McClellan clarified the president's abrupt reversal:

" 'The president is following through on his commitment to a
multi-pollutant strategy that will significantly reduce pollutants,' Mr.
McClellan said. 'CO2 should not have been included as a pollutant
during the campaign. It was a mistake.' "   —IBID.

Profile in Courage:
Bush and Leadership

Campaigning, Bush would often stress the **theme** *of his* **decisiveness,** *making sure that viewers received the* **message** *that, as president, he would never be afraid to* **take a stand.**

> "My opponent won't tell you where he stands on this issue. He is afraid to offend somebody, but that's not what a leadership is about. You got to stand strong. If you don't stand for anything, you don't stand for anything. If you don't stand for something, you don't stand for anything."
>
> —*AUSTIN AMERICAN-STATESMAN,* NOVEMBER 2, 2000

> "Our leaders should be judged by results, not by entertaining personalities and cute sound bites."
>
> —*ALL THINGS CONSIDERED,* NPR, NOVEMBER 8, 1999

> "I'm a decisive person."   —*NATIONAL JOURNAL,* AUGUST 7, 1999

However, while his **message** *was decisive, the* **candidate** *was generally* **not.** *By and large, his spine was obviated either by the need to keep his true position hidden from the rational majority or by his fear of losing the extremist members of his base.*

ABORTION RIGHTS

"Those are all questions that have to be answered given the context
of the moment."   —*NEW YORK TIMES*, JULY 15, 1998

*Thus Bush addressed the question of his possible support for an abortion rights can-
didate on the party ticket. Such cautiousness infuriated Gary Bauer, who, throughout the GOP debates, attempted endlessly, without success, to force the governor to
"stand strong" against abortion.*

BAUER: I want to ask you a simple yes-or-no question.
               Will you commit tonight to having a pro-life run-
               ning mate? I'm willing to say that Governor
               Christie Todd Whitman of New Jersey, the pro-
               abortion Republican governor, doesn't need to
               stick close to her phone. I won't be calling her to
               be my running mate.
                        Are you willing to make a similar commitment
               for a pro-life running mate?
BUSH: I think it's incredibly presumptive for someone
               who has yet to earn his party's nomination to be
               picking vice presidents. I'll tell you what I *will* do.
               I'll name somebody—I'll name somebody who
               can be the president. That ought to be the main
               criteria for any one of us who has the opportunity
               to pick a vice president, Gary. It's going to be, can
               that person serve as president of the United States?
               —GOP DEBATE, DES MOINES, DECEMBER 12, 1999

*As things turned out, Bush did, of course, pick "a pro-life running mate" in Dick
Cheney.*

GAY RIGHTS

"I have no idea whether the children ought to be removed or not removed."   —*DALLAS MORNING NEWS,* MARCH 23, 1999

This was Bush's comment on a Texas bill that would require the forced removal of children from foster homes in which parents are gay, lesbian, or bisexual.*

STAY, PAT, STAY

In the fall of 1999, Pat Buchanan was assailed by all sides for suggesting, in his book A Republic, Not an Empire, *that Hitler waged his war against the West because the governments of France and Britain forced him into it, and that the Fuehrer had in any case not posed a threat to the United States.*

Such revisionism was not a new thing for Buchanan, who had always shown a Reich-sized soft spot for the Nazis. What was new for the feisty commentator was his blunt stand against "free trade." That position was a late expression of his anachronistic isolationism—and, no doubt, the primary reason why his views were now so noisily condemned.

Whatever mainly drove it, the condemnation of Buchanan's views on World War II expressed a broad and firm consensus against Nazism. This created a dilemma for George W. Bush, who didn't want to alienate those members of his party who did not necessarily agree with that consensus.

---

*As far as his own record was concerned, Bush had a lot to hide from gay Americans:
"Many supporters characterize Bush as a gay-friendly presidential candidate who condemns discrimination in all forms and campaigns for gay votes. Yet in his six years as Texas governor, Bush has rarely met an antigay measure he didn't like, starting with the state's sodomy law, which he once defended as a 'symbolic gesture of traditional values.'
"Even more troubling for gay activists is state legislation that would have barred gays from adopting or serving as foster parents. The bill ultimately failed last year, but Bush never distanced himself from a provision that would have allowed the state to strip gay parents of the children who have already been placed in their homes." *The Advocate,* July 24, 2000.

BOB NOVAK:	Pat Buchanan is considering leaving the Republican Party, becoming the nominee of the Reform Party. Would you personally ask Pat Buchanan not to take that step?
BUSH:	Yes, I would.
NOVAK:	Call him up and ask him?
BUSH:	I may just decide to ask him today on the stage in Ames, Iowa. Because—we're standing next to each other for the photo op. I will turn to him and say, "Pat, I hope you don't leave the Republican Party."

—*EVANS, NOVAK, HUNT & SHIELDS,* CNN,
AUGUST 14, 1999

"I don't want Pat Buchanan to leave the party. I think it's important, should I be the nominee, to unite the Republican Party. I'm going to need every vote I can get among Republicans to win the election." —*NEW YORK TIMES,* SEPTEMBER 25, 1999

After catching flak for such a frank admission of political concern, Bush retroactively invented a more civic-minded motive for himself:

| LARRY KING: | Let's touch a lot of bases. When Pat Buchanan thought about leaving, you said, Stay, we need every vote. Were you wrong? |
| BUSH: | Well, actually, what I said was, stay, I'd like to debate his philosophy of isolationism and protectionism. I wanted the Republican Party to hear what he had to say and to hear what I had to say. And I was convinced that my view of free trade and America leading the world to peace would be the philosophy that would be accepted. I wanted to reject his kind of politics in the primary. |

KING: So are you—your father said, in the end, he was
                   probably glad that [Buchanan is] not in the party.
                   Are you?
BUSH: Well, now that he's chosen to go, you bet. I mean,
                   see you later.
                                    [*Laughter*]
                         —*LARRY KING LIVE,* CNN, DECEMBER 16, 1999

KING: Should the Reform Party candidate be a partici-
                   pant in the national debates when candidates are
                   selected?
BUSH: You need to ask me that question later on.
KING: Well, you can have an opinion on it. If Buchanan's
                   the nominee, should he in the debates?
BUSH: I'll reserve my opinion. I will reserve my opinion.
                         —*LARRY KING LIVE,* CNN, DECEMBER 16, 1999

THE STARS AND BARS

TIM RUSSERT: South Carolina: big issue—
BUSH: Yes.
RUSSERT: —whether to fly the Confederate flag.
BUSH: Yeah.
RUSSERT: A flag [that] to many black Americans represents
                   slavery. Should South Carolina take that flag down?
BUSH: It's up to the people of South Carolina.
RUSSERT: It doesn't bother you that they fly it?
BUSH: It's up to the people of South Carolina to make
                   the decision as to what to do with their flag, just
                   like it's up to the people of Texas to decide
                   whether we're going to have a lottery or not.
RUSSERT: Do you think the Confederate flag represents
                   slavery?

BUSH: I think the Confederate flag creates all kinds of emotions amongst different groups of people. But it is up to the people of South Carolina to make that decision.

—*MEET THE PRESS*, NBC, NOVEMBER 21, 1999

BRIAN WILLIAMS: Governor Bush, a few blocks from here, on top of the state capitol building, the Confederate flag flies with the state flag and the U.S. flag. It is, as you can hear from the reaction of tonight's crowd of three thousand people from South Carolina, a hot-button issue here. The question is: Does the flag offend you personally?

BUSH: The answer to your question is—and what you're trying to get me to do is to express the will of the people of South Carolina is what you're trying to get—

WILLIAMS: No, I'm asking you about your personal opinion—

BUSH: The people of South Carolina. Brian, I believe the people of South Carolina can figure out what to do with this flag issue. It's the people of South Carolina—

WILLIAMS: If I may—

BUSH: I don't believe it's the role of someone from outside South Carolina and someone running for president to come into this state and tell the people of South Carolina what to do with their business when it comes to the flag.

WILLIAMS: As an American citizen, do you have a visceral reaction to seeing the Confederate flag—?

BUSH: As an American citizen, I trust the people of South Carolina to make the decision for South Carolina.

—WEST COLUMBIA, SOUTH CAROLINA,
GOP DEBATE, JANUARY 17, 2000

UNIDENTIFIED REPORTER:	Here's your favorite topic: the flag. If you were to fly the Confederate flag outside the statehouse of Texas—I think you said that you wouldn't because of the symbolism, but it was never followed. What symbolism?
BUSH:	That means that—what that means is that some people have—people have strong feelings about that. Some people feel one way about it, some people feel the other way about it. And the people of South Carolina can make up their own mind. Yeah?
REPORTER #2:	But Governor, if I could just follow that?
BUSH:	My strong feeling is that the people of South Carolina can make up their mind. I've answered that question all I'm going to answer it today.
REPORTER #3:	Governor, one more time.
BUSH:	No, no, no.
REPORTER #3:	You're aspiring to be a national leader, not the governor. You're trying to be the president, the leader of the party of Lincoln. And yet you're concerned about the Republicans getting labeled as being insensitive to minorities. Don't you see that your position on that Confederate flag sends that kind of signal?
BUSH:	No. I don't see that at all. I don't think it reflects my heart at all. It reflects the understanding that the people of South Carolina can make up their own mind on that issue, just like they can make up their own mind on the lottery issue. I don't—I don't believe that.

—*NIGHTLINE,* ABC, JANUARY 12, 2000

Pushed to the wall, Bush started breaking down. In this exchange, the governor's last word on the subject was a burst of wild non sequiturs.

JUAN WILLIAMS: Well, Governor, one of the things that stood out
to me when I looked at the polls here in New
Hampshire was that 51 percent of the voters said
that George W. Bush says what we want to hear.
He'll just tell us whatever it is that we want to
hear in order to please us, in order to win this office. And I was reminded [of] your stand on the
flag issue in South Carolina. You said, "It's up to
the people of South Carolina"—as if you have no
historical context, as if you don't have a position
there of your own.

BUSH: Juan, I've got a position.

WILLIAMS: Your position is, Leave it up to the people.

BUSH: No, no, my position is the people of South Carolina can decide. You may not like my position.
But that's a position. And I don't believe the polls
said that. I don't read the polls. But I suspect that
when you look closely at what the people of this
state like, they like somebody who tells them exactly what my record is, what my philosophy is.

　　　I don't make decisions based upon polls or
focus groups, Juan. I'm the person who laid out a
tax-cut plan that has stood the test of time. I'm
not the candidate that, when the heat got on,
started, kind of, fine-tuning the tax-cut plan.

　　　　　　　　　　　—FOX NEWS SUNDAY, JANUARY 30, 2000

BOB JONES UNIVERSITY

TIM RUSSERT: "Compassionate conservative."

BUSH: Yes, sir.

RUSSERT: That's how you've described yourself. A lot of
eyebrows were raised when you made an appearance at Bob Jones University.

BUSH: Yeah, yeah.

RUSSERT: Now, let me show you a picture of Gov. George
             W. Bush and the gentleman there to your right.
             On the left of the screen is Bob Jones III. Let me
             show you what he said about your dad, which I
             think is rather chilling. And I'll put it on the
             screen for you and our viewers:

             "I believe that Mr. Reagan came to office with
             good intentions, but he broke his promise to us
             when he took on Mr. George Bush, a devil, for his
             vice president. . . . Mr. Reagan has become a trai-
             tor to God's people."

             How could you sit with a man who called
             your dad "a devil"?

BUSH: Well, you know, each of us change in life, and now
             he doesn't believe George Bush is a devil.

RUSSERT: Did he tell you that?

BUSH: No, he would have told me that, I presume. I pre-
             sume he was an honest enough man if he invited a
             son who is—completely loves his dad like I do. As
             you know, I'm a warrior for my dad. I wouldn't
             stand for that. And as a matter of fact, he was very
             complimentary of my dad. People change, Tim.
             People change and—

RUSSERT: The reason he called your dad a devil is because
             your dad said that university should lose its tax-
             exempt status because it discriminated.

BUSH: Well, as I said, the man didn't bring up my dad at
             all. I was invited to go to the campus. There were
             six thousand students and voters there. I went be-
             cause I wanted to get out my message of compas-
             sionate conservatism. My views on my dad haven't
             changed, just because he said that some eighteen
             years ago.

RUSSERT: But—well, let me show you what Mr. Jones's current thinking is and put it on the screen, because
this is just as disturbing:

"We believe that the Lord God created races
with distinctions and that races are meant to be
separate from one another. We basically accept that
there are three races: Caucasians, Negroes, and
Orientals. Caucasians can't date Orientals.
Orientals can't date Caucasians, and neither of
them can date Negroes."

That's what he believes in.

BUSH: Yeah. Well, I disagree with that, too. That was also
said in 1983, if you notice on that one.

RUSSERT: It's still the policy of the university.

BUSH: Well, it's not a good policy. And I didn't—when I
go to speak to voters, I don't necessarily have to
embrace the policies of the university.

RUSSERT: But you're giving affirmation to that institution.

BUSH: I am not giving affirmation. I'm giving affirmation—quite the contrary. I'm giving affirmation to
somebody who's going to unite our country. I
stood up there and said, "Let's march together
toward a better tomorrow." How can I go into a
university like that and subscribe to those views
when my little brother, the great governor of
Florida, married a girl from Mexico in my own
family?

RUSSERT: Why go, Governor? You wouldn't go to a Ku
Klux Klan rally.

BUSH: That's exactly right. I sure wouldn't.

RUSSERT: You wouldn't go to hate groups?

BUSH: I would not go to hate groups. But this is a group
that's based upon—this is a religious group.

RUSSERT: Well—

BUSH: This is not a hate group.

RUSSERT: —I checked their Internet [site] yesterday. You
                 know what it says? That Mormonism and
                 Catholicism are "cults."

BUSH: Well, I disagree.

RUSSERT: That's in the president's letter.

BUSH: You're not a cultist. I agree.

RUSSERT: No, I'm not. But let me show you what the chan-
                 cellor said about the Pope. The Pope—I openly
                 acknowledge I'm a Catholic. Let me put it on the
                 screen:

                 "The pope is the greatest danger we face
                 today. . . . He is doing more to spread Antichrist
                 communism than anyone around. The papacy is
                 the religion of the Antichrist and is a Satanic
                 system."

BUSH: But, Tim—

RUSSERT: Not just—What do you think the Catholic voters
                 in Michigan and New York and California see or
                 think when they read that and know that you as-
                 sociate yourself with that school?

BUSH: Well, but look, I don't associate myself with the
                 thought. First of all, that was a 1982 quote by a
                 man who's now passed away.

RUSSERT.   He's the chancellor. He was the chancellor.

BUSH: And I'm not—he's not—Mr. Jones—I don't
                 agree with that, Tim. Do not subscribe—I mean,
                 you know, you cannot subscribe those views to
                 me because I went to a university to speak to try
                 to convince six thousand people to be on my
                 team.
                      Ronald Reagan went there and spoke. Do you
                 think the Catholics in Michigan rejected Ronald
                 Reagan when he asked for their vote for the presi-

dency? Of course not. They listened to what Reagan had to say, and they looked at Ronald Reagan's heart.

And I do not agree with this notion that somehow if I go to try to attract votes and to lead people toward a better tomorrow, somehow I get subscribed to some—some doctrine gets subscribed to me. I don't accept that, and neither should you. And it's unfair.

RUSSERT: But people who know you and respect you and like you say, "George W. Bush, Thomas Burch and Bob Jones III aren't your kind of people. Why are you associating with them?"

BUSH: Well, first of all, Burch shows up because he represents a veterans' group, and he said, "I want to support your candidacy."

You know, I've got thousands of supporters who support me for one reason or another. I went to Bob Jones University because I wanted to convince people that my brand of conservatism is the right brand of conservatism for the Republican Party and is the right brand of conservatism for the country. That's why I went. That's what a leader does. A leader doesn't shirk. A leader leads. A leader stands up and sets an agenda. And that's what I'm going to do.

—*MEET THE PRESS*, NBC, FEBRUARY 13, 2000

"I did denounce it. I de—I denounced it. I denounced interracial dating. I denounced anti-Catholic bigacy—bigotry. . . . No, I—I—I—I spoke out against interracial dating. I mean, I support inter—the policy of interracial dating."

—*CBS EVENING NEWS*, FEBRUARY 25, 2000

BUSH ON AMERICAN
GOVERNANCE

"Many of them are good personal friends of mine. I'm confident
that we'll be able to get along pretty well."

—*NATIONAL JOURNAL,* AUGUST 7, 1999

Bush was referring to his relations with Congress.

"The legislature's job is to write law. It's the executive branch's job to
interpret law."   —AUSTIN, TEXAS, NOVEMBER 22, 2000; *SLATE*

"I am mindful of the difference between the executive branch and
the legislative branch. I assured all four of these leaders that I know
the difference, and that difference is they pass the laws and I execute
them."   —WASHINGTON, D.C., DECEMBER 18, 2000; *SLATE*

THE SHAPE OF THINGS
TO COME

"I think it is a little early to project the amount of money the Legislature will be dealing with. And, as you know, I hope I'm not here to
have to deal with it."   —*DALLAS MORNING NEWS,* JULY 14, 2000

*Bush was referring to the possibility of a shortfall in the Texas budget. As it turned
out, the governor's large tax cuts wreaked havoc with the state's economy, leaving a
"once-healthy surplus . . . nearly erased by budget overruns, particularly from health
care costs like Medicaid," the* New York Times *reported on February 12, 2001.
"We made tax cuts because we thought we had this huge surplus," recalled one Republican state senator. "I might have voted a little differently on all those tax cuts
had I realized that we were only funding 23 months of these [Medicaid] programs."*

This testament to Bush's "leadership" as governor pertains directly to his presidential vision since, Reagan-like, he entered national office calling for the same kind of radical tax-cutting plan that had lately ravaged his own state—although it paid off nicely for the very richest people there.

A NEW BROOM

"The administration I'll bring is a group of men and women who are focused on what's best for America, honest men and women, decent men and women, women who will see service to our country as a great privilege and who will not stain the house."

—GOP DEBATE, DES MOINES, IOWA, JANUARY 15, 2000

"I've been consistent throughout the course of the campaign that my Supreme Court will be people that will not use the bench from which to legislate."   —*USA TODAY,* NOVEMBER 3, 2000

Following Election Day 2000:

**REPORTER
(OFF MIKE):**   At what point do you think this dispute [will end]?

BUSH: You know, that's hard to tell. I think it's—that this is certainly unprecedented in modern times. Now, the more quickly this gets resolved, the better off it is for the nation. And we believe that the responsible course of action is to be well-prepared. It's in our nation's best interest that—that—that should I assume the presidency, that this is an administration that has planned well and is prepared to assume the highest office of the land. And it will be. And we will be prepared.

—BUSH CAMPAIGN PRESS BRIEFING,
NOVEMBER 10, 2000

"This morning I talked to Secretary Cheney. We had a very good conversation. He sounded really strong, and he informed me that, as a precautionary measure, he went into the hospital. He was feeling chest pains, and turns out that subsequent tests, blood tests, and the initial EKG showed that he had no heart attack. I'm pleased to report that I know all Americans join me and Laura in wishing him all the best.

"Looking forward to talking to him this afternoon to continue strategizing about this election and the election results. I am disappointed with last night's ruling by the Florida Supreme Court. We believe the justices have used the bench to change Florida's election laws and usurp the authority of Florida's election officials. . . .

"Secretary Cheney will make a great vice president.

"And as I reported today—I'm pleased to report that he sounded very strong on the telephone. And he did the right thing. He felt some warning signs, and he went into the hospital and had them checked out. And he's going to make a great vice president. And America's beginning to see how steady and strong he is. . . .

"I'm looking forward to a good Thanksgiving meal, I might add, with my family. And Dick Cheney is healthy. He did not have a heart attack."

—BUSH CAMPAIGN PRESS BRIEFING, NOVEMBER 22, 2000

Secretary Cheney had, in fact, just had a heart attack. Either Bush's staff had kept the truth from him, or he knew it and was lying.

TIM RUSSERT:	How important is that for a president, to be able to read people, understand the nuances—body language?
BUSH:	Oh, it's incredibly important for a lot of reasons. First of all, it's important to be able to have a—a— s—be able to delegate to people whose instincts you trust. Micromanagers fail when it comes to big CEO positions. And in order to be a good

manager, you've got to surround yourself with people who've got the right judgment, which means you better have the good judgment.

—CNBC NEWS, DECEMBER 30, 2000

In presenting Al Gonzales, his new White House counsel, Bush used much the same Horatio Alger narrative that George H. W. Bush had used in selling Clarence Thomas, even though Gonzales did not need that sort of pitch. In any case, "a two-bedroom house" is not a hovel, nor is it necessarily a sign of poverty to have a lot of siblings.

BUSH: But he's a guy who grew up in a two-bedroom house. His mother and daddy working, you know, as hard as they possibly can to bring up—six brothers and sisters?

GONZALES: I have seven siblings.

BUSH: Seven siblings. Eight in the family. And now he's going to be sitting at the right hand of the president of the United States.

To me, these appointments—and each . . . each person has got their own story that is so unique, stories that really explain what America can and should be about. And so I welcome them. I can't tell you how good of folks they are, not only in terms of the jobs they'll have but just in the quality of character.

—PRESS CONFERENCE, DECEMBER 18, 2000

"The person who runs FEMA [Federal Emergency Management Agency] is someone who must have the trust of the president because the person who runs FEMA really is the first voice oftentimes that someone whose lives have been turned upside down hears from."   —PRESS CONFERENCE, JANUARY 4, 2001

"I do remain confident in Linda [Chavez]. She'll make a fine labor secretary. From what I've read in the press accounts, she's perfectly qualified."   —PRESS CONFERENCE, JANUARY 8, 2001

BUSH:	Yeah?
REPORTER:	The European Union and Japan have filed a challenge in the WTO against a rule in the Agriculture Appropriations Bill that would allow steel companies to receive money from antidumping duties.
BUSH:	Say again now?
REPORTER:	It's an agriculture appropriations bill. President Clinton opposes this language in there that would allow companies to receive receipts from antidumping duties.
BUSH:	I think the administration needs to do what they think is right, and I'll address all these issues once I'm sworn in as the president.
REPORTER:	Thank you very much.
BUSH:	Thank you.

—PRESS CONFERENCE, DECEMBER 22, 2000

All the World's a Stage:
Bush on Foreign Policy

I'm not going to play like I've been a person who's spent hours involved with foreign policy. I am who I am.
—GEORGE W. BUSH, *NEWS HOUR WITH JIM LEHRER*

"Kosovians can move back in."
—*INSIDE POLITICS,* CNN, APRIL 9, 1999

"Keep good relations with the Grecians."
—*THE ECONOMIST,* JUNE 12, 1999

"If the East Timorians decide to revolt, I'm sure I'll have a statement."
—*NEW YORK TIMES,* JUNE 16, 1999

"The only thing I know about Slovakia is what I learned firsthand
from your foreign minister, who came to Texas."
—KNIGHT RIDDER, JUNE 22, 1999

*Bush made that comment to a Slovak journalist. In fact, it was the foreign minis-
ter of Slovenia whom he had met in Texas.*

Such gaffes inspired a local TV journalist, Andy Hiller of WHDH in Boston, to ask Bush the names of several foreign leaders. Hiller started out by asking Bush if he considered himself weak on foreign policy.

BUSH: Nah. I've got a clear vision of where I want to lead America.

HILLER: Can you name the president of Chechnya? [Aslam Maskhadov]

BUSH: No. Can you?

HILLER: Can you name the president of Taiwan? [Lee Tung-Hui]

BUSH: Yeah: Lee.

HILLER: Can you name the general who's in—

BUSH: Wait a minute, is this a—is this a *Fifty Questions?*

HILLER: No. It's four questions of four leaders in four hot spots.

Hiller asked Bush to name Pakistan's leader, Pervaiz Musharaf.

BUSH: The new Pakistani general has just been elected. He's not elected—this guy took over office. He appears he's going to bring stability to the country, and I think that's good news for the subcontinent.

HILLER: And you can name him?

BUSH: General—I can't name the general. General.

HILLER: And the prime minister of India? [Atal Bihari Vajpayee]

BUSH: The new prime minister of India is—no. Can *you* name the foreign minister of Mexico?

HILLER: No, sir. No, sir. But I would say to that, I'm not running for president.

BUSH: I understand. I understand, but the point I say to you is, is that, you know, if what you're suggesting

is, is that—what I'm suggesting to you is if you
can't name the foreign minister of Mexico, therefore, you know, you're not capable of what you
do. But the truth of the matter is, you're is—you
are, whether you can or not.★

—REBROADCAST ON *THE NEWS*, MSNBC,
NOVEMBER 4, 1999

"When I'm the president, we're not going to obfuscate when it
comes to foreign policy."

—NEW HAMPSHIRE GOP DEBATE, JANUARY 7, 2000

*During this period of heightened concentration on his foreign policy credentials, Bush
was asked if he had "any take at all" on Vladimir Putin, Boris Yeltsin's successor
as Russia's head of state.*

"I really don't. I will if I'm the president."

—*MEET THE PRESS*, NBC, NOVEMBER 21, 1999

BRIT HUME: Do you think that President Bush could have
done the job he did in assembling and holding together the Gulf War coalition, composed of many
very varied nations, had he not had the knowledge
of the world that he had from years of experience
and diplomacy and politics at the UN?

BUSH: In order to be a good president when it comes to
foreign policy, it requires someone with vision,
judgment, and leadership. I've been the governor

★In trying to turn the tables on his questioner—"Do you?"—Bush was trying the tactic that
his father had used so successfully against Dan Rather back in 1988. (See p. 84.)

of the second biggest state in the United States. If it were a nation, it would be the eleventh largest economy in the world. I was overwhelmingly re-elected because the people in my state realized I know how to lead, and I've shown good judgment.

A couple of weeks ago, at the Reagan Library, I talked about my vision for peace. My goal, should I become the president, is to keep the peace. I intend to do so by promoting free trade, which, in my judgment, promotes American values across the world. I intend to do so by strengthening alliances, which says America cannot go alone [*sic*]; we must be peacemakers, not peacekeepers. And I intend to strengthen the military to make sure that the world is peaceful.

HUME: With all respect, sir, I don't think you answered the question.

BUSH: Well, I gave you my qualifications why I think I'll be a good foreign policy leader.

—GOP DEBATE, NEW HAMPSHIRE,
DECEMBER 2, 1999

Bush had just recited the same litany of his achievements in his answer to Hume's question about his daily reading. (See p. 126.)

As we have seen, Bush often represented his refusal to discuss his own as further evidence of his concern for children (see pp. 103ff.). He made the same sentimental move in calling for increased "free trade" with Mexico—despite NAFTA's catastrophic impact on the air and water in the border regions.

"I understand why people are coming [to America], family values do not stop at the Rio Grande River. If you're a mother or dad in

Mexico and you've got mouths to feed and you hear there is good work in a state, and you are going to come to feed your children, it's part of loving a child. It's part of what it means to be a mother or dad. And that's why I'm such a strong backer of trade with Mexico and trade in our hemisphere."

—*LARRY KING LIVE*, CNN, SEPTEMBER 26, 2000

"I'm honored. . . . He understands our belief in free trade. He understands I want to ensure our relationship with our most important neighbor to the north of us, Canadians, is strong."

—*WALL STREET JOURNAL*, MARCH 3, 2000

Here Bush was referring to "Prime Minister Jean Poutine," who, according to a humorous questioner, had just endorsed the governor's campaign. "Poutine" was not prime minister of Canada, however, but a hearty French Canadian lunch of french fries, cheese curds, and gravy.

"Discussing terrorism and other foreign threats, Bush vowed to 'use our technology to enhance uncertainties abroad.' "

—*NEW YORK TIMES*, MARCH 6, 2000

"Oh. I thought you said 'some band.' The Taliban in Afghanistan! Absolutely. Repressive."　　　　　—*GLAMOUR*, JUNE 2000

This was a reply to a question in another journalistic pop quiz. When asked about the Taliban, Bush shook his head and stood there mute until the reporter hinted: "repression of women in Afghanistan . . . ?"

"The fundamental question is, Will I be a successful president when it comes to foreign policy? I will be, but until I'm the president, it's going to be hard for me to verify that I think I'll be more effective."   —*NEW YORK TIMES,* JUNE 28, 2000

"We'll let our friends be the peacekeepers and the great country called America will be the pacemakers."

—HOUSTON, TEXAS, SEPTEMBER 6, 2000; *SLATE*

"I will have a foreign-handed foreign policy."

—REDWOOD, CALIFORNIA, SEPTEMBER 27, 2000; *SLATE*

"A key to foreign policy is to rely on reliance."

—*WASHINGTON POST,* NOVEMBER 1, 2000

Among friends—as he believed he was when chatting with the Weekly Standard's Tucker Carlson—Bush took a different tone on foreign policy, casually conceding his bone-ignorance of basic information.

"Nobody needs to tell me what I believe. But I do need somebody to tell me where Kosovo is."   —*TALK,* SEPTEMBER 1999

BA-DA-BOOM!

As he did with many other of his weaknesses, Bush eventually defused the issue of his global ignorance by playing it for self-effacing laughs.

"[W]e just had some really good news out of Yugoslavia. I'm especially pleased that Mr. Milosevic has stepped down. That's one less Polyslavic name for me to remember."

—AL SMITH MEMORIAL DINNER, NEW YORK, OCTOBER 19, 2000

AT THE HELM

"It's about past seven in the evening here, so we're actually in different time lines."   —*NEW YORK TIMES,* JANUARY 30, 2001

President Bush, in Washington, was speaking on the telephone to Gloria Macapagal Arroyos, the new president of the Philippines, in her office in Manila.

At his joint press conference with British prime minister Tony Blair:

Q: A question for both of you: There's been a lot said about how different you are as people. Have you already in your talks found something maybe that you—some personal interests that you have in common, maybe in religion or sport or music?

BUSH: We both use Colgate toothpaste.

—*AP ONLINE,* FEBRUARY 23, 2001

A few weeks later, the president met with South Korean president Kim Dae Jung, who had lately won the Nobel Peace Prize for his efforts to stabilize relations with his northern neighbor. Bush dealt Kim's hopes a heavy blow by making clear that he did not intend to maintain the Clinton policy of missile talks with North Korea. The patent flimsiness of his excuse was further evidence that he and his cabal prefer that North Korea be "our" enemy so as to justify more big spending on missile defense and other costly chunks of pie-in-the-sky.

"Today Mr. Bush made it clear that he had little intention of following Mr. Clinton's path, at least not now. In a brief exchange with reporters after meeting Mr. Kim in the Oval Office, Mr. Bush said: 'We're not certain as to whether or not they're keeping all terms of all agreements.'

"But the United States has only one agreement with North Korea—the 1994 accord that froze North Korea's plutonium processing at a suspected nuclear weapons plant. And at a briefing this afternoon two senior administration officials, asked about the president's statement, said there was no evidence that North Korea is violating its terms.

"Later, a White House spokesman said that Mr. Bush was referring to his concern about whether the North would comply with future accords, even though he did not use the future tense. 'That's how the president speaks,' the official said."

—*NEW YORK TIMES,* MARCH 8, 2001

Commander in Chief

Ellington AFB, Tex., March 24, 1970—George Walker Bush is one member of the younger generation who doesn't get his kicks from pot or hashish or speed. Oh, he gets high all right, but not from narcotics. . . . Lt. Bush, who is 23, is due to complete his pilot training June 23. He will then be released from active duty and assume reserve status in the Air National Guard. He plans to fly as much as possible with the Air Guard and work in his father's campaign. Beyond that, he hasn't any plans.

As far as kicks are concerned, Lt. Bush gets his from the roaring afterburner of the F-102.

"Flying, the whole thing, is kicks," he said. "But afterburner is the real kick."

—PRESS RELEASE, OFFICE OF INFORMATION, TEXAS AIR
NATIONAL GUARD; QUOTED IN MINUTAGLIO,
FIRST SON, PP. 130–31

In 1968, Bush was slipped into the Texas Air National Guard, joining the 147th Fighter Wing—"the Champagne Unit," as it was later known, because of all the wealthy young Houstonians whom it kept Stateside during the war in Vietnam. Promoted, in just a few months, to second lieutenant (an extraordinary rise), Bush went on to have a lot of fun, first in training at Moody Air Force Base in Georgia, then at Ellington Air Force Base near Houston. His buddies liked him ("He was a real

*outgoing guy," remembers one), and the system pampered him, prizing his A-1 con-
nections to the top.*[84] *He had the glamour of a VIP and was allowed to go on leave
for many a political assignment—helping out the GOP's congressional campaigns
in Florida and Alabama, and dating Tricia Nixon at her dad's request. (That happened only once.)*

*However, Bush's military service offered more than space for partying and time
for politicking. Our future leader learned to be an able pilot, mastering the F-102
Interceptor that the guard used for training purposes (and which was being phased
out of use in Vietnam). This was no mean feat, as Bush himself would later on remind the voters—or try to. "I'm not suggesting I was any great war hero, but I want
you to know that flying F-102 fighters, putting the thing in afterburner at the end
of a runway, was something other than not being a part of the military," he said at
one point, in what may be the most anticlimactic statement in the history of military reminiscence.*[85]

*While Bush did learn to fly, however, his military service evidently taught him
very little about strategic thinking* off *the campaign trail. Although trained as a potential officer, Bush came away unable to articulate the simplest doctrine—such as,
for example, the concept of deterrence that he tried repeatedly to propagate throughout the presidential race.*

*The concept is a valid and important one, and now and then Bush did phrase
it with the necessary clarity:*

> "I'm worried about the fact that our mission is not clear. It ought to
> be to have a military that's properly trained and equipped to be able
> to fight and win war, and, therefore, prevent war from happening in
> the first place."
>
> —CAMPAIGN SPEECH IN MICHIGAN; FEDERAL NEWS SERVICE,
> NOVEMBER 3, 2000

*The crucial phrase there is "be able to fight"—the military's blatant readiness and
might inhibiting attack themselves, as the mere presence of well-muscled bouncers will
discourage brawls in nightclubs. For the most part, Bush just could not get it straight,
his garbled comments casting the ability to fight—the key component of the whole*

equation—as secondary. This had him repeatedly saying that you deter war best by fighting it—a proposition that he made in several slightly different ways.

For example, the military's proper mission is to fight wars and be capable of winning them, which will deter them:

> "The mission of the military is to fight and be able to win war, and therefore prevent war from happening in the first place."
>
> —GOP DEBATE, FEBRUARY 15, 2000

Or maybe it's the military's double job to fight and win wars and also be able—somehow—to prevent them from occurring:

> "The purpose of the military is to fight and win war. And to be able to deter war."   —NEW HAMPSHIRE GOP DEBATE, JANUARY 6, 2000

On the other hand, it could be the purpose of our military to deter wars by reversing the old-fashioned formula of fight and win:

> "We ought to have a commander in chief who understands how to earn the respect of the military, by setting a clear mission, which is to win and fight war, and therefore deter war."
>
> —THIS WEEK, ABC, JANUARY 23, 2000

Since the basic point of all such statements was to underscore the need for a "clear mission," Bush's muddy utterances were not too promising. In any case, the doctrine as he mostly put it—deterring war by fighting it—is logically absurd (and morally untenable), a mere restatement of the slogan "Kill for Peace," which the Fugs once sang, satirically.

And yet this quibbling is irrelevant; for, in making all such statements, Bush's aim throughout the race was not to offer a coherent military policy but simply "to earn the respect of the military," as that last entry puts it. In short, his purpose was, as usual, political: Win the soldiers' votes, and reassure the Pentagon and weapons manufacturers that he meant business—literally. As his early presidential actions have made obvious, Bush's military vision is based wholly on the drive by those great interests to commit the nation to the costliest, and looniest, of weapons systems: a "missile shield," and, later, other giant space-based novelties. Defense Secretary Donald Rumsfeld has long championed that Reagan-era program—as has Lockheed Martin, the defense contractor closest to this White House and the GOP in general.

Bush's statements on the military "theme" betrayed no knowledge of or interest in the pertinent issues, despite the tutelage of Condoleezza Rice. His only aims appeared to be the demonstration of his deference to the Pentagon and the frequent venting of alarmist rhetoric of the sort that helps to grow the military budget. (For his part, Al Gore spoke more expertly, but just as deferentially, straining to out-hawk the jut-jawed W, arguing that he would raise the military budget even higher and retrospectively saluting the preposterous invasions of Grenada and Panama.) On other matters, Bush showed his usual disengagement.

BUSH:	I am for "Don't ask, don't tell." This is a policy that Colin Powell thoughtfully put in place—
ROWLAND EVANS:	That's the Clinton policy.
BUSH:	Well, if that's the Clinton policy, I support that.

—CNN, AUGUST 14, 1999

KOSOVO

"Uh, I support winning. And, uh, the strategy must—America must be slow to engage militarily, but once we engage, we must do so to win."

—*INSIDE POLITICS,* CNN, APRIL 7, 1999

"That's dependent upon the military advisers that would be advising me."

—ON WHETHER HE WOULD HAVE DEPLOYED TROOPS IN KOSOVO; *AP ONLINE,* MAY 28, 1999

NUCLEAR WEAPONS

"That's going to depend upon generals helping me make that decision, Tim."

> —ON THE ACCEPTABLE LEVEL OF NUCLEAR WEAPONS
> FOR BOTH THE U.S. AND RUSSIA; *MEET THE PRESS,* NBC,
> NOVEMBER 21, 1999

"That depends upon my advisers and the people who know a heck
of a lot more about the subject than I do."

> —ON WHETHER, IN THE START II TALKS,
> HE WOULD DECREASE THE NUMBER OF
> NUCLEAR WARHEADS TO ONE THOUSAND; IBID.

"My point is, is that I want America to lead the nation—lead the
world—toward a more safe world when it comes to nuclear
weaponry."   —*NEW YORK TIMES,* JANUARY 27, 2000

"A WORLD OF MADMEN"

"This is still a dangerous world. It's a world of madmen and uncer-
tainty and potential mential losses [*sic*]."

> —*FINANCIAL TIMES,* JANUARY 14, 2000

*That assertion, made at a well-attended oyster roast in South Carolina, evidently
mystified all hands: "Bush's spokespeople could not immediately explain what a
mential loss was, but it seemed only distantly related to missile launches," the* Financial Times *reporter wrote.*

" 'When I was coming up, it was a dangerous world, and you knew
exactly who they were,' he said. 'It was us versus them, and it was

clear who them was. Today, we are not so sure who the they are, but we know they're there.' "

—IOWA WESTERN COMMUNITY COLLEGE,
JANUARY 21, 2000; *SLATE*

"This is a world that is much more uncertain than the past. In the past we were certain, we were certain it was us versus the Russians in the past. We were certain, and therefore we had huge nuclear arsenals aimed at each other to keep the peace. That's what we were certain of. . . . You see, even though it's an uncertain world, we're certain of some things. We're certain that even though the 'evil empire' may have passed, evil still remains. We're certain there are people that can't stand what America stands for. . . . We're certain there are madmen in this world, and there's terror, and there's missiles, and I'm certain of this, too: I'm certain to maintain the peace, we better have a military of high morale, and I'm certain that under this administration, morale in the military is dangerously low."

—ALBUQUERQUE, NEW MEXICO; *WASHINGTON POST,*
MAY 31, 2000

"We cannot let terrorists and rogue nations hold this nation hostile or hold our allies hostile."   —IOWA, AUGUST 21, 2000; *SLATE*

"I don't want nations feeling like that they can bully ourselves and our allies. I want to have a ballistic defense system so that we can make the world more peaceful, and at the same time I want to reduce our own nuclear capacities to the level commiserate with keeping the peace."

—DES MOINES, IOWA, OCTOBER 23, 2000; *SLATE*

CHARLIE ROSE: OK. What if you thought Saddam Hussein, using the absence of inspectors, was close to acquiring a nuclear weapon?

BUSH:	He'd pay a price.
ROSE:	What's the price?
BUSH:	The price is force, the full force and fury of a re-action.
ROSE:	Bombs away?
BUSH:	You can just figure that out after it happens.

—*READERS DIGEST ONLINE,* AUGUST 2000

TOM BROKAW: Governor Bush, you have said that you supported the idea of rejecting the test ban treaty, and you want to build a missile defense system. If you were the president—if you were Pres. Jiang Zemin in China, or you were Pres. Boris Yeltsin in Russia, wouldn't you be saying to your military personnel, and to your scientists, "They want to start it up again. We've got to do everything that we can to go on a hair trigger. And we've got to expand our own nuclear arsenal"?

BUSH: No, they'd be hearing a different message. They'd be hearing a message that the United States is a peaceful nation—that we intend to keep the peace. But we're not going to sit by and allow rogue nations to hold any of our friends hostage. That we're not going to allow for accidental launches. And we've got the technology necessary to keep the peace.

Mr. Yeltsin will hear from President Bush that "I intend to give you a chance to join us in the development of theater- based and national antiballistic missile systems. But after a short period of time, if you choose not to, we'll withdraw from the treaty." Because we're a peaceful nation.

But we're not going to miss an opportunity, Tom, if I'm the president, to say to our friends and allies, "We're going to provide a shield so you

won't be blackmailed." We're going to say to our
friends, the Israelis, "We'll provide you a shield
and work with you, so you won't become blackmailed by Iranians or Iraqis."

No, our country must not retreat. We must not
worry about what the Russians and Chinese
think. What we need to do is lead the world to
peace. And that's exactly the kind of president I
intend to be.

—GOP DEBATE, DES MOINES, IOWA,
DECEMBER 13, 1999

MEANWHILE, BACK ON
PLANET EARTH . . .

"That's Washington. That's the place where you find people getting
ready to jump out of the foxholes before the first shot is fired."
—WESTLAND, MICHIGAN, SEPTEMBER 8, 2000; *SLATE*

*As an airman, Lieutenant Bush had no need to be taught that nervous ground
troops don't jump out of foxholes just before the shooting starts—unless they've lost
their minds.*

AT THE HELM

"In another clear reversal of a campaign promise, President Bush
reportedly plans to slash fiscal year 2002 Department of Energy
funding for nonproliferation programs with Russia.

"During his campaign, Bush supported threat reduction (Nunn-
Lugar) programs, stating in November 19, 1999, 'I will ask the
Congress to increase substantially our assistance to dismantle as many
of Russia's weapons as possible as quickly as possible.'

"While the budget for the DOE nonproliferation programs was

slated to reach $1.2 billion in fiscal 2002, Bush instead plans to cut funding to $800 million from $872 million.

★★The Materials Protection, Control, and Accounting (MPC&A) program, which improves physical security at Russian nuclear weapons facilities, will reportedly lose $31 million.

★★The Nuclear Cities Initiative, a program to prevent Russian "brain drain" by creating civilian jobs for weapon scientists at "closed" nuclear cities, is slated to lose $20 million.

★★A program to help Russia dispose of its excess weapons-grade plutonium will receive a small increase, but far less than the doubling of funds that was expected.

"These and related programs run by the Defense and State departments reduce U.S. security threats posed by Russia's Cold War nuclear 'leftovers'—more than 22,000 nuclear weapons, 1,000 metric tons of highly enriched uranium, and 150 metric tons of plutonium. The materials are stored in low security facilities and are susceptible to theft or sale to hostile countries or terrorists.

" 'The reversal represents a stunning retreat from campaign pledges and a serious blow to U.S. security,' said John Isaacs, President of Council for a Livable World. 'President Bush must be breathing too much carbon dioxide.' added Isaacs."

—PRESS RELEASE, COUNCIL FOR A LIVABLE WORLD

EDUCATION FUND, MARCH 16, 2001

It's the Economy,
Your Excellency

I don't care what the polls say [about economics]. I don't. I'm doing
what I think what's wrong.

—*NEW YORK TIMES,* MARCH 15, 2000

"[E]ntrepreneurship equals freedom."

—*NATIONAL JOURNAL,* AUGUST 7, 1999

"It's clearly a budget. It's got a lot of numbers in it."

—REUTERS, MAY 5, 2000

"The best way to relieve families from time is to let them keep some
of their own money."

—WESTMINSTER, CALIFORNIA, SEPTEMBER 13, 2000; *SLATE*

"It's your money. You paid for it."

—LACROSSE, WISCONSIN, OCTOBER 18, 2000; *SLATE*

In the event of a global financial crisis:

"I would have my secretary of treasury be in touch with the financial centers not only here but at home."
—PRESIDENTIAL DEBATE, BOSTON, OCTOBER 3, 2000

"I mean, these good folks are revolutionizing how businesses conduct their business. And, like them, I am very optimistic about our position in the world and about its influence on the United States. We're concerned about the short-term economic news, but long term I'm optimistic. And so, I hope investors, you know—secondly, I hope investors hold investments for periods of time—that I've always found the best investments are those that you salt away based on economics."
—AUSTIN, TEXAS, JANUARY 4, 2001; FEDERAL NEWS SERVICE

BRING ME YOUR TIRED, YOUR RICH

On the subject of economics, Bush's choicest gaffes were evidence not of stupidity but of a rich kid's utter insincerity. Repeatedly, in trying to communicate how much he cared about the poor and middle-class, he would mangle the attempt as surely as his father did before him. This Bush, however, did not use inappropriate upscale locutions like "a splash of coffee" but simply burst into illiterate howlers that betrayed the awful truth.

"I know how hard it is for you to put food on your family."
—GREATER NASHUA, NEW HAMPSHIRE, JANUARY 27, 2000

(It was also in the downscale setting of New Hampshire that Bush Sr. had announced, "Message: I care.")

"I understand small business growth. I was one."
—*NEW YORK DAILY NEWS,* FEBRUARY 19, 2000

"This campaign not only hears the voices of the entrepreneurs and the farmers and the entrepreneurs, we hear the voices of those struggling to get ahead." —DES MOINES, AUGUST 21, 2000; *SLATE*

"One of the features in my plan, John, says to the single mom with two children making forty thousand dollars a year, you get a 53 percent tax cut. For single moms with children who make less than forty thousand a year get—get bigger tax cuts. My question to you is, in reviewing of your plan, that single mom with children—two children, making forty thousand—get no tax cut. And I'm wondering why." —GOP DEBATE, DES MOINES, DECEMBER 13, 1999

In this question to John McCain, the governor—as usual—had trouble credibly envisioning a family in straitened circumstances. Either those "two kids" have excellent part-time jobs, or they get quite a nice allowance from their "single mom." In any case, the governor made clear, those children ought to get a tax cut.

Bush's inability to take a walk in someone else's modest shoes was once again apparent in the third presidential debate, when a woman named Lisa Key asked him about his tax plan.

KEY: How will your tax proposals affect me as a middle-class, twenty-four-year-old single person with no dependents?

BUSH: . . . You're going to get tax relief under my plan. You're not going to be targeted in or targeted out. Everybody who pays taxes is going to get tax relief. If you take care of an elderly in your home, you're going to get the personal exemption increased.

I think also what you need to think about is not the immediate, but what about Medicare? You get a plan that will include prescription drugs, a plan that will give you options. Now, I hope people understand that Medicare today is important, but it doesn't keep up with the new medicines. If you're a Medicare person, on Medicare you don't get the new procedures. You're stuck in a time warp in many ways. So it'll be a modern Medicare system that trusts you to make a variety of options for you.

You're going to live in a peaceful world. It'll be a world of peace because we're going to have a clearer, clear-sighted foreign policy based upon a strong military and a mission that stands by our friends, a mission that doesn't try to be all things to all people, a judicious use of the military which'll help keep the peace.

You'll be in a world hopefully that's more educated, so it's less likely you'll be harmed in your neighborhood, seeing an educated child is one much more likely to be hopeful and optimistic.

You'll be in a world in which fits into my philosophy [sic]: you know, the harder work—the harder you work, the more you can keep. That's the American way. Government shouldn't be a heavy hand. That's what the federal government does to you. It should be a helping hand. And tax relief in the proposals I just described should be a good helping hand.

—PRESIDENTIAL DEBATE, OCTOBER 17, 2000

SOCIAL SECURITY

On the coming crisis:

"There's not going to be enough people in the system to take advantage of people like me."

—WILTON, CONNECTICUT, JUNE 9, 2000; *SLATE*

This gaffe was another inadvertent truth from Bush's "heart," since it betrayed the plutocratic view that Social Security is just a socialistic burden on the rich—the many "people in the system" being allowed by Washington "to take advantage of people like me"—i.e., multimillionaires.

On whether Social Security recipients would, under his plan, receive the same benefits as they did under the present system:

"Maybe, maybe not."   —*WASHINGTON POST,* NOVEMBER 1, 2000

"Bush said he has 'ruled out no new Social Security taxes.' "
                        —*WASHINGTON POST,* OCTOBER 1, 2000

Bush meant to say that he had ruled out new Social Security taxes.

"They want the federal government controlling Social Security like it's some kind of federal program."
                        —*USA TODAY,* NOVEMBER 3, 2000

TAXATION

"I think we need not only to eliminate the tollbooth to the middle class, I think we should knock down the tollbooth."
                        —NASHUA, NEW HAMPSHIRE, *NEW YORK TIMES*
                        (GAIL COLLINS), FEBRUARY 1, 2000

"It is not Reaganesque to support a tax plan that is Clinton in nature."
                        —LOS ANGELES, FEBRUARY 23, 2000; *SLATE*

"A tax cut is really one of the anecdotes to coming out of an economic illness."

    —*THE EDGE WITH PAULA ZAHN,* CBS, SEPTEMBER 18, 2000

LARRY KING: [Gore] said: If you lopped off the top 1 percent
        that you are giving tax relief . . . you could pay for
        the cost of every other program.

BUSH: Oh, I don't—you know, I hadn't—I'm not so sure.
        I'm not quick in my mind at math, but I don't believe in trying to pick and choose winners when it
        comes to tax relief.

    —*LARRY KING LIVE,* CNN, SEPTEMBER 26, 2000

"It's going to require numerous IRA agents."

    —*HOUSTON CHRONICLE,* OCTOBER 15, 2000

The governor was referring to Gore's tax plan and the huge new bureaucracy it would create, somewhere in Dublin.

"Mr. Vice President, in all due respect, it is—I'm not sure 80 percent of the people get the death tax. I know this: 100 percent will get it if I'm the president."   —PRESIDENTIAL DEBATE, OCTOBER 17, 2000

BUT SERIOUSLY, FOLKS . . .

"[M]y opponent keeps saying I give too much tax relief to the top 1 percent, but he hadn't heard my latest proposal. The bottom 99 percent will do well when they get to split Dick Cheney's stock options."

        [Laughter]

    —AL SMITH MEMORIAL DINNER IN NEW YORK,

        OCTOBER 19, 2000

"At one point, Bush thundered that Mr. Gore believes that the federal surplus 'is the people's money.' He meant to say that Mr. Gore considers the surplus the 'government's money.' But he took his mix-up in stride and paraphrased Ronald Reagan to laugh at himself. 'Excuse me,' he said, 'There I go again,' and the crowd lapped it up.

—*NEW YORK TIMES,* OCTOBER 31, 2000

AT THE HELM

"A lobbying campaign led by credit card companies and banks that gave millions of dollars in political donations to members of Congress and contributed generously to President Bush's 2000 campaign is close to its long- sought goal of overhauling the nation's bankruptcy system.

"Legislation that would make it harder for people to wipe out their debts could be passed by the Senate as early as this week. The bill has already been approved by the House, and Mr. Bush has pledged to sign it.

"Sponsors of the bill acknowledge that lawyers and lobbyists for the banks and credit card companies were involved in drafting it.★ The bill gives those industries most of what they have wanted since they began lobbying in earnest in the late 1990's, when the number of personal bankruptcies rose to record levels. . . .

"Consumer groups describe the bill as a gift to credit card companies and banks in exchange for their political largess, and they complain that the bill does nothing to stop abuses by creditors who

---

★"Among the biggest beneficiaries of the measure would be MBNA Corporation of Delaware, which describes itself as the world's biggest independent credit card company. Ranked by employee donations, MBNA was the largest corporate contributor to the Bush campaign, according to a study by the Center for Responsive Politics, an election research group.

"MBNA's employees and their families contributed about $240,000 to Mr. Bush, and the chairman of the company's bank unit, Charles M. Cawley, was a significant fund-raiser for Mr. Bush and gave a $1,000-a-plate dinner in his honor, the center said. After Mr. Bush's election, MBNA pledged $100,000 to help pay for inaugural festivities." *New York Times,* March 13, 2001.

flood the mail with solicitations for high-interest credit cards and loans, which in turn help drive many vulnerable people into bankruptcy.

" 'This bill is the credit card industry's wish list,' said Elizabeth Warren, a Harvard law professor who is a bankruptcy specialist. 'They've hired every lobbying firm in Washington. They've decided that it's time to lock the doors to the bankruptcy courthouse.' "

—*NEW YORK TIMES,* MARCH 13, 2001

The Nation's Health

"For those that are uninsured, many of the uninsured are able-bodied, capable people capable of buying insurance choose not to do so."

—INTERVIEW IN MANCHESTER, NEW HAMPSHIRE,
WITH WMUR, NOVEMBER 10, 1999

Tim Russert asked Bush if he would support a person's right to sue his or her HMO. Bush's yes turned out to be a tacit no, but seeing this required your careful concentration.

BUSH: Yes.

RUSSERT: Republicans in Congress don't like that. They voted three to one against it.

BUSH: I think it's important for people to have access to the courts of law if, in fact, there is a—if, in fact, once they have had an opportunity to have their claims heard, and if the findings of the arbitration panel, called an "independent review organization," are ignored, there ought be a cause of action. People ought to have some kind of access to express their concerns, both in an arbitration panel, and, ultimately, in the courts.

       Listen, I'm a tort reformer. I've fought for tort

reform in the state of Texas. I signed seven pieces of major tort legislation because our civil justice system was unfair.

—*MEET THE PRESS,* NBC, NOVEMBER 21, 1999

"I'm sorry. I wish I could wave a wand."

—*NEW YORK TIMES,* FEBRUARY 18, 2000

Such was the governor's compassionate response to a mother who had asked him how he planned to deal with cases like her own. a son with a chronic, life-threatening illness and a medical insurance plan that would not cover the expenses of his care. Although she had asked the candidate to talk about his policy on health insurance, he replied as if she'd asked him for a handout.

"I don't know the statistics he's using, but I do know that there's a lot of women who are covered."

—*60 MINUTES II,* CBS, MARCH 7, 2000

The governor had just been asked if Al Gore was correct in saying that Texas ranked forty-ninth among the fifty states for the number of its female residents with health-care coverage.

DAN RATHER: Al Gore has said that in Texas, where you're governor, that, among women with health care, Texas ranks number forty-ninth, children with health insurance ranks number fifty. Is that true, and what does this tell us about your governorship?

BUSH: Well, I think you can kind—find all kinds of statistics to make all kinds of cases. I rest my—I rest most of my case on the fact that people in Texas like the job I have done.   —IBID.

"Well, there'll be a health-care debate, and there'll be a health-care issue that I'm going to—I mean, a health-care speech and policy that I lay out. I talk about health care all the time at these one on ones when asked. It's on people's minds."

—CNN INTERVIEW, MARCH 8, 2000

"We will promote individual choice. We will rely on private insurance."   —FOX NEWS REPORT, APRIL 11, 2000

"I don't think we need to be subliminable about the differences between our views on prescription drugs."

—ORLANDO, FLORIDA, SEPTEMBER 12, 2000; *SLATE*

"FUZZY MATH"

GORE: Some people who say the word "reform" actually mean "cuts." Under the governor's plan, if you kept the same fee for service that you have now under Medicare, your premiums would go up by between 18 and 47 percent—and that's the study of the congressional plan that he's modeled his proposal on, [the study] by the Medicare actuaries.

Let me just give you one quick example. There's a man here tonight named George McKinney from Milwaukee. He's seventy years old. He has high blood pressure. His wife has heart trouble. They have income of twenty-five thousand dollars a year. They cannot pay for their prescription drugs. And so they're some of the ones that go to Canada regularly in order to get their prescription drugs.

Under my plan, half of their costs would be

paid right away. Under Governor Bush's plan, they
would get not one penny for four to five years,
and then they would be forced to go into an
HMO or to an insurance company and ask them
for coverage. But there'd be no limit on the premiums or the deductibles or any of the terms and
conditions.

BUSH: I cannot let this go by—the old-style Washington
politics of, "We're going to scare you in the voting
booth." Under my plan, the man gets immediate
help with prescription drugs. It's called "immediate helping hand." Instead of squabbling and
finger-pointing, he gets immediate help.
Let me say something. Now I understand—

JIM LEHRER: Excuse me, Governor.

GORE: Jim, can I—

LEHRER: All right, three and a half minutes is up. But we'll—

GORE: Could I make one other point?

BUSH: Wait a minute.

GORE: They get twenty-five thousand a year income.
That makes them ineligible.

BUSH: Look, this is a man, he's got great numbers. He
talks about numbers. I'm beginning to think not
only did he invent the Internet, but he invented
the calculator.
    It's fuzzy math. It's a scaring—trying to scare
people in the voting booth. Under my tax plan,
that he continues to criticize, I set a third—the
federal government should take no more than a
third of anybody's check. But I also drop the bottom rate from 15 percent to 10 percent because by
far the vast majority of the help goes to the people
at the bottom end of the economic ladder. If
you're a family of four in Massachusetts making
fifty-thousand dollars you get a 50 percent cut in

the federal income taxes you pay. It's from four thousand to about two thousand.

Now, the difference in our plans is, I want that two thousand dollars to go to you, and the vice president would like to be spending the two thousand on your behalf.

—PRESIDENTIAL DEBATE, OCTOBER 3, 2000

Bush's rhetoric was fuzzier by far than Al Gore's math. Rather than rebut Gore's claims—or even deny them—Bush simply changed the subject from his Medicare proposal to his tax plan, which he then defended by relying on a riff he knew by heart.

"Drug therapies are replacing a lot of medicines as we used to know it."   —PRESIDENTIAL DEBATE, OCTOBER 17, 2000

"It's one thing about insurance, that's a Washington term."

—PRESIDENTIAL DEBATE, OCTOBER 17, 2000

"If I'm the president, we're going to have emergency room care, we're going to have gag orders, women will have direct access to OB-GYN."   —PRESIDENTIAL DEBATE, OCTOBER 17, 2000

"And, folks, it's important we get this right because we're a compassionate nation. We're a nation that says, when somebody cannot help themselves, we will as a government. We're a nation that says, anytime anybody has to choose between food and medicine: 'That's not right. That's not our vision of America. That's not what America's all about as far as we're concerned.'

[*Applause*]

"So one of our priorities is to say to Congress, both Republicans and Democrats, 'Let's solve this problem. Let's make sure prescription drugs are a part of the Medicare plan for every senior. Let's help the poorest of seniors be able to afford the medicines of the future. Let's give people options in the Medicare program. Let's trust seniors to be able to make decisions about what's best for them.'

"Now, I know there's a lot of talk about Medicare, and you've heard the debates about spending this money here and that money there, and this plan here and that plan there. It's got to be kind of confusing to some, and I understand that.

"But one thing they can't run and hide from is this fact: In 1992, they crossed our country—'they' being my opponent and his friend, our president. They crossed our country and they said: 'Oh, just give us a chance. We'll do something on Medicare.' And you may remember, in 1996, they had to say it again. And here we are now, eight years after the initial promise was made, and they're still saying it!'

"And the message of this campaign is, 'We're tired.' [*sic*] The vice president says, 'You ain't seen nothing yet.' Well, he's right. We haven't seen anything yet!

[*Applause*]

"This campaign is sending a clear message. It's a clear message. Leadership is going to bring people together to solve this important problem. That's what a leader does, is solve problems:

"*We're* not going to use Medicare as a political issue! It's time to put that kind of thinking aside!"

—KALAMAZOO, MICHIGAN, OCTOBER 27, 2000;
FCDH POLITICAL TRANSCRIPTS

The Color Line

Herein lie buried many things which if read with patience may show the strange meaning of being black here in the dawning of the Twentieth Century. This meaning is not without interest to you, Gentle Reader; for the problem of the Twentieth Century is the problem of the color-line.

—W. E. B. DUBOIS, *THE SOULS OF BLACK FOLK*

"The color-line" observed by the exact DuBois is surely just as grave a problem as it was a century ago. It is, however, also harder to perceive than it was then—in part because of the disarming "color line" deployed today by politicians of the right. By putting on big multicolored shows of "tolerance," the GOP misrepresents itself—the party of Strom Thurmond, Trent Lott, Bob Barr, Rush Limbaugh, William Rehnquist, David Duke, and Bob Jones University thereby appearing as if somehow dedicated to the same ideal of racial justice that they all have worked against for years. Thus they hand Americans, and black Americans in particular, a "color line" the way a deft seducer will assure some foxy feminist that he believes in women's rights and always has.

At such salesmanship our president works hard—as he has had to do, since in the realm of race relations he has so much to hide, not only in the GOP but in his own background. His "victory" in Florida—an upset based directly on the systematic racial profiling of that state's voters (see p. 275)—was but the climax of a personal history replete with hints of (let us call it) Southern comfort. The Skull and Bones connection, for example, doesn't augur well for Bush's sensitivity on race. In his day, Bonesman Prescott Bush, our president's grandfather, reportedly dug up Geronimo's grave and snatched the warrior's skull, which they say is still hidden in the club's dark monolithic quarters on Yale's campus, along with other Indian re-mains. (The story was reported by Ron Rosenbaum.) According to the Greenwich Village Gazette, *moreover, the ghastly treasures kept inside the Skull and Bones retreat reportedly include a set of Hitler's silverware, which the initiates are said to dine with once a year—a fixed tradition by the time George W. Bush became a mem-ber back in 1964.*[86]

Although such tales cannot be verified beyond a shadow of a doubt—although no Bonesman will deny them outright—there is abundant further evidence of Bush's lifelong blindness toward racism. Although not as lurid, the evidence is just as un-encouraging as those Gothic rumors. First of all, there is Bush's absolute oblivious-ness to the fact of racial segregation in the Midland of his childhood, which is thus idyllically described on page 18 of his campaign autobiography, A Charge to Keep:

> Midland was a small town, with small-town values. We learned to respect our elders, to do what they said, and to be good neighbors. We went to church. Families spent time together, outside, the grown-ups talking with neighbors while the kids played ball or with marbles and yo-yos. Our homework and schoolwork were important. The town's leading citizens worked hard to attract the best teachers to our schools. No one locked their doors, because you could trust your friends and neighbors. It was a happy childhood. I was surrounded by love and friends and sports.

That glimpse of paradise does not reveal—except between the lines—that Midland was a wealthy compound for whites only. The city's affluence is ably hidden by those Norman Rockell touches: "small-town values," "marbles" and "yo-yos" do not quite square with "country club," although the privileged kids there all belonged to one. Likewise, the passage's hypnotic emphasis on "neighbors" leads us to forget, or not to think, that Midland was a little Eden strictly segregated. The few black peo-ple there were menials. "The blacks couldn't wear dress clothes going downtown, only overalls or a uniform," recalls Otha Taylor, the Bushes' black maid, who minded lit-tle George, Jeb, Neil, and Marvin from 1958.[87] *There is no known instance of the eldest Bush boy ever mentioning that he grew up in a de facto state of apartheid—*

a lifelong silence that suggests that the arrangement didn't bother him, assuming that he even noticed it.

As governor of Texas, Bush demonstrated that his comfort zone with white supremacy is just about as big as all outdoors. For instance, in November 1999—when he was in full gallop toward the White House—Bush made Charles Williams, police chief in the town of Marshall, chairman of the Texas Commission on Law Enforcement Standards and Education. It was a curious choice for such a post, especially in light of Bush's own embrace of "education" as his main concern. A year before his elevation, Williams testified, in a discrimination lawsuit, that the epithets "porch monkey" and "black bastard" are not offensive. "If it's a general statement, no, I don't consider it a racial slur," he said in deposition. He has not modified that view. "You just have to show me where it's a racial slur. It just depends on how it's used and who it's used toward," he told the Associated Press in April 2000. Bush showed the same peculiar tolerance of racist ideology when he appointed Dr. William "Reyn" Archer (son of Representative Bill Archer, GOP powerhouse) as a state health commissioner. In 1998 Dr. Archer gave a speech in which he claimed that blacks value loyalty far more than honesty (unlike Republicans) and that they "don't buy" civilized arrangements such as marriage. Dr. Archer later made more waves when he suggested that the state's high rates of teenage pregnancy reflect a powerful Hispanic yen for having babies. By nature, the commissioner suggested, Texas's Chicano citizens are disinclined to feel that "getting pregnant is a bad thing" and so they just keep reproducing, wed or not.[88]

Bush's friends insist that there is not a biased bone in his whole body, just as he himself has often advertised his "heart" as innocent of all such nastiness. If true, it is beside the point. Far more damaging than his promotions of unreconstructed white supremacists or his refusal to condemn the use of the Confederate flag in South Carolina or his mating dance with Pat Buchanan was his extraordinary stewardship of the Texas criminal justice system—the busiest outpost of a larger national system that vastly overconcentrates on African-Americans.

The statistics are astonishing. As governor, Bush came to oversee, in Molly Ivins's words, "the largest prison system on the planet Earth." According to a study published in August 2000 by the Justice Policy Institute in Washington, D.C., Texas—population 20 million—has over 163,000 of its citizens in jail, with well over 700,000 under some form of juridical control. With one out of every twenty of the state's adults in prison, on parole, or on probation, Texas can account for one-

fifth of all the people jailed throughout the nation in the 1990s. For every 100,000 of its citizens, Texas has 700 behind bars—248 more than the national average. If Texas were a separate country, the JPI concluded, "it would have a higher incarceration rate than Russia, China, the United States, and the rest of the industrialized and nonindustrialized world."

Such are the results, in Texas, of the nation's "drug war"—which is in fact a race war waged by legal means. Although 72 percent of all illicit drug users are white and only 15 percent black, African-Americans account for 36.8 percent of those arrested on drug charges, constituting 42 percent of those held in federal prisons for narcotics and nearly 60 percent of those held in state jails. In the 1990s the number of black inmates busted for narcotics increased by 60 percent, while that of whites increased by 46 percent. In state courts, white drug users are less likely to do time than blacks, with 32 percent of all convicted white defendants going to jail, while 46 percent of blacks end up imprisoned.

It is this racist trend—and not, as Bush believes, the hippies' influence—that has played hell with "family values" in poor black communities. "Crime control policies," note two scholars in American Psychologist, *"are a major contributor to the disruption of the family, the prevalence of single parent families, and children raised without a father in the ghetto," and have contributed as well to unemployment rates among the poor. The move to lock them up has also had disastrous civic consequences. By 1997, 1.46 million black men—out of a total voting population of 10.4 million—had lost the right to vote because of felony convictions. According to Human Rights Watch: "Thirteen percent of all adult black men—1.4 million—are disenfranchised, representing one-third of the total of disenfranchised population and reflecting a rate of disenfranchisement that is seven times the national average."*[89]

As governor of Texas, Bush was by far the nation's proudest and most diligent enforcer of this racist trend—and reaped a large electoral benefit from doing so, his tough stance winning the approval of a clear majority of Texans. It is therefore no surprise that very few blacks voted for him in the last election; and considering his cynicism, it is also no surprise that he would keep on trying to win them over, with many earnest words and tolerant gestures.

"In terms of being a president that says there's no place in racism [*sic*], it starts with saying there's no place for racism in America. . . . And that's what leadership needs to do. Leadership needs to stand up and say, and condemn racism and condemn prejudice and hold people accountable as an individual, not as a group."

—MICHIGAN GOP DEBATE, JANUARY 10, 2000

"This month in particular, we remember the stories of those who have helped to build our nation and advance the cause of freedom and civil rights. We remember the bravery of the soldiers of the Fifty-fourth Massachusetts Infantry Regiment and the sailors of the USS *Mason* in service to our country. We remember those who marched on Washington, sat at whites-only lunch counters, and walked rather than use segregated buses. And we remember those, known only to each of us, who helped to build our families, places of worship, and communities.

—"NATIONAL AFRICAN-AMERICAN HISTORY MONTH, 2001: A PROCLAMATION BY THE PRESIDENT OF THE UNITED STATES," FEBRUARY 1, 2001

"I don't remember any kind of heaviness ruining my time at Yale."

—MINUTAGLIO, *FAVORITE SON,* P. 117

Bush was here referring to the Civil Rights movement of the 1960s, among other struggles of that time.

As a presidential candidate, Bush discussed his racial target marketing with the same frank cynicism that marked all his campaign self-assessments.

"As he traveled through East Texas last week, Bush acknowledged that his campaign has a specific Hispanic strategy but no specific Hispanic message.

" 'I think the message is the same. I've never been one to tailor my message to one group of people versus another group of people,' he said. 'In the case of Hispanic voters, it is a combination of developing a theme that says to the Hispanic community, "This guy understands . . . and he can speak the language somewhat." '

"Bush, in words and ads, believes Hispanic issues are the issues of everyone: opportunity, education and the like. He is airing two Spanish radio ads, one stressing education, the other heavy on personal responsibility.

"Luis Garcia of KJS, the San Antonio advertising firm handling the Hispanic campaign for Bush, said it's the effort, as much as the message, that makes it work.

" 'This is a campaign that recognizes the importance of Hispanics and does it in a way that shows what Governor Bush represents, which is exactly what's important to the Hispanic community,' Garcia said.

"Things got a little trickier in seeking black voters, something Bush also hopes to be able to do in record numbers for a Texas Republican.

" 'Same thing,' he said, explaining that, as with Hispanics, there will be no special message for blacks. 'But obviously, the Spanish component is not there. But it is the same type of idea. It's how you make sure the message is heard.' "

—*AUSTIN AMERICAN-STATESMAN,* AUGUST 23, 1998

BUSH: First of all, Cinco de Mayo is not the independence day. That's dieciséis de Septiembre, and—

CHRIS MATTHEWS: What's that in English?

BUSH: Fifteenth of September.

—*HARDBALL,* MSNBC, MAY 31, 2000

"Dieciséis de Septiembre" means "September sixteenth." What Bush meant was "decimoquinto."

On Native-American rights:

"My view is that state law reigns supreme when it comes to the Indians, whether it be gambling or any other issue."

—AP, NOVEMBER 4, 1999

Although Texas has a large Native-American population, Governor Bush was evidently unaware that the U.S. government's treaties with the Indians take precedence over state laws.

"No one wants racial profiling to take place in any state. The governor of this state doesn't, the governor of my state doesn't. I'm interested in fair justice. I think we ought to hold people accountable if they break the law, regardless of the color of their skin."

—PRESIDENTIAL DEBATE, OCTOBER 11, 2000

"I mean, there needs to be a wholesale effort against racial profiling, which is illiterate children."

—IBID.

"People shouldn't read into venue locations someone's heart."

—AP, JANUARY 12, 2000

Bush was responding to complaints about his having given a speech at a former slave plantation in Lexington, South Carolina.

"What I am against is quotas. I am against hard quotas, quotas they basically delineate based upon whatever. However they delineate, quotas, I think vulcanize society. So I don't know how that fits into what everybody else is saying, their relative positions, but that's my position."

—*SAN FRANCISCO CHRONICLE* (MOLLY IVINS), JANUARY 21, 2000

At the third presidential debate, a woman named Norma Kirby asked the governor a pertinent question:

KIRBY: How will your administration address diversity, inclusiveness, and what role will affirmative action play in your overall plan?

BUSH: I've had a record of bringing people from all walks of life into my administration, and my administration is better off for it in Texas. I'm going to find people that want to serve their country. But I want a diverse administration, I think it's important.

I've worked hard in the state of Texas to make sure our institutions reflect the state, with good smart policy, policy that rejects quotas. I don't like quotas. Quotas tend to pit one group of people against another. Quotas are bad for America. It's not the way America is all about. But policies that give people a helping hand so they can help themselves. For example, in our state of Texas, I worked with the legislature, both Republicans and Democrats, to pass a law that said if you come in the top 10 percent of your high-school class, you're automatically admitted to one of our—one of our higher institutions, higher institutions of learning, college. And as a result, our universities are now more diverse. It was a smart thing to do; I called it—I labeled it affirmative access.

I think the contracting business in government can help, not with quotas but help meet a goal of ownership of small businesses, for example [*sic*]. The contracts need to be smaller, the agencies need to be, you know—need to recruit and to work hard to find people to bid on the state contracts. I think we can do that in a way that represents what America's all about, which is equal opportunity and opportunity for people to realize their potential, so to answer your question, I support, I guess the way to put it is affirmative *access*. And I'll have an administration that'll make you proud.

JIM LEHRER: Vice President Gore?

GORE: . . . I don't know what "affirmative access" means. I do know what affirmative *action* means. . . .

Now, I just believe that what we have to do is enforce the civil rights laws. I'm against quotas. This is—with all due respect, Governor, that's a red herring. Affirmative action isn't quotas. I'm against quotas. They're illegal. They're against the American way. Affirmative action means that you take extra steps to acknowledge the history of discrimination and injustice and prejudice, and bring all people into the American dream because it helps everybody, not just those who are directly benefitting.

LEHRER: Governor, what is your—are you opposed to affirmative action?

BUSH: No, if affirmative action means quotas, I'm against it. If affirmative action means what I just described, what I'm for, then I'm for it. You heard what I was for. [The] Vice President keeps saying I'm against things. You heard what I was for, and that's what I support.

LEHRER: What about—Mr. Vice President, you heard what he said.

GORE: He said if affirmative action means quotas, he's against it. Affirmative action doesn't mean—

BUSH: Good.

GORE: —quotas. Are you for it *without* quotas?

BUSH: Well, I may not be for your version, Mr. Vice President, but I am for what I just described to the lady. She heard my answer.

GORE: Are you for what the Supreme Court says is a constitutional way of having affirmative action?

(Bush turned to Lehrer, to get him to change the subject.)

BUSH:	Jim—!
LEHRER:	Let's go onto another—another—
GORE:	I think that speaks for itself.
LEHRER:	It's a question—
BUSH:	No, it doesn't speak for itself, Mr. Vice President. It speaks for the fact that there are certain rules in this that we all agreed to. But evidently rules don't mean anything.

> —PRESIDENTIAL DEBATE, OCTOBER 17, 2000

WOOPS

"Unfairly but truthfully [*sic*], our party has been tagged as being against things. Anti-immigrant, for example. And we're not a party of anti-immigrants. Quite the opposite. We're a party that welcomes people."   —CLEVELAND, JULY 1, 2000; *SLATE*

The Unborn

On the white-hot subject of abortion, Bush became extraordinarily vague—even by his special standard—whenever he was forced to range beyond his usual sound-bites about "life."

"Part of ushering in the responsibility era, which I talk a lot about, is for folks to understand the preciousness of life. It's not only life for the unborn, it is life for the elderly, it is life of the young, it is life of the living."   —*MEET THE PRESS,* NBC, NOVEMBER 21, 1999

"I'm going to lead the country to understanding the value of life— the preciousness of life. Life for the living and life for the unborn."
          —*THIS WEEK,* ABC, JANUARY 23, 2000

"There's a larger issue than just abortion, and it's valuing life, a culture of life. It's not just life of the child or the unborn; it's life of the living."   —*LARRY KING LIVE,* CNN, JULY 20, 2000

"I don't know. Probably down."   —*TALK,* SEPTEMBER 1999

This was Bush's answer to the question as to whether the number of abortions had gone up or down in Texas since he had been elected governor. On hearing this, top campaign aide Karen Hughes was quick to set the record straight: "We've doubled

the number of adoptions in Texas. You've done a lot to cut abortions." Hughes's col-
league David Sibley agreed: "That's right. The crisis pregnancy centers." The gov-
ernor replied, "We don't fund crisis pregnancy centers."

"I think it's important for those of us in a position of responsibility
to be firm in sharing our experiences, to understand that the babies
out of wedlock is a very difficult chore for mom and baby alike. . . . I
believe we ought to say there is a different alternative than the culture that is proposed by people like Miss [Naomi] Wolf in society.
. . . And, you know, hopefully, condoms will work, but it hasn't
worked."   —*MEET THE PRESS,* NBC, NOVEMBER 21, 1999

"States should have the right to enact reasonable laws and restric-
tions, particularly to end the inhumane practice of ending a life that
otherwise could live."   —CLEVELAND, JUNE 29, 2000; *SLATE*

JACK FORD: Governor, you have talked a great deal over this
                   past week about your position on the issue of
                   abortion. Assume for a minute, if indeed you were
                   the president, if indeed *Roe versus Wade* was over-
                   turned, if indeed there was a constitutional
                   amendment banning abortions—what would you
                   think would be the right thing to happen for a
                   doctor who performed an abortion? Should that
                   doctor be criminally prosecuted?

BUSH: You mean if abortions were illegal?

FORD: Yes.

BUSH: Yeah, I mean that's a huge "if."

FORD: Right.

BUSH: This country needs a president who can lead us to
                   understanding of life. There's a lot of people who
                   disagree with what you just said, and there is good
                   people on both sides of this issue.

(It was unclear what the governor meant by "what you just said.")

The real fundamental question is, Can our party and our nation have a president who leads us to respect life?

FORD: But if we got to—

BUSH: But I mean, eventually—well, eventually if the law is broken, of course there needs to be some kind of prosecution.

FORD: Would we also then find ourselves in a situation where if a woman had an abortion that she would also be criminally prosecuted?

BUSH: No, I don't think that would be the case.

—*GOOD MORNING AMERICA,* ABC,
JANUARY 25, 2000

CHRIS MATTHEWS: Abortion—is it going to be an issue in this campaign? Should it be?

BUSH: I think—I think the—the life issue is an issue. And I—I—one of my jobs is to set an ideal for America that says we'll protect life, life of the elderly.

MATTHEWS: Yeah.

BUSH: I think one of the issues that faces Amer—that America faces—I know you oftentimes worry out loud, what should America be like is one of your concerns.

MATTHEWS: Yeah, what kind of a country you want to live in?

BUSH: What kind of country you live in. When—

MATTHEWS: Let me ask you—

BUSH: Let me—let me—let me answer that, because—

MATTHEWS: Sure.

BUSH: —I—I'm pretty good about asking myself the own question [*sic*], then answering it, see?

MATTHEWS: OK.

BUSH: I—well, the country I want to live in is a country
             that respects life, and—and—and respects life of
             the unborn and the living, respects life of people
             living in tough neighborhoods and good neigh-
             borhoods, and respects the elderly. That's the ideal
             world, and that's what I intend to lead toward.

             I understand not everybody agrees with me,
             but that's not going to deter me from trying to set
             the right tone for America.

MATTHEWS: President Clinton promised when he ran—he
             made a number of promises the—for people—
             people who work hard and play by the rules.

BUSH: Yeah.

MATTHEWS: He also said he was going to make abortion safe,
             legal, and rare, which I think helped him with
             Roman Catholic voters that last one.

BUSH: It's a pretty interesting line.

MATTHEWS: Do you buy it? Do you think he's made it rare?

BUSH: Do I buy that—no; otherwise, he would not have
             vetoed a ban on partial-birth abortion.

MATTHEWS: Right.

BUSH: I think there's a lot of things we can do to work
             together to reduce abortions. I think there's a lot
             of things we can do to increase adoptions.

MATTHEWS: Do you think abor—banning abortion would
             work? Step aside from the morality for a second. If
             you outlawed it, if you banned it in the states, the
             states all separately banned it after *Roe versus
             Wade*—

BUSH: Yeah.

MATTHEWS: —was overruled, or whatever, wouldn't we go
             back to the 1950s we grew up with? The movie
             stars all went to Denmark, people—You can go
             to—you can go to—

BUSH: There's going to be abo—if—

MATTHEWS: —walk to Windsor, Canada, and have an abortion.

BUSH: Yeah.

MATTHEWS: You can take a bus ride or a car ride to Vancouver. How can you stop people from getting an abortion if they want one?

BUSH: You can't. You can't. I—I—

MATTHEWS: So why ban it?

BUSH: Well, I—I don't—I—I don't—I think the key is, is to change the culture first and foremost. I don't think anybody is under—I don't believe people believe it can be banned. I believe we can do everything we can to make it, as the president said, more rare.

MATTHEWS: Yeah.

BUSH: I believe we can ban partial-birth abortion. That's clearly an issue that people on both sides of the political—

MATTHEWS: Right.

BUSH: —fence should be able to come and agree on. And—

MATTHEWS: What about a woman who's forty-eight years old, and she's listening to the biological clock, and she knows all the arguments morally, and she's been raised by her par—her parishioner—she's—by a priest who say not to have an abortion, but she decides she wants one. Whose decision is that under—under God? Whose decision is that?

BUSH: Well, here's—here's—here—here's the thing. I mean, you can bring up every hypothetical—

MATTHEWS: All right.

BUSH: —situation on this issue and what I—

MATTHEWS: Well, we'll—we'll come right back. We'll be right back with Governor Bush—

BUSH: Wait a minute.

MATTHEWS: —for his answer. It's not hypothetical. It's every woman you talk to.

BUSH (ON VIDEOTAPE):   [*Commercials*]

My job will be to lift the spirits of America, to set our sights higher. My job will be to usher in the Responsibility Era—a culture that will stand in stark contrast to the last few decades, which has clearly said to America: "If it feels good, do it. And if you've got a problem, blame somebody else."

MATTHEWS: We're back with Governor Bush. Thank you, Governor. Sorry for interrupting. You want to— you said it was a hypothetical case. I want to give you a chance to expand on that. When it really comes down to it, after all the advice a woman gets, all the state laws are passed, federal laws are *not* passed or whatever, whose final decision is it whether you have an abortion or not? Who has the final call?

BUSH: You know, I would hope that the person would make the decision, for example, to put the child up for adoption.

I'm gonna talk about the ideal world, Chris. I've read—I understand reality. If you're asking me as the president, would I understand reality, I do.

MATTHEWS: OK.

BUSH: I do. The—but the role of the president is to set a tone and a—and a—and a—and a—and to appreciate life. I've said a lot in the campaign, I want the goal for America to be that born and unborn children be protected in law and welcomed to life. That's the goal. That's—that's the ideal world and that's exactly where I intend to lead.

—*HARDBALL,* MSNBC, MAY 31, 2000

Death Row

The offender never pardons.

—GEORGE HERBERT, *OUTLANDISH PROVERBS*

BUSH:	You should head down to Sixth Street.
REPORTER:	Why, what's there?
BUSH:	Bars. Lots of 'em.
REPORTER:	Should I mention your name?
BUSH:	[laughing] Well, if you do, and end up in jail, you ain't never gonna get out!

—*THE TIMES* (LONDON), FEBRUARY 15, 1999

"I like the law the way it is right now."

—*FORT WORTH STAR-TELEGRAM,* APRIL 3, 1999

Governor Bush said this in opposition to a legislative effort to exempt the mentally retarded from the Texas execution law.

On Karla Fay Tucker:

LARRY KING:	All you could have done was give her thirty days, right?
BUSH:	That's right.
KING:	Why didn't you give it to her, the thirty days?

BUSH: Because my job is to uphold the law of the land. My job is to ask the question, innocence or guilt. My job is not to judge hearts. That's not the job of the governor.

—*LARRY KING LIVE,* CNN DECEMBER 16, 1999

On the execution of Gary Graham, whose impending punishment had been the cause of widespread protests:

"This case has had full analyzation and has been looked at a lot. I understand the emotionality of death penalty cases."

—*SEATTLE POST-INTELLIGENCER,* JUNE 23, 2000

"The only thing that I can tell you is that every case I have reviewed, I have been comfortable with the innocence or guilt of the person that I've looked at. I do not believe we've put a guilty—I mean, innocent person to death in the state of Texas."

—*ALL THINGS CONSIDERED,* NPR, JUNE 16, 2000

On the murderers of James Byrd:

GORE: I think [hate] crimes are different. I think they're different because they're based on prejudice and hatred, which gives rise to crimes that have not just a single victim but they're intended to stigmatize and dehumanize a whole group of people.

JIM LEHRER: You have a different view of that.

BUSH: No, I don't, really.

LEHRER: On hate crimes laws?

BUSH: No. We've got one in Texas, and guess what: The three men who murdered James Byrd—guess what's going to happen to them? They're going to

be put to death. A jury found them guilty and—
it's going to be hard to punish them any worse
after they get put to death. And it's the right cause,
so it's the right decision.

—PRESIDENTIAL DEBATE, OCTOBER 11, 2000

BUSH: I want to repeat, if you have a state that fully supports the law, like we do in Texas, we're going to
go after all crime, and we're going to make sure
people get punished for the crime. And in this
case, we can't enhance the penalty any more than
putting those three thugs to death, and that's
what's going to happen in the state of Texas.

—IBID.

*The mere transcript cannot convey the look of pleasure that lit up George Bush's
face as he foretold the fate of James Byrd's murderers. (See pp. 52–53.) The look
struck one viewer in particular—a black man named Leo Anderson, who at the next
debate implored the governor to say it wasn't so.*

ANDERSON: In one of the last debates held, the subject of capital punishment came up. And in your response to
the question, you seemed to overly enjoy—as a
matter of fact, [be] proud that Texas led the nation
in execution of prisoners. Sir, did I misread your
response, and are you really, really proud of the
fact that Texas is number one in executions?
BUSH: No, I'm not proud of that. The death penalty's
very serious business, Leo. It's an issue that good
people obviously disagree on. I take my job seriously. And if you think I was proud of it, I think
you misread me. I do.
           I was sworn to uphold the laws of my state.

During the course of the campaign in 1994, I was asked, "Do you support the death penalty?" I said I did if administered fairly and justly. Because I believe it saves lives, Leo, I do. I think if it's administered swiftly, justly, and fairly, it saves lives.

One of the things that happens when you're a governor, oftentimes you have to make tough decisions. And you can't let public persuasion sway you because the job's to enforce the law. And that's what I did, sir. There've been some tough cases come across my desk. Some of the hardest moments since I've been the governor of the state of Texas is to deal with those cases.

But my job is to ask two questions, sir. Is the person guilty of the crime? And did the person have full access to the courts of law? And I can tell you looking at you right now, in all cases those answers were affirmative.

I'm not proud of any record. I'm proud of the fact that violent crime is down in the state of Texas. I'm proud of the fact that we hold people accountable. But I'm not proud of any record, sir. No.

—PRESIDENTIAL DEBATE, OCTOBER 17, 2000

That reply was noteworthy, first of all, for the skill with which Bush charmed his questioner, not only with that deferential "sir" but, after the debate had ended, by making a beeline for Anderson and giving him the whole full-body treatment. The governor's mendacity is also worth remarking. As Texas's chief executive, he was never known to spend—at most—a minute more than half an hour on any business, death penalty appeals included. Moreover, the claim that "violent crime is down in the state of Texas" was disingenuous. "Crime has dropped in Texas," the Toronto Globe and Mail had reported some weeks earlier, "but at a significantly slower rate than in the rest of the country, and well behind states of similar size, such as New York." ("Texas Tops All States in Prison Population," Toronto Globe and Mail, August 29, 2000.)

Message: I'm Real

"I don't feel like I've got all that much too important to say on the kind of big national issues." —*20/20*, ABC, SEPTEMBER 15, 2000

"The important question is, How many hands have I shaked?" —*NEW YORK TIMES*, OCTOBER 23, 1999

The primitive grammatical mistake in that much-quoted gaffe is far less troubling than the point that Bush was trying to make: that "the important question" in his case was not exactly where he stood on "the kind of big national issues," and not (of course) his suitability for higher office, but only the extent and vigorousness of his campaigning. In part, Bush's overemphasis on minor matters like handshaking was a way to keep on underemphasizing complicated or contentious issues, which might cost him votes if he were forced to talk about them.

And yet his constant focus on his own campaigning was not only an evasive measure. First of all, such talk betrayed the governor's assumption that his arduous campaigning was itself enough to justify his being elected. "How many hands have I shaked?" The note of self-congratulation—and self-pity—in that question gave away his view that he should be rewarded not for his deserts but for so stoutly going through the long ordeal of running.

"I don't want to win? If that were the case, why the heck am I on the bus 16 hours a day, shaking thousands of hands, giving hundreds

of speeches, getting pillared in the press and cartoons and still staying
on message to win?" —*NEWSWEEK,* FEBRUARY 28, 2000

*A politician, one would think, must take all that abuse in stride—the long days "on
the bus," the speechifying, the criticism in the press—and stay "on message" in the
face of it; and yet Bush seemed to think that he deserved a medal for such labors.
Beyond his laziness, however, the candidate's incessant yammering about his job performance as a candidate bespoke a general uninterest in all other subjects. With his
campaign—his governance included—what finally mattered was not good and bad
or right and wrong. Despite the heavy Christian props, on Bush's stage the only
thing that played was "theme" and "message."*

Bush would sometimes sound as if he might be talking about something deeper.

"There's nothing like the humbling experience of getting whipped
pretty bad in New Hampshire to cause a man to re-evaluate."
—*NEW YORK TIMES ONLINE,* MARCH 15, 2000

*Despite that hint of introspection, the governor wound up that nonconfession right
back on the surface:*

"And I re-evaluated my message and I re-evaluated how I was con-
ducting myself as a candidate." —IBID.

*At best, such relentless self-reflection—the messenger repeatedly delivering the mes-
sage that he'd done a really great job as a messenger repeatedly delivering a message—was merely comic in its flagrant emptiness.*

"I've changed my style somewhat, as you know. I'm less—I pontifi-
cate less, although it may be hard to tell it from this show. And I'm
more interacting with people."
—*MEET THE PRESS,* NBC, FEBRUARY 13, 2000

"People make suggestions on what to say all the time. I'll give you an example; I don't read what's handed to me. People say, 'Here, here's your speech, or here's an idea for a speech.' They're changed. Trust me."   —*NEW YORK TIMES,* MARCH 15, 2000

CARL CAMERON: What premium price [*sic*] do you put on a harmonious convention, and why?

BUSH: Well, this is an event, and a big event in the course of a long campaign. You and I have been through several of them. The kickoff of the campaign was a big event.

The primaries, of course, were big. And since—had I not won, I wouldn't be sitting here.

The period between the primaries and the convention has been an important period.

And, of course, the convention—and the convention is important because it gives a sense of who I am, and I think if we do our job right, to lead our party and lead the country, I think what you are going to find is that this is going to be a convention that spells out what we're for.

—*FOX SPECIAL REPORT WITH BRIT HUME,*
JULY 19, 2000

At its worst, the endless dwelling on mere "message" evidenced the sort of moral bankruptcy that finally did in Richard Nixon:

"I readily concede I missed an opportunity at Bob Jones; I'd have been a hero. If I had gone down there and said, 'We're all God's children; we can receive redemption in all different kinds of ways; the Catholic religion is a great religion, Judaism is a great religion.' It's all I would have needed to have said. One sentence."

—*NEW YORK TIMES ONLINE,* MARCH 15, 2000

"LET ME PULL THE MOTE OUT OF THINE EYE"

Despite—or as an expression of—his own unremitting calculation (see also "Profile in Courage," pp. 178ff.), Bush was always quick to wonder righteously at the unremitting calculation of the Democrats.

"If somebody's so calculating that they spend their whole life calculating the path to the presidency, when they become president, they'll be calculating. I mean, calculation is a part of their being."
—*READERS DIGEST ONLINE*, AUGUST 30, 2000

"I've been, frankly, amazed at the amount of polling that goes on to determine the behavior in the White House. Starting with, for example, where to take a summer vacation. I was floored."
—*MEET THE PRESS*, NBC, NOVEMBER 21, 1999

Even Bush's very protestations that he wasn't calculating were themselves apparent calculations, clearly memorized (including, in this case, his stubborn use of "resignate" for "resonate").

"They said, 'You know, this issue doesn't seem to resignate with the people.' And I said, you know something? Whether it resignates or not doesn't matter to me because I stand for doing what's the right thing, and what the right thing is hearing the voices of people who work [*sic*]."   —PORTLAND, OREGON, OCTOBER 31, 2000; *SLATE*

"There are a lot of nice pundits. And other kind of pundits. They say, they say, you know this issue doesn't seem to resignate. And I said, you know something, whether it resignates or not, that doesn't matter to me because I stand for doing what's the right thing."
—*ST. PETERSBURG TIMES*, NOVEMBER 2, 2000

In short, it matters not that Bush spoke as a malapropist, but that such statements were so hypocritical. The same is true of his reply to a question as to whether he was using the Elian Gonzalez case for mere political advantage:

"You subscribe politics to it. I subscribe freedom to it."

—AP, APRIL 6, 2000

HE CAN DISH IT OUT . . .

"Other Republican candidates may retort [*sic*] to personal attacks and negative ads."

—FROM A BUSH/CHENEY FUND-RAISING LETTER,
WASHINGTON POST, MARCH 24, 2000

Although his own political attacks were blatant, Bush seemed not merely to be feign-ing outrage at others' countermoves against himself. As thin-skinned as his father (and his father's mentor), he was always quick to charge his adversaries with doing the sort of thing to him that he had done—and was still doing—to them. This is a venerable propaganda trick—although it's not entirely tactical but also symptomatic of a paranoid approach to combat, whether martial or electoral.

"The senator [McCain] has got to understand if he's going to have—he can't have it both ways. He can't take the high horse and then claim the low road."

—FLORENCE, SOUTH CAROLINA, FEBRUARY 17, 2000; *SLATE*

In fact, McCain's attack on Bush was nothing in comparison with Bush's on McCain—a massive smear job that entailed push-polling (telephonic rumor-mongering disguised as polling), racist innuendo (by subtly using pictures of Mc-Cain's adopted Asian daughter), frank impugnment of the senator's record as a champion of veterans' rights (notwithstanding his war-hero status), and accusations of religious prejudice (because the senator had rashly criticized the Christian right).

Then, having thoroughly trashed McCain in South Carolina, Bush abruptly craved the senator's forgiveness, and endorsement—despite the fact that he himself could never have forgiven such a libel if he had been its target (as he never was).

"I think we agree, the past is over."

—*DALLAS MORNING NEWS,* MAY 10, 2000

In the presidential contest, Bush was always quick to cry that he was getting hit below the belt—although the Democratic campaign propaganda was remarkably impersonal, considering the governor's many failings (and the GOP's astounding record of ad hominem assaults on Clinton/Gore). Indeed, Bush always used the loud complaint about his adversaries' "negative campaigning" as a way to shut down all discussion of his dismal record as the governor of Texas.

"Well, that's going to be up to the pundits and the people to make up their mind. I'll tell you what is a president for him, for example, talking about my record in the state of Texas. I mean, he's willing to say anything in order to convince people that I haven't had a good record in Texas."   —MSNBC, SEPTEMBER 20, 2000

Meanwhile, Bush always represented his attacks as mere defenses—even when his team struck first. Thus he justified one of his anti-Gore commercials:

"The point is, this is a way to help inoculate me about what has come and is coming."   —*NEW YORK TIMES,* SEPTEMBER 2, 2000

In Bush's view, Gore/Lieberman's chicanery knew no bounds. He even thought that Gore had stooped to plagiarizing Bush's own material—an accusation based on his belief that the cliché "a fresh start" was an invention of his own campaign and that the Democrats had stolen it.

"Bush poked fun at Gore's suggestion, in an interview with *USA Today*, that a Gore administration would be a 'fresh start,' noting that the phrase had been an early slogan of his own.

"Aides passed around a copy of Bush's 1999 collection of speeches entitled *A Fresh Start for America*.

" 'Unbelievable, isn't it?' Bush said."   —AP, AUGUST 11, 2000

PLAYING POLITICS WITH
PEOPLE'S LIVES

During the 1992 Republican convention, Larry King interviewed George W. and Jeb Bush. At one point the subject turned to a New York Times *article suggesting that the president had been politically motivated in mounting Operation Desert Storm.*

KING: What do you make of the *New York Times* piece today and your father's angry reaction to it?

BUSH: I think it's lousy journalism. I think for the *New York Times* to say that George Bush would commit U.S. lives to Iraq for political purpose stinks. And American people ought to be outraged at that kind of journalism. That's what we call impact journalism. And it seems like to me that, on the verge of this convention, they're trying to impact my good dad's chances of sending out a positive message to the American people.

                —*LARRY KING LIVE*, CNN, AUGUST 16, 1992

According to two Time *reporters, the younger Bush's jubilation after Desert Storm was gleefully, aggressively political:*

"Despite [President] Bush's deliberately leaked exhortation that his aides should avoid inserting partisan politics into foreign policy, the president's intensely partisan eldest son, George W. Bush, universally known as 'Junior,' couldn't help but exult on *Air Force One* during the flight back to Maine: 'Do they think the American people are going to turn to a *Democrat* now?' "

—MICHAEL DUFFY AND DAN GOODGAME, *MARCHING IN PLACE: THE STATUS QUO PRESIDENCY OF GEORGE BUSH* (1992), P. 200

"Desert Storm was one of the great achievements of the twentieth century. And it had a shelf life of about a month."

—*TEXAS MONTHLY*, NOVEMBER 2000

WOOPS

And yet, for all his own chicanery, at times the governor could not help almost blurting out the truth.

"If you're sick and tired of the politics of cynicism and polls and principles, come and join this campaign."

—HILTON HEAD, SOUTH CAROLINA, FEBRUARY 16, 2000; *SLATE*

"The fact that [Gore] relies on facts—says things that are not factual—are going to undermine his campaign."

—*NEW YORK TIMES*, MARCH 4, 2000

The Making of the President
2000

Anyway, after we go out and work our hearts out,

after you go out and help us turn out the vote,

after we've convinced the good Americans to vote—

and while they're at it, pull that old George W. lever, if
I'm the one—

when I put my hand on the Bible,

when I put my hand on the Bible, that day when they
swear us in,

when I put my hand on the Bible,

I will swear to not—to uphold the laws of the land.
—GEORGE W. BUSH, TOLEDO, OHIO, OCTOBER 27, 2000

"We're pleased to welcome the Cheneys and Andy Card here, and
we're just going to continue our discussions about the future. And as I
said yesterday, I think it's responsible that Dick and I and others con-
template a potential administration. [See "A New Broom," pp. 191ff.]

"First Lady Bush will be arriving here soon."
—BUSH CAMPAIGN PRESS BRIEFING, NOVEMBER 11, 2000

REPORTER: Governor, why did you decide to go forward and
              seek the injunction in Florida?

BUSH: I think you ought to call Jim Baker and let him—
he made the explanation today, and I thought it
was a very sound and reasoned explanation. And if
you've got any further comment—questions about
that—just call him. Call his office. He'll be the person in charge of explaining our position as to why
we don't think there needs to be three elections.

—IBID.

REPORTER: Governor, do you plan to appeal the Florida
Supreme Court decision?

BUSH: We will refer you to my lawyers in Florida. Jim
Baker is doing a good job.

REPORTER: What options are you considering?

BUSH: I refer you to our folks in Florida. They are—Jim
Baker is in charge of the team in Florida, and he's
doing a really good job down there.

—BUSH CAMPAIGN PRESS CONFERENCE,
NOVEMBER 22, 2000

BUSH: Well, I'm—we're both being kept abreast of the
options and opportunities. I decided that it was
best to take our case to the Supreme Court of the
United States, which will be heard tomorrow. All
options are on the table. But one of our strategies
is to get this election ratified. And the sooner the
better for the good of the country.

REPORTER: Governor, how do you respond to the criticism
that in fact your legal team, through your decisions, are in essence delaying—not delaying, but
sort of running out the clock to prevent the addi-
tional ballots, disputed ballots, from being
counted?

BUSH: As I recall, the facts are these: On election night

we won. And then there was a recount, and we
won. And there was a selected recount as a result
of different legal maneuverings, and we won that.
And I believe one of these days, that all this is
going to stop, and Dick Cheney and I will be the
president and the vice president.

—BUSH CAMPAIGN PRESS CONFERENCE,

NOVEMBER 30, 2000

"As far as the legal hassling and wrangling and posturing in Florida, I
would suggest you talk to our good team in Florida led by Jim Baker."

—IBID.

REPORTER: Governor, now that the Supreme Court has had
             its hearing, how do you feel your prospects stand
             right now?

BUSH: Well, I—we'll wait and see what they say [at] the
             Supreme Court, and all these different courts.
             Dick and I felt like we won the first three elec-
             tions. The first election three times.
                 And we're confident that when it's all said and
             done, that—that he and I will be honored to be
             the president and the vice president. That's why
             we're having these meetings. That's why we're in
             the process of preparing to assume the offices to
             which we feel like we've been elected.

             —BUSH CAMPAIGN PRESS CONFERENCE,

             DECEMBER 2, 2000

"I felt like the Supreme Court of the United States made a very positive statement on our behalf. And I think that the important—what
I—the sentiment I want to convey is this: that I am comforted by
the fact that the highest court of our land heard our case and will

make sure this election is fair. I think that's—I think that's very important for our citizenry to hear.

"And as far as what the legislature does in Florida, that's going to be up to the leadership in the legislature."

—BUSH CAMPAIGN PRESS CONFERENCE, DECEMBER 4, 2000

BUSH: I felt like [the Florida Supreme Court's] decision was not a fair decision at the time, and I felt like they had rewritten a law and—you know, so therefore.

REPORTER: But are you saying you will abide by the rulings of any law courts in this matter?

BUSH: Well, I think the court system is very important in the country. But I felt like in the case of the Florida Supreme Court, like I said in my statement, and like Secretary Baker said in his statement, that they changed the rules. And the Supreme Court reviewed that. And now remember, many of the—many of the experts were saying, "Well, the Bush team has no chance to get their case heard by the Supreme Court." Not only was the case heard, but the Supreme Court acted in a way that I think is a positive—positive for our campaign.

—IBID.

"The great thing about America is everybody should vote."

—AUSTIN, TEXAS, DECEMBER 8, 2000

AT THE HELM

"See, I believe in the power of the people. I truly do. I do."

—*NEW YORK TIMES*, MARCH 7, 2001

AFTERWORD

The fetters imposed on liberty at home have ever been forged out of the weapons provided for defense against real, pretended, or imaginary dangers from abroad.

—JAMES MADISON, FEBRUARY 23, 1799

Our system suffers from a grave disorder at the top—both in the nation's capital, where a callow and illiterate president sits unelected, gamely fronting for a far-right oligarchy, and throughout the mainstream media, whose personnel do not perceive the evidence before their very eyes. As we have seen, that dual disorder is suggestive of dyslexia, which blocks perception of the written word. It is even more suggestive of *amnesia*. Indeed, the president's peculiar language is the language of forgetfulness—which is also the language of TV, the medium, despite its ever-swelling archive of taped moments, tending always to transfix the audience in an eternal *now*.

The oblivious effect of Bush's speech is as complex as his illiteracy. On the one hand the president's forgetfulness is tactical: a *willed* amnesia, meant to be contagious. Like the father's, the son's talk is intended largely to induce us to forget whatever ugly thing we may suspect or know about his life or record. Through mere lying, and/or by blitzing questioners with claims half true or intimidating or distractingly emotional, both Bushes, despite their intellectual dimness, have always been astute enough to change the subject when confronted with embarrassing reminders of the past: HW's criminal participation in Iran-Contra; W's nonpolitical transgressions, whether felonies or misdemeanors, and his dirty doings as governor of Texas. More important, both men have always been as ready to deny the dark parts of the nation's past as they have been to sanitize their own. Although not as skilled at such nostalgic improv as Ronald Reagan (who, with his archaic haircut and pretelevisual quips, was himself a walking fiction of "the way things used to be"), neither Bush was ever a mean hand at whiting out America's past—as when the father vowed, before a gathering of ex-fascists, "I will never apologize for the United States of America—I don't care what the facts are"; or as when Bush the Younger thus summed up the Cold War's "lessons": "[O]ur nation's greatest export to the world has been, is, and always will be the incredible freedoms we understand in the great land called America."

Of course, all politicians try to talk away their priors, and all rightists prettify the national past. In his forgetfulness, however, this Bush has no peer; for his speech does not just cause forgetfulness in others but is *itself* essentially oblivious—its very sound and sense determined by amnesia. At his clearest, Bush tends to speak in serial declaratives, very short and simple, and linked together, quasi-Biblically, with "and."

> As I recall, the facts are these: On election night we won.
> And then there was a recount, and we won.
> And there was a selected recount as a result of different legal maneuverings, and we won that.
> And I believe one of these days, that all this is going to stop, and Dick Cheney and I will be the president and the vice president.

The statement is amnesiac, then, not only in its meaning—"the facts" that Bush claimed to "recall" all being fabrications. He and President Cheney had *not* "won" on "election night," nor had there ever been a *manual* recount, which was the only kind of "recount" that the Democrats were calling for. Thus his statement was to some extent *deliberately* oblivious, like his evasive answers to the question of his past drug use.

While such forgetfulness was surely tactical, however, Bush's statement, typically, was itself also structured by *his own* amnesia—its bite-sized syntactic units being the only kind that he can handle. When he tries for a grammatical arrangement more complex than see-Dick-run, Bush often breaks down in mid-effort, having just . . . forgotten how he started out, and where he ought to go.

> I felt like their decision was not a fair decision at the time, and I felt like they had rewritten a law and—you know, so therefore.

As it dictates the endless parataxis of his sentences, so does the president's amnesia often have him flailing in supreme rhetorical confusion, blurting out disjointed bits of prose until some propaganda tag line pops into his head, which then gives him something clear to say, repeatedly. It is because of such forgetfulness—and not stupidity per se—that Bush has always been averse to speaking off the cuff, and tries to keep all such appearances as rare and imperceptible as possible.*

Whether it's a handicap that he was born with or a consequence of youthful boozing and/or drug abuse, our president is not alone in his forgetfulness: TV, too, is thoroughly amnesiac—an entity with little memory and one that also urges its forgetfulness on those who watch.[90] It is therefore not surprising that TV was quick to reconfirm the president-select's forgetful take on what had taken place in Florida and, since the inauguration, eager to keep on forgetting—and to have *us* keep forgetting—what really happened. To understand what's going on today, then, we must resist TV's oblivious influence and first of all remember what went down after Election Day. We must also look much further back, for that coup was the climax of a history far richer, darker, and more complicated than TV, as we now know it, ever could convey. To understand what really hap-

---

*Running for re-election in 1998, Governor Bush took every step to minimize the audience of his sole debate against opponent Garry Mauro—holding it in remote El Paso, and scheduling the face-off for a Friday night during Texas's high school football season. Similarly, President Bush held no official press conference for over a month after his inauguration—then quickly called one on February 23, in the wake of the big news that Hugh Rodham, Hillary Clinton's brother, had taken several hundred thousand dollars as a lobbyist for certain felons seeking presidential pardons. Thus Bush held his first press conference on the same day that Senator Clinton also answered questions from reporters—a stroke of timing whereby his performance was protectively upstaged by the latest chapter of his precedecessor's very long ordeal.

pened, we must look back to the very dawn of time—as far as TV is concerned—so that we might begin to understand how, for the House of Bush, it all finally came together in the year 2000: every antidemocratic force in the United States converging to suppress the will of the majority. Only such a longer view can help us start to see just how the Bush team "won," and everybody lost.

Although it has its partial precedents in U.S. history, the Rehnquist putsch was something new. First of all, it was effected by a GOP that is not only dominated by the super-rich (who also own much of the Democratic Party) but managed by a host of vengeful ultrarightists whose alliance is peculiar to this time and place: Nixon men still seething over Watergate; military men still smoldering over Vietnam; Southerners still livid over the desegregation of the schools, the end of lynch law, the extension of the franchise, and the burning of Atlanta; Christian Fundamentalists still steaming over rock 'n' roll, the Scopes trial, and modernity in general; Catholics fuming over *Roe v. Wade*. The whole enterprise is funded, and its larger moves dictated, by the corporate network of big oil and petrochemicals, "defense," tobacco, pharmaceuticals, insurance, pesticides, and automotives, among other industries, their top brass and top shareholders all still smarting at the heavy hand of "regulation"—as if there were a lot of that in the United States.

Each of those angry factions is forced forward by a toxic memory, or illusion, of defeat. What has now made them all especially dangerous, however, is a victory: the fall of Soviet communism. We cannot afford to underestimate the trauma—or ignore the consequences—of that disappearance. On the one hand, the whole huge bureaucracy of national security is still in place, but lacks a global enemy to justify its appetite. That system needs a state of war—just like its Soviet counterpart (which was finally ruined by the cost of that requirement). And yet the need is not only material but psychological. For as long as Stalin's empire shared the planet with us, the wildest of our citizens—and not just grassroots kooks but many high-and-mighty maniacs—were suitably preoccupied by that external threat. Although they did great harm to the Republic in pursuit of their apparent mission ("McCarthyism," the war in Vietnam, the Watergate conspiracies,

33 ISSUES FREE!

THE NEW YORKER

YES! Please start my money-saving subscription to THE NEW YORKER.

☐ 1 year (46 issues) – just $49.95.
That's like getting **33 ISSUES FREE!**

Name _____
(please print)

Address/Apt. _____

City/State/Zip _____

E-Mail Address _____

☐ I prefer 2 years (92 issues) for just $79.95.

☐ Payment enclosed   ☐ Bill me later

J3CS33

and Iran-Contra being only the most infamous examples), the patriots never went so far as to subvert our democratic institutions openly—the way that rightists did in other countries, with ample CIA support. Fixated on the dictatorial Other, American extremists by and large respected the legality and peacefulness of our elections, ritually proclaiming them as blessed examples to the wider world.

But all that changed with the collapse of communism. In general, wars tend to leave a certain stubborn rage among the soldiers and the masses— an emotional holdover that is easily manipulated by domestic interests that have scores to settle or want to strengthen their position. Our Cold War was no exception. Fifty years of mass mobilization left this country with a boiling residue of paranoid anxiety that, now lacking any foreign object, had to find some other focus. That need was more than answered by the born-again Republicans, who swiftly turned their wrath on Washington it-self, the Democrats, "the liberals"—Nixon's enemies, but now assailed with an unprecedented violence and sophistication, far surpassing even the right-wing crusade against the Roosevelts.

Thus our system has been profoundly damaged by a subtle form of blowback, the savage forces roused against the Soviets now wreaking havoc here in the United States. That dynamic had atrocious consequences na-tionwide when, in the hospitable climate of "the Gingrich Revolution," with Rush Limbaugh, among others, calling openly for gunplay, far-right activists started committing racist murders, taking shots at Jewish children, assassinating doctors who performed abortions, and, most shockingly, blowing up a federal office building in Oklahoma City—the worst act of domestic terrorism in American history. (Although quick to credit the old fantasy that "Commie propaganda" was a fatal snare, Limbaugh waxed in-dignant at the charge that his incitements might have had some conse-quence.)

It was, of course, the White House that lay directly in the sights of all those propaganda guns (and at least one real gun)*—a consequence not of

---

*On the afternoon of October 29, 1994, twenty-six-year-old Francisco Martin Duran, armed with a Chinese-made SKS semiautomatic assault rifle, fired up to thirty rounds at the front of the White House, hitting the mansion with at least eight bullets. To carry out that mis-

the president's behavior but of that aggravated need for some new enemy. There is no other explanation for the rightist animus against Bill Clinton—who, in calmer times, would surely stand out as a great Republican, what with his winning economic policies, tolerance of Reagan-style deregulation, tough approach to crime and (yet) FDR-like popularity among the nation's have-nots. That he has been cast as a *leftist* has to do exclusively with cultural and generational mythology,* as exploited by the GOP.[91] Especially in the South, Bill Clinton seemed to carry all the sins of the detested '60s counterculture. His youthful disapproval of the war in Vietnam, and clear avoidance of the draft, whipped American revanchists into a seditious frenzy. (Meanwhile, such patriots ignored the military records of those rightists who, while hawkish on that war, found ways to keep from fighting in it: Limbaugh, Gingrich, Quayle, and Cheney, among other war supporters who had dodged the draft for sound careerist reasons.) The peacenik Clinton also was a figure of demonic hippie hedonism, smoking pot (although denying it) and, as everybody knows, getting it on with as many chicks as Charlie Manson. While linking him to the Aquarian ideal of sex, drugs, and rock 'n' roll (his White House staff was "Berkeley, California, with an Appalachian twist," one vilifier wrote),[92] the fiction also played on ancient racist fears of Negro sexuality. "Our first black President," as friend and foe alike soon deemed him, Clinton bore the mark of Ham because of his unusual rapport with African-Americans, whose fondness for him was, in rightist eyes, just one more strike against him. (The myth of Clinton's negritude is something of a miracle, considering how many African-Americans were sent to prison while the brother was

---

sion, Duran had driven all the way to Washington from Colorado Springs, Colorado, where he worked as an upholsterer. (According to his neighbors, he always dressed in camouflage—a habit that he picked up in the Army, where he had served from 1987 to 1991.) There were bumper stickers on the gunman's pickup truck: FIRE BUTCH RENO and THOSE WHO BEAT THEIR GUNS INTO PLOWS WILL PLOW FOR THOSE WHO DON'T.

*Such cultural mythicizing was squarely based, however, on the pathological hatreds of a few of Clinton's far-right enemies in Arkansas—in particular, the bloody-mouthed archsegregationist "Justice Jim" Johnson, who had loathed Clinton ever since his own failed run against Senator William Fulbright in the state's 1968 Democratic primary. (Clinton, who had once berated Johnson to his face, worked for Fulbright in that contest.) See Joe Conason and Gene Lyons, *The Hunting of the President: The Ten-Year Campaign to Destroy Bill and Hillary Clinton* (New York: Thomas Dunne Books, 2000), pp. 67–82 et passim.

in office.)* And, of course, the negative effect of all those anticountercul-
tural clichés—draft dodger, pothead, hippie swinger, nigger-lover—was
amplified immeasurably by Clinton's marriage to the polarizing Hillary,
whose lawyerly demeanor, unapologetic liberal activism, ever-changing
hair, and blunt disdain for cookie-baking quickly set her up for rightist di-
abolization as the Anti-Mom, America's Worst Lady—a terrifying spectre
of the '60s' "women's lib."

The Clintons' actual flaws and/or misdeeds bore no relation to that
crackpot vision of pure evil. Likewise (to compare small things to great), the
Soviets' true record and intentions were irrelevant to the Cold War's wildest
agitators—who were also the most effective of the champions of that crusade. While there were surely anticommunists of principle—many of them
socialists—who did their best to tell the world what Leninism really meant,
the crucial animus in Cold War anticommunism came not from them but
from the fierce emotion of a certain lunatic plurality, roused and guided on
behalf of powerful interests in both parties and in the world of what they
used to call "big business." That mighty undertow—which flowed through
Nixon's mind and J. Edgar Hoover's and James Forrestal's and James An-
gleton's and all throughout the CIA and U.S. military as well as through the
Joe McCarthy cult and the John Birch Society—is a factor that revisionist
historians forget, or downplay, in their efforts to reglamourize the great U.S.
propaganda drive against the Reds. And that same warlike sentiment, peddled in the grassroots by the propagandists of the right, dominated U.S. politics throughout the '90s, and finally helped the House of Bush to put their
boy in office. While Clinton had the genius to survive the long attack

---

*According to a study by the Justice Policy Institute, released in February 2001, under Clin-
ton the number of Americans jailed increased by 673,000—as opposed to an increase of
478,000 under Reagan. Throughout the Clinton years, the prison population overall jumped
from 1.4 million to over 2 million, and the racial disproportion only worsened in that time.
Under Reagan/Bush, the rate of African-Americans imprisoned rose from 1,156 per 100,000
black men to about 2,800. Under Clinton, that rate grew to 3,620 per 100,000 black men.

Of course, Clinton was not himself responsible for such acceleration, which was built
into the system that the state in general created. Nor did Clinton loudly champion such mass
imprisonment, as did, for example, Governor Bush. Rather, he colluded in that evil passively
by not making any fuss about it, for political reasons—or perhaps because he always had a gun
pointed at his head.

against him, Al Gore lacked the crucial smoothness. Therefore, among the reasons for that Democrat's defeat we must include the winning GOP campaign to replace the Soviets with Clinton/Rodham Clinton/Gore in U.S. far-right demonology. Although it failed to finish Clinton, the slander stuck to Gore sufficiently to drive up Bush's numbers in the heartland so that the Republican endgame in Florida became decisive.

U.S. interference with democracy is nothing new. Indeed, it was the very hallmark of U.S. Cold War foreign policy. As the world learned in the 1970s, the CIA had long routinely meddled in the politics of other lands— from Italy to Ecuador, from Iran, Guatemala, and the Philippines to Vietnam, Cambodia, and Chile—using violence and every other kind of dirty trick to jar electorates into voting for "our" choices, not their own. The same sort of subversive operation was exposed by Watergate, which chillingly revealed that it could happen here—and did in 1972, George McGovern's very candidacy having been arranged through covert means by Nixon's team.* Iran-Contra was another major crime against democracy, the zealots in the White House and the CIA conspiring to ignore Congressional constraints on their worldwide jihad against the Reds. "We're too timid. The attitude is 'Don't stick your neck out. Play it safe.' This kind of crap is smothering us," CIA Director William Casey grumbled at one agency conclave.[93] And so the Reagan/Bush team forged an international arms-trading network answerable only to themselves, so as to fund the Contras by selling arms covertly to Iran's extremist government, in violation of the law and official U.S. policy.† Aside from the hefty profits real-

---

*Under orders from Charles Colson, Nixon's henchmen worked the eminently beatable McGovern into place primarily by wrecking the campaign of front-runner Ed Muskie. Through an impressive range of dirty tricks, including forgery and fabricated libel, the Nixon team sowed many anxious doubts about the candidate's trustworthiness and sanity. At length their efforts paid off handsomely when, on February 26, 1972, Muskie, campaigning in New Hampshire, threw a tearful fit outside the offices of the Manchester *Union Leader,* whose far-right publisher, William Loeb, had first run a piece insulting Muskie's wife and then a letter charging that the candidate had laughed at a pejorative description of the state's French Canadians ("Canucks"). The letter had been drafted by a Nixon operative.

†There is still abundant evidence—which a subsequent Congressional investigation scrupulously overlooked—that the Reagan/Bush team had come to power in the first place through

ized by certain of the principals, for the true believers in "the Enterprise," its main attraction lay in their apparent role as deputies of God. "Sometimes you have to go above the written law," as Fawn Hall, Oliver North's loyal secretary, put it at the Iran–Contra hearings, to justify her having taken part in the illegal shredding of official documents.

The belief that they were acting in the name of freedom kept such patriots on the job from the founding of the CIA until the fall of Soviet communism. Certainly there were a lot of cynics in that company, hard-boiled players who were only in it for the savage fun. However, such adventurism was always tacitly legitimized by the official view that the clandestine struggle was a necessary evil in the face of worldwide communist subversion—and there were agents who did not just pay lip service to that view but held it fervently. But whether they were opportunists or fanatics, or both at once, *all* Cold War activists could justify their antidemocratic coups, both foreign and domestic, as moves essential to the rescue of democracy.

That position was absurd and self-destructive—just like the Leninist defense of vast repression in the name of vast emancipation. And yet, although irrational, the antidemocratic argument of either side *was* justified, to some extent, by the other side's mere presence on the planet. That self-perpetuating face-off, which lasted until 1989, was already evident by the end of 1946, as Martin Walker has observed. "The more each side became convinced of its image of the other, the more they were locked into hostility."[94] Thus, for all their crimes against democracy, the busy agents of the CIA—as well as Nixon, Kissinger, Haldeman and Ehrlichman, Reagan, Bush, Weinberger, North, and Casey—always had a pretty good excuse (as did their Soviet counterparts).

---

an earlier covert arrangement with Iran. As Gary Sick first suggested—and as later reports have reconfirmed—in 1980 the Reagan campaign, under William Casey's management, may well have persuaded the lieutenants of the Ayatollah Khomenei not to free the U.S. hostages that they had taken in the coup of 1979 but to wait at least until Election Day. That delay would keep the incumbent Jimmy Carter from negotiating an "October surprise"—a sudden, joyous liberation of the men and women who had been imprisoned in Teheran for months—and associate such liberation with the new U.S. regime. As it happened, the timing of the hostages' release could not have been more flattering to Reagan/Bush, with emancipation coming *at the very moment* that the Gipper was sworn in. TV's split-screen spectacle of those two simultaneous events was an exhilarating propaganda coup.

There is no excuse for President George W. Bush. The coup that elevated him was a first in U.S. history. This time the plotters offered no dire warnings of an imminent takeover by the foreign Other—the crucial touch in every U.S. rightist insurrection from the Federalist crackdown of 1798 (in which the enemy of choice was France) to the federal move against dissent during World War I (the enemy then being Germany), up through the anti-Soviet campaign whose consequences we are living with today. The Bush campaign's unprecedented silence on the foreign threat was, first of all, necessitated by the simple fact that there *was* no such threat and had not been for quite some time. Despite much strenuous effort to concoct a foreign stand-in for the Soviets—"narcoterrorists," Islamic fundamentalists, China and/or one or all of the "rogue states"—no recent surrogate has had the staying power of the mammoth tyranny that quickly fell apart on Bush the Elder's watch—much to his obvious chagrin.

In any case, Bush/Cheney had no need for the old xenophobic rationale because the GOP had long since managed to convince the mad plurality of voters that the Democrats were now the most sophisticated enemies of the United States. Thus did the propagandists of the U.S. right finally accomplish what the tiny U.S. ultraleft had tried to do back in the latter days of SDS: "Bring the war home." Long persuaded that the neoliberal Democrats were Communists if not Satanists, the GOP's fringe-dwelling fellow travelers were aroused almost to violence by the innuendo coming from the party's operatives in Miami, Palm Beach, Washington, and Austin. As soon as Karl Rove, James Baker, Limbaugh, Novak, Bennett, and the rest had started hinting darkly that the Democrats were up to some generic "mischief" (a charge accompanied by not a shred of evidence), there were grassroots paranoids converging on South Florida—some common citizens showing up with guns, to help prevent *Al Gore* from stealing the election—while the campaign's somewhat cooler players ran the show.

And yet there also was a deeper reason why Bush/Cheney did not justify their moves by pointing scarily abroad. They offered no excuse because they didn't really see the need for one, the interruption of democracy not being such a bad thing in their eyes. Of course, if such a coup had taken place in *Russia*—a ballot recount halted, say, by a judicial bloc of five ex-

Stalinists so that the likely loser of a presidential contest was proclaimed the winner—the very players who made it happen here would be expressing steely outrage, and blaming it on Clinton, and calling for more spending on "defense." But it did happen here—and with exactly the same ruthless cynicism and subversive cunning that the right has always claimed to find appalling in the *Communists*. To anyone who ever heard the standard diatribe against the Soviets' global strategy of terror, the tactics used to put this President in office had to seem uncannily familiar. "Terrorism attempts to erode the legitimacy of democratic institutions," wrote one patriot in Ronald Reagan's time. "Its real and lasting effects cannot be measured in body counts or property damage but by its long-term psychological impact and the subsequent political results. The terrorists' cry is: Don't trust your government, your democratic institutions, your principles of law. None of these pillars of an open society can help you. Give in to our demands."

When Vice President Bush spoke those words in January 1987, he was, of course, referring to the governments of Libya, Nicaragua, and Cuba, El Salvador's FMLN, Colombia's M-19, and all related "murderous outfits."[95] (His purpose was to counteract the general "perception," as he put it, "that this Administration traded arms for hostages" in terrorist Iran.) As a reflection on the true intentions of those states and movements, it was a statement typically dishonest and sensational. As a prophetic self-description, on the other hand, it was as right as rain. "Don't trust your government, your democratic institutions, your principles of law." Thus did the Bush revanchists tell America throughout their postelectoral propaganda drive to smear the ballot and the courts—but only insofar as those great institutions threatened to assist the Democrats. The rightists would support our system, and assert its health, but only if it did their bidding. If it did not, they would proclaim it hopelessly corrupt and get their goons and others to dismantle it. In short: "Give in to our demands." It is indeed a strategy as un-American as Bush and all his cohorts liked to claim it was. The fact that they have used it to enthrone his son against our wishes now makes one thing finally clear—that it was always *they themselves* who posed the greatest danger to democracy, not whatever alien subversive movement they might rail against to keep themselves in power.

The spectacle of all those rightist factions working in overt collusion—religious maniacs and corporate lobbyists, radical free-marketeers and diehard segregationists, GOP opportunists and impatient military men—is quite a lurid picture. It is also incomplete, because it leaves out what is surely the most influential of the interests that have ravaged our democracy. Crucially, the mainstream media, and TV in particular (although not just TV), has helped the rightists out at every turn, as we have seen—throughout the race by always giving their preposterous candidate a passing grade, despite the daily evidence of our own senses, and largely snickering at his adversary for his loud sighs and makeup. Then, throughout the slo-mo postelectoral coup, they glossed over all the right's immense self-contradictions, always tactfully refraining from investigating the copious and graphic evidence of major "mischief" by the GOP and authoritatively demanding, early on, that Al Gore pack it in and do it graciously—as if it had been stipulated in our Constitution that the media, and not America's electorate, decides who should be president. And then, as soon as Bush had finished reading his inauguration speech, they instantly and totally forgot everything that had just happened, hailing the new president for his aplomb (which was apparent to no viewer) while always noting solemnly the "slender margin" of his "victory," and otherwise repressing the stark fact that *he was not elected*. The GOP helped make it just a little easier to manage that denial, first by neutralizing Jesse Jackson—the foremost champion of our learning how the vote had really gone in Florida—by leaking word of his love child to the *National Enquirer*, and then by orchestrating a whole new postpresidential reimpeachment drive against the Clintons, for their having taken certain items from the White House, and for the pardon of Marc Rich. However dubious those deeds may have been, they were nothing in comparison with stealing an election; but the watchdogs of the media went along with it enthusiastically—as if they felt grateful for the opportunity to turn their eyes, and ours, away from the subversion of democracy.

It is unlikely that the media will keep up this particular distraction. The anti-Clinton craze—a frenzy never broadly popular to start with—is certain shortly to become old news, however many more misdeeds or errors may be left to bring to light. (It may be old news by the time you read this.)

On the other hand, the president's own closet is well-known to be packed tight with skeletons, any one of which might do the trick should some elite subgroup decide that he must go. The tales are mostly rumors, and yet rumors, as the Clinton era has taught us, are certainly enough to paralyze a president—or do him in. For instance, the media may report, as if it were a fact, that Bush still drinks, or that he was arrested more than once for driving drunk, or that he got his girlfriend an abortion back in 1970 or that he *was* arrested for possession of cocaine in 1972, or—still more fantastic— that, when newly married to his Laura, he fathered a love child on the family's Chicana maid, and his parents paid the woman off to go and raise the girl in Mexico. The media may even find occasion to report, as if it were the truth, that Laura, in her youth, committed murder or manslaughter with her car—running down her boyfriend in the heat of passion after fighting with him. Such rumors are no wilder—and no better founded— than all the Gothic tales of treachery and depravity that swirled for years around the Clintons. Some or all of them may therefore end up in the news all day and night, for weeks and months on end, regardless of their truthfulness, if our president should ever anger the wrong people or make some other serious mistakes.

Such payback would gratify a lot of Democrats, just as Nixon's people have for years been tickled pink by Clinton's woes. To those of us concerned about democracy, however, that next wave of scandals, if and when it comes, cannot provide the slightest consolation, even if it finishes the House of Bush. For even at their gamiest, such revelations are simply not important. Indeed, it is encouraging that finally, most Americans could not care less about those epoch-making blowjobs in the Oval Office, or even about Clinton's disappointing "cover-up"—a squalid lie about a private episode. Such matters were irrelevant when Jefferson used them to slander Hamilton and when Jefferson's own enemies used them to slander him—and they are still irrelevant, despite the frequent plaints about "the death of outrage" vented by the likes of William Bennett, Robert Bork, and other big-time founts of natural gas. As the custodians of a government empowered to represent their interests, the citizens of a democracy must face the world as adults—not like children sitting in a Sunday school or watching some big patriotic movie. What *should* stir public outrage—and what *does*, despite TV—is the subversion of democracy; and when that crime does not work anybody up, and only then, it will be time to call it quits.

The petty morals charges are not just beside the point. Such titillating fare is yet more evidence of how our media system actually regards us: as nasty-minded dimwits, able to grasp nothing but the dumbest arguments, incapable of thinking past the next Big Mac, and interested only in the dirty parts of any story. Thus the media gave us almost no real news throughout the long electoral campaign. The coverage stuck to trivialities, in large part by adhering strictly to the tried-and-true Coke/Pepsi para-digm of Democrats/Republicans, *neither* of whose candidates made any waves on "free trade," military spending, foreign policy, "the drug war," the death penalty, campaign-finance reform—or media deregulation. With Nader noted only as a spoiler, so as to intensify the thrill-a-minute horse-race aspect of the narrative, there was no way to broaden "the debate" be-yond the usual foot-wide consensus. (When that inconvenient candidate was threatened with *arrest* unless he left the premises of the first debate—an antidemocratic stroke as shocking as the mob effort to disrupt the Miami recount—the media ignored the crime, as did the Democrats.) Such deliberate narrowness of focus was, at best, paternalistic—the media's employees protecting us from all complexity for their, and our, own good.

And yet their motivation was really not that simple; for if those em-ployees were mainly driven to protect the interests of their parent compa-nies, the anchors and reporters might just as easily have been pro-Gore, both men being near-impossible to tell apart on media-related issues, and Gore being, by a nose, the people's choice. Rather, what finally seemed to drive the anti-Democrat consensus at the top end of the mediocracy—among the likes of Brian Williams, Chris Matthews, Tim Russert, Cokie Roberts, and Sam Donaldson—was their wish to make it clear to all that *they* are in control. While certainly no flaming liberal, Gore did at least make sense and knew his stuff and otherwise evinced a certain civic ex-pectation of the audience—that they would listen carefully to what he had to say, and make their judgments based on reason. His references to the Dingell-Norwood bill for a patients' bill of rights made this clear—too clear for the tribunes of the media, who seemed resentful of such efforts to engage the viewers in terms a little more complex than those of advertising, TV news, and other forms of supersimple propaganda. And so they finally sneered at Gore—as they had done at Clinton—for knowing much of anything, and for replying with long sentences. On the other hand, the ill-prepared and incoherent Bush was literally more their style. Repeating his catchphrases endlessly and making errors that got easy laughs, he spoke no language but the language of TV—which, in their eyes, made him fit for office, whether he was voted in or not.

Thus we Americans have been tricked out of our democracy by a vast and very smart conspiracy of stupid talkers—people deftly talking *down* to us, so as to sell us shoddy goods of slightly different kinds. Throughout the GOP there are the rustic-seeming demogogues, kickin' back 'n' talkin' folksy to the TV audience—as if they were not fronting for the multinationals, and/or working for theocracy to benefit the Christian ultraright. That oppressive spectacle is moderated—and its darker hints ignored or laughed away—by telejournalists who talk the talk of advertising, constantly assuring us that they know what we'll buy and what it takes to sell us.

On either side of the equation, the political and the commercial, the populist pretense can barely hide the absolute contempt that all those talkers really feel for us, the people—whose show, lest we forget, this is supposed to be. Nor, of course, is that contempt apparent only in this latest, most egregious, of electoral thefts. The gradual suppression of democracy has taken place on many fronts, by varied means: through the GOP's refusal to update the methods of the national census, a tactic that has disenfranchised some three million voters, mostly black; through the "drug war," which has likewise had disastrous civic consequences, by sidelining a few million more minority voters, among others, in the system's federal and for-profit jails; through sophisticated union-busting methods, which have helped to keep America's workers isolated, anxious, and compliant; through "tort reform" and other steps to limit the prerogative of juries. At the top, all such moves are variously certified by a Supreme Court whose far-right majority—the dearest legacy of Reagan/Bush—invariably finds against the people on behalf of state, industrial and/or commercial *power,* whether its representatives are prison guards or corporate lobbyists, TV-station own-

ers or insurance companies, media barons or right-wing presidential candidates. It is that overriding interest, not "states rights" or "strict construc-
tionism," that guides the legal thinking of the Rehnquist bloc—whose
champions, meanwhile, keep on sounding off against "judicial activism."

And day by day the media cartel facilitates this huge infringement of
democracy, primarily by failing to report it. That cartel's aim is not to
serve us but to serve us up to advertisers; so increasingly its "journalism"
is all murder stories, sports and weather, showbiz items, corporate ads disguised as news, and lurid scandals that amount to nothing. Thus we are
deprived of the routine illumination on which all democracy depends—
that a general blackout has lately disenfranchised all of us, regardless of class,
creed or color. It was precisely to prevent just such a national catastrophe
that Jefferson and others pushed the First Amendment, ensuring freedom
of the press. It is a sign of just how hostile to democracy "the press" itself
has now become that its own managers invoke the First Amendment to
deny the public any worthwhile news—perversely arguing that it would
violate *their* free-speech rights if they were forced to serve "the public
interest"—and justify their massive exploitation of the public airways by
giving us a little noncommercial fare. (Rehnquist et al. buy that argument.)*

---

*For example: "In a major victory for large cable television companies, a U.S. appeals court
on Friday set aside federal rules that limit the number of customers one cable company can
serve.

"The unanimous decision by a three-judge panel of the appeals court in Washington,
D.C., could ultimately clear the way for AT&T Corp. and AOL Time Warner Inc., the nation's largest cable companies, to strengthen the grasp they already have on the U.S. cable
market.

"AT&T . . . and AOL Time Warner challenged the FCC's rules that say one company
can serve no more than 30 percent of the U.S. cable market. The companies also challenged
the agency's rule preventing companies from putting channels in which they hold a financial
interest on more than 40 percent of a system's offerings.

"The companies argued the rules violate constitutional free speech rights and are arbitrary and capricious. The court ruled the FCC never justified the basis for its limits, and sent
the rules back to the FCC to be reworked. . . .

"A spokeswoman for AOL Time Warner said it is "a good day for cable operators' 1st
Amendment rights." ("Court Sets Aside Limits to the Number of Customers One Cable Firm
Can Serve," *Chicago Tribune,* March 3, 2001.)

That such monopolistic sway must pose a threat to *the people's* First Amendment rights
is a fact not mentioned in such litigation—or in most news reports on all such findings.

A media system thus deregulated does not benefit its audience with more robust protection from the state. On the contrary: The mightier and less accountable that system, the *closer* its relations with the state's top dogs. Its journalists cannot afford to be too enterprising—as we have lately seen. One anecdote should make the point. A few days before Election Day, British journalist Greg Palast broke the story of how Gov. Jeb Bush's minions had illegally purged the names of over 64,000 voters, mostly Democrats, from the rolls in Florida. That revelation having gotten major play in Britain, as well as in *Salon,* Palast heard from a CBS News producer interested in doing a version of the story. Palast provided her with all his information on that scandal—and then gave her the makings of what would have been another hot exclusive:

> I also freely offered up to CBS this information: The office of the governor of Florida, brother of the Republican presidential candidate, had illegally ordered the removal of the names of felons from voter rolls—real felons, but with the right to vote under Florida law. As a result, thousands of these legal voters, almost all Democrats, would not be allowed to vote.
>
> One problem: I had not quite completed my own investigation on this matter. Therefore CBS *would have to do some actual work,* reviewing documents and law and obtaining statements. The next day I received a call from the producer, who said, "I'm sorry, but your story didn't hold up." Well, how did the multibillion-dollar CBS network determine this? Why, "we called Jeb Bush's office." Oh. And that was it.

While it appalled him, that lame response did not surprise him, Palast writes, since it is now "standard operating procedure for the little lambs of American journalism. One good, slick explanation from a politician or corporate chieftain and it's case closed, investigation over."[96] So much for the democratic ardor of "the liberal media"—an institution every bit as docile and reactionary, in its own ironic way, as the Fourth Estate in Baghdad or Havana.

The whole show, in a word, has gotten out of hand. To take it back, and finally master that production, we will have to pay some close attention to the boring stuff that made the TV people laugh throughout the last, abortive presidential race: campaign finance reform, thorough media reform, electoral reform. Only then will we be able even to discuss, much less effect, those larger changes that are also now required—in economics, criminal justice, education, national health care, foreign policy, environmental regulation, and all the other areas that our new unelected president so dimly understands.

And yet before we talk about reforms, there is something everyone now disenfranchised can and must do right away. We need to realize that the United States has been transformed—before our very eyes—into an outright plutocracy. The likes of Jefferson and Madison would never recognize this land of ours, whose major media serve only multinational corporations, and where the will of the majority no longer matters. It is a grim and painful situation; and yet we cannot rectify it until we've looked at it unflinchingly, just as Jefferson and Madison would do—and as the talking heads today will not.

In short, before we can recover any democratic possibility, we must first face the fact that we don't live in a democracy—and that we still deserve it, and can manage it.

POSTSCRIPT: YEAR ONE

THIS LAND IS MY LAND

After Governor Bush became our president, his tongue continued to betray his se-crets to the world, or at least to anybody who was paying attention. Sometimes he would accidentally state his real position loud and clear, despite his careful posture of "compassion." There was this blunt confession—and quick retraction—in his first budget speech:

> "Education is not my top priority!"
> [*Applause*]★
> "Education is my top priority!"   —FEBRUARY 27, 2001†

Similarly, when he would try to green himself, Bush sometimes fell off-message, let-ting slip his true concern:

★The moment's inadvertent honesty included the congressional Republicans, who frankly cheered the president's confession.
†Unless otherwise noted, all quotations of the president and his associates are taken from the transcripts published daily by the Federal News Service (FNS).

"I also strongly believe that we can explore for natural gas in Alaska without damaging the economy—the environment. And I believe that's necessary to do that!"

[*Applause*]

—ORLANDO, FLORIDA, DECEMBER 4, 2001

And in his ad-libs after 9/11, now and then the president would inadvertently bring up the dark side of his "war on terrorism," as if acknowledging the consequences— or the purpose—of his large-scale crackdown on our civil liberties:

"We are resolved to rout out terror wherever it exists to save the world from freedom!"

[*Applause*]

—ATLANTA, GEORGIA, JANUARY 31, 2002; FDCH POLITICAL TRANSCRIPTS

While he continued to reveal the truth at unexpected moments of lucidity, Bush also kept revealing what he really thought by often losing touch with English when attempting to feign sentiments that were not his. Thus he would speak nonsense, for example, when departing from his scripts on education, thereby confirming that that area was surely not his "top priority." He said as much in his remarks at the Hispanic Scholarship Fund Institute:

"If a person doesn't have the capacity that we all want that person to have, I suspect hope is in the far distant future, if at all."

—MAY 22, 2001

He evinced the same conviction in speaking to the National Urban League:

"Year after year, children without schools are passed along in schools without standards."   —AUGUST 1, 2001

Unclear when speaking on constructive subjects, throughout his first year Bush was especially uncompelling when he tried to sell the cause of peace. That failure was unfortunate, to say the least, since talk was just about the only thing the president

would do to leash the dogs of war. Concerning Israel, for example, where the blood flowed ever heavier throughout the summer, he promised only to keep telling both sides to stop fighting, please: "The United States will continue to stay actively involved in urging there to be calm, in urging both parties to resist the temptation to resort to violence," Bush offered on July 13. A born cheerleader, he sometimes called for "peace" as if demanding one more touchdown. "And if the Palestinians are interested in a dialogue, then I strongly urge Mr. Arafat to put a hundred percent effort," he said on August 24, "into—into—into solving the terrorist activity, into stopping the terrorist activity." The limp conclusion of that sentence, after such a rah-rah start, made all too clear that Bush was bored stiff by the prospect of conciliation—which came across, in his unconscious prose, as boring diplomatic rituals and preachy talking.

"These terrorist acts and the responses have got to end in order for us to get the framework—the groundwork, not framework—the groundwork to discuss a framework, to lay the—all right."
—AUGUST 13, 2001

Although, after 9/11, Bush now and then asserted that the United States loves peace and always has, his ad-libbed comments on that theme were still completely uninspiring, while some of them were just as cryptic as his weirdest prewar utterances:

"And so one of the areas where I think the average Russian will realize that the stereotypes of America have changed is that it's a spirit of cooperation, not one-upsmanship; that we now understand one plus one can equal three, as opposed to us, and Russia we hope to be zero."
—NOVEMBER 15, 2001

Whether it was international "cooperation" or "children without schools" or "the environment," or any other point of light, Bush was at risk rhetorically whenever he assayed a do-good theme. Even his own altruistic pretext for the bombing of Afghanistan would sometimes lead him into verbal trouble—which is not surprising, since he really couldn't have cared less about the people living there. When, six months before Election Day, the governor was asked about the Taliban, his reply was cursory and glib (p. 199). Four months into his term, the president expressed the same jocose indifference to Afghanistan—the place, he said facetiously, "where them loonies shoot up the statues."[97] *But when the Taliban became our latest enemy, Bush suddenly perceived the horror of their antifeminist atrocities—much as his dad had done with General Noriega back in 1989, and with Saddam Hussein the following year, both monsters having been acceptable enough until the state saw fit to demonize them. Whether this Bush had been soft on Mullah Omar's movement out of simple apathy, or because of some back-channel oil-related dealings with the Taliban, from 9/11 on he condemned their cruelty as if it had been galling him for years—although, as usual, his unruly mouth would sometimes give the game away:*

"We're freeing women and children from incredible impression!"
[*Cheers, applause*]
— AURORA, MISSOURI, JANUARY 14, 2002

On the other hand, when speaking of his war as punishment and nothing else, the president was clear, his grammar sound, his syntax unconfused—just as it had been when, as a candidate, he had defended execution by the state (pp. 242–45).

"We're not into nation-building. We're focused on justice. And we're going to get justice."   —SEPTEMBER 25, 2002

Bush's incapacity for lucid idealism raises a disturbing question: How does the president of the United States conceive of the United States? Certainly he has the highest praise for this "great land"—a "fabulous country," "a fantastic country," "the greatest country on the face of the earth," etc. Such demagogic cries of vague approval prompt us to ask what, exactly, makes the United States so "fabulous" in Bush's eyes; for the greatness of America has everything to do with the ideals that drove our founders to create this nation in the first place—yet those ideals do not come up in Bush's frequent paeans to "America." What, then, does this country mean to him?

Bush started to address that question out in Crawford, in the dog days of our final prewar summer. Those presidential musings were the centerpiece of a new propaganda campaign called "Communities of Character"—a drive intended to improve our leader's standing in the polls. Alarmed by his earthbound approval ratings, the White House hoped to highlight Bush's "warmth" and demonstrate "the ease with which he understands and talks about issues," as one official put it. ("We've got to find a way to bring those elements out," he added wishfully.)[98] "Communities of Character" placed Bush in woodsy volunteerist settings and had him giving vent to much transcendent hogwash about "values" as the source of "character" (or vice versa). He tried it, for example, at a YMCA camp in Colorado:

> "The spirit of America is found in the character of our citizens, the value base that makes America, I think, such a different kind of place—a place that—a country that values family and friendship, a place where people learn values and character. One of the things that—when I try to describe America to somebody who has never been here, I say, 'We're a country stitched together by communities of character.' "

He noted the sublime tableau of the surrounding Rockies—which, he said, were not just "beautiful."

> "There's also a grand vision embodied in these mountains. And the vision is that we can teach our children right from wrong. And we can teach them good, sound values, so that when they get older they'll make the right choices in their life."
> —AUGUST 20, 2001

Aside from trying to make the president seem kindly and on top of things, such nonsense was meant also to serve certain other propaganda purposes: plug the volunteerist enterprise of "faith-based" operations (as alternatives to federal assistance); discreetly pander to the "heartland," where the president had most of his electoral support; and, through the scenic backdrops, further obfuscate his grim environmental plans. For all the ingenuity behind the packaging, however, that sentimental drive did nothing to reverse, or even slow, Bush/Cheney's downward spiral. The White House policies were too right-wing for the majority, and Bush's act completely unconvincing—because he didn't care a fig about "communities of character" (whatever that phrase meant), and his indifference clearly showed.

After 9/11, the president worked the "values" pitch into his unending wartime

pep talk. America, he claimed repeatedly, is great because its people are so good—a
line that never moved him to "Churchillian" heights:

"And it's my duty as the president of the United States to use the
resources of this great nation, a freedom-loving nation, a
compassionate nation, a nation that understand values of life, and
rout terrorism out where it exists."   —OCTOBER 11, 2002

"Oftentimes I've spoke—when I speak around the nation, I talk
about the great strength of the nation lies in the hearts and souls of
our citizens. I was using military terms at times even before the war
began. I talked about 'armies of compassion.' I truly believe that's one
of the wonderful strengths of America—that we have got armies of
compassion all across our country."   —NOVEMBER 20, 2001

"And it's going to be a great year, primarily because Americans
have—have taken a look inward, reassessed our values, and realized
that some of the basics in life are that which is most important—love
of faith, love of family—and as a result, our communities will be
stronger. So I'm—I'm—I'm really looking forward to 2002."
                                              —DECEMBER 31, 2001

"It is the momentum of a millions of acts of kindness that take place
all across America, that's how we stand up to evil. And if any country
can do it, it is this country, because this is a—
                           [*Applause*]
—because this is a nation that is loving and strong, compassionate,
God-fearing, a nation that will not relent when it comes to our most
precious value, and that value is freedom."   —FEBRUARY 8, 2002

Thus, in his continuing paean to "America," the president consistently applauded
"values" rather than "ideals." Between those terms there is an all-important differ-
ence. Certainly the former carries quite a pungent whiff of cultural conservatism, in-
voking the nostalgic fantasy of "family values"—Dad makes the rules, Mom bakes
the bread, the kids are right with Jesus, and there's no safe sex, or any sex at all.
However, while it surely does invoke that vision, Bush's emphasis on "values" is ac-

tually more quietist than theocratic. Whereas America's ideals inspire us to a certain civic activism, Bush's "values" urge us all away from any effort at self-rule—the most important "value" of them all, according to our founding documents. In Bush's view, this land is "great" because its people happen to be "good" themselves—too good, in fact, to call the shots. "Strong and decent and compassionate," those paragons don't ever step outside the narrow sphere of "family" and "faith," except to run some kindly errands in the neighborhood. "Freedom-loving" they may be, yet they would never think to exercise their freedom to participate in government—or, indeed, "to institute new Government, laying its Foundation on such Principles, and organizing its Powers in such Form, as to them shall seem most likely to effect their Safety and Happiness," to quote the Declaration of Independence. Thus Bush's "strong" Americans make lousy citizens—but first-rate soldiers, always eager to fight "evil," and to follow orders.

Of course, the president's aversion to democracy was no big secret, since he had been vaulted into power against the will of the electorate. Still, it was always something of a shock when he would make the feeling obvious, as he did at some unguarded moments.

STUDENT:	What's your most favorite thing?
BUSH:	Most favorite thing—helping people, to make a difference in people's lives, setting a good example, so that youngsters like yourself realize that democracy is—can be a very good system, that politics is a noble calling.*

—CRAWFORD ELEMENTARY SCHOOL,
CRAWFORD, TEXAS, AUGUST 27, 2001

And yet, as usual, it was when he tried to fake it that his deep uninterest came across most vividly. On his first Independence Day as president of the United States, Bush tried to capture the peculiar democratic majesty of the occasion:

REPORTER:	What's the occasion, Mr. President?
BUSH:	Wanted to come over. We're looking out our window every day at the Jefferson. It's a beautiful day.

Politics As a Noble Calling—a book that Bush may well have read—is the memoir of F. Clifton White, Goldwater's chief strategist and mentor to Reagan's major operatives.

Wanted to come over and begin the beginning of the Fourth of July celebration at the Jefferson Memorial. It's an opportunity to say hello to some of our fellow Americans.

REPORTER: What does the Fourth mean to you, Mr. President?

BUSH: Well, it's an unimaginable honor to be the president during the Fourth of July in this country. It means what these words say, for starters. The great inalienable rights of our country. We're blessed with such values in America. And I—it's—I'm a proud man to be the nation based upon such wonderful values.

I can't tell you what it's like to be in Europe, for example, to be talking about the greatness of America. But the true greatness of America are the people.   —JULY 2, 2001

On the subject of America, however, Bush did not always sound like someone coming out of anesthesia. When trying to extoll democracy and our "inalienable rights," he was completely incoherent. On the other hand, when improvising on his private piece of this "great land" of ours, the president was not just comprehensible but sometimes almost eloquent—his ownership inspiring him to much the same unwonted clarity that baseball, war, and executions also seem to call from him.

"Anyway, you can kind of get a feel. These little cleared-out areas now, they'll be full of windflowers in the spring. And the greens will come out. This place was emerald green in the spring. I mean, it's hard to envision, and you probably think I'm exaggerating, but we had enough rain to really green this place up. It was spectacular."

—AUGUST 25, 2001

"We're making great progress in one of our—one of the bottom areas that was heretofore relatively inaccessible. One of these days I'll take you down there. It's a beautiful place. It's a Bois d'Arc grove. The Bois d'Arc tree is a native tree, real hard wood, that grows these giant green, kind of apple-looking things."

—DECEMBER 28, 2001

*Moved almost to poetry by the thought of his own grounds, while speaking mainly gibberish on the subject of our fundamental rights, our unelected president was just the man to sit atop this system, which we might call "America without democracy."
In his first State of the Union address, Bush boldly advertised that system to the world, and did it with no gaffes, and no apologies:*

"We have no intention of imposing our culture, but America will always stand firm for the nonnegotiable demands of human dignity: the rule of law, limits on the power of the state, respect for women, private property, free speech, equal justice and religious tolerance."

—JANUARY 29, 2002

That Bush's catalog omits "democracy," exalts "the rule of law" to paramount importance, and puts "private property" ahead of "equal justice" and "free speech" says everything we need to know about his patriotic vision.

"THANKS FOR THE $600 REBATE CHECK": A SCAM

Although the "war on terrorism" certainly improved his act, prior to 9/11 there had been some home-front battles that the president had also fought with noticeable confidence. Much like his grandiose world "crusade," those national drives allowed him to exert the "war mentality" that is his special gift,* enabling him to stay on message largely without blowing any lines.

Bush's first such fight concerned his giant tax cuts. To whip up popular support for that ambitious bill—from which the populus would realize no benefits—the president kept pounding on his bully pulpit with an awesome single-mindedness and staggering perverseness that suggested something not unlike intelligence. At his May 11, 2001, press conference, for example, he answered question after question, after some preliminary jive, with the same blunt, urgent call to Congress—a repetition so hypnotic that you might have failed to notice that each answer was beside the point, and false to boot.

---

*"Freaked out, the girls are. Wife's OK. She understands we're at war—got a war mentality. And so do I." "Bush Cheers N.Y. Rescue Workers," AP, September 15, 2001.

Q: Mr. President, a lot of families are struggling to pay for gasoline at record prices. What can you do to help them in the short term? Will your energy report address that? And do you agree with your Energy secretary that OPEC bears some responsibility for these prices?

BUSH: . . . [T]he best way to make sure that people are able to deal with high energy prices is to cut taxes, is to give people more of their own money, so they can meet the bills, so they can meet the high energy prices. . . .

Q: Your party in the past has argued in favor of either suspending or rolling back the federal gasoline tax. Will you consider doing either?

And secondly, what would you say to American families who may pay as much as $3 at the pump this summer at the same time the oil companies in this country are experiencing and enjoying record profits?

BUSH: . . . [T]he Congress needs to cut taxes as quickly as possible, to give people money to be able to deal with this situation. . . . But the quickest way to get money in people's pockets to deal with prices is tax relief. . . .

Q: Mr. President, are you really going to let Republicans and Congress go home for the next recess without some kind of other short-term relief? You know the Democrats are after you and the vice president, saying you're a couple of former oil men protecting the industry. Would you at least support the Republican bill in the House which would ease some emission standards in California?

BUSH: . . . Let's get the tax relief done and do it quickly. I hope there is no intention to delay. There needs to be money in the pockets of our consumers as quickly as possible. . . .

Q: What about that emissions bill?

BUSH: I'll look at all options, but the clearest way to get things done quickly is tax relief. . . . The quickest way to help people with their energy bills is tax relief. That is the quickest, surest way to do so. . . .

Q: Mr. President, on the question of repealing the gas tax, even some Republicans have questioned the leadership and the clarity of voice from this White House about what they should do. I've talked to several Republican leaders who have said the White House has said, look, if you can figure out a way to pass it, we'll say it's okay, but we're not going to propose it. And what they say is if the White House would say they're for it, it would be easier for us to pass it. Can you tell the American people right now—

BUSH: . . . Pass the tax relief as quickly as possible. That's the quickest way to help consumers. . . . Pass the tax relief package as quickly as possible. . . .

Q: Given what's going on with energy prices and the difficulties in the economy, can you assure the American people at the start of your term that they will be better off at the end of it than they are today? And if they're not, should they blame you?

BUSH: . . . I'm not really that concerned about standing in polls. I'm doing what I think is the right thing to do, and the right thing to do is to have proposed a tax relief package. . . . I proposed the plan, I cam-paigned on the plan. . . . If I had my way, I'd have it in place tomorrow so that people would have money in their pockets to deal with high energy prices, so people would have money in their pockets to be able to plan for the future. . . .

What that mesmerizing nonexchange did not convey—since none of the reporters would come out and say it—was that those Americans now "struggling to pay for gasoline," and whom Bush claimed to want to "help" by getting his "tax relief pack-

age [passed] as quickly as possible," were not included in the package, and therefore were not getting tax relief. In any case, as should be clear by now, the purpose of the president's robotic pitch for "tax relief" was to distract the general audience from two gigantic rip-offs: one at the gas pumps, the other shortly to be authorized by Congress.

The president's bill was passed on May 26—and yet his fight did not stop there. For months thereafter he kept defiantly repitching what appeared to be the most attractive feature of the bill: the "tax rebates"—$300 for individuals, $600 for couples filing jointly—that had started coming right away (preceded by a special mailing from the IRS, which emphasized the president's responsibility for such largesse, and promised further tax cuts in the future).

"You know, this really isn't a gift from the government. This is a refund of your own money—money you've earned and money you will now be able to spend. In February, I told the American people that our federal government was overcharging them. I said the federal government was overcharging them, and, on your behalf, I demanded a refund. Congress worked with me in a bipartisan way, and now your money is on its way back to you."

— FROM ITALY, JULY 20, 2001

"Driving into the high school here, I saw a sign that said, 'Thanks for the $600 rebate check.'

[Applause]

"But what I should have—what I should have done was stopped and said, 'You don't need to thank me. It's your money to begin with!'

[Cheers, applause]

"Some of them in our nation's capital say $600 doesn't matter to a family. Well, what they ought to do is get out of the capital—I presume they are—and come out and talk to the working people of America, and find out what $600 means. I was in a Harley Davidson plant yesterday in Milwaukee. A lot of the workers came up and said, 'Thanks for my 600.' One fellow said, 'I built a deck. You need to come over and have a beer with me.'

[Laughter]

"I said, 'I quit drinking.'

[Laughter, cheers, applause]

"He said, 'How about root beer?'"

[*Laughter*]

—HARRY S. TRUMAN HIGH SCHOOL,
INDEPENDENCE, MISSOURI,
AUGUST 21, 2001

"I can't tell you how proud I am to be traveling around the country and people walk up and say, 'Thanks for the $600.' Now there are some cynics who say 600 doesn't mean anything to a working family in America. That's not what I hear. I hear it means a lot to people."

—CRAWFORD, TEXAS, AUGUST 24, 2001

"You see, there's a big debate in Washington about the money in Washington. Sometimes, folks up there lose sight about whose money it is. That money is not the government's money; it's the people's money. And we did the right thing with sharing that money with the people who pay the bills.

"We've taken action. As you can see, this is an administration that, when we see a problem, we move. We don't stick our finger in the air trying to figure out which way the wind is blowing. I don't need a poll or focus group to tell me what to think. I do what I think is right for the American people. And we'll just let the political chips fall where they may. And the right thing to do was to cut the taxes."

—PITTSBURGH, PENNSYLVANIA, AUGUST 26, 2001

Bush showed his "war mentality" in the convincing zest with which he kept reminding us of all that he had done for us—i.e., of all that they had tried to take away from us. They were "the federal government" and/or "some in the nation's capital," those (Democratic) "cynics" who do not appreciate "what $600 means to a working family." Of course, they also naturally included Clinton—who did always "need a poll or focus group" to tell him what to think, whereas this president just "cut the taxes," sending out those blessed checks because it was "the right thing to do."

It was a breathtaking performance, all the more impressive for its general gaffe-lessness—because the whole thing was a bald and screaming lie. First of all, the Democrats were understandably annoyed by the president seizing credit for that "refund," which he and the Republicans had actually opposed. *When Bush signed on to the Democrats' request for short-term tax relief, it was late in the game, and he did it only to secure the Democrats' agreement to those long-term rate cuts that he really wanted, since they would "help" not "working families" but his peers.*[99]

But far more stunning than that merely partisan deception is the basic fact that each such modest check was not a "refund," or a "rebate," but a mere advance— *as you may know by now, especially if you had to pay it back. If, after filing, you had no refund coming from the IRS in 2002, you would owe that prior "refund" to the government; while, if you were due such a refund, you would find the prior "refund" now deducted from it.*

Indeed, the only way most people could find out the truth about the "rebates" was by such delayed discovery that they weren't "rebates" at all—the media having failed to point it out. "I, like millions of others, got my notice from the IRS just yesterday, saying that I'm going to get a $600 rebate the week of August 6. That's good news for the Russert family! Isn't this good news for all of America?" Tim Russert asked Tom Daschle on July 22, with a happy gleam of avarice in his eyes—suggesting that he didn't know the score. (Oddly, Daschle didn't set him straight.) The corporate press repeated the same fiction endlessly, and thereby reconfirmed the president's big lie—which he repeated in his first State of the Union speech (so as to push those rate cuts for the rich):

"Good jobs depend on sound tax policy. Last year—

[*Applause*]

—some in this hall—last year some in this hall thought my tax relief plan was too small. Some thought it was too big.

[*Applause*]

"But when the checks arrived in the mail, most Americans thought tax relief was just about right.

[*Cheers, applause*]

"Congress listened to the people and responded by reducing tax rates, doubling the child credit and ending the death tax. For the sake of long-term growth and to help Americans plan for the future, let's make these tax cuts permanent."

[*Cheers, sustained applause*]

—JANUARY 29, 2002

DUBYA AGONISTES

As soon as they took office, the president and his associates, flush with their electoral success, moved swiftly to impose a militant antiabortion program on as many fronts as possible—a bold assault, since Bush the candidate had posed as moderate on that issue (see pp. 236–41). The blitzkrieg started with Bush/Cheney's nomination of John Ashcroft as attorney general. Ashcroft had been agitating for a constitutional abortion ban since 1972—a year before he entered politics, and three years prior to Roe v. Wade. As his state's attorney general, then governor, the dour Missourian said not a word to stem the rising tide of "pro-life" violence against abortion clinics. Indeed, Ashcroft had been a warm supporter of the Infant's Protection Act, which would have legalized the use of violence to halt abortions in Missouri.[100] *(When the bill was stopped by Governor Mel Carnahan, Ashcroft called the veto "tragic.")*

Despite such evidence of his extremism (also including his defense of the Confederacy), Ashcroft made it through his confirmation hearings early in Bush/Cheney's honeymoon. Nor was there any real impediment to Bush's second "pro-life" move—an executive order barring federal support for family planning services abroad that might perform abortions, or even recommend them. (This meant that such clinics' personnel could not even discuss abortion, other than to speak against it, or else they would risk losing all U.S. support.) And then, that same week, the president announced his opposition to stem cell research, hinting that he would soon reinstate the federal ban that had been put in place by Reagan/Bush—and that Bill Clinton had then overturned in 1993. Although Bush Jr. ruled out only such research that might require aborted fetuses, his staff made clear that he meant all stem cell research, as he had seemed to say throughout the presidential race.

Here the White House finally overreached. The GOP's hard ranks were all together on the Ashcroft nomination, while Bush/Cheney's new executive order was too technical, and its consequences too remote, to rouse much protest. On the question of stem cell research, however, there was some potent opposition to the party line—which didn't seem to make a lot of sense to any but the most exacting pro-life propagandists, since it was soon clear that such research could thrive without the use of stem cells from aborted fetuses. Because the research promised to alleviate much human suffering, scientists and doctors lined up solidly in opposition to a ban—as did most Americans, and many pro-life activists, including certain big shots in the GOP itself.

Thus our new president was in a bind of his own making—not unlike the early bind that Clinton had created for himself by pushing right away for letting gays serve in the military without fear of punishment. If Bush had played down the issue instead of talking tough about it, he would have had more leeway to finesse the issue. Now, however, he could not give in without appearing as a traitor to his base (cf. "Read my lips!"). If, on the other hand, he stuck to that severe minority position, he'd end up looking pretty uncompassionate, with all those Alzheimer's survivors (including Nancy Reagan), and quadriplegics (including Christopher Reeve), and other high-profile afflicted people blinking tearfully on Sixty Minutes.

And so the best thing Bush could do—or so the White House evidently thought—was spin that tough political decision as an epic philosophical ordeal. Such a game plan seemed to promise several propaganda benefits. First of all, by dragging out the whole affair and playing up the vast complexity and difficulty of the issue, the president might be shielded from eventual criticism. The more he seemed to agonize, the likelier it was that his old comrades, or the other side, might cut the guy a little slack if he should finally have to disappoint them. And there could be other, longer-term advantages. By overdramatizing his alleged inner struggle, the president's propagandists helped obscure some uninspiring aspects of his character. There was Bush's famed aversion to long books and heavy thinking—and here he was discussing Life Itself with theologians, ethicists, geneticists! And now the same man who, as governor, had been notoriously casual about approving executions—taking thirty minutes, tops, reviewing every case—was now engaged in months of wondering deeply at the ethical and moral consequences of his final word, whatever it might be. And there was, of course, the necessary implication, or reminder, that the president was not Bill Clinton, who would have sought out pollsters to decide the matter for him—whereas this issue was too serious for politics.

Here again, in short, Bush was at war—trying to disarm his critics on both sides, fighting our impression of him, tacitly assailing Clinton. The war analogy was fixed within the president's own mind, or so his chief political advisor claimed. "Karl Rove said the president compared this in magnitude to if he had to commit troops," said one awed congressman, after Rove had briefed a group of GOP House members in July.[101] While overblown (if not absurd), the president's analogy was apt, since Bush was once again surprisingly capacitated by his sense of being under fire.

Throughout the long, long build-up to his speech, he did what was for him a cred-
itable job suggesting what a heavy mental/moral struggle he was going through:

"This is a very serious issue that has got a lot of ramifications to it,
and I'm going to take my time because I want to hear all sides. I
want to fully understand the opportunities and to fully think
through the dilemmas.

"And so I will make an announcement in due course, when I'm
ready. And it doesn't matter who is on what side, as far as I'm
concerned. This is a decision I'll make. And somehow to imply that
this is a political decision is—I guess either doesn't understand how
I—somebody doesn't understand how I think or really doesn't
understand the full consequence of the issue. This is way beyond
politics.

"This is an issue that speaks to morality and science and the
juxtaposition of the both. And the American people deserve a
president who will listen to people and to make a serious, thoughtful
judgment on this complex issue. And that's precisely how I'm going
to handle it."   —JULY 23, 2001

Ari Fleischer on the president's ordeal:

"As the president approaches this decision, he's thinking very
carefully and very thoughtfully about different people's perspectives
on this issue, and many of those perspectives include things that are
individual and things that are personal, and the president is very
aware that there is a balance on this issue, where there is so much
potential for health and for breakthroughs. On the other hand, the
president is very concerned about preserving a culture of life, and
both sides of the issue have very compelling, important personal
stories to tell. And the president is a good listener and he's going to
have a very thoughtful approach to this."   —JULY 9, 2001

"It is a very complicated and nuanced decision, and it's something
the president is approaching in a very thoughtful and deliberative

fashion. I think, frankly, it's a fashion which the American people will take comfort that the decision the president makes on stem cell research will be based on careful thought, careful deliberation and a lot of listening. And he will make the decision on his own timetable. And he is going to listen to a lot of parties and face the complexities that this issue raises for everybody in our American society."

—JULY 11, 2001

"He's listening and he's thinking. He's weighing the arguments that people have presented to him, both proponents and the opponents. And he's giving it very careful consideration. He's weighing the moral implications of the issues that are presented to him from all sides, the scientific implications, and the powerful promise of science implications, as well as the implications for what it means for someone who respects a culture of life. And many of these are conflicting pieces of information that are brought to him, and he's carefully weighing them and considering them, thinking about them.

"And as you heard him say last week, he'll make up his mind on his own timetable, and when he does, he will share the reasons on how he arrived at the decision, what it was that he weighed, and how he came to the decision he'll ultimately come to."

—JULY 25, 2001

" 'He seems to be going over it again and again,' says someone in the administration who has discussed the issue with him."

—*TIME,* JULY 23, 2001

"PRESIDENT STRUGGLING WITH STEM CELL ISSUE."

—UPI, JULY 26, 2001

And Laura Bush:

"I think he is making up his mind, but I'm not really sure where he is right now on it. I think it's a very serious issue. It's a very serious moral and ethical issue and scientific issue. And he's heard from a lot

of different people, a lot of experts in a lot of different fields. And
when he makes up his mind, he'll let everyone know."

—INSIDE POLITICS, CNN, JULY 30, 2001

*And even after Bush had made his speech, the White House kept it up. The next
day, Karen Hughes conducted an interminable briefing on the Big Decision, going
on and on and on and on as if to hypnotize the stunned reporters into full appreciation of her boss's newfound gravitas.*

"This is an issue that I think almost everyone who works at the
White House, the president asked them their opinion at some point
or another. And not only did he ask your opinion, but he also asked
really probing questions about, you know, what leads you to that
conclusion, what ethical considerations did you give that? He didn't
stop at knowing what you thought about this issue, he wanted to
know the moral underpinnings, the rationale, the reasons that you
held that position. And I think literally virtually everybody who
works in the White House has been asked at one point or another
on this issue by the president about our positions.

"One of the things that struck me during all the meetings was the
profound nature of this decision. Almost everyone who came into
the Oval Office to talk with the president on—no matter what their
position, no matter what side of the issue they took—talked about
the tremendous ramifications. Several people told him, you know,
this may be the most important decision of your presidency, or this is
one of the most important decisions you will make, this has more
ramifications than, you know, almost anything else you will do as
president. And a number of people made that point to him. . . ."

*"Karen," one reporter broke in desperately, "I've never known you or the president
to detail the background of a decision like this, in such laborious detail. Why does
the president think it's important to share all of this with the American people?"
But still she soldiered on—reading from the notes she took on Bush's meetings with
the ethicists, listing his encounters with the scientists, and finally turning to the
books the president had used as props the night before.*

"I did bring—forgot to mention these books. A few people have asked about the books that were on the table next to the president during his address last night.

"These were the books. And these were the books that—this is a—the National Institutes of Health report on the science that was prepared at the request of Secretary Tommy Thompson when the president asked that we look in depth into the science."

She turned to Jay Lefkowitz, general counsel of the OMB.

HUGHES:	I think that was in March of this year?
LEFKOWITZ:	I think in late—
HUGHES:	Maybe in February of this year. And so this is the report that came out right as we were about to go to Europe in July, from the National Institutes of Science. And this is a briefing book that Jay prepared for the president and members of our senior staff, that has a very balanced view of all the different arguments, ethical arguments—
LEFKOWITZ:	Legal issues—
HUGHES:	—legal issues—
LEFKOWITZ:	—scientific—
HUGHES:	—scientific issues—
LEFKOWITZ:	—background papers.
HUGHES:	—background papers on this very complex issue.

To hammer home her point about the president's heroic cogitations, she would have shown some actual footage of his pulsing brain, if such a video had been available. It was, to put it mildly, overkill; and yet the White House propaganda choristers kept killing anyway, those working for the press continuing the song. After granting that Ms. Hughes's dog-and-pony show had been a little much, the Wall Street Journal's *Paul Gigot, commenting on PBS's* Newshour with Jim Lehrer, *himself belatedly joined in:*

"But I think it's genuine in the sense that I think he *did* grapple with this. I mean, I talked to people who, quite apart from the White House, [were] just reporting other stories. Medicare reform,

for example. . . . 'Bush would say, "What do *you* think about the
stem cell research?" It was an hour meeting, and we spent forty-five
minutes on stem cell and fifteen minutes on Medicare!' So I think
that that was legitimate."

—*NEWSHOUR WITH JIM LEHRER*, PBS, AUGUST 10, 2001

*And what about the speech itself? After all that agonistic hooha, with Bush and all
his henchmen endlessly asserting how "profound," "complex," and "difficult" the
issue is, the long-awaited speech itself expressed no thoughts at all (although it kept
on stressing the profundity, complexity, and difficulty of the issue). First Bush sen-
timentally affirmed the sanctity of all those teeny customers—"each embryo is
unique," he said, and added that, if he were going to allow their use for research purposes, he'd do so with "a heavy heart." But then, when he finally said that he* would
*let the scientists use those stem cell lines that were already extant, he expressed no
sorrow for those embryos—nor did he offer any explanation as to why* that *use of
embryonic tissue was okay:*

> "Embryonic stem cell research offers both great promise and great
> peril. So I have decided we must proceed with great care. As a result
> of private research, more than sixty genetically diverse stem cell lines
> already exist. They were created from embryos that have already
> been destroyed, and they have the ability to regenerate themselves
> indefinitely, creating ongoing opportunities for research. I have
> concluded that we should allow federal funds to be used for research
> on these existing stem cell lines, where the life-and-death decision
> has been made. Leading scientists tell me research on these sixty lines
> has great promise that can lead to breakthrough therapies and cures."

*Thus Bush finally skated over the complexities and difficulties, rendering a split-the-
difference verdict meant to placate either side (and that his team had been devising
all along, while he supposedly sat clutching at his head). And as it was a failure intellectually and morally, so did the oration fail politically. Those who had been lobbying against stem cell research were bitterly, and rightly, disappointed—Bush having
simply dumped the very principle that they had been defending all along. And yet
the speech also perplexed the scientists, who knew that there weren't over sixty viable stem cell lines, and that the prospects of the ones that did exist were surely not
as bright as Bush had said.*[102]

The speech, in short, was but another scam, its purpose only to confuse and neutralize his critics, while making him look "deep" as well as "strong" and "sure." And if the president could screw up a decision that ostensibly preoccupied him over months and months, what of all those countless others that he's rendered with his usual impulsiveness?

STUDENT:	Is it hard to make the decisions as President?
BUSH:	Is it hard to make decisions as President? Not really. If you know what you believe, decisions come pretty easy.

—CRAWFORD ELEMENTARY SCHOOL,
CRAWFORD, TEXAS, AUGUST 27, 2001

HOME IS WHERE THE HEART IS

As president, Bush continued to come out with memorable tautologies: "Our nation must come together to unite," he cried in Tampa (June 4, 2001), and, at the Summit of the Americas in Quebec City, he made it clear that "commerce and trade go hand in hand" (April 21, 2001). Such accidental gems were, as ever, good for laughs, but they were not as telling, or important, as the grand tautology that Bush has often reconfirmed in one way or another— that he is who he is, knows what he knows, believes what he believes.

He put that gnomic self-description most explicitly the first time he expressed it, on PBS's NewsHour with Jim Lehrer (see p. 195): "I'm not going to play like I've been a person who's spent hours involved with foreign policy. I am who I am." Since becoming president he has now and then restated that position, less mystically, perhaps, but just as bluntly. Strolling with his wife in Rome soon after the police riot in Genoa, he offered playfully to give the crowd a speech. ("The steps where the orators used to speak is right over there—is anybody interested?") A reporter asked him if his views on globalization had been influenced in any way by the protests in Genoa, and— "to the confusion of some of the listening journalists," according to Reuters—Bush replied:

"I know what I believe. I will continue to articulate what I believe and what I believe—I believe what I believe is right."—JULY 23, 2001

And a month later, fielding questions from a grade-school class in Crawford, Bush was asked if it was hard for him to make decisions as the president. He answered that it really wasn't, and continued:

"If you're one of these types of people that are always trying to figure out which way the wind is blowing, decision-making can be difficult. But I find that—I know who I am. I know what I believe in, and I know where I want to lead the country. And most of the decisions come pretty easily for me, to be frank with you."

AUGUST 27, 2001

As that reply made clear, Bush sees iron self-assurance as a sign of "character"—a confidence based squarely on good "values," and therefore totally unlike the spineless pandering that we would always get from What's-His-Face. But, of course, there is another way of looking at it (although that fact is not self-evident to those who just believe what they believe is right). While it's a fine thing to have principles—depending on what they might be—it's not so good to have a mind that's closed as tight as a full oil drum, or a clam. While it's very easy for the president to make decisions, once he's made them it's impossible, apparently, for him to reconsider them, no matter what. "I'm the kind of person that when I make up my mind, I'm not going to change it," he boasted in mid-August.[103] While such inflexibility may be a plus in theocratic circles, it's not a quality that suits the leader of this great democracy, whether we're at war or not.

The World

"I appreciate diplomatic talk, but I'm more interested in action and results."   —OCTOBER 11, 2002

Japan's Foreign Minister Makes
Inappropriate Remark About Bush

"On June 17, a day before Foreign Minister Makiko Tanaka would be meeting U.S. Secretary of State Colin Powell, Ms. Tanaka visited Germantown [Friends] School in Philadelphia, where she studied for two years when she was a high school student.

   "The alumnae of the high school gave Ms. Tanaka a grand

welcome. She enjoyed a class reunion and talking with her old classmates. Ms. Tanaka did not accompany interpreters and stenographers. She made a remark about George Bush during her conversation with her classmates and her words will remain in the history of Japan's foreign ministers.

". . . Ms. Tanaka's visit to Washington, D.C., was agreed to by the Japanese government. The objective of her trip was to vindicate what she expressed about U.S. foreign policies at meetings with her counterparts from other countries. She conveyed her messages of criticisms about the foreign policies of the U.S. government to them. She must have told them faithfully what she believed. . . .

"During the conversation with her old classmates at the reception in Germantown [Friends] School, *The Weekly Post* learned that Ms. Tanaka made a remark about George Bush, 'He is totally an asshole,' in English.

"The majority of her classmates seemed to support the Republican Party; however, they were critical about Mr. Bush's new missile defense plan. When Ms. Tanaka made this remark, the classmates in the room were reportedly excited.

"There has never been a statesman in Japanese history who called a U.S. president 'an asshole.' "

—*THE WEEKLY POST* (JAPAN), JUNE 15–JULY 1, 2001

In the international arena, Bush's perfect certainty is not a virtue but a major danger, as it has threatened to transform the United States into the mightiest rogue nation of them all. Although he ran as something of an isolationist, our president has now turned out to be another sort of global player entirely. We might call him an aggressive solipsist: he is what he is, knows what he knows, and who cares what you think? That posture was apparent well before he was made president—most notably when he flunked that infamous pop quiz on foreign leaders in the fall of 1999 (pp. 196–97). While people all around the world were shocked by his blithe ignorance, the moment didn't play too badly for him here, where even certain Democrats defended him and faulted the reporter for impertinence. Not knowing anything at all about the world would seem to be a major defect in a presidential candidate, yet it was finally cast as further proof of Bush's unpretentiousness, its risky implications overlooked.

From Day One of his term, the president continued to display an awesome un-
awareness of the world beyond our continental borders. There was an awkward
moment during the inaugural festivities.

"Teenage soprano Charlotte Church looks back with fondness, I'm
told, on her encounter with George Dubya Bush when she sang at
his inauguration ceremony in January. By way of making
conversation when they were introduced, the Texan charmer asked
where this lovely lil' lady hailed from. 'I'm from Wales,' she said.
'What state is that in?' he replied. 'It's in Great Britain.' There was a
pause, and a crease of perplexity appeared in the presidential brow.
'Oh, really?' he said. 'I'll have my people look into that.'
Church tells friends she found him 'kind of stupid.' "

—*DAILY TELEGRAPH* (UK), APRIL 19, 2001

Abroad himself, Bush went on showing the world how much attention he had paid
to it:

"Africa is a nation that suffers from incredible disease, and it suffers
from poverty as well."

—FROM GOTEBORG, SWEDEN, JUNE 14, 2001

Q:	Mr. President, why did you decide to stop bombing exercises at Vieques Island? Were you swayed by the protests of the Puerto Rican people or were there political factors involved, such as the concerns of Hispanic-Americans?
BUSH:	He's referring to the fact that upon assuming office, I was presented, like I had been on other issues, with an agreement between Puerto Rico and the United States government that we would conduct exercises off the island of Vieques for the United States Navy.
	My attitude is that the Navy ought to find somewhere else to conduct its exercises, for a lot of reasons. One, there's been some harm done to

people in the past. Secondly, these are our friends
and neighbors and they don't want us there.

—IBID.

*In fact, those "friends and neighbors" are all U.S. citizens, as Bush might have re-
called from the Republican convention, where, as usual, there was a Puerto Rican
delegation.*

"There are a lot of proud Philippines living in America."

—NOVEMBER 20, 2001

*Such lapses were not all that serious—although some Puerto Ricans, Africans, and
Welsh did find them unencouraging. And yet loose lips can do real damage far and
wide, especially when they are attached to presidential faces that have lightly fur-
nished minds behind them.*

"I think it's very important for President Musharraf to make a clear
statement to the world that he intends to crack down on terror. And
I believe that if he does that and continues to do what he's doing, it
will provide the—it'll provide relief, pressure relief, on a situation
that's still serious.

"I don't believe the situation is defused yet, but I do believe there
is a way to do so, and we are working hard to convince both the
Indians and the Pakis there's a way to deal with their problems
without going to war."   —JANUARY 7, 2002

Dubya Shoots from the Lip, Again

"President Bush dropped one of his trademark clangers on Monday,
referring to Pakistanis as 'Pakis,' a term that is considered an ethnic
slur, especially in Britain.

"The gaffe came when Bush told reporters that the US is
'working hard to convince both the Indians and the Pakis there's a
way to deal with their problems without going to war.' The White
House clarified soon after that the President meant no disrespect to
the Pakistani people.

" 'The president has great respect for Pakistan, the Pakistani people, and the Pakistani culture. Pakistan has been a strong member of the international coalition in the war against terrorism,' White House spokesman Scott McClellan said.

"Even well-versed American commentators—as well as many Indians—routinely use the terms 'Paks' and 'Pakis' to describe Pakistanis, unaware that the expression is as insulting as other etiquette-busters such as 'Japs,' 'Red Indians,' and 'Negroes.' "

—*TIMES OF INDIA,*
JANUARY 9, 2002

Although that slur was coined in Britain, there was no excuse for Bush's public use of it. Just four months earlier, his own vice president had caught some flak for much the same mistake: "Let me simply say we have had discussions with the Paks," Dick Cheney said on Meet the Press *on September 16—a gaffe that earned some very audible rebukes, including one from William Safire: "Innocent intent is an excuse only once; now he is sensitized, as are we all," he wrote too optimistically.★[104] That Bush had not been properly prepared to talk about the Pakistanis tells us something of the disarray within his White House—for his use of "Pakis" was objectionable not because it was a grave offense against political correctness, but because it was a serious diplomatic error. Bush's team was just then struggling to improve the fierce relations between India and Pakistan (a clash that had been worsened by the U.S. "war on terrorism"). His use of "Pakis" therefore was unhelpful, since it betrayed a bias in that standoff, the slur having long been used "by many Indians," as the* Times of India *points out.*

Prior to 9/11, the White House had already sent destructive diplomatic signals through the media—when Dick Cheney, in a rambling Q & A with Tony Snow on Fox News Channel, stomped into another very dicey situation, bluntly taking sides as if he weren't vice president of the United States but just another CEO with strong opinions:

★Bush and Cheney weren't the only ones who didn't get it. On December 12, Trent Lott told Larry King that "the Pakis have been very helpful, and I believe that we will be able to find a way to get [Osama bin Laden], whether he's in Pakistan or Sudan or wherever he tries to flee."

SNOW:	Israel now has a policy of assassinating opposition leaders.
CHENEY:	In Israel, what they've done, of course, over the years, is occasionally, in an effort to preempt terrorist activities, is to go after the terrorist. And in some cases, I suppose, by their lights, it is justified. If you've got an organization that had plotted or is plotting some kind of suicide bomber attack, for example, and they have hard evidence of who it is and where they're located, I think there's some justification in their trying to protect themselves by preempting.

A little birdie seemed to tell the veep that maybe he had gone too far:

CHENEY:	Clearly, it would be better if they could work with the Palestinians and the Palestinian authorities and the terrorists of whatever stripe could be headed off and imprisoned and tried, rather than having them actually assassinated.
SNOW:	Have they given us any indication that these are, in fact, preemptive strikes?
CHENEY:	I think that's their claim. I do know, in some cases, they have, in fact, gone to the Palestinian authorities with names and locations and asked that the Palestinians take action against the terrorist in Palestinian territory. And when the Palestinians have failed to do that, then the Israelis have gone forward and launched a strike.

—AUGUST 2, 2001

These instances bespeak a problem far more serious than simple ignorance of diplomatic protocol. Dick Cheney's readiness to shoot off his mouth in a most explosive situation—a readiness at which the president would soon outdo him with his wild allusion to the "axis of evil"—indicates a deep aversion to diplomacy itself. Whereas the diplomat attempts to get each side to see things differently, the fella who believes what he believes just doesn't need to hear about it. And while the diplomat would have each side give up a little bit, so that all sides might finally gain, this possibil-

ity has no appeal for those who want the whole damn thing, and want it now, and figure that they have the troops to take it. Such bullies have no use for diplomats, because they actually prefer the endless clash that diplomats attempt to interrupt. It's always them and theirs against the world—and yet the diplomats keep trying to stop the violence, and drag the world in for another boring round of complicated "talks."

Bush showed his preference for stark confrontation over any genuine discussion when he took his first official trip to Europe. There he would not budge an inch on any of the issues that concerned the other heads of state—above all, global warming and missile defense—but merely kept restating his position, much as Bush/Quayle had "negotiated" with Saddam Hussein during Operation Desert Shield. Nor is that comparison far-fetched, since this Bush really did perceive the Europeans—our allies—as a pack of enemies, as he made clear in a candid interview with the adoring Peggy Noonan shortly after his return:

> " 'With all due modesty, I think Ronald Reagan would have been proud of how I conducted myself. I went to Europe a humble leader of a great country, and stood my ground. I wasn't going to yield. I listened, but I made my point.
>
> " 'And I went to dinner, as Karen [Hughes] would tell you, with 15 leaders of the EU, and patiently sat there as all 15 in one form or another told me how wrong I was about the Kyoto accords. And at the end I said, "I appreciate your point of view, but this is the American position because it's right for America.' " Mr. Bush said the issue of a missile defense was similar to global warming, though to a certain degree there was 'a different attitude' among the EU leaders; they were 'a little more forward leaning' on it.
>
> " 'My point is that I was holding my ground on issues I think are important for our country. And I believe in missile defense in particular, that as a result of standing my ground based on principle, not based on hostility but based upon a positive point of view, that I'll be able to reach an accord with Putin.' "
>
> —*WALL STREET JOURNAL,* JUNE 25, 2001

To be "forward leaning" is, in Bush's view, to go along with him (or, perhaps, bend over for him). And to go along with him means taking "the American position," which is determined by what's "right for America." Therefore, all "forward leaning" people will agree to do what's "right for America," while only "backward leaning" types will not agree, presumably for their own selfish reasons. Such was "the American position"—"based on principle," and "patiently" articulated by "a humble leader."★

It was a tacit ultimatum, not much different from the outright threat that Bush would make repeatedly from 9/11 on: *"You're either with us or against us."* According to the worldview powering that ultimatum, any action that the U.S. president decides upon is good, since it will do the United States some good, he says. That such an action might have nasty consequences for the other nations—and for the United States—just doesn't signify, because the president can't see the consequence. In his view, there is no pressing need to act on global warming, whatever certain scientists may say, because, as far as he's concerned, the most important thing is to keep selling lots of oil and gas. Nor—whatever certain experts say—could missile defense pose any threat to world stability, because, as far as he's concerned, a missile shield will simply *"keep the peace."* From where he sits, such worries have no merit, and so those voicing them are not worth listening to—indeed, aren't really there at all, as far as he's concerned.

As far as he's concerned, in fact, is always just as far as Bush can go. Devoid of empathy, and quick to write off those who will persist in seeing things another way, he talks most easily to those who strike him as reflections of himself. That narcissistic tendency may help explain his strange response to Vladimir Putin, whom he embraced with all the warmth that wasn't in his powwows with the Europeans. On June 16, with the lupine KGB man standing right beside him at Brdo Castle in Slovenia, the president came out with this amazing testimonial:

> "I looked the man in the eye. I found him to be very straightforward and trustworthy. We had a very good dialogue. I was able to get a sense of his soul—a man deeply committed to his

---

★Although he wouldn't listen to a word the Europeans had to say, before Bush left he urged them to appreciate how carefully he'd listened to them: "Well, I hope the notion of a unilateral approach died in some people's minds today, here. Unilateralists don't come around the table to listen to others and to share opinion. Unilateralists don't ask opinions of world leaders. I count on the advice of our friends and allies. I'm willing to consult on issues. Sometimes we don't agree, and I readily concede that, but there is a lot more that we agree upon than we disagree about." June 13, 2001.

country and the best interests of his country. And I appreciated so
very much the frank dialogue."   —JUNE 16, 2001

*It was an eerie turn (especially since Stalin also thought that he could gauge a man's
trustworthiness by looking deep into his eyes). Back home, predictably, there were
strong protests: Jesse Helms released a statement criticizing Bush for that "excessively
personal endorsement," and many on the right gave thanks to the insurgent senator. The flap was reminiscent of the time when Ronald Reagan fell for Mikhail Gorbachev in 1986—and yet the similarity is limited. While Reagan was apparently
impelled by a utopian desire for some dramatic peace agreement (a breakthrough that
Nancy Reagan also wanted him to make, for history's sake), Bush seems to have
liked Putin because Putin seemed to Bush a lot like Bush.*

*The president found his Russian counterpart attractively inclined, as he made
clear (albeit rather oddly) on his next trip to Europe:*

"I thought he was very forward leaning, as they say in diplomatic
nuanced circles."   —JULY 23, 2001

*It was, however, evidently not the Russian's openness to Bush's missile program that
appealed to Bush, but a deeper similarity, which he could not stress enough.*

"I very much enjoyed our time together. He's an honest,
straightforward man who loves his country. He loves his family. We
share a lot of values."   —JUNE 16, 2001

BUSH:	He is a physical fitness person and I bet he'd like to get up and go for a long walk.
Q:	He's probably seen nothing like it.
BUSH:	I'd love to show him the canyons. I will show him the canyons. And I think he'll like it out here. . . . I think he'd like to spend some time in Washington and do both, go to Washington and Crawford.

—AUGUST 25, 2001

"And it's my honor to welcome to Central Texas a new style leader,
a reformer, a man who loves his country as much as I love mine, a

man who loves his wife as much as I love mine, a man who loves his daughters as much as I love my daughters, and a man who's going to make a huge difference in making the world more peaceful by working closely with the United States."   —NOVEMBER 15, 2001

"A physical fitness person," just like Bush, and one who loved his country, wife, and daughters just as Bush did, Putin wouldn't seem to have deserved the bloody soubriquet "The Butcher of Chechnya." And yet the Russian's readiness to heat up his own "war on terrorism" seems to have been in Bush's mind a few months prior to 9/11.

"As you know, I'm going to see him in a couple of weeks. I look forward to continuing what has been a very good relationship. And it's important that I have a good relationship with Mr. Putin, because it's good for the—it's good for our nations, and it's also good for the world for us to develop a good relationship, so we can work together to make the world more secure.

"And we share common interests. He's deeply concerned about extremism and what extremism can mean to Russia. And, as you know, I am, too. He recognizes there are new threats in the twenty-first century. The United States is not a threat. And we can work cooperatively to address the new threats of the twenty-first century."
                                                              —JULY 6, 2001

However Putin may have figured into it, the "war on terrorism" was a dream come true for this extremely certain president, who will find all the enemies he needs— despite the facts, despite his friends, and never mind the consequences for the rest of us.

"Some of these regimes have been pretty quiet since September eleventh. But we know their true nature. North Korea is a regime arming with missiles and weapons of mass destruction while starving its citizens. Iran aggressively pursues these weapons and exports terror, while an unelected few repress the Iranian people's hope for freedom. Iraq continues to flaunt its hostility toward America and to support terror. The Iraqi regime has plotted to develop anthrax and nerve gas and nuclear weapons for over a decade. This is a regime that has already used poison gas to murder thousands of its own citizens, leaving the bodies of mothers huddled over their dead children. This is a regime that agreed to international inspections, then kicked out the inspectors. This is a regime that has something to hide from the civilized world.

"States like these and their terrorist allies constitute an axis of evil, arming to threaten the peace of the world. By seeking weapons of mass destruction, these regimes pose a grave and growing danger. They could provide these arms to terrorists, giving them the means to match their hatred. They could attack our allies or attempt to blackmail the United States. In any of these cases, the price of indifference would be catastrophic."★ —JANUARY 29, 2002

The Nation

Bush cuts as defiantly parochial a figure on the national as on the global stage. He has been not a "president of all the people" but a president of all the people who were moved to vote for him. Shortly after the Supreme Court chose him to be president, Bush publicly foretold the narrowness of his appeal by journeying to Austin, and announcing his accession from the statehouse there. And as his popularity declined perceptibly from early June, Bush did the opposite of outreach, concentrating only on the "heartland,"† where he'd sing the praises of those locals who were in his camp and pointedly exalt their "values" as the (only) ones that made this country "fabulous."

"I do want to remind you all that one of the things that makes this country so unique is our value system: the values of hard work, family, faith, values that sound pretty much like the heartland of

---

★The president seems not to have known exactly what the Axis was. Speaking in Japan on February 22, he made a statement happily erasing World War II from the history of U.S.-Japanese relations: "My trip to Asia begins here in Japan for an important reason. It begins here because for a century and a half now, America and Japan have formed one of the great and enduring alliances of modern times. From that alliance has come an era of peace in the Pacific."

†As an Illinoisan born and bred, I hereby mean no disrespect to the so-called fly-over states. There is as much provincialism on the Upper West Side of Manhattan as there is in, say, Nebraska, and the one is just as tiresome as the other.

America to me. We're winding down the legislative session here, and I hope a week from tomorrow that Congress takes off and gives all of us a break.

[*Laughter*]

"And I'm heading back to the heartland. I'm going back to Crawford, Texas, where Laura and I have got some property. . . .

"But it's important for all of us in Washington to stay in touch with the values of the heartland because they're values that really are unique. It basically says that values—a value system of basic inherent values that override politics and different demographics and different religions. It's what makes America so unique and great. . . . You should never be afraid of embracing the values you find in the heartland of America, the values you bring to Washington, D.C."

—TO THE FUTURE FARMERS
OF AMERICA, JULY 27, 2001

"You know, next month I'll be going to my ranch in Crawford, where I'll work and take a little time off. I think it is so important for a President to spend some time away from Washington, in the heartland of America. And whenever I go home to the heartland, I am reminded of the values that build strong families, strong communities and strong character, the values that make our people unique. Every society depends on trust and loyalty, on courtesy and kindness, on bravery and reverence. These are the values of Scouting and these are the values of America."

— NATIONAL SCOUT JAMBOREE,
BOWLING GREEN, VIRGINIA, JULY 30, 2001

"In a few days, I'm headed home to the heartland to listen to the American people and to talk about the values that unite and sustain our country."   —AUGUST 3, 2001

White House to Move to Texas for Awhile

"When Bush retreats to his ranch, aides say, the White House just changes location. 'He'll be returning to Texas and operating out of Crawford,' says Karen Hughes, counselor to the president, referring

more to the small town where reporters will gather than the exact
site of Bush's command center. He'll be seven miles down narrow,
winding Prairie Chapel Road.

"Hughes rattles off a list of things that will take up the president's
time, from daily national security briefings to whatever national and
international matters may come up.

"Bush will make brief outings to 'celebrate some of the values
that strengthen America,' she says."   —USA TODAY, AUGUST 3, 2001

Q: Ari, the president has billed this trip as "going
               home to the heartland," a place where he says the
               values are superior or what they should be. And
               I'm wondering, what exact region does he, you
               know, ascribe these values to? Where is the "heart-
               land," and—?

FLEISCHER: Well, he's never said that he finds the values supe-
               rior. The president has never said anything like
               that.

Q: Well, he's said he's found it correct or what, you
               know, America stands for—

FLEISCHER: But he's never said anything about "superior,"
               because that implies it's superior to someone
               else's, and the president has never discussed it like
               that.
                  But what the president believes is, first of all, he
               has a home in Texas. That is his home.

                                          —AUGUST 3, 2001

"You know, I've told the people of the nation's capital there that I
was coming back to the heartland to herald the values of the
heartland, the values that make America so different and so unique.
And one of those values is neighbors helping neighbors. It's a value
that has existed for a long period of time. But no president should
ever take that value for granted. And so that's why Laura and I are
so honored to thank the volunteers who are here and to remind
our fellow Americans that if we're interested in a decent tomorrow
for every citizen, if we want the American dream to extend its

reach in every community, that all of us must work hard in our
communities to help a neighbor in need."

—WACO, TEXAS, AUGUST 8, 2001

"But it's also important to get out and see the people, too. It's
important to keep balance and perspective. We find that on our
ranch in Central Texas, and I find it as I travel the heartland. No
better place to come than the great state of Colorado, where people
are down to earth and work hard and adhere to great American
values. And I want to thank you for the warm welcome I received
today."   —DENVER, COLORADO, AUGUST 14, 2001

*For all its treacly emphasis on "kindness," "trust," and "neighbors helping neigh-
bors"—and notwithstanding Ari Fleischer's lame denial—that "heartland" stuff was
meant to be invidious. The hint of militant provincialism was, in part, a tactical attempt to reassure Bush/Cheney's more conservative constituents that this administration wasn't soft on coons or fags or any of those other coastal types who'd gone for
Clinton. Bush's willingness to speak on "character" and "values" at the National
Scout Jamboree suggested that he backed the outfit when its longtime ban on gays
had just become a cause of controversy. Not long before the "heartland tour" began,
moreover, the White House had been embarrassed by reports that it was quietly working with the Salvation Army to ensure that "faith-based" groups not be obliged by
law to hire gay people. Around the same time, the White House pointedly turned
down an invitation from the NAACP to address its ninety-second annual convention (soon after Ari Fleischer had mistakenly announced that Kweisi Mfume was
no longer the organization's president). Such gestures made it clear that this administration didn't feel the need to reach beyond the "heartland" for more votes.[105]*

*And yet Bush's doggedly provincial thrust was not just tactical, but an expres-
sion of his deep hostility to anyone too different from himself. Several months before the "heartland tour," when he was still enjoying his honeymoon, the president
made his own preference very clear upon his first return to Crawford after the inauguration:*

"Mr. Bush told party guests that there was a reason beyond his own
pleasure to retreat to the area around his ranch, a place he loves like

no other. 'I want to stay in touch with real Americans,' he
explained."   —*NEW YORK TIMES*, FEBRUARY 19, 2001

*Bush reconfirmed his bias, albeit in a very different tone, on his first presidential visit
to New York:*

"One hundred and seventy-one days after he was sworn in, George
W. Bush paid his first visit as president to New York State yesterday,
proposing ways to ease immigration and paying tribute to Cardinal
John O'Connor. But Mr. Bush expressed something short of pure
delight at being back in the state that he lost by nearly 25 percentage
points last November and that his advisers view as politically out of
reach for 2004.

" 'How do you like New York, Mr. President?' a reporter asked
Mr. Bush as he posed for a photograph with a small cluster of
Democrats and Republicans in front of New York Harbor, moments
after leading 29 new citizens at a V.I.P.-packed naturalization
ceremony on Ellis Island in the Pledge of Allegiance. 'It's a beautiful
day,' Mr. Bush responded tersely.

"Fellow Republicans at his side, including Mayor Rudolph W.
Giuliani and Gov. George E. Pataki, froze for about five awkward
seconds, and Mr. Bush reconsidered his response. 'I love New York,'
he proclaimed, to the evident relief of his hosts."

                                        —*NEW YORK TIMES*, JULY 11, 2001

*After 9/11, of course, the president discovered a new fondness for New York—
especially after its unhappy citizens had given him a hero's welcome.* But after a
few months at "war," Bush went back to his old ways.*

---

*Bush's animus no doubt bore some relation to his furtive efforts not to make good on the $20
billion that he pledged for the rebuilding of Manhattan shortly after 9/11. Although he quickly
promised New York's senators that they would have the money soon ("You've got it"), it took
six months of stubborn lobbying behind the scenes before the president came through—
boasting, when he finally did, of how this too proved the value of his word. When the deal was
finally done, moreover, it turned out that tax credits made up some $5 billion of the total. See
Michael Tomasky, "The Out-of-Towners," *New York*, October 1, 2001; "Panel Defeats Effort
to Give Billions More to New York," *New York Times*, November 15, 2001; "Bush Gives New
York More, but Lawmakers Demand All," *New York Times*, November 17, 2001; "Bush Restates

"But it's great to be back here in the great state of Missouri, and Springfield. I want to thank the chamber of commerce for hosting this event. It gives me a chance to share some of my thoughts with our fellow citizens as I work my way down to the heartland of America. I was—started earlier in Moline, Illinois, at a factory that makes John Deere tractors. I—I am here to talk to farmers. I'm on my way down to New Orleans to remind people that much of what we grow and produce in America is shipped overseas out of that port.

"I'm really here to remind people of the great values of our country lived in your everyday lives. So I want to thank you all for coming."   —SPRINGFIELD, MISSOURI, JANUARY 14, 2002

A LOVING GUY

Before

"So when the President was here [in Philadelphia] on July 4, I had the opportunity to shake his hand. I wasn't sure if that was a good idea or not but I did it anyway, and said to him, 'Mr President, I hope you only serve four years. I'm very disappointed in your work so far.'

"He kept smiling and shaking my hand but answered, 'Who cares what you think?' His face stayed photo-op perfect but his eyes gave me a look that said [that] if we'd been drinking in some frathouse in Texas, he'd've happily answered, 'Let's take it outside.' A nasty little gleam. But he was (fortunately) constrained by presidential propriety.

"But that was the end of it, until I turned away and started scribbling the quote down in my notepad, so as to remember The Gift forever. When he saw me do that he got excited and craned his neck over the rubberneckers to shout at me, 'Who are you with?

Commitment for Government to Give $20 Billion to New York," AP, February 6, 2002; "Bush Offers Details of Aid to New York Topping $20 Billion," *New York Times,* May 8, 2002.

Who are you with?' People started looking so he made a joke: 'Make sure you get it right.' But he kept at it: 'Who do you write for?' I told him I wasn't 'with' anybody and pointed to one of his staff people, who knows me a little, and said, 'Ask him, he'll tell you.' Then I split.

"Half an hour later, my boss (who had helped organize the event we were at) came up to me and said, 'did you really tell the President that he was doing a "lousy fu*king job"'? No way, I said, I was very polite, I just told him what I thought. Fortunately, he believed me. He wasn't happy with me, but he believed me. But anyway, if you ever wondered if the Prez really was kind of a jerk, I'm here to tell you, he is, and I got The Gift to prove it."

—E-MAIL FROM BILL HANGLEY JR., JULY 9, 2001

Hangley's e-mail, which he had sent out to twenty-five friends, soon spread like wild-fire on the Internet, leading to a few stories in the press.

"White House spokesman Scott McClellan said, 'I don't think I'm going to dignify something so ridiculous with a response.' "

—*NEW YORK DAILY NEWS,* JULY 28, 2001

"It's a tragic loss of life that occurred. It's also tragic that many police officers have been hurt, men and women who have been trying to protect democratically elected leaders and our necessary right to be able to discuss our common problems."

—GENOA, ITALY, JULY 21, 2001

Bush was referring to the death of Carlo Giuliani, a twenty-three-year-old Roman activist who had been killed by the police in Genoa the day before, amid the violence outside the G-8 summit meeting on "free trade." Giuliani had been shot twice—once in the face—and then run over by a police vehicle.

The president's response was striking, first, for its equation of Giuliani's "loss of life" with the injuries sustained by the police—mainly cuts and bruises, according to Italian press reports, while one carabiniere did receive a bad blow to the eye. Although no picnic, certainly, such hurts were hardly "tragic." Moreover, "many po-

lice officers" were not *injured—but many demonstrators and reporters* were. *While roughly thirty officers were treated and released, scores of people on the other side were badly hurt: 180 were in the hospital by the end of that one day alone.*

The police ran wild in Genoa—as the Italian government's own investigators noted one week later, and as Italy's police chief, Gianni De Gennaro, admitted shortly after that. While keeping their hands off the hard-core marauders of the in-famous "Black Bloc"—a tight-knit corps of German and Italian "anarchists"—the cops went after the nonviolent majority, and members of the press, with terrifying fury. At the time, their misbehavior was deplored by many of the dignitaries gathered in Genoa.

Our president's position, on the other hand, was closer to the view of Sylvio Berlusconi, who had only praise for his police, and criticism only for the victims. ("The left is masochistic," he later told La Repubblica, *"and out to defend violent protesters.")*[106]

Toward the summer's end, as he continued losing points, the president became more obviously prickly. Reporters now began to get a snootful of his inability to brook dissent or deal with probing questions.

Q: On stem cells, you said that the sixty stem cell lines could be experimented on. It now turns out that they've been mixed in the laboratory with mice cells under FDA guidelines. Apparently they could have no practical effect. Did you know that when you made this decision—that these possibly couldn't be used?

That query got under the presidential skin:

BUSH: Here's what I knew. I knew that I sat down with the NIH experts, the people who were—the people who are charged by our federal government to follow the research opportunities on all fronts, and they feel like the existing stem cell lines are ample to be able to determine whether or not embryonic stem cell research can yield the results necessary to save lives.

               This is their opinion. And I can think of no

better opinion on which to make my—base my judgment. And so I haven't changed my opinion in the least. As a matter of fact, I read some comments today where the NIH scientists again confirmed that we've got enough existing stem cell lines to do the research necessary to determine whether or not the promise of embryonic stem cells will be met.

Q: Sir, to follow up: Why is it that the [*Inaudible*]—

BUSH: The NIH came into the Oval Office, and they looked me right in the eye, and they said, "We think there is ample stem cells—lines to determine whether or not this embryonic stem cell research will be—will work or not." And I appreciated their candor and I appreciated their advice.

The nettled POTUS shifted his attention to another journalist in the crowd—Jay Root of the Fort Worth Star-Telegram. *It is relevant to note that one of the prime contractors for the V-22 Osprey is Bell Helicopter Textron, located in Fort Worth. It is also relevant that Root does not have lots of hair.*

BUSH: Root! Good to see you, my boy!

Q: Sir, you talked about the need to—

BUSH: How are you?

Q: Doing good, I'm good.

BUSH: Used to cover me as governor.

Q: You talked about—

BUSH: Fine lad, fine lad!

[*Laughter*]

Q: You talked about the need to maintain technological—

BUSH: A little short on hair, but a fine lad! Yeah.

[*Laughter*]

Q: I am losing some hair.

You talked about the need to maintain technological superiority. Given some of its well-known problems, do you think that a part of that would include the V-22? And do you think, given some

	of the budget problems that have been discussed, that it compromises maybe your ability to go forward with the V-22, the F-22, and the Joint Strike Fighter?
BUSH:	Root represents Forth Worth.
	[*Laughter*]
SECRETARY	
RUMSFELD:	I never would have guessed!
	[*Laughter*]

—AUGUST 24, 2001

On September 5, Bush held his first state dinner, in honor of Mexican president Vicente Fox. At an informal press conference with his old friend earlier that day, he had told reporters to "shut up" in broken Spanish, and then cut off inconvenient questioners by adding, "No puedo oirle" (I can't hear you), much to the amusement of his guests. At 11:00 that night—a Wednesday—the Bushes ended their big party with a fifteen-minute show of fireworks that terrified the city, the White House having failed to let its neighbors know that the display was coming. Audible as far north as Mt. Pleasant and as far south as Alexandria, the 769 shells launched from the Ellipse in Fox's honor "lit up the sky and rattled windows miles away," the Hous-ton Chronicle reported. Hundreds of Washingtonians complained, having thought the Capitol was under terrorist attack. "I thought, 'This is it! We're being bombed!' " said one nervous resident of DuPont Circle.[107]

Locally, the consensus was that Bush's big bang had been supremely thought-less, even arrogant. "I don't know, maybe the president is cocky as hell and thinks the neighborhood is not really a neighborhood," a man from Foggy Bottom told the Washington Post. *"But we're all his neighbors, and we already put up with quite a lot." Despite the grassroots hue and cry, however, the national press did not see fit to say much on the matter—a near-silence very different from the orgy of bad press that followed Clinton's fabled haircut-on-the-runway in Los Angeles. Although that haircut had, in fact, caused no delays at LAX, as* Newsday *ultimately proved, the myth gave rise to damning stories in the thousands. (When the truth came out, there were just three retractions.) By contrast, there were only a few dozen brief print items on the later fireworks show, which had demonstrably upset a lot of people. Bush's blowup was not only inconsiderate, moreover, but profligate—although the*

White House, typically, would not reveal the cost of those explosions, or even say who'd paid for them; and yet the press ignored those questions, too.[108]

> "[Laura Bush spokeswoman Ashleigh] Adams said the display was paid for by the State Department because it was tied to a diplomatic function—and she referred questions about its cost to the department.
>
>   " 'Oh, I was told that it was the White House,' a State Department press official said.
>
>   "Another agency official said only the White House could comment on a state dinner."
>
> —*NEW YORK DAILY NEWS,* SEPTEMBER 7, 2001

On Thursday, the following day, the First Lady's office sent out a brief note of apology for the disturbance. The president made no comment.

After

A month into the "war on terrorism," Bush made a trip to China, where he came out with another of his telling jests (see pp. 122 and 155) about the democratic press.

> "Once the press conference was under way the next day, Mr. Bush seemed to enjoy China's authoritarian flair. Mr. Jiang [Zemin] cut short the brief question-and-answer period by announcing, 'That is the end of the press conference. Thank you.'
>
>   "Mr. Bush remarked later, 'I like the way the Chinese do it when it comes to press conferences.' "
>
> —*NEW YORK TIMES,* OCTOBER 21, 2001

Visit Highlights Education, Work Programs, Unemployment Climbs

"President Bush, pushing community colleges as the best way to retrain laid-off workers, met with unemployed people, students and Portland Community College officials Saturday at a Northeast Portland job center partly run by the school. . . .

"Bush began his three-hour, two-stop visit to Portland at the Oregon Air National Guard base near Portland International Airport, where he greeted about 150 Guard members and their families. At least 500 members have been called to full-time duty since the Sept. 11 attacks, mostly for domestic air patrols. Portland firefighters Dwight Englert, Wesley J. Loucks, Neil Martin and Ed[d] Hall also welcomed Bush as he stepped off Air Force One. They joined the recovery effort at the World Trade Center days after the terrorist attacks, and were invited by Sen. Gordon Smith, R-Ore., to meet Bush."

—*SUNDAY OREGONIAN,* JANUARY 6, 2002

An Interview with Edd Hall

SIERRA CLUB: Of all the things you could've said to President Bush in that five-second encounter, you chose to tell him not to drill in the Arctic National Wildlife Refuge. Why?

EDD HALL: I thought about what I could say that he'd be able to hear quickly, rather than explain something like the effects of huge tax cuts for corporations, for example.

It came down to the Arctic being on top of the list. Bush is an oil guy, and also, even if you take away all the environmental arguments against drilling the Arctic National Wildlife Refuge, all the reasons they want to drill don't make sense. Will it decrease our dependence on oil and increase energy security? No. Will we get the oil immediately? No. Increase our oil supply? Only negligibly. That's how I came to telling him not to drill in the Arctic: It was the shortest, most concise statement that could fit it in the time I had, and it also is a top priority issue for the environmental community.

SIERRA CLUB: How did you feel about his response of, "Yeah, then we'll run out of energy"?

HALL: I was disappointed. I think the quick look that he gave me said more than his answer did. The change in his eyes. He kept his composure, but in his eyes was something like, "How did you get in here?" Now I know that's my perception, and perception is entirely owned by the perceiver.

SIERRA CLUB: But you wanted him to say something like, "Thanks, I always like to hear what the American public is thinking."

HALL: Yeah. But I could tell my comment wasn't appreciated.

—SIERRA CLUB WEB SITE

*On "promoting fatherhood":**

"I've been to war. I've raised twins. If I had a choice, I'd rather go to war."

—AP, JANUARY 27, 2002

More on Vladimir Putin:

"She—he is—he knows about women's rights and the importance of them, because he's raging—raising two teenage daughters.
[*Chuckles*]
"He and I share something in common."

—CRAWFORD, TEXAS, NOVEMBER 15, 2001

9/11

Contrary to the fiction that our president was fundamentally transformed by 9/11, the crisis soon revealed—or reconfirmed—exactly who he is: a person very different from the sudden paragon of popular imagination, and also very different from the natural leader who, according to Karl Rove, had been there all along. A total change of character is not too likely in the case of any fifty-five-year-old—and it would have been impossible for Bush, who even in his youth was hardly flexible. Post-9/11, the president was the same man he had been before the fact—the same man who speaks so tellingly throughout these pages.

---

*"Promoting fatherhood was a commitment I made as governor, it's a commitment I make as president, and it's a commitment I have made every day since our little girls were born in Dallas, Texas." June 7, 2001.

The lack of empathy that marks his sense of humor (see pp. 120–22) was apparent also in his own emotional response to 9/11. Aside from his distasteful jokes about the terrorist attacks (see pp. 348–49), there was his apparent incapacity for any show of sorrow, at least in public. Without a script, he seemed unable to assimilate the tragic aspect of the crisis, or even face it, but would just look right on past it to the happy, happy day of our eventual revenge. Where Mayor Giuliani let himself perceive the horror of it all, and therefore could convey some sense of it— "The number of casualties will be more than any of us can bear ultimately"—*the president kept trying to qualify the sadness with reminders of how angry we all were.*

"First of all, I can't tell you how sad I am, and America is, for the people of New York City and the tri-state area. I want to let you know there is a quiet anger in America that really is real."

—SEPTEMBER 13, 2001

"You know, through the tears of sadness I see an opportunity. Make no mistake about it, this nation is sad. But we're also tough and resolute."

—SEPTEMBER 13, 2001

"Make no mistake about it: underneath our tears is the strong determination of America to win this war. And we will win it."

—SEPTEMBER 15, 2001

"Behind the sadness and the exhaustion, there is a desire by the American people to not seek only revenge, but to win a war against barbaric behavior, people that hate freedom and hate what we stand for."

—SEPTEMBER 15, 2001

That emotional tic, which Bush expressed spontaneously, soon found its way into his scripted oratory:

"Our grief has turned to anger, and anger to resolution."

—SEPTEMBER 20, 2001

And later:

" 'All Americans are sad and angry to learn of the murder,' Bush said. 'May God bless Daniel Pearl.' "

—*AP ONLINE*, FEBRUARY 22, 2002

If this were a psychobiography, we might look deeply into Bush's tendency to jump away from grief and straight to rage.★ *However, his one-note trumpet call was infinitely less important as a symptom of his psychic wounds, if any, than as a winning propaganda stimulus—for that insistent call to arms made all the difference at that crucial time. In this case it was not the media that mainly drove the nation down the military road (as had occurred in August 1990) but the president, with his repeated reassurance that America would make the evildoers pay for this. That promise, and his many telegenic declarations of his own "determination" and "resolve," made any course but war all but unthinkable—his voice, and face, predominating over every other.*

It was only natural that a people so horrifically attacked should want to hit back hard (although that feeling was not universal, and was less obvious in New York City than elsewhere in the nation). That it was natural did not make it wise or right, however. A less impetuous response might make more sense, not only morally but also for the national security, as the New York Times *suggested in a thoughtful editorial that came out the day after.*

"What we live with now, beyond shock and beyond the courage witnessed on the streets in New York and Washington yesterday, is an urge for reprisal. But this is an age when even revenge is

---

★Unlike his predecessor, and also unlike Ronald Reagan, this president appears to be afraid of any strong emotion that might lead to tears—an aversion that may lie behind his frequent swaggering and constant hard-edged teasing. Something of that fearfulness came through in a preinaugural interview on NBC. "Not since John Kennedy was inaugurated," Tom Brokaw noted, "have both parents been present to watch their son sworn in as president of the United States." Bush replied:

"I'm going to stay focused. I think I will be able to. I—I'm—you know, I'm worried about Mother and Dad. Not worried about them, I just—they're emotional, as well, and I can't imagine what's going to be going through their mind. But I will, I will be focused on the oath, and I'll be focused on my speech. And I'm—and I'm not going to turn around and spend too much time looking at them because it will be an emotional moment for them and for me. But yes, I can get through it." *NBC Nightly News*, January 15, 2001.

complicated, when it is hard to match the desire for retribution with the need for certainty. We suffer from an act of war without any enemy nation with which to do battle. The same media that brought us the pictures of a collapsing World Trade Center shows us the civilians who live in the same places that terrorists may dwell, whose lives are just as ordinary and just as precious as the ones that we have lost. That leaves us all, for now, with fully burdened emotions, undiminished by anything but the passage of the few hours that have elapsed since midmorning yesterday. There is a world of consoling to be done."   —SEPTEMBER 12, 2001

That, however, was the road not taken. Built only for attack (and no doubt in the service of a larger plan not yet revealed to us), the president could not console, but worked to channel everybody's shock and sadness into a great national campaign for "retribution," which he started that same day.

"The deliberate and deadly attacks which were carried out yesterday against our country were more than acts of terror. They were acts of war. This will require our country to unite in steadfast determination and resolve. Freedom and democracy are under attack.

"The American people need to know that we're facing a different enemy than we have ever faced. This enemy hides in shadows, and has no regard for human life. This is an enemy who preys on innocent and unsuspecting people, then runs for cover. But it won't be able to run for cover forever. This is an enemy that tries to hide. But it won't be able to hide forever. This is an enemy that thinks its harbors are safe. But they won't be safe forever.

"This enemy attacked not just our people, but all freedom-loving people everywhere in the world. The United States of America will use all our resources to conquer this enemy. We will rally the world. We will be patient, we will be focused, and we will be steadfast in our determination.

"This battle will take time and resolve. But make no mistake about it: We will win. . . .

"I want to thank the members of Congress for their unity and support. America is united. The freedom-loving nations of the world

stand by our side. This will be a monumental struggle of good versus
evil. But good will prevail."   —SEPTEMBER 12, 2001

*Thus did the president distract us from the world of consolation. And when he
pointed forward to the day when that horrific memory might no longer pain us, he
did so not to reassure us that this suffering too shall pass but only to suggest that
he would not forget—and not stop fighting to avenge those "acts of war."*

"They have roused a mighty giant. And make no mistake about it:
we're determined.

"Oh, there will be times when people don't have this incident on
their minds, I understand that. There will be times down the road
where citizens will be concerned about other matters, and I
completely understand that. But this administration, along with those
friends of ours who are willing to stand with us all the way through,
will do what it takes to rout terrorism out of the world."

—SEPTEMBER 16, 2001

THE REASON WHY

*At that time of terror, the president's peculiar inability to feel our pain did not dis-
credit him. As we have seen, his air of grim determination scored him many points
with the domestic audience, who were above all grateful that he didn't seem bewildered or afraid, and so were surely not inclined to hold his lack of empathy against
him. Not that everyone was utterly content with the slim range of his emotions. The
national adulation of the tough-but-tender Giuliani was, implicitly, a vote against
the payback-happy Bush—as was the startling U.S. cult of Tony Blair. After two
memorably compassionate and idealistic speeches of support for the United States (on
October 3 and October 4), the prime minister became a hero to Americans, 41 percent of whom would have supported him for president, according to the* London
Sunday Telegraph. *("I found myself becoming envious that he was Britain's leader,
and not America's," one Yank wrote the British embassy in Washington. "He gave
voice to what is in the heart of most Americans better than any American leader.")
Still, while the people, in their heart of hearts, may have longed for a president more*

comforting and/or uplifting, they seemed largely grateful for Bush's air of warlike certainty.

And so his obvious hard-heartedness, which his tense handlers had been struggling to conceal throughout the summer, was suddenly a big mark in his favor. Now there was no need for him to natter on about "communities of character," or otherwise to fake some "warmth," because his who-cares-what-you-think obtuseness was, at the time, an aspect of what seemed to be his strength. And just as his emotional constriction was a big advantage for him in those weeks of trauma, so were his intellectual limitations something of a plus—for people didn't really want to think at that nightmarish time but only to feel better; and so there was a general readiness to trust his claims as if they added up. Although his crucial statements were, in fact, irrational, they played well with the shattered audience. Thus Bush's simplemindedness—formerly a national running joke—now served at once to elevate him and sell us on the military option.

For instance, his claim that the attacks were "acts of war" was legally unsound and, far more significant, strategically dubious. The perpetrators acted not as soldiers of a national entity but as members of a criminal conspiracy, and so did not deserve to be exalted to the status of legitimate warriors. And as Sir Michael Howard noted in a speech before the Royal United Services Institute, a full-scale military counterstrike, with its inevitable toll on innocent civilians, would only serve to turn more hearts and minds against us, and thereby make the terrorist menace all the greater in the long run. "I can only suggest that it is like trying to eradicate cancer cells with a blowtorch," said the military historian, observing how the counterstriking British had made matters infinitely worse in Northern Ireland, Palestine, and Cyprus.[109] Although it was a cogent argument, it seldom came up in the U.S. press (the speech itself appeared belatedly in Harper's), our commentators and reporters, for the most part, merely parroting the "acts of war" assertion. This was understandable, considering the general fear. It was less understandable when, four months later, no reporters thought to ask why, if we were fighting in response to "acts of war," those captured by our forces in Afghanistan were not being classed as "prisoners of war" but only "detainees," unprotected by the Geneva Convention.★

★"They will be handled not as prisoners of war, because they're not, but as unlawful combatants," Secretary Rumsfeld said on January 11, 2002. "As I understand it, technically, unlawful combatants do not have any rights under the Geneva Convention." That diktat held dire implications for our own soldiers, should any of them end up captured by the enemy—a problem noted not by U.S. journalists but, eventually, by Colin Powell.

And as the U.S. press accepted Bush's claim that "acts of war" had been committed on our soil, so did they buy his speculation on the purpose of the terrorist attacks. Such acquiescence was remarkable, since the entire U.S. counterwar was predicated squarely on the president's compelling theory. What had the killers hoped to bring about? Somehow, Bush knew the answer to that fundamental question less than twelve hours after he had raced to Air Force One and promptly lit out for the territories. Without any pertinent intelligence, the president was certain that the terrorists—because they "hate our freedom"—had simply meant to spook us into wimping out and shutting down:

> "These acts of mass murder were intended to frighten our nation into chaos and retreat. But they have failed; our country is strong."
>
> —SEPTEMBER 11, 2001

On September 13, Karl Rove elaborated.

> " 'I think what they're trying to do is to cower our society,' he said. 'I think they're attempting to undermine its openness and its freedom and its ability to dissent, to be different. I think they're attempting to force America back into itself. To make America tepid and afraid of the world. To destroy our confidence and our society.' "
>
> —*THE NEW YORKER,* OCTOBER 1, 2001

While not as pithy as Bush's formulations ("We're a nation that can't be cowed by evildoers," said the president on September 16), Rove's comment reconfirmed the notion that the terrorists had wanted mainly to demoralize us. A few days later, the vice president assayed a more specific version of the same argument, repeating the then-widespread notion that Osama bin Laden—driven by "intense hatred" of "freedom and democracy"—had hoped to drive the United States from the Middle East.

> "And his objective, *obviously,* is to try to influence our behavior to force us to withdraw from that part of the world, and clearly he's not going to be successful. . . .
>
> "The fact of the matter is that the—we'll not allow him to achieve his aims. We're not about to change our policies or change our basic fundamental beliefs. What we are going to do is aggressively go after

Mr. bin Laden, *obviously,* and all of his associates, and even if it takes a long time, I'm convinced eventually we'll prevail."
—*MEET THE PRESS,* NBC, SEPTEMBER 16, 2001 (EMPHASIS ADDED)

Clearly, the entire administration was in full agreement on the perpetrators' aims and, therefore, on the proper national response to the attacks. To put it in the president's own words: "Evil people," consumed with "hatred of our freedoms," had tried "to frighten our nation into chaos and retreat." Of course, those evil ones had failed. ("I think he seriously misreads the American people," said Cheney of bin Laden.) Rather than "retreat," "our country [will] unite in steadfast determination and resolve," and hit back hard—wherever necessary, and for just as long as it might take—to wipe out (as Bush said on September 15) "the curse of terrorism that is upon the face of the earth."

It is striking that the president's view exerted so much influence, not just inside the White House but throughout the nation—for there was not a shred of evidence, at the time or afterward, to bolster the contention that the terrorists had aimed "to cower our society." Bush's intuition said far less about the point of the attack than it revealed about himself and his shocked audience, who badly needed the illusion of empowerment that he offered them by promising that "we will win." In sounding off about the terrorists' motives and intentions, the president was, as ever, speaking not from any actual experience or information but merely from his gut. Being who he was, and believing just what he believed, Bush would require no expert briefings to assist him in deciding what was right for everyone. As Condolleeza Rice explained admiringly on September 13, the president's reaction was "almost immediate." While everybody else was caught up in the moment, Bush kept his eye squarely on the ball.

". . . [I]n his very first statement to his National Security Council he said: 'This was an attack on freedom and we're going to define it as such, and we're going to go after it, and we're not going to lose focus; and we're going to minister to the country and deal with the horrors that people are experiencing and the consequences; and we're going to get through our period of mourning, but we're not going to lose focus and resolve on what happened here and what this means for the United States of America in its leadership role to mobilize the world, now, to deal with this scourge.'

"And I think it was much quicker with him than it probably was with any of the rest of us."

—WEB SITE FOR THE OFFICE OF INTERNATIONAL
INFORMATION PROGRAMS, STATE DEPARTMENT
(WWW.USINFO.STATE.GOV), SEPTEMBER 13, 2001

Taking his show on the road, the president got lots of folks a-hootin' and a-hollerin' by trotting out his theory that "their intended act," as he said on October 11, "was to destroy us and make us cowards and make us not want to respond":

"They think they can run and they think they can hide, because they think this country is soft and impatient. But they are going to continue to learn the terrible lesson that says: Don't mess with America!"

[*Applause*]

—ONTARIO, CALIFORNIA, JANUARY 5, 2002

"Our enemies rely upon surprise and deception. They used to rely upon the fact that they thought we were soft. I don't think they think that way anymore!"

[*Extended applause*]

—THE PENTAGON, JANUARY 10, 2002

"The enemy made a mistake. They thought this nation was soft. They thought because we're a wealthy nation, that we wouldn't rise to the occasion. Oh my, are they wrong!"

[*Applause*]

—JOHN DEERE HARVESTER WORKS,
EAST MOLINE, ILLINOIS, JANUARY 14, 2002

"We are a strong, strong nation, and I am so proud to be the president of such an incredible land! You know, the enemy, when they hit us on 9/11, really didn't understand America. They thought we were soft. I guess they were watching too much TV!"

[*Laughter*]

—CHARLESTON REGIONAL AIRPORT,
CHARLESTON, WEST VIRGINIA, JANUARY 22, 2002

"The terrorists are beginning to realize they picked the wrong enemy!

[*Cheers*]

"As I like to put it, they must have been watching too much daytime TV!

[*Laughter*]

"They thought we were soft. They thought we would roll over. My, oh, my! They hadn't got us figured out!'

—EGLIN AIR FORCE BASE, FLORIDA, FEBRUARY 4, 2002

"You know, when the enemy hit us on September the eleventh, they must have not figured out what we were all about. See, they thought we weren't determined. They thought we were soft. They obviously had never been to a National Cattlemen's Convention before!

[*Laughter, applause*]

"Now what they're finding out is this great land is determined, and patient, and steadfast, and strong to defend freedom."

[*Applause*]

—NATIONAL CATTLEMEN'S ASSOCIATION CONVENTION, DENVER, COLORADO, FEBRUARY 8, 2002

BUSH: It's hard for me to figure out what was going through the minds of those who planned and attacked America. They must have thought we were soft!

SOLDIER: They were wrong!

BUSH: Yes, they were!

[*Laughter*]

They thought we were so materialistic that we didn't understand sacrifice and honor and duty. They must have been watching some lousy movies!

[*Laughter*]

They didn't know that this great nation would rise up in unison to send a clear message that we will do whatever it takes to defend our freedoms,

that this great nation is resolved to find the killers
one by one and bring them to justice!

[*Applause*]

—TO U.S. TROOPS IN ANCHORAGE, ALASKA; FEBRUARY 16, 2002;

FDCH POLITICAL TRANSCRIPTS

Meanwhile, outside of the United States, there was a general consensus—based on the work of scholars and reporters who actually knew something on the subject— that the terrorists, in fact, had not "thought we would roll over": on the contrary. "The terrorism of September 11 was above all a provocation—albeit a provocation of gigantic proportions," wrote political scientist Gilles Kepel. "Its purpose was to provoke a similarly gigantic repression of the Afghan civilian population and to build universal solidarity among Muslims in reaction to the vicitmization and suffering of their Afghan brothers." "9-11 was not just a mad act," claimed journalist Guillaume Dasquie, who, with Jean-Charles Brisard, has studied the Taliban extensively. "It was a political act meant to create a good ground for a big war in all Central Asia. Mullah Omar and bin Laden wanted to rally Muslims in Central Asia." To those who had been following bin Laden's career, 9/11 would have come as no surprise. "Osama bin Laden continues to build sound theological foundations for escalating the jihad," Yossef Bodansky wrote in 1999.

"He has repeatedly summed up his belief in a statement usually
made while waving his own ornate Koran. 'You cannot defeat
heretics with this book alone, you have to show them the fist.' He
also elucidated his vision of the relentless, fateful, global jihad against
the United States in a book entitled *America and the Third World War.*
The draft manuscript is already being circulated among key Islamist
leaders and commanders in the original Arabic and in translation
into several South Asian languages. In this book bin Laden
propounds a new vision, stressing the imperative of a global uprising.
. . . For the Islamists there can be no compromise or coexistence
with Western civilization."[110]

According to this other view, in short, the terrorists did not *think "we were soft," and actually had "figured out what we were all about." They* hoped *to drag us into war, so that we might, in Cheney's words, "aggressively go after Mr. bin Laden and all his associates" wherever they may be, for years to come. Such a massive and protracted counterdrive throughout the Muslim world would hardly faze the radicals, since it would give them just the sort of unifying stimulus that they require, so as to split the world in two, believers versus infidels, or—as our president so often puts it—"good versus evil."*

IT TAKES ONE TO KNOW ONE

Early in the crisis, Bush got himself into a peck of trouble with our Muslim allies, because of an unfortunate aside. "We haven't seen this kind of barbarism in a long period of time," he said on September 16, and then, in passing, used a word that rather jarred our allies in Karachi, Kabul, Oman, Tunis, and Jakarta:

> "And this is a new kind of evil—and we understand, and the American people are beginning to understand, this **crusade,** this war on terrorism, is going to take a while, and the American people must be patient."   —SEPTEMBER 16, 2001

Q: The president used the word "crusade" last Sunday, which has caused some consternation in a lot of Muslim countries. Can you explain his usage of that word, given the connotations to Muslims?

FLEISCHER: I think what the president was saying was—had no intended consequences for anybody, Muslim or otherwise, other than to say that this is a broad cause that he is calling on America and the nations around the world to join. That was the purpose of what he said.

Q: But having used that word, Ari, will he not use it again in the context of talking about this effort?

FLEISCHER: I think, to the degree that that word has any connotations that would upset any of our partners or anybody else in the world, the president would regret if anything like that was conveyed. But the

purpose of this conveying it [*sic*] is in the traditional English sense of the word. It's a broad
cause."   —SEPTEMBER 18, 2002

The discomfort of our Muslim friends was understandable—and so was Bush's ca-
sual use of the offending word. It was a classic instance of cross-cultural misappre-
hension, since most westerners don't have a clue about the long bloodbath of
1096–1271, while Muslims can't forget about it. (Many westerners don't have a
memory of historical events before last week, but that's another problem.) In any case,
the president was thenceforth pretty careful not to say "crusade" again in public. It
was a whole five months before he slipped again.

"They [the Canadians] stand with us in this incredibly important
crusade to defend freedom, this campaign to do what is right for
our children and our grandchildren."
                    —ANCHORAGE, ALASKA, FEBRUARY 16, 2002

Finally, the flap over "crusade" was a distraction from Bush/Cheney's deeper lim-
itations. Like the president's allusion to "the Pakis," his reference to "this crusade"
did arguably reconfirm his team's exceptional obtuseness on the diplomatic front.
There was, however, a real danger at issue here—and it was not that Bush misspoke
but that, as usual, he accidentally told a certain truth. Whether he used the word
"crusade" or not, the president was all fired up in the reckless, buccaneering spirit
of the Crusaders, as he made quite clear in the peroration of his war speech to Con-
gress—a pious testament that went unquestioned by the press, or by the Democrats:

"I will not yield, I will not rest, I will not relent in waging this
struggle for freedom and security for the American people.
    "The course of this conflict is not known, yet its outcome is
certain. Freedom and fear, justice and cruelty, have always been at
war—and we know that God is not neutral between them."
                    [*Applause*]
                                    —SEPTEMBER 20, 2001

Bush has had no doubt that God is on his side.

"He believes, [friends and aides] say, that he has come face to face with his life's mission, the task by which he will be defined and judged.

" 'He frequently says that we will be known to history by the way we approach this great cause,' said one of his top White House aides, adding that Mr. Bush had made that statement to the religious leaders with whom he met in the White House just hours before his address to Congress on Thursday night.

"One of the president's close acquaintances outside the White House said Mr. Bush clearly feels he has encountered his reason for being, a conviction informed and shaped by the president's own strain of Christianity.

" 'I think, in his frame, this is what God has asked him to do,' the acquaintance said. 'It offers him enormous clarity.' "

—*NEW YORK TIMES*, SEPTEMBER 22, 2001

Bush's grandiose and absolutist vision is, in part, expressive of "the president's own strain of Christianity"(pp. 110–16, 147–54), which links him to the fiercest elements in his administration and constituency. In that strain, and in those groups, there is a stubborn trace of the medieval zeal that once drove the Crusaders to kill Jews and Muslims, and the Christians of Constantinople, by the tens of thousands. In Bush himself that strain has long been overlooked, because of reportorial timidity, his winning air of frat-house bonhomie—and also by the looming figure of the just-about-berserk attorney general, whose paranoid religiosity has always upstaged Bush's own. (There is a widespread misconception that the awkward and eccentric Ashcroft is a rogue within the Bush administration, and that, if he went too far, the president would rein him in: Machiavelli, wherever he is now, must be amused.) For all the president's disarming calls for tolerance of every creed, John Ashcroft's pride of place as head of our judicial branch sends quite a different message: God, he clearly thinks, backs him and his, and no other believers. He showed his feelings toward the Church of Rome when he told the folks at Bob Jones University—where the Church is still "the Whore of Babylon" and its pope the Antichrist—"I thank God for this institution and for you"; and there he also advertised his vision of the Jews[111] in this revealing (and largely unreported) passage from his speech at BJU:

"Unique among the nations, America recognized the source of our character as being godly and eternal, not being civic and temporal. And because we have understood that our source is eternal, America has been different. We have no king but Jesus.

"My mind, thinking about that, once raced back a couple of thousand years when Pilate stepped before the people in Jerusalem and said, 'Whom would ye that I release unto you? Barabas? Or Jesus, which is called the Christ?' And when they said 'Barabas,' he said, 'But what about Jesus? King of the Jews?' And the outcry was, 'We have no king but Caesar.'

"There's a difference between a culture that has no king but Caesar, no standard but the civil authority, and a culture that has no king but Jesus, no standard but the eternal authority. When you have no king but Caesar, you release Barabas—criminality, destruction, thievery, the lowest and the least. When you have no king but Jesus, you release the eternal, you release the highest and best, you release virtue, you release potential." —MAY 8, 1999★

And having spoken thus on Judaism as a senator, Attorney General Ashcroft set his sights on Islam—awkwardly enough, it being months into the "war on terrorism":

"The American-Arab Anti-Discrimination Committee (ADC), the largest Arab-American civil rights organization, called on President George W. Bush to distance himself from anti-Islamic statements attributed to Attorney General Ashcroft and demanded the latter's immediate resignation.

"ADC President Ziad J. Asali and Vice President Khalil E. Jahshan, wrote President Bush to express Arab-American condemnation of the Ashcroft statement which they described as 'inflammatory, fanatical and inexcusable, particularly coming from the Attorney General of the United States.'

★See www.spectacle.org/0201/ashcroft.html.

"In an article by Cal Thomas in Crosswalk.com News Channel, Ashcroft is quoted as saying that 'Islam is a religion in which God requires you to send your son to die for him. Christianity is a faith in which God sends his son to die for you.' "

—*COUNTERPUNCH WIRE,*

FEBRUARY 8, 2002

The attorney general's otherwordly sureness as to Good and Evil, Right and Wrong, sheds light on his peculiar conduct as America's top law enforcement officer: his refusal to take evidence from pro-choice citizens who had been targeted by terrorists; the indefinite imprisonment of several hundred Middle Eastern and Asian men because of hypothetical connections to Al Qaeda; his eagerness to do away with constitutional protections for anyone whom he and/or the president decides is guilty; his charge that those objecting to such measures "only aid terrorists"; and so on.★

Ashcroft's tendency to see the world, or universe, as twain asunder, totally and neatly riven into warring camps of good and evil, light and dark, is Bush's tendency as well. As his associates noted to the New York Times, *the president "was interpreting this juncture in grand, emphatic and even Manichaean terms."*

"And what we have to do is not just go after these perpetrators, and those who gave them haven, but the whole curse of terrorism that is upon the face of the earth."   —SEPTEMBER 15, 2001

"We will rid the world of the evildoers."   —SEPTEMBER 16, 2001

"America says, 'We don't care how you help, just help. Either you're for us, or you're against us.' "

[*Applause*]

—OCTOBER 4, 2001

★"That—that John Ashcroft," Bush stammered to Tom Brokaw on January 15, 2001, "is a open-minded, inclusive person."

"Across the world and across the years, we will fight these evil ones, and we will win!"

[Cheers, applause]

—NOVEMBER 21, 2001

"I said there are no shades of gray in this fight for civilization; there are no shades of gray. Either you're with the United States of America or you're against the United States of America."

[Applause]

—JANUARY 5, 2002

"I don't see many shades of gray in this world. Either you are with us or against us. This great nation stands on the side of good."

—FEBRUARY 7, 2002

And yet, while Bush's worldview is identical to Ashcroft's, he did not come by it as Ashcroft did. Whereas the latter learned his Pentacostalist creed from early on, in a family that belonged to the Assemblies of God, Bush was born again in middle age, having been raised a straight-ahead Episcopalian. Thus the president did not derive his Manichaean view from Sunday school per se, as he himself has sort of said:

"The unexpected, obviously, was September the eleventh, when evil people decided to attack America. I say 'evil people' because I don't view this as a religious war. I view this as a struggle of good versus evil. And, make no mistake about it, good will prevail."

[Applause]

—JANUARY 5, 2002

Rather than absorb his worldview from his religious fundamentalism, Bush seems to have been drawn to fundamentalism because of its appeal to his worldview (and also, to some extent, because of its political advantages). His either/or perception of reality was well established by the time Billy Graham inquired if he was "right with God." That way of seeing is no doubt partly temperamental—and partly cultural, Bush having long ago imbibed it as an adolescent growing up in Eisenhower's

America. The president who now believes that God and History have chosen him to cleanse the world of "terrorism" is but a taller and more grizzled version of the lad who watched a lot of westerns on TV, and liked to play with guns.

"Now, the mission is to rout terrorists, to find them and bring them to justice, or as I explained to the prime minister [Koizumi] in western terms, to smoke 'em out of their caves, to get 'em runnin' so we can get 'em."   —SEPTEMBER 25, 2001

"There's no cave deep enough for him to hide. He can run, and he thinks he can hide. But we're not going to give up until he and every other potential killer and every other body who hates freedom will be brought to justice."
                 —PITTSBURGH, PENNSYLVANIA, FEBRUARY 5, 2002

"Even though George W. Bush is president, Neil Bush can still see in him the sixteen-year-old who gave him and his younger brother ten seconds to start running down the hall before firing BB pellets at them."   —*UTAH COUNTY DAILY HERALD*, MARCH 2, 2002

Q: Are you saying you want him dead or alive, sir? Can I interpret your—

BUSH·   I just remember—all I'm doing is remembering when I was a kid, I remember that—they used to put out there in the old West a "wanted" poster; it said " Wanted Dead or Alive." All I want, and America wants him brought to justice. That's what we want.
                                        — SEPTEMBER 17, 2001

Here Bush was not, of course, recalling his own childhood back in 1885, but only harking back to something that he'd watched as a preadolescent couch potato: Wanted Dead or Alive, a Four Star Productions show that CBS ran on Saturday nights from 1958 to 1961. The program made a star of Steve McQueen, and clearly made a big impression on the president-to-be.

While schooled by countless TV shows, and movie matinees, to root against the bad guys (and the Indians), the young Bush also honed his Manichaean impulse as a would-be baseball star and all-around sports fanatic. It is significant that he stood out as a cheerleader at Andover, as he would later show the same extraordinary knack for group incitement, as the nation's Rallier-in-Chief post-9/11. For all the towering hubris of his self-display, the baseball diamond never seemed to be entirely absent from his mind:

Bush Keeps Terror Photo "Scorecard"

"As the war on terrorism began, President Bush ordered aides to produce a photo 'scorecard' of Osama bin Laden's al-Qaida terrorist network, crossing off faces with an 'X' as members were captured or killed.

"The president also asked the State Department to develop a detailed catalogue of the status of U.S. government requests to nearly 100 governments across the world, listing responses received and actions taken, the *Washington Post* reported Sunday.

" 'I'm a baseball fan, I want a scorecard,' Bush told the newspaper. 'And I understood that when you're fighting an enemy like al-Qaida, people—including me—didn't have a sense of whom we were fighting. And I actually got a chart.'

"The president pointed to a photo and thumbnail biography of Muhammad Atef, bin Laden's military chief and the leading planner of the Sept. 11 attacks.

" 'There's an "X" right there,' Bush said. Atef is known to have been killed during the U.S. bombing of Afghanistan in November."

—AP, FEBRUARY 3, 2002

As we have seen, the president's performance has been much improved by the "enormous clarity" with which the Lord has blessed his mind. Indeed, such merely verbal clarity, along with his don't-mess-with-Texas body language, was Bush's great achievement after 9/11—the only one, in fact, that we can confidently grant him at this point. And yet that simple spectacle did not make matters clearer, but merely served to mask a very deep confusion. Certainly his policies are every bit as murky as his statements (sometimes) sound precise. His military strategy might be summed up as follows: "Let's just buy it all and use it everywhere!" His foreign policy, meanwhile, is fraught with irresolveable self-contradictions.

On the one hand, his "Bush Doctrine" seems to force ("Make no mistake!") an absolute divide between the evil states that "harbor terrorists"and those good states that don't. And yet the latter list, as far as he's concerned, includes Saudi Arabia—the very epicenter of Wahhabist terrorism—as well as Lebanon and Syria; while the former list, as far as he's concerned, includes those three new "axis" powers that actually have no relationship to one another and two of which aren't harboring any terrorists to speak of.

And yet, beneath the pea-soup fog of Bush's policies, there is a grand confusion deeper still—arising not from notions or distinctions ill-thought-out but from the president's own profound resemblance to the enemy. That fact too has been concealed by the "enormous clarity" of his wartime remarks—which often sound like what the Mullah Omar too would say, and with the same conviction. The belief that God is on his team; his eagerness to fight forever ("I will not yield, I will not rest") throughout a world that has "no shades of gray," and where you're either with him or against him; his fixed conviction that his struggle is defensive always, and so always just; his hard refusal to consider any compromise; his inability to see how anybody else might see the situation: all of these are psychic features common both to Bush and to bin Laden, and to their respective teams. And as they share those traits, so do both sides alike promote a suicidal program—suicidal, at any rate, for those who can't seek refuge in the big guy's cave or bunker.

> "Our forefathers would salute the modern-day sacrifice of the brave passengers on Flight 93, who after reciting the Lord's Prayer, said, 'Let's roll,' and stormed the hijackers taking the plane down, probably saving thousands of lives on the ground."
>
> [*Applause*]
>
> —TO CALIFORNIA BUSINESS LEADERS,
> SACRAMENTO, OCTOBER 17, 2001

In short, the founders might see something un-American about this "war on terrorism." It is a jihad by another name—and one that has entailed a broad executive attack upon the very freedoms that would make this democracy worth fighting for. In this way too the Bush team is a pale reflection of the radical Islamist net-

work that would also crack down hard on any dissidence. An administration that would suspend habeas corpus, hold military trials in secret, and listen in on conversations between suspects and their lawyers; that warns the people to "watch what they say," and has the FBI investigate Americans for their reading or opinions, and grants the CIA authority to spy on U.S. citizens, and urges people to start snooping on their neighbors; and that sets up, in the Pentagon, an "Information Awareness Office" to combine and organize the data from the government's surveillance systems and that pushes for the final corporate concentration of the media so that independent voices must be shunted off into the furthest margins—such a junta does not champion our "freedom." On the contrary, its aim appears to be to (as it were) "cower our society" and "undermine its openness and its freedom and its ability to dissent."

Those who would thus abrogate the Bill of Rights—after having come to power despite the voters' will—are not, of course, dispersed throughout the Muslim world. They are in power right here, right now, forever warning us of the enormous danger posed to our democracy by those fanatical Islamists, Ba'athist fascists, North Korean communists—warnings that all sound like jokes, because they actually describe the very people making them:

"Americans are asking, 'Why do they hate us?'

"They hate what they see right here in this chamber: a democratically elected government. Their leaders are self-appointed. They hate our freedoms: our freedom of religion, our freedom of speech, our freedom to vote and assemble and disagree with each other."   —SEPTEMBER 20, 2001

"They hate progress and freedom and choice and culture and music and laughter and women and Christians and Jews and all Muslims who reject their distorted doctrines.

"They love only one thing. They love power, and when they have it, they use it without mercy."
—CHARLESTON, SOUTH CAROLINA, DECEMBER 11, 2001

"I worry about a regime that is closed and not transparent."
—ON NORTH KOREA (*NEW YORK TIMES,* FEBRUARY 20, 2002)

BUSINESS AS USUAL

Q: How much sacrifice are ordinary Americans going
            to have to be expected to make in their daily lives
            and their daily routines?

BUSH: Our hope, of course, is that they make no sacrifice
            whatsoever. We would like to see life return to
            normal in America.   —SEPTEMBER 15, 2001

"Now, the American people have got to go about their business. We
cannot let the terrorists achieve the objective of frightening our
nation to the point where we don't—where we don't conduct
business, where people don't shop."   —OCTOBER 11, 2001

*After 9/11, people wanted, naturally enough, to do something—anything. Many
charitable souls pitched in to help the victims, while young folks thronged to join the
military and the CIA, or, alternatively, took to other idealistic courses, working in
the streets or on the campuses to make the world a saner place. There was also speculation, both by talking heads and actual human beings, that "terrorism" might now
prove to be our Great Depression/World War II/Cold War—a national ordeal that
would deliver us from e-mail, fast food, shopping malls, and trash TV and introduce
us, finally, to the hardiness and pluck that made the "Greatest Generation" so
grown-up.*

*Although he did all that he could to feed that yearning, the president was also
very careful not to call for "sacrifice," as in "Ask not what your country can do for
you" or "I have nothing to offer but blood, toil, tears and sweat." It's possible that
Bush and his imagineers did not think that the viewers would really like a lot of
sacrifice, however popular the works of Tom Brokaw and Stephen Ambrose. It's also
possible, though, that the president refrained from asking us for sacrifice not just because that theme turned off the focus groups, but—as is more likely—because mass
sacrifice would mean huge losses for Bush/Cheney and their friends. This administration is for more and bigger SUVs, more snowmobiles and dirt bikes in the
wilderness, less fuel economy in every motor-driven vehicle, a lot more plastic pack-*

aging, and any other measure that might mean more oil and gas burned up per capita. The sort of market self-denial that was urged on people during World War II—gas rationing, victory gardens, patching up old tires—is just the sort of thing that Bush does would not want anybody thinking of, since it might lead to timelier notions of sustainable development.

For his part, Bush did everything he could to help his sponsors milk the "war on terrorism." Not long after the attacks, he did a big-time favor for the Travel Industry Association of America (TIA), allowing them to use him as a pitchman in a TV ad promoting tourism inside the United States. The ad replayed the president's request that good Americans fly off to national "destination spots" for lots of fun ASAP—fun that wouldn't do much for the overall economy but that would surely benefit one of Bush/Cheney's major donors.

Bush's Star Role in TV Travel Ad May Shine On

"Hotelier and Republican donor Bill Marriott helped create the spot after meeting with Karl Rove and other Bush advisers. The ad—opening with the post–Sept. 11 speech to Congress where Bush says, 'Americans are asking, "What can we do?"' and urges them to travel—was due to end this week. But the U.S. Travel Industry Association weighs an extension; it's raising $20 million for TV time from ailing airline, hotel and car-rental members.

" 'It is very unusual' for presidents to allow use of their image for commerce, former Federal Election Commission counsel Larry Noble says. For favor-seeking industries, he adds, it could be a bad precedent. But Rove says the nation confronts "an extraordinary situation." The commercial has aired 1,035 times during network news, pro football games and cable shows. The industry group reports 'phenomenal response'—except for daily gripes from Democratic viewers.

"Nearly all of Marriott International Inc.'s $754,000 for 2000 elections went to Bush and other GOP causes."

—*WALL STREET JOURNAL*, DECEMBER 12, 2001[112]

With the winter Olympics as a backdrop, Bush did a bit of stealthy advertising for another group that had helped put him where he is today.

"On the afternoon of Friday, February 8, George W. Bush spoke at the National Cattlemen's Beef Associations annual meeting in Denver. 'We want the people in China eating U.S. beef,' the President stated to thunderous approval. He reminded them that he has done much for the beef industry and cattle ranchers, and that he plans to do more.

"No doubt, Bush's appearance at this event netted thousands of dollars in campaign contributions for the GOP. In each of the last three election cycles, the National Cattleman's Beef Association gave nearly a half a million dollars in political contributions, for a six-year total of nearly $1.3 million. Roughly 85 percent of these donations in each of the last three election cycles have gone to Republicans.

"Later that same day, Bush traveled to Utah and participated in the Opening Ceremonies of the Winter Olympics. After appearing in the national anthem ceremony, Bush showed up sitting in the stands amongst the U.S. athletes. NBC showed him humbly perched next to a shocked and giggly young lady who handed Bush her cell phone so he could say hi to her mommy. The young girl was figure skater Sasha Cohen. A few nights later, NBC interviewed Sasha and played up the Presidential encounter, including a quick interview with the mother. Sasha gushed about her fondness for the President. . . .

"Of the 211 members of the U.S. Olympic squad, guess which one has the unique distinction of being the official youth spokesperson for the National Cattlemen's Beef Association? . . . Sasha was elevated to the post just a few days after the events of 9-11. James Sease, Chairman of the SC Beef Board, said at the time: 'We are so fortunate to have Sasha on board. This is a great way to reach the consumers of tomorrow—and today.'

"And the Beef Association is planning to put their new spokesperson to good use. On February 6 (just two days before Bush's appearance at their annual convention), the Beef Association announced plans for an April 2002 media blitz featuring Sasha. 'To reach young girls with a positive message about beef,' the Beef folks will run one-page, full-color ads featuring Sasha 'in 11 high-profile youth publications beginning in April.' The youth program Sasha is the spokesperson for targets what the Beef Association calls 'tween girls . . . between ages 8 and 12 . . . who will be moms in not too many years' and they just want these youngsters to 'understand the benefits of including beef in their diets.' The Association gloats: 'This ad campaign is projected to provide more than 13 million impressions to the targeted age group through magazines they read.'

"How convenient for the Beef industry that their youth spokesperson was featured in a heartwarming photo shoot with our commander in chief viewed by 70 million TV viewers just a few weeks before launching a major media blitz featuring that spokesperson. No doubt this ad campaign as well as their youth spokesperson's profile will get a huge boost thanks to Bush's Olympic shenanigans. I wonder how much that kind of publicity costs?"

—ALAN BALCH, *BUZZFLASH.COM,* FEBRUARY 26, 2002[113]

A CHINK IN THE ARMOR

Q: When was the last time you talked to either Mr. Lay or any other Enron official about the—about anything? And did the discussions involve the financial problems of the company?

BUSH: I have never discussed with Mr. Lay the financial problems of the company.

The last time that I saw Mr. Lay was at my mother's fund-raising event for literacy in Houston. That would have been last spring. I do know that Mr. Lay came to the White House in—early in my administration, along with, I think, twenty other business leaders to discuss the state of the economy.

It was just kind of a general discussion. I have not met with him personally.

—JANUARY 10, 2002

Thus began the president's first and, for a long spell, only scriptless statement on his own connection to the blazing wreck that had been Enron. Thereafter, the White

House took especial pains to keep him closed up tight on that most damaging of sub-jects, letting him speak only when he'd been well prepped with lines that might help make him look as if he also had been outraged by the scandal. Such heightened cau-tiousness was understandable, since Enron was just the sort of topic on which Bush could not ad-lib without revealing his true sympathies. Here, for example, is the last bit of his January 10 performance, which gave the game away, despite the staffer's effort to bring down the curtain:

Q:	What can you do about the pensioners—
STAFF:	Thank you.
BUSH:	Who?
Q:	What can you do about pensioners now? Isn't that horse already out of the barn—?
BUSH:	Well, we—our group is meeting, and they will bring recommendations—recommendations here. They'll look at—fully investigate what went on.
	I am—my concern, of course, is for the share-holders of Enron, but—and—but my—I have—I have great concern for the stories—for those I read about in the stories who put their life savings aside and for whatever reason, based upon some rule or regulation, got trapped in this awful bank-ruptcy and have lost life savings.
	And one of the things this group is going to do is take a good, hard look at it.

At that Q&A, however, Bush was hurt not by his native inability to empathize with those who'd been ripped off ("Who?") but by the starker fact that, as soon as he was asked about his old friend "Kenny Boy" Lay, Bush started lying like a rug:

Q:	How much of this is to inoculate yourself and the administration politically from—[*Inaudible*]?
BUSH:	Well, first of all, Ken Lay is a supporter, and **I got to know Ken Lay when he was a head of the—what they call the Governor's Business Council in Texas.**

**He was a supporter of Ann Richards in my run
in 1994, and she had named him head of the
Governor's Business Council, and I decided to
leave him in place, for the sake of continuity.**

**And that's when I first got to know Ken and
worked with Ken,** and he supported my candidacy
for—and—but this is what—what anybody's going to
find, if—is that this administration will fully investigate
issues such as the Enron bankruptcy to make sure we
can learn from the past and make sure that workers are
protected.

—JANUARY 10, 2002

*It was the sort of blunt and open fib that almost always means disaster. In the 1994
gubernatorial race in Texas, Lay had given the aspiring Bush three times more cash
than Governor Richards—$37,500 to him, $12,500 to her. In the summer of
2001, moreover, Lay himself had told PBS's* Frontline *that he'd been a Bush supporter in that race—and friends with Dubya for much longer than the president had
claimed: "But I was very close to George W. and had a lot of respect for him, had
watched him over the years, particularly with reference to dealing with his father when
his father was in the White House, and some of things he did to work for his father,* and so did support him."*[114]

In its baldness, Bush's lie recalled another presidential whopper:

"Now I have to go back to work on my State of the Union speech,
and I worked on it till pretty late last night. But I want to say one
thing to the American people. I want you to listen to me. I'm going
to say this again: **I did not have sexual relations with that
woman,** Miss Lewinsky. I never told anybody to lie, not a single
time. Never. These allegations are false. And I need to go back to
work for the American people."   —FNS, JANUARY 26, 1998

---

*According to Greg Palast, one of the things that Bush "did to work for his father" was to
make a phone call back in 1988, urging the government of Argentina to sell Enron the
pipeline carrying water from Chile into Buenos Aires. Because of Bush's help, Enron now
owns the city's water supply. See www.gregpalast.com/detail.cfm?artid=125&row=1.

348 Mark Crispin Miller

And yet, while Bush's lie was every bit as bald as Clinton's—and Enron's crimes, and Bush's links to them, of infinitely greater consequence than Clinton's links with Miss Lewinsky—the press played down the former lie as irresonsibly as it played up the latter one. Throughout the month after Clinton's lie was suddenly exposed in August 1998, the networks replayed that notorious denial forty-two times and never really let it go. By contrast, in the month after Bush's lie—which was exposed at once—the networks replayed it only seven times and then forgot about it.

THAT'S MY BUSH!

A few months after 9/11, the president relaxed enough to crack some jokes about it.

Q: One thing, Mr. President, is that you have no idea how much you've done for this country. And another thing is that—how did you feel when you heard about the terrorist attack?

BUSH: . . . Well, Jordan, you're not going to believe where—what state I was in when I heard about the terrorist attack. I was in Florida. And my chief of staff, Andy Card—well, actually I was in a classroom, talking about a reading program that works. And it—I was sitting outside the—the classroom, waiting to go in, and I saw an airplane hit the tower of a—of a—you know, the TV was obviously on,★ and I—I used to fly myself, and I said, "Well, there's one terrible pilot!"

Something—perhaps the fact that nobody laughed—told him that he hadn't struck the proper note.

★This was a strange misremembrance, unless that TV was receiving broadcasts from another planet: CNN did not tune in to the disaster until after it had happened, and had no footage of that first crash until well after 9:00 A.M.

BUSH: And I said, "It must have been a horrible accident."

—ORLANDO, FLORIDA, DECEMBER 4, 2001

In late November, Mitch Daniels, Bush/Cheney's budget director, gave a luncheon speech at the National Press Club:

"The president had said throughout his campaign, and long before these events were visible to us, that he hoped to always operate in the black and, in fact, at levels beyond the Social Security surplus, but that there were three conditions under which a deficit would be acceptable, those being war, recession, or emergency. And as he said to me shortly after the eleventh, 'Lucky me, I hit the trifecta.' "

[*Laughter*]

—NOVEMBER 28, 2001

"And we've got a job to do at home, as well. You know, I was campaigning in Chicago and somebody asked me, 'Is there ever any time where the budget might have to go into deficit?' I said only if we were at war or had a national emergency or were in recession.

[*Laughter*]

Little did I realize we'd get the trifecta.

[*Laughter*]

But we're fine.

—CHARLOTTE, NORTH CAROLINA, FEBRUARY 27, 2002

RING IN THE NEW

"But all in all, it's been a fabulous year for Laura and me."

—DECEMBER 21, 2001

NOTES

PREFACE: NOW MORE THAN EVER

[1]"short-sighted party operatives": "Bush Told to Water Down His Right-Wing Agenda," *Independent* (UK), 5/26/01.

[2]"a first-order disaster": Michael Kramer, "Bully Boy Bush's Big Blunder," *New York Daily News*, 5/24/01.

[3]"a wake-up call": "A Question of Governing from the Right," *The New York Times*, 5/25/01; "There is only": "Many in G.O.P. Remain Bullish in Face of Loss," *New York Times*, 5/31/01; "personal interest": "Bush Defends His Stance Despite Stinging Defection," *New York Times*, 5/25/01; "hanky panky": "Bush Told to Water Down His Right-Wing Agenda," *Independent* (UK), 5/26/01.

[4]"everything is A-OK": "Americans Like Bush for Personal Traits, Honesty," AP, 4/27/01.

[5]Bush environmental policies pretty close to Clinton/Gore's: This was, of course, a point made often by Ralph Nader, who revisits the issue throughout his campaign memoir, *Crashing the Party: How to Tell the Truth and Still Run for President* (New York: St. Martin's Press, 2002). Three months into the Bush presidency, Greg Easterbrook made exactly the same case—although not damningly but in a spirit of approval, the journalist being a conservative Democrat. See "Health Nut," *The New Republic*, 4/30/01. (The article is online at www.tnr.com/043001/easter brook043001.html.)

[6]"enfeebled politically": "A Chastened Bush Goes to Europe," *The Guardian* (UK), 6/8/01; "a certain inexperience": Safire on *Meet the Press*, NBC, 6/24/01; "Mr. Bush's European tour": "Bush Loses Favor Despite Tax Cut and Overseas Trip," *New York Times*, 6/21/01.

[7]"Mr. Bush's inattention": Ibid.; "Hear me loud and clear": Bush/Gore debate, 10/4/01; 42 percent of his first year: "A White House on the Range," *Washington Post*, 8/7/01; "I'm getting a lot done": "President Chats with Crawford Neighbors," AP, 8/9/01; "job seems to follow you around": "Bush Brothers Take on Each Other at Golf," Reuters, 7/7/01.

[8]"To me, he hasn't": "For Some Voters, President Has Yet to Prove Himself," *Washington Post*, 8/5/01; "I go around the state": "Economy Sobers Bush's Ratings," *Washington Times*, 8/26/01; *That's My Bush!*: "Pushed Out 'Bush' Eyes the Big Screen," *Daily Variety*, 8/3/01.

[9]"communities of character": "Bush Plans Values-Based Initiative to Rev Up Agenda," *Washington Post*, 7/29/01; "After Six Months, Bush Team Plans Change of Focus," *New York Times*, 8/5/01.

[10]"Some House Republicans": "Thanksgiving on the Hill?" *Roll Call*, 9/6/01; "potholes and landmines": Stuart Rothenberg quoted in "Bush Facing Big Hurdles; Full Plate of Issues Awaits As Vacation Comes to End," *Houston Chronicle*, 9/3/01.

[11]"It was unclear," William Bennett: "A Day Of Terror: The President; A Somber Bush Says Terrorism Cannot Prevail," *New York Times*, 9/12/01; "not our best moment," "I am stunned": "After The Attacks: The Events; In Four Days, a National Crisis Changes Bush's Presidency," *New York Times*, 9/16/01; "Bush should have insisted": William Safire, "New Day of Infamy," *New York Times*, 9/12/01.

[12]"And he will not waver!": "President Bush: A Leader Thrust into Global Crisis," CNN, 10/20/01; "When he said, 'Let's roll' ": *Larry King Live*, CNN, 11/8/01; "From Where Does George W. Bush": Howard Fineman and Martha Brant, " 'This Is Our Life Now,' " *Newsweek*, 12/3/01; "It's been a while": Christopher Buckley, "War and Destiny: The White House in Wartime," *Vanity Fair*, February, 2002, p. 84.

[13]"utterly irrelevant": Berke quoted in David Talbot, "Democracy Held Hostage," *Salon.com*, 9/29/01; the *New York Times* on the Florida recount: Gore Vidal, "*Times* Cries Eke! Buries Al Gore," *Nation*, 12/17/01.

[14]Bin Laden family and the Carlyle Group: "Bin Laden Family Is Tied to U.S. Group," *Wall Street Journal*, 9/27/01 (surprisingly, Judicial Watch—a rightist pressure group that had supported Paula Jones against Bill Clinton—sent out a fervent press release to drum up broader media interest in the *Journal*'s story); Salem bin Laden and Arbusto Energy: James Hatfield, "Why Would Osama bin Laden Want to Kill Dubya, His Former Business Partner?" *Online Journal*, 7/3/01 (www.online journal.com/Special__Reports/Hatfield-R-091901/hatfield-r-091901.html) (see

also J. H. Hatfield, *Fortunate Son: George W. Bush and the Making of an American President*, 2nd ed., paperback [New York: Soft Skull Press, 2001], pp. 54–56); "On Sept. 26": "Arms Buildup Is a Boon to Firm Run by Big Guns," *Los Angeles Times*, 1/10/02.

[15]John O'Neill: Jean-Charles Brisard and Guillaume Dasquié, *Ben Laden: La Vérité Interdite* (Paris: Editions Donoël, 2001) (see also Nina Burleigh, "Bush, Oil and the Taliban," *Salon.com*, 2/8/02; www.salon.com/politics/feature/2002/02/08/forbidden/print.html); one brief story: "Oil Diplomacy Muddled U.S. Pursuit of bin Laden, New Book Contends," *New York Times*, 11/12/01 (oddly enough, there is no mention of these findings in the *Times*'s long year-end piece about the U.S. failure to forestall the terrorist attacks [Judith Miller, Jeff Gerth, and Don van Natta Jr., "Planning for Terror but Failing to Act," *New York Times*, 12/30/01], although the article quotes O'Neill, referring to his change of jobs without explaining *why* he left the FBI; Seymour M. Hersh on the CIA: "Annals of National Security: What Went Wrong," *The New Yorker*, 10/8/01; "I can't thank you": GWB to CIA employees, Langley, Va., 9/26/01; White House interference with congressional investigation into 9/11: "Veep Tries to Stop 9/11 Spy Probe," *New York Post*, 1/30/02.

[16]A. J. Brown and Barry Reingold: "Political Dissent Can Bring Federal Agents to Door," *Christian Science Monitor*, 1/8/02; Matthew Rothschild, "The New McCarthyism," *The Progressive*, 1/1/02. See also Duncan Campbell, "Anti-War Profs Targeted," *The Guardian* (UK), 12/19/01; Nat Hentoff, "Eroding American Freedoms," *Washington Times*, 1/28/02; "FBI Software Sidesteps Detection," *New York Daily News*, 1/8/02; David Corn, "The FBI's Black Magic?," *TomPaine.com*, 1/7/02; Michael Connor, "Brave New Web," *Austin Chronicle* (on Alternet, www.alternet.org/story.html?StoryID=12142); "Is the Bush Administration Really Imperiling Freedom for the Sake of Security?," *The Economist*, 12/6/01; "Four Commanders Seek Staff Role for the F.B.I.," *New York Times*, 11/20/01; "Feds Investigating Student Org's," AP, 12/20/01; Charles W. Gittins, " 'Military Commissions' Wrong Response to September 11," *Washington Times*, 11/28/01; Julian Borger, "For Their Eyes Only," *The Guardian* (UK), 3/6/02.

[17]Bush being fundamentally transformed: Haynes Johnson made this point on *Odyssey*, Chicago Public Radio, 10/31/01; "You can never tell": Margaret Wente, "The Making of a President," *Toronto Globe & Mail*, 9/25/01; "some divine guidance": *Meet the Press*, NBC, 12/23/01.

[18]"a great leader all along": "The Rove Review: 'Clarity,' 'Compassion,' " *Washington Post*, 12/12/01; "Moments of Crisis: In the White House, a Sense of What History Can Teach," *New York Times*, 1/9/02; "In a lot of ways": *Meet the Press*, NBC, 12/23/01.

[19]"Bush's recent performance": "The Rove Review," *Washington Post*, 12/12/01; "Has Mr. Bush changed?": "America As Reflected in Its Leader," *New York Times* 1/6/02.

[20]"These are times": from a reader's review on Amazon.com, posted on 1/31/01; "Anyone who has watched": "America As Reflected in Its Leader," *New York Times*, 1/6/02.

[21]Enron's internal propaganda: Michael Tomasky, "Do Unto Others . . . Oh, Never Mind," *Washington Post*, 2/3/02.

[22]Bush's military budget: Center for Defense Information, "U.S. Military Transformation: Not Just More Spending, but Better Spending," 1/31/02 (www.cdi.org/mrp/transformation.cfm); Center for Defense Information, "Highlights of the FY'03 Budget Request," 2/4/02 (www.cdi.org/issues/budget/FY03Highlights -pr.cfm). Sarah Left, "Bush's Offensive Budget," *The Guardian* (UK), 1/24/02.

LOOK WHO'S TALKING

[23]"discharge the complicated," "who cannot spell": John William Ward, *Andrew Jackson: Symbol for an Age* (New York: Oxford University Press, 1955), p. 64; "A barbarian who": John T. Morse Jr., *John Quincy Adams* (Boston, 1891), p. 242, quoted in William A. DeGregorio, *The Complete Book of U.S. Presidents* (New York: Barricade Books, 1996), p. 118.

[24]"everyday businesslike sanity": Bernard Bailyn, *The Ideological Origins of the American Revolution* (Cambridge, Mass.: Belknap Press of Harvard University Press, 1967), p. 19; Attorney General Crittenden on Fillmore's sensible speech: Robert J. Rayback, *Millard Fillmore: Biography of a President* (Buffalo: Buffalo Historical Society, 1959), p. 335.

[25]"If we wish": Alyn Brodsky, *Grover Cleveland: A Study in Character* (New York: St. Martin's Press, 2000), p. 39; Eisenhower's editorial acumen: Emmet John Hughes, *The Ordeal of Power: A Political Memoir of the Eisenhower Years* (New York: Atheneum 1963), pp. 24–25; "His mental cassettes": Lou Cannon, *President Reagan: The Role of a Lifetime* (New York: Simon & Schuster, 1991), p. 293.

[26]"It's no exaggeration": Campaign rally in Troy, Ohio, 10/21/88; "You cannot be": Campaigning in Dover, New Hampshire, 1/15/92: both gaffes are included in *Bushisms: President George Herbert Walker Bush in His Own Words,* a volume compiled by the editors of *The New Republic* (New York: Workman, 1992); "inarticulate as though": "Campaign Trail," *New York Times*, 11/4/88; "cramped down on": "Bush

Works on Image, but Says He Must 'Be Me,' " *New York Times*, 8/8/88; "We have made mistakes": *Financial Times*, 5/9/88. (What the vice president had meant to say, apparently, was "setbacks.") "The most important": *San Antonio Express News*, 1/30/00. (Bush was trying to say that the duties of parenting should come before the obligations of one's job.)

[27]"like a sixteen-year-old": "Bush Works on Image," *New York Times*, 8/8/88; "This election is": "Quayle, in South, Accuses Dukakis of Lacking Issues," *New York Times*, 9/3/88; "We understand the importance": "Two Campaigns Have Same Emphasis and Tone; Quayles Borrows Bush Props, Malaprops," *Los Angeles Times*, 9/16/88; "There is nothing": "Quayle Discards His Script on Military Issues and Raises Eyebrows," *New York Times*, 9/9/88. ("The audience was left wondering whether the Senator favored offensive or defensive weapons," noted the reporter, Lisa Belkin.)

[28]"Looking back": Maureen Dowd, "The Education of Dan Quayle," *New York Times Magazine*, 6/25/89, p. 20; "really is the studious sort": "Quayle's No. 1 Colleague Hits the Campaign Trail," *New York Times*, 9/11/88.

[29]George H. W. Bush's reading: "For Bush, Culture Can Be a Sometime Thing," *New York Times*, 19/27/88; "Bush's Tastes Down Home to Less So," *New York Times*, 5/1/90; "He jogged and drove his boat": Dan Quayle, *Standing Firm: A Vice-Presidential Memoir* (New York: HarperCollins, 1994), pp. 252–53.

[30]Baseball cards: Gail Sheehy, "The Accidental Candidate," *Vanity Fair*, October 2000, p. 168.

[31]"A guy who's been": "Shades of Gray Matter; The Question Dogs George W. Bush: Is He Smart Enough? There's No Simple Answer," *Washington Post*, 1/19/00.

[32]"Behold, then": George Bancroft on Andrew Jackson, quoted in Richard Hofstadter, *Anti-Intellectualism in American Life* (New York: Knopf, 1963), p. 159.

[33]"calculated bluntness": Kenneth Cmiel, *Democratic Eloquence: The Fight over Popular Speech in Nineteenth-Century America* (New York: William Morrow, 1990), p. 63; "the rich richer": quoted in DeGregorio, p. 119. For a detailed study of how cautiously the franchise was, in fact, extended in the heyday of "Jacksonian Democracy," see Alexander Keyssar, *The Right to Vote: The Contested History of Democracy in the United States* (New York: Basic Books, 2000), pp. 53–76.

[34]"I'll answer some questions": "Presidency Takes Shape With No Fuss, No Sweat," *New York Times*, 2/10/01.

[35]"TV is still," "vaudeville": Michael R. Beschloss, *Taking Charge: The Johnson White House Tapes, 1963–1964* (New York: Simon & Schuster, 1997), p. 253, n. 3.

[36]"I'm not a bit": Memo to H. R. Haldeman, May 9, 1971, in Bruce Oudes, ed., *From the President: Richard Nixon's Secret Files* (New York: Harper & Row, 1989), p. 251.

[37]"I don't think": Robert Odle Jr. quoted in Gerald S. Strober and Deborah Hart Strober, *Nixon: An Oral History of His Presidency* (New York: HarperCollins, 1994), p. 49.

[38]"One weakness in": Oudes, *From the President,* pp. 203–4.

[39]"Need now to establish": Entry for July 21, 1969, in H. R. Haldeman, *The Haldeman Diaries: Inside the Nixon White House* (New York: Putnam, 1994), pp. 73–74.

[40]Nixon's readings in philosophy: Monica Crowley, *Nixon in Winter* (New York: Random House, 1998), p. 344 ("When I walked," " 'No wonder the Greeks' "), p. 347 (" 'Boy, there's the truth!' "), p. 353 (" 'It's so complex' "); Nixon on "little Negro bastards," homosexuals, etc.: From an Oval Office conversation taped on May 13, 1971, transcribed by James Warren, "Nixon on Tape Expounds on Welfare and Homosexuality," the *Chicago Tribune* (11/7/99), and reprinted as "All the Philosopher King's Men" in *Harper's,* February 2000, 22–24.

[41]Barbara Bush on Geraldine Ferraro: *New York Times,* 10/4/84, 10/5/84; *Houston Chronicle,* 10/6/84; "bozos," "Ozone Man": "Bush, Clinton Begin Finish Line Sprint; Upbeat President, Charged by Polls, Steps Up Rhetoric," *Washington Post,* 10/30/92; "asshole": Minutaglio, *First Son,* p. 223; "He had on": Barbara Bush, *Barbara Bush: A Memoir* (New York: Scribner's, 1994), p. 37.

[42]"It's not that he": Monica Crowley, *Nixon Off the Record* (New York: Random House, 1996), p. 46; "Oh, yes": Bush made this remark to historian Barbara Tuchman, quoted in an AP story, 8/13/88; "A lot of people": AP, 10/19/87.

[43]Bush's pitch: Richard Ben Cramer, *What It Takes: The Way to the White House* (New York: Random House, 1992), pp. 26–29. (Throughout, Cramer's book offers an incisive view of Bush's background and temperament.) The supermarket scanner flap: "Bush Encounters the Supermarket, Amazed," *New York Times,* 2/5/92; "That Amazing Scanner," *Washington Post,* 2/12/92; Howard Kurtz, "The Story That Just Won't Check Out," *Washington Post,* 2/19/92; "Bush wrongly ridiculed about grocery scanner," *Houston Chronicle,* 2/25/92.

[44]Charles Colson to Pat O'Donnell, 7/24/71: "We should always consider using George Bush more often as a good speaking resource. He is very good on his feet, he generally can get media attention, he does have Cabinet rank and he takes our line beautifully. I would make more on an effort to get him into things as you find good forums than we have done in the past": Oudes, *From the President,* p. 302; "I am convinced": letter of 7/23/74, in George Bush, *All the Best, George Bush: My Life in Letters and Other Writings* (New York: Scribner, 199), pp. 181–82;

"a political jackpot": Kevin Buckley, *Panama: The Whole Story* (New York: 1991), p. 254.

[45]"He connects with": Bush media adviser Lionel Sosa, quoted in the *Pittsburgh Post-Gazette,* 10/29/98.

[46]This judgment was confirmed by the Brookings Institution, which, on 11/13/00, released a useful overview: *How the Television Networks Covered the 2000 Presidential Campaign.* (Parts of the report are available online at www.brookings.edu/comm/transcripts/20001113.htm.)

[47]"I remember what": Governor Bush on *Larry King Live,* CNN, 9/29/00; "twice mopped the floor": Dennis Byrne, "Even great intellects have dumb days," *Chicago Sun-Times,* 11/1/00; "The intelligentsia said": George Will, "Demeanor Does Matter: It Can Denote Political Sentiment," *Sun-Sentinel* (Ft. Lauderdale, Fla.), 10/29/00; "The country can afford": Michael Kelly, "Dumb vs. Dishonest," *Washington Post,* 9/27/00; "A Gore administration": George Will, "The Case for Bush," *Washington Post,* 11/5/00.

[48]"grammatical English": Rush Limbaugh, *The Way Things Ought To Be* (New York: Pocket Star Books, 1993), p. 206.

[49]"Bush's ambling on the": George Will, "Demeanor Does Matter: It Can Denote Political Sentiment," *Sun-Sentinel* (Ft. Lauderdale, Fla.), 10/29/00.

[50]"Because he is black": George Will, "The Way the Media Treat Jackson," *Washington Post,* 1/28/88. For more background on the episode, see "Jackson Faults Media Minority Portrayals; Says Press 'Poisons Minds' in Speech at Sacramento Fund Raiser," *New York Times,* 1/20/88.

[51]"You don't have to be": "Fellow Governor Touts Texan with a Double-Edged Anecdote," *Washington Post,* 6/1/2000.

[52]"political campaign terrorist": Mary Matalin quoted in Minutaglio, *First Son,* p. 260; "soul of an alley cat": Rusher quoted in Strober and Strober, *Nixon: An Oral History,* p. 50; "He'll do positive things": Nixon to Charles Colson, Oval Office conversation, 1/2/73, in Stanley Kutler, *Abuse of Power: The New Nixon Tapes* (New York: Free Press, 1997), p. 193. Bush's contribution to his father's terroristic presidential drive in 1988 has been noted by all his biographers, but it is J. H. Hatfield whose account is most detailed. See "Home Run" in *Fortunate Son,* pp. 75–96.

[53]"If you're not": "Behind Bush Juggernaut, an Aide's Labor of Loyalty," *New York Times,* 1/11/00.

[54]"went up the walls": Harlow quoted in Greg Mitchell, *Tricky Dick and the Pink Lady: Richard Nixon vs. Helen Gahagan Douglas—Sexual Politics and the Red Scare,*

1950 (New York: 1998), p. 40; "A total Nixon man": Elizabeth Mitchell, *W: Revenge of the Bush Dynasty* (New York: Hyperion, 2000), p. 116.

[55]"Just wait will": Ibid., p. 63; "While Kennedy was running": Fitzhugh Green, *George Bush: An Intimate Portrait* (New York: 1989), p. 64; "I may not be eloquent": from Bush's acceptance speech at the 1988 Republican National Convention; "in love with the Kennedys": Peggy Noonan, *What I Saw at the Revolution: A Political Life in the Reagan Era* (New York: Random House, 1990), pp. 6, 9.

[56]Georgetown dinner party: Barbara Bush, *Barbara Bush: A Memoir*, p. 67.

[57]"The country—we turned": Oval Office conversation between President Nixon and Alexander Haig, 5/16/73, in Kutler, *Abuse of Power*, p. 506.

[58]"The Beatles went though": Minutaglio, *First Son;* "There is an arrogance": *All the Best, George Bush*, p. 182.

[59]"I don't remember": Minutaglio, *First Son*, p. 117; "we in Texas": Parmet, *George Bush: The Life of a Lone Star Yankee*, p. 130.

[60]"I'm a warrior": Bush on *Larry King Live*, CNN, 8/16/92; "WHAT HAS HE": Minutaglio, *First Son*, p. 286.

[61]Andover classmate Bob Marshall, quoted in Minutaglio, *First Son*, p. 66.

[62]"only a cigarette burn": "Branding Rite Laid to Fraternity," *New York Times*, 11/8/67.

[63]The Telecommunications Act of 1996—a bill essentially dictated by the media industries themselves, and stealthily approved by Congress—proclaimed the outright giveaway of the digital television spectrum to the same great corporate players that already dominate the media, both "new" and "old." As a sop to those who took exception to that massive theft of public property, President Clinton asked Al Gore to chair a commission whose ostensible purpose was to come up with a (voluntary) code of public service obligations for the broadcasters, who might thereby "give something back" for being given such a handsome oligopoly. The commission included media activists as well as corporate heavy hitters—a group that could arrive at no agreement without some moral leadership, which Gore did not provide. Of all the public service obligations that the group might have discussed at length (educational programming, noncommercial local shows, a limit on ads aimed at children, etc.), the only one that the commission entertained was a minimal requirement of free broadcast time for the top contenders during campaign seasons. The group's corporate types rejected even that, and so the "Gore Commission" finally came up empty. See Robert W. McChesney, *Rich Media, Poor Democracy* (Urbana, Ill.: University of Illinois Press, 1999), pp. 70–76, 146–59.

[64]"ABC and CBS": Colson to Haldeman, 11/17/70, in Oudes, *From the President,* p. 171.

[65]The poll by Fairness and Accuracy in Reporting (FAIR) in available online at www.fair.org/reports/journalist-survey.html.

[66]"He has made": "Bush's Selections Signal a Widening of Cabinet's Role," *New York Times,* 12/31/00; "What happens in": William Safire, "Bush's Two Pumpkins," *New York Times,* 1/1/01.

[67]"Only the most": Hughes, *The Ordeal of Power,* p. 319; "I can't be": "Bush Works on Image, but Says He Must 'Be Me,' " *New York Times,* 8/8/88; "Bush is always": Meg Greenfield, *Newsweek,* 4/2/90; "What these tics": Michael Kinsley, "Introduction," *Bushisms,* p. 2.

[68]"The receptivity of": Adolf Hitler, *Mein Kampf,* trans. Ralph Manheim (Boston: Houghton Mifflin, 1943), p. 180.

[69]Prescott Bush's financial involvement with the Nazis is a story that has long been tactfully ignored, for obvious reasons. The bare facts are these: On October 20, 1942—almost a year after Pearl Harbor—the U.S. government impounded the Union Banking Corp. under the Trading with the Enemy Act. All Union Banking's stock shares were siezed by the U.S. Alien Property Custodian. The shares were held by Prescott Bush, managing partner of Brown Brothers Harriman, and six other men: three Bush associates, including E. Roland "Bunny" Harriman, and three Nazi executives, who were instruments of the mighty pro-Nazi industrialist Fritz Thyssen.

On October 28, the government siezed two more Nazi entities run by Union Banking: the Holland-American Trading Corp. and the Seamless Steel Equipment Corp. On November 17—as U.S. troops were fighting in North Africa—the U.S. government siezed the Nazi interests in the Silesian-American Corp., which Prescott Bush had co-managed with his father-in-law, George Herbert Walker. (The government did not their impound their shares.)

In its volumes for the 1930s and 1940s, the *New York City Directory of Directors* has Bush listed as a director of Union Banking Corp. from 1934 through 1943.

See: John Loftus and Mark Aarons, *The Secret War Against the Jews: How Western Espionage Betrayed the Jewish People* (New York: St. Martin's Press, 1994); Wesley G. Tarpley and Anton Chaitkin, *George Bush: The Unauthorized Biography* (Washington, D.C.: Executive Intelligence Review, 1992).

THE MADNESS OF
KING GEORGE

[70]On the Republican party's employment of ex-Nazis and ex-fascists, see Christopher Simpson, *Blowback: America's Recruitment of Nazis and Its Effects on the Cold War* (New York: Weidenfeld & Nicholson, 1988), and Russ Bellant, *Old Nazis, the New Right and the Republican Party* (Boston: South End Press, 1991).

[71]On the *Lawrence Eagle-Tribune*'s treatment of the Horton case, see Steve Burkholder, "The *Lawrence Eagle-Tribune* and the Willie Horton Story," *Washington Journalism Review,* July–August 1989. On the Bush/Quayle campaign's use of the Horton episode, see Sidney Blumenthal, *Pledging Allegiance: The Last Campaign of the Cold War* (New York: HarperCollins, 1990), pp. 295–96, and Jack W. Germond and Jules Witcover, *Whose Broad Stripes and Bright Stars?: The Trivial Pursuit of the Presidency, 1988* (New York: Warner Books, 1989), pp. 262–64.

[72]The atrocity tales about Saddam Hussein's invasion were, necessarily, purveyed through every medium. However, the best-known and most comprehensive source of such inventions was Jean P. Sasson, *The Rape of Kuwait* (New York: Knightsbridge, 1991), a quickie paperback that suddenly appeared in several thousand U.S. bookstores, drugstores, and supermarkets—and in bulk on every U.S. military base in Saudi Arabia—about a week before Desert Storm began, heavily advertised (on a six-figure budget) with the commanding tag line, "Read it, and you'll know why we're there." According to the publisher's chief executive, the book was circulated among U.S. troops "with the help of the Saudis." "Book Notes," *New York Times,* 1/9/91. On Nayirah al-Sabah, see John R. MacArthur, *Second Front: Censorship and Propaganda in the Gulf War* (New York: Hill & Wang, 1992), pp. 57–60. In general, my assertions about the propaganda side of Desert Storm are based on my own research on that episode, which I intend to analyze at length in a forthcoming study.

THE YOUNG PRETENDER

[73]Myron Magnet, *The Dream and the Nightmare: The Sixties' Legacy to the Underclass* (New York: William Morrow, 1993), p. 35.

[74]Aaron Latham, "How George W. Found God," *George,* September 2000.

[75]J. H. Hatfield, *Fortunate Son: George W. Bush and the Making of an American President* (New York: Thomas Dunne Books, 1999), pp. 237–44.

[76]"Shades of Gray Matter; The Question Dogs George W. Bush: Is He Smart Enough? There's No Simple Answer," *Washington Post*, 1/19/00.

[77]It is instructive to compare Chace's book, which appeared in 1998, with Carolyn Eisenberg's *Drawing the Line: The American Decision to Divide Germany, 1944–1949*, which had come out two years earlier from Cambridge University Press—and which Chace fails even to include in his bibliography, much less discuss, even though it contradicts certain of his claims about Dean Acheson. It is no less instructive to compare the copious mainstream praise for Chace's book with the near-total mainstream silence about Eisenberg's, despite the great newsworthiness of her discoveries and the universal praise her book received from academic reviewers. See Mark Crispin Miller, "When Good Books Vanish," *Free Inquiry*, Fall 2000, pp. 16–18.

[78]Peter Conrad, *Television: The Medium and Its Manners* (Boston: Routledge & Kegan Paul, 1982), p. 48.

[79]On Celtie Johnson: "Woman Promotes Teaching of Creationism in Kansas Public Schools," *Kansas City Star*, 11/26/99; "Developing any book": Gerry Rising, "Creationism Kansas Style," *Buffalo News*, 9/13/99.

[80]Dr. Ed Young, pastor at Houston's Second Baptist Church, is quoted in Latham, "How George W. Found God," *George*, September 2000; Fawn Hall's crucial testimony at the Iran-Contra hearings is quoted in William S. Cohen and George J. Mitchell, *Men of Zeal: A Candid Inside Story of the Iran-Contra Hearings* (New York: Viking, 1988), pp. 130–36.

[81]The data are available on the Web site of the Center for Responsive Politics, at www.opensecrets.org.

[82]For background on the Boston Harbor ad, see Blumenthal, *Pledging Allegiance*, and Germond and Witcover, *Whose Broad Stripes and Bright Stars?*, as well as Kathleen Hall Jamieson, *Dirty Politics: Deception, Distraction and Democracy* (New York: Oxford University Press, 1992), pp. 105–6. For a visual analysis of the ad, see Mark Crispin Miller, "The 1988 Campaign: Decoding the Hidden Messages," *Columbia Journalism Review*, Jan./Feb. 1992, 36–39.

[83]*AP Online*, 5/28/99.

[84]Col. Ralph Anderson, quoted in Hatfield, *Fortunate Son*, p. 45.

[85]Ibid., p. 43.

[86]Rosenbaum's article is included in *The Secret Parts of Fortune: Three Decades of Intense Investigations and Edgy Enthusiasms* (New York: Random House, 2000), pp.

155–72; On the possibility that Skull and Bones keeps some of Hitler's silverware, see Toby Rogers, "Sympathy for the Devil, Part 5," *Greenwich Village Gazette*, available online at www.gvny.com/columns/rogers/page5.html.

[87]Gail Sheehy, "The Accidental Candidate," *Vanity Fair*, October 2000.

[88]Paul Begala, *Is Our Children Learning?: The Case Against George W. Bush* (New York: Simon & Schuster, 2000), pp. 103–5.

[89]"The largest prison system": Molly Ivins and Lou Dubose, *Shrub: The Short But Happy Political Life of George W. Bush* (New York: Vintage, 2000), p. 141 (and see pp. 141–55); JPI study: "Texas Tops All States in Prison Population," *Toronto Globe and Mail*, 8/29/00; racial percentages on incarceration for drug charges: Substance Abuse and Mental Health Services Administration, *National Household Survey on Drug Abuse: Summary Report 1998* (Rockville, Md.: National Institution Drug Abuse, 1999), p. 13; racial percentages on state court convictions: David J. Levin, Patrick A. Langan and Jodi M. Brown, *State Court Sentencing of Convicted Felons, 1996* (Washington, D.C.: U.S. Department of Justice, 2000), p. 8; "Crime control policies": Craig Haney and Philip Zimbardo, "The Past and Future of U.S. Prison Policy: Twenty-five Years After the Stanford Prison Experiment," *American Psychologist*, vol. 53, no. 7 (July 1998), 716; disenfranchisement: "Study Suggests Black Male Prison Rate Impinges on Political Process," *Washington Post*, 1/30/97; Human Rights Watch: Jamie Fellner and Marc Mauer, "Losing the Vote: The Impact of Felony Disenfranchisement Laws in the United States," (Washington, D.C.: Human Rights Watch and the Sentencing Project, 1998), p. 8. These and further pertinent data are available at www.drugwarfacts.org/racepris.htm.

AFTERWORD

[90]TV's inordinate focus on the *now* is but one aspect of the medium's inherent rightist bias, according to Jeffrey Scheuer, whose book *The Sound Bite Society: Television and the American Mind* (New York: Four Walls Eight Windows, 1999) offers an invaluable discussion of TV's impact on U.S. politics.

[91]Certain aspects of the Clinton bogey were not propaganda calculations but mere semiotic accidents. The USA's first baby-boomer chief executive was in big trouble, first of all, because he had been born too late to wear the sort of buttoned-up, quasi-paternal gravity that many people still expected from "the president." In 1988 George W. Bush could say that he believed the elder Bush should be elected "because he's been a great dad," and no one laughed at him for saying it. While appropriate for throwbacks like the Gipper and George Bush, such filial emotion is

not a civic possibility here in the culture of TV, where dads dress down and kids cool out and presidents have got to chill in public. Clinton roused reactionary fury just for being on this side of the big postwar divide; and his victories over Bush, then Dole—each an uptight poster boy for what Tom Brokaw calls "the greatest generation"—only magnified his reputation as a juvenile delinquent.

[92]Gary Aldrich, *Unlimited Access* (Washington, D.C.: Regnery 1996), quoted in Jeffrey Toobin, *A Vast Conspiracy: The Real Story of the Sex Scandal That Nearly Brought Down a President* (New York: Simon & Schuster, 1999), p. 96.

[93]Joseph Persico, *Casey: From the OSS to the CIA* (New York: Viking Penguin, 1990), p. 290.

[94]Martin Walker, *The Cold War: A History* (New York: Henry Holt, 1993), p. 47.

[95]George Bush, "Uniting Against Terrorism," a speech delivered at an international conference on terrorism sponsored by the magazine *Discover* on January 20, 1987; *Department of State Bulletin,* April 1987, pp. 3–5.

[96]Greg Palast, "Silence of the Lambs: The Election Story Never Told," posted on the *Media Channel* at www.mediachannel.com.

POSTSCRIPT: YEAR ONE

[97]"where them loonies": quoted in Christopher Hitchens, "Worst of the Worst," *Newsweek,* 7/9/01.

[98]"the ease with which he": Micholas E. Calio quoted in "After Six Months, Bush Team Plans Change of Focus," *New York Times,* 8/5/01.

[99]Bush and the Democrats' plan for short-term tax relief: "Notebook: Fact Checks," *The New Republic,* 2/11/02.

[100]Ashcroft and Infant's Protection Act: Adele M. Stan, "License to Kill?" *Salon.com,* 1/18/01.

[101]"Karl Rove said": "President Struggling with Stem Cell Issue," UPI, 7/26/01.

[102]Those against stem cell research: For a full articulation of the orthodox Catholic view, see "Bishop Paul S. Loverde on President Bush's Stem Cell Decision," *Arlington Catholic Herald,* 8/23/01, also on the Web site of the Culture of Life Foundation, at www.christianity.com/partner/Article__Display__Page/0,,PTID4211| CHID102753|CIID784904,00.html (weeks before the president's speech, in fact,

the opponents of such research had made clear that they would disapprove the very sort of compromise that Bush finally announced: "Richard Doerflinger of the National Conference of Catholic Bishops said such a compromise would be unacceptable. 'I don't see it as a compromise, but as a transitional step' to a 'full blown' policy of federally financing embryonic research, Doerflinger said, adding that if researchers found the experiments on the small number of lines promising, they would want to create even more lines, and that would create pressure to allow tax dollars to be used for more experiments." "Bush Said to Be 'Struggling's with Stem Cell Decision," *CNN.com*, 7/4/01); stem cell speech perplexed many scientists: "Bush Compromise Raises Doubts over Stem-Cell Resilience," *Nature*, 8/16/01; "Stem Cell Research Faces FDA Hurdle; With Mouse Cell Base, Tough Rules Apply," *Washington Post*, 8/24/01; "Mouse Cells in Stem Lines May Limit Use," *Wall Street Journal*, 8/24/01.

[103]"I'm the kind of person": *Weekly Compilation of Presidential Documents*, 8/20/01. The full exchange is noteworthy for the president's clear annoyance that his speech had not shut down all further questions.

Q:	One more question on stem cells, if I may?
BUSH:	You can ask it, but I've already answered it.
Q:	Well, I'll ask and—
BUSH:	I answered it Thursday night, when I gave an address to the nation.
Q:	But sir, since then, some pro-life activists have said that you're—
BUSH:	You know something? I gave the statement I thought was right. I spent a lot of time on the subject. I laid out the policy I think is right for America, and I'm not going to change my mind. I'm the kind of person that when I make up my mind, I'm not going to change it.

There are going to—people have got all kinds of opinions. I gave mine, and I gave it to the country. And it's a policy that's well thought out. Understand that there's a moral issue—moral issue, plus there's a chance that we can save people's lives. And I've laid out the path to do that.

[104]"Innocent intent": William Safire, "Words at War," *New York Times Magazine*, 9/30/01.

[105]Boy Scouts: "Scouts Divided," *Newsweek*, 8/6/01; Salvation Army: "Charity Cites Bush Help in Fight Against Hiring Gays; Salvation Army Wants Exemption

from Laws," *Washington Post,* 7/10/01; NAACP: John Nichols, "W Picks Golf over NAACP," *Capitol Times* (Madison, Wisc.), 7/12/01.

[106]Genoa: "Genoa Riot Inquiry Says Police Were Too Violent," *The Times* (London), 8/1/01; "Italy's Police Chief Admits Police Excesses During G8," Agence France Presse, 8/8/01; "Evidence Shows Summit Police Using Guns," *Scotland on Sunday,* 8/5/01; "Is Silvio Berlusconi Bad News?," *BusinessWeek Online,* 8/1/01.

[107]"shut up": FNS, White House briefing, 9/5/01; "Bush, Fox Talk Immigration Reform," AP, 9/5/01; "lit up the sky": "D.C. Residents Blast Bush over 'Big Bang,' " *Houston Chronicle,* 9/9/01; " 'This is it!' ": "Look! Up in the Sky!; It's a Late Wake-Up Call from a White House Party," *Washington Post,* 9/7/01.

[108]"I don't know": "Look! Up in the Sky!" *Washington Post,* 9/7/01; Clinton's haircut-on-the-runway: "Bill's Coif: The Myth; Runway Trim Delayed No One," *Newsday,* 6/30/93; Jonathan Schell, "Haircut: A Tale with a Life of Its Own," *Newsday,* 7/18/93. See also "Covering Clinton," David Shaw's three-part series in the *Los Angeles Times,* 9/15–9/17/93.

[109]Sir Michael Howard's speech: "Stumbling into Battle," *Harper's,* 1/2/02, pp. 13–17.

[110]"The terrorism of September 11": Gilles Kepel, *Jihad: The Trail of Political Islam,* tr. Anthony F. Roberts (Cambridge, Mass.: Harvard University Press, 2002), p. 4; "9/11 was not": quoted in Nina Burleigh, "Bush, Oil and the Taliban," *Salon.com,* 2/8/02; "Osama bin Laden continues": Yossef Bodansky, *Bin Laden: The Man Who Declared War on America* (New York: Prima Publishing, 2001), pp. 387–88. See also Noam Chomsky, *9-11* (New York: Seven Stories Press, 2001), and the pertinent writings of Simon Jenkins of *The Times* (London) and Robert Fisk of *The Independent* (UK).

[111]Ashcroft's vision of the Jews: Like many Christian fundamentalists, Ashcroft is ambivalent about Jews—on the one hand, mindful of the Jews' important role in Christian eschatology (and, therefore, pro-Zionist); on the other hand, repelled by what he sees as the Jews' secularist and cosmopolitan influence. For a friendly reminiscence of the former inclination, see Tevi Troy, "Washington Diarist: My Boss the Fanatic," *The New Republic,* 1/29/01.

[112]"Bush's Star Role": "Washington Wire," *Wall Street Journal,* 12/21/01.

[113]Alan Balch, "Why Did Bush Sit Next to Sasha Cohen at the Olympics? Just Ask 'Where's the Beef?,' " *BuzzFlash.com,* 2/26/02 (www.buzzflash.com/contributors/2002/02/022602__Cohen__Beef.html).

[114]Lay and Bush: "Records Show Enron CEO Supported Bush, Not Richards, in '94 Texas Race," *Dallas Morning News,* 1/12/02.

RECOMMENDED READING

GEORGE H. W. BUSH

Blumenthal, Sidney, *Pledging Allegiance: The Last Campaign of the Cold War* (New York: HarperCollins, 1990).

Cramer, Richard Ben, *What it Takes: The Way to the White House* (New York: Random House, 1996).

Duffy, Michael, and Dan Goodgame, *Marching in Place: The Status Quo Presidency of George Bush* (New York: Simon & Schuster, 1992).

Parmet, Herbert S., *George Bush: The Life of a Lone Star Yankee* (New York: Scribner's, 1997).

Parry, Robert, *Lost History: Contras, Cocaine, the Press & "Project Truth"* (Arlington, Va.: The Media Consortium, 1999).

Tarpley, Webster G., and Anton Chaitkin, *George Bush: The Unauthorized Biography* (www.tarpley.net/bush2.htm).

Walsh, Lawrence E., *Firewall: The Iran-Contra Conspiracy and Cover-Up* (New York: W. W. Norton, 1997).

GEORGE W. BUSH

Abraham, Rick, *The Dirty Truth: The Oil & Chemical Dependency of George W. Bush* (Houston: Mainstream Publishers, 2000).

Begala, Paul, *"Is Our Children Learning?": The Case Against George W. Bush* (New York: Simon & Schuster, 2000).

Carlson, Tucker, "Devil May Care," *Talk,* September 1999, pp. 103–10.

Didion, Joan, "God's Country," *The New York Review of Books,* 11/2/2000 (www.nybooks.com/nyrev/WWWarchdisplay.cgi?20001102068F).

Hatfield, J. H., *Fortunate Son: George W. Bush and the Making of an American President* (New York: Soft Skull Press, 2000).

Ivins, Molly, and Lou Dubose, *Shrub: The Short But Happy Political Life of George W. Bush* (New York: Vintage Books, 2000).

Krugman, Paul, *Fuzzy Math: The Essential Guide to the Bush Tax Plan* (New York: W. W. Norton, 2001).

Lemann, Nicholas, "The Redemption," *The New Yorker,* 1/31/00, pp. 48–63.

Minutaglio, Bill, *First Son: George W. Bush and the Bush Family Dynasty* (New York: Times Books, 1999).

Mitchell, Elizabeth, *W: Revenge of the Bush Dynasty* (New York: Hyperion, 2000).

Moore, Michael, *Stupid White Men . . . and Other Sorry Excuses for the State of the Nation* (New York: Regan Books, 2002).

Sheehy, Gail, "The Accidental Candidate," *Vanity Fair,* October 2000, pp. 164–95.

POLITICAL BACKGROUND

Bellant, Russ, *Old Nazis, the New Right, and the Republican Party* (Boston: South End Press, 1991).

Blumenthal, Sidney, *Rise of the Counter-Establishment: From Conservative Ideology to Political Power* (New York: HarperCollins, 1988).

Brock, David, *Blinded by the Right: The Conscience of an Ex-Conservative* (New York: Crown, 2002).

Conason, Joe and Gene Lyons, *The Hunting of the President: The Ten-Year Campaign to Destroy Bill and Hillary Clinton* (New York: St. Martin's Press, 2000).

Engelhardt, Tom, *The End of Victory Culture: Cold War America and the Disillusioning of a Generation* (New York: Basic Books, 1995).

Gibson, James William, *Warrior Dreams: Violence and Manhood in Post-Vietnam America* (New York: Hill & Wang, 1994).

Irons, Peter H., *A People's History of the Supreme Court* (New York: Penguin, 2000).

Johnson, Chalmers, *Blowback: The Costs and Consequences of American Empire* (New York: Metropolitan Books, 2000).

Lazarus, Edward, *Closed Chambers: The Rise, Fall and Future of the Modern Supreme Court* (New York: Penguin, 1999).

Rosenfeld, Richard N., *American Aurora: A Democratic Republican Returns* (New York: St. Martin's Press, 1997).

Simpson, Christopher, *Blowback: America's Recruitment of Nazis and Its Effects on the Cold War* (London: Weidenfeld & Nicholson, 1988).

Toobin, Jeffrey, *A Vast Conspiracy: The Real Story of the Sex Scandal that Nearly Brought Down a President* (New York: Touchstone, 1999).

ON MEDIA

Gitlin, Todd, *Media Unlimited: How the Torrent of Images and Sounds Overwhelms Our Lives* (New York: Metropolitan Books, 2002).

Hertsgaard, Mark, *On Bended Knee: The Press and the Reagan Presidency* (New York: Farrar, Straus & Giroux, 1988).

McChesney, Robert W., *Rich Media, Poor Democracy: Communication Politics in Dubious Times* (New York: New Press, 2000).

Palast, Gregory, "Silence of the Lambs: The Failure of U.S. Journalism," 3/1/01; available at www.gregpalast.com/columns.cfm.

Schechter, Danny, *The More You Watch, the Less You Know: News Wars/[sub]Merged Hopes/Media Adventures* (New York, Seven Stories Press, 1998).

Scheuer, Jeffrey, *The Sound Bite Society: Television and the American Mind* (New York: Four Walls Eight Windows, 1999).

ELECTION 2000

Bugliosi, Vincent, *The Betrayal of America: How the Supreme Court Undermined the Constitution and Chose Our President* (New York: Thunder's Mouth Press/ Nation Books, 2001).

Danielson, Catherine, "Vote Fraud in Tennessee: Worse Than Florida?" *Alternet,* 3/13/01, www.alternet.org/story.html?StoryID=10589.

Dershowitz, Alan, *Supreme Injustice: How the High Court Hijacked Election 2000* (New York: Oxford University Books, 2001).

Grann, David, "Quiet Riot," *The New Republic,* 12/25/00, pp. 16–17.

Kaplan, David A., *The Accidental President: How 413 Lawyers, 9 Supreme Court Justices, and 5,963,110 Floridians (Give or Take a Few) Landed George W. Bush in the White House* (New York: William Morrow, 2001).

Nader, Ralph, *Crashing the Party: How to Tell the Truth and Still Run for President* (New York: St. Martin's Press, 2002).

Nichols, John, with David Deschamps, *Jews for Buchanan: Did You Hear the One about the Theft of the American Presidency?* (New York: New Press, 2001).

Palast, Gregory, "What Really Happened in Florida?" *Newsnight,* BBC News, 2/16/01. This transcript of Palast's BBC appearance—along with his invaluable newspaper columns on Bush/Cheney's vast electoral mischief—is available at www.gregpalast.com.

Schechter, Danny, and Roland Schatz, eds., *Hail to the Thief: How the Media "Stole" the U.S. Presidential Election 2000* (Bonn, Germany: Innovatio Verlag, 2001).

Simon, Roger, *Divided We Stand: How Al Gore Beat George Bush and Lost the Presidency* (New York: Times Books, 2001).

Toobin, Jeffrey, *Too Close to Call: The Thirty-Six-Day Battle to Decide the 2000 Election* (New York: Random House, 2001).

9/11

Brisard, Jean-Charles, and Guillaume Dasquié, *Ben Laden: La Vérité Interdite* (Paris: Editions Donoël, 2001).

Chomsky, Noam, *9-11* (New York: Seven Stories Press, 2001).

Cooley, John K., *Unholy Wars: Afghanistan, America and International Terrorism* (Sterling, Va.: Stylus Publishing, 2000).

Griffin, Michael, *Reaping the Whirlwind: The Taliban Movement in Afghanistan* (London: Pluto Press, 2001).

Hersh, Seymour M., "Annals of National Security: What Went Wrong," *The New Yorker,* 10/8/01.

Kepel, Gilles, *Jihad: The Trail of Political Islam,* tr. Anthony F. Roberts (Cambridge, Mass.: Harvard University Press, 2002).

Rashid, Ahmed, *Taliban: Militant Islam, Oil and Fundamentalism in Central Asia* (New Haven, Conn.: Yale University Press, 2001).

ONLINE RESOURCES

Alternet, www.alternet.org

Bushwatch, www.bushwatch.com

BuzzFlash, www.buzzflash.com

Center for Public Integrity, www.publicintegrity.com

Center for Responsive Politics, www.opensecrets.org

The Daily Howler, www.dailyhowler.com

Democracy Now!, www.democracynow.org

Democratic Underground, www.democraticunderground.com

Fairness and Accuracy in Reporting (FAIR), www.fair.org

Guerilla News Network, www.guerillanews.com

Make Them Accountable, www.makethemaccountable.com

The Media Channel, www.mediachannel.org

"The Meria Heller Show," www.Meria.net

Online Journal, www.onlinejournal.com

openDemocracy, www.opendemocracy.net

The Project on Media Ownership (PROMO), www.promo.org

Redrock Eater News Service, e-mail to: rre-on@lists.gseis.ucla.edu

TomPaine.common sense, www.tompaine.com

Truthout, www.truthout.org

WorkingForChange (Working Assets), www.workingforchange.com